The Politically Incorrect Guide® to Communism

The Politically Incorrect Guides® to...

American History
Thomas Woods
9780895260475

The Bible
Robert J. Hutchinson
9781596985209

The British Empire
H. W. Crocker III
9781596986299

Capitalism
Robert P. Murphy
9781596985049

Catholicism
John Zmirak
9781621575863

The Civil War
H. W. Crocker III
9781596985490

The Constitution
Kevin R. C. Gutzman
9781596985056

Darwinism and Intelligent Design
Jonathan Wells
9781596980136

English and American Literature
Elizabeth Kantor
9781596980112

The Founding Fathers
Brion McClanahan
9781596980921

Global Warming
Christopher C. Horner
9781596985018

The Great Depression and the New Deal
Robert Murphy
9781596980969

Hunting
Frank Miniter
9781596985216

Islam (And the Crusades)
Robert Spencer
9780895260130

Jihad
William Kilpatrick
9781621575771

The American Revolution
Larry Schweikart and
Dave Dougherty
978-1-62157-625-9

The Middle East
Martin Sieff
9781596980518

The Presidents, Part 1
Larry Schweikart
9781621575245

The Presidents, Part 2
Steven F. Hayward
9781621575795

Real American Heroes
Brion McClanahan
9781596983205

Science
Tom Bethell
9780895260314

The Sixties
Jonathan Leaf
9781596985728

Socialism
Kevin D. Williamson
9781596986497

The South (And Why It Will Rise Again)
Clint Johnson
9781596985001

The Vietnam War
Phillip Jennings
9781596985674

Western Civilization
Anthony Esolen
9781596980594

Women, Sex, and Feminism
Carrie L. Lukas
9781596980037

The Politically Incorrect Guide® to Communism

Paul Kengor

REGNERY PUBLISHING
A Division of Salem Media Group

Cataloging-in-Publication data on file with the Library of Congress

ISBN 978-1-62157-587-0
e-book ISBN 978-1-62157-615-0

Published in the United States by
Regnery Publishing
A Division of Salem Media Group
300 New Jersey Ave NW
Washington, DC 20001
www.Regnery.com

Manufactured in the United States of America

10 9 8 7 6 5 4 3 2 1

Distributed to the trade by
Perseus Distribution
www.perseusdistribution.com

*To the countless millions who suffered and died
at the hands of the idiotic, insane, ignorant, asinine,
lying, conniving, criminal, horrific, destructive, dehumanizing,
diabolical, bloody, brutal, barbarous, ridiculous, pernicious, atrocious,
hellacious, murderous, monstrous, malicious, malignant,
moronic, godless, and all-around stupid, vile, vicious,
and evil ideology known as communism*

Contents

CHAPTER 1

Educating for Ignorance

> **Did you know?**
> ★ American high school students have recently put on events celebrating communism
> ★ To school teachers, the real villains are the "red-baiting" anti-communists
> ★ Communism killed ten times as many people as Nazism

Graduating seniors at Cottonwood Classical Preparatory school in Albuquerque, New Mexico, picked the perfect theme for their 2015 spring prom. The killer concept they picked for the premier dance of the year? "Prom-munism."[1]

The grand event would unfold under the banner—the literal red flag—of Lenin, Stalin, Mao, Marx, and Castro. For their big party, the students looked to The Party. They invoked a different kind of Party animal—the rapacious mass murderers whose marquee event was a carnival of carnage, a legacy of over a hundred million dead victims.

Now there's something to dance about.

Perhaps North Korea's Kims could spin some records? The Kim boys—Kim Il-Sung, Kim Jong Il, Kim Jong Un—were wild party animals. The second Kim was Hennessy's number one private purchaser of cognac, which he guzzled along with his personal harem of bleach-blonde party girls—the permanent sex slaves that comprised his "Satisfaction Corps" of women specially trained by the state to administer to his sexual gratification.[2] He also boasted the world's largest private collection of pornography, which he bequeathed to his son, who has partied with some of America's best—notably,

NBA bad-boy Dennis Rodman. The current Kim's harem is known as his Pleasure Squad. And his regime peddles Rohypnol, the notorious date-rape drug.[3]

Mao Zedong, too, was quite the party animal. Not only was he responsible for between sixty and seventy million dead Chinese. He also sired hundreds if not thousands of Chinese children—and passed along his venereal diseases to the countless virgin girls supplied for his satisfaction by his Red Guard.[4]

"Our students are in the International Baccalaureate program, so they are very academically focused," said one Albuquerque school official, explaining the educational inspiration for the concept. "One of the classes they enjoy the most is a world history class."

A student named Cole Page—a sensible sophomore who betrayed an insight into communism the seniors somehow hadn't gleaned from the high school's history classes—expressed a different perspective: "I honestly don't think it's that funny."[5]

"*Glee* Meets the Russian Revolution"

Unfortunately, "Prom-munism" wasn't a fluke.

Three years earlier, in September 2012, a band at New Oxford High School near Gettysburg, Pennsylvania, home of one of the great moments in American history, gave a salute to one of the worst moments in history. They performed a halftime show titled "St. Petersburg 1917," a musical commemoration of the Bolshevik Revolution. The band's website posted a photo of the beaming students holding the hammer and sickle, the symbol that Vladimir Lenin and Leon Trotsky elevated in St. Petersburg in 1917.

Here again, not everyone was laughing.

"There is no reason for Americans to celebrate the Russian revolution," said one irate parent. "I am sure the millions who died under communism would not see the joy of celebrating the Russian revolution by a school 10 miles from Gettysburg." He added, "It was *Glee* meets the Russian Revolution. I'm not kidding you. They had giant hammers and sickles and they were waving them around." He asked, "Who thought this was a good idea?"

Said another parent, "If I was Lithuanian, Estonian, or Ukrainian, I'd be a little hot. I'd be really hot. It's insulting to glorify something that doesn't need to be glorified in America."

The parent wondered what the reaction might have been if the band had chosen a Nazi theme, "celebrating the music of 1935 Berlin."

The superintendent of the school defended her students. "It's a representation of the time period in history, called 'St. Petersburg 1917,'" she objected. "I am truly sorry that somebody took the performance in that manner. I am." She continued: "If anything is being celebrated it's the music.... I'm just very sorry that it wasn't looked at as just a history lesson."[6]

As a history lesson, it deserves a giant F.

How is this happening, in America today, a century after the Bolshevik Revolution that launched a global killing spree from Kiev to Cambodia, from Havana to Hungary?

What Americans are witnessing here is a direct by-product of decade after decade of little to no education—correction, *mis*education—on the malicious menace of deadly communism, which America devoted so many precious lives and resources to defeat. We won the Cold War in the political arena, but lost it in the classroom. If and when communism is taught at all in American schools, the communists are often lauded for their idealism, their devotion to equality for women and minorities. Their actual track record—the politically created famines, the wars of aggression, the body count in the tens of millions—is too frequently passed over in silence. It's not that no villains are called out, but they're the *anti*-communists like Senator Joe McCarthy. At best, the teacher assumes a position of moral neutrality, as if, to borrow from President Ronald Reagan's "Evil Empire" speech, the Cold War was simply "one giant misunderstanding," in which the free West occupied no moral high ground.

Back in the time of the Cold War, Reagan exposed the folly of moral equivalence between the communist world and the free West. He urged Americans to "beware the temptation of pride—the temptation of blithely declaring yourselves above it all and label both sides equally at fault, to ignore the facts of history and the aggressive impulses of an evil empire." He urged his countrymen not to remove themselves "from the struggle between right and wrong and good and evil."

The fact is, there was right and wrong and good and evil in the battle against Soviet communism. And though America, as Reagan admitted, had its faults—indeed, its "sins"—it could not hold a candle to the blowtorch of fiery evils emanating from behind the Iron Curtain.

The "Softer Side" of Communism

I could fill this book with story after painful story relayed by my own students—a parade of appalling ignorance in our education establishment. One former student named John, Grove City College class of 2000, told me about his first assignment as a teaching assistant in a nearby high school history class. He had been a double major in education and history, so he told his supervising teacher he'd be happy to cover the Soviet Union in the 1930s. She agreed. So John methodically taught about the famine in the Ukraine, Stalin's purges and Great Terror, and the Hitler-Stalin Pact. He gave carefully sourced figures on the millions of victims.

John was pleased at how the students were engaged by the lessons, with many hands in the air. Clearly, they were learning all of these hideous things for the first time. But he also noticed the dirty looks from his supervisor stationed at the back of the room, arms folded, eyes glaring. At the end of his presentation, the teacher testily reprimanded him, "Look, John, I want you to ease up on the Red-baiting and commie-bashing. Besides, these students are going to get a decidedly different view on communism from me." She promised to teach "a softer side of communism."

Imagine if the teacher had said something similar about Nazism: *Look, John, I want you to ease up on the Nazi-baiting and Hitler-bashing. Besides, these students are going to get a decidedly different view on fascism from me.* What if she had promised to teach a "softer side" to the Third Reich?

Another student of mine—Sean, Grove City College class of 2001—told me about the elite Christian private school he attended in northern Ohio where a newly hired teacher fresh out of college from a major university in Pennsylvania told the students that he was a "Christian communist." In fact, he argued that anyone who is a Christian should be a communist. "Communism is misunderstood," was the teacher's refrain.

Too bad Karl Marx wasn't there to tell the shockingly ill-informed teacher that "communism begins where atheism begins." In the Soviet Union, Christians literally could not be members of the Communist Party. And teachers could not be Christians.

Harry Truman Explains the Difference between Christianity and Communism

President Truman colorfully said he was willing to believe in an ideal "Honest Communism," with Christians holding all their goods in common as "set out in the Acts of the Apostles." But every actual instance of communism, he pointed out, was something quite different: "They all start with a wrong premise—that lies are justified and that the old, disproven Jesuit formula, the ends justify the means, is right and necessary to maintain the power of the government." He said, "Russian Godless Pervert Systems won't work."[7]

★ ★ ★

JFK on Why Communism and Christianity Are Incompatible

According to John F. Kennedy, communists allow "no room for God": "The claim of the state must be total, and allow no other loyalty, and no other philosophy of life, can be tolerated." They "make the worship of the State the ultimate objective of life."[8] President Kennedy spoke of the "struggle for supremacy between two conflicting ideologies: freedom under God versus ruthless, godless tyranny."[9]

A freshman student in a 1996 course I taught at Robert Morris University told me about the successful propaganda of one Allegheny County school district teacher, who convinced the entire class that Marxism was a "wonderful" but "misunderstood" system that had never really been tried. "He absolutely brainwashed us," she told me bitterly. The teacher did a bang-up job covering the calamities of Nazism, and rightly so. The leftists who dominate education are never negligent in exposing the atrocities of an ideology that they consider an extreme "right-wing" one. They do yeoman's work hammering the Holocaust and its catastrophe, as they should. But high school teachers who give equal time to the evils of the communist ideology, which killed ten times the number of people the Nazis annihilated, are vanishingly rare.

These are just three anecdotal examples from my own backyard—which, incidentally, is a fairly conservative backyard. Pittsburgh isn't San Francisco. Western Pennsylvania and eastern Ohio are not New England and Chicago. Robert Morris University is not Columbia University. The incidents I have recounted here are the tip of the iceberg. I speak on the crimes of communism at colleges all over the country, and I hear accounts like these everywhere.

Honestly, I have never given a talk where some young person has not paused to tell me stories like this. The students are often quite resentful, knowing they have been misled, misinformed, and betrayed.

We talk about "educating for excellence." But in reality, in American high schools and colleges across the West, we are educating for ignorance.

This *Politically Incorrect Guide® to Communism*, which is really simply a Politically Accurate Guide to Communism, endeavors to provide the corrective. It is a stake in the chest of the Marxist-Leninist monster, the Bolshevik vampire that deserves to be forever interred aside Vladimir Lenin in Red Square. Expose the hissing creature to the sunlight of truth and watch him shriek and shrivel.

So, dear reader, grab a stake and a hammer (but not a sickle)—and maybe even a cross and a little holy water. Let the pounding begin.

CHAPTER 2

How Many People Have These Bastards Killed?

"Communism has only killed 100 million people. Why not give it another shot?"

That was the quip on a T-shirt given to me by a former student. The mordant comment was a bittersweet joke. No ideology has been as singularly deadly as communism.

That's a damned big killing field, comrade.

And the butcher's bill is not even the whole story. No political ideology has produced as much wretched poverty, rank repression, and sheer violence as communism. In country after country, across vastly different nationalities, traditions, and ethnicities, communists have consistently engaged in egregious violations of the most basic human rights, from free speech to the right to assemble, from press freedom to property rights, from conscience rights to religious liberty. Communist regimes have routinely refused their citizens the right to exit—that is, to escape—the misery and destruction they have implemented within their own borders. In some cases, they erected walls to lock the masses into their workers' paradise: cement barriers patrolled by secret police with guns aimed not outward

Did you know?

★ Communism has killed well over a hundred million people worldwide

★ The communists in Cambodia killed at least a quarter and perhaps as many as half of the population

★ Stalin alone killed about six times as many people as Hitler

A Book You're Not Supposed to Read

Alexander Solzhenitsyn begins *The Gulag Archipelago*, his majestic history of the Soviet forced-labor-camp system, with a shocking story. He cites an article in the journal *Nature*, which informed its readers, in a strictly scientific fashion, about the discovery of a perfectly preserved prehistoric fish in Siberia.

"Flouting the higher claims of ichthyology," narrated Solzhenitsyn, and "elbowing each other to be first," the men who made the discovery chipped away the ice, hurried the fish to a fire, cooked it, and bolted it down. No doubt, said Solzhenitsyn, *Nature* impressed its readers with this account of how a ten-thousand-year-old fish had been preserved over such a long period. But only a narrower group of readers could decipher the true meaning of this "incautious" report. That smaller club was Solzhenitsyn's fellow survivors of the Gulag.[1] When your goal is survival, you survive, even if it means hurriedly devouring something that in a normal world would be carefully transported to a museum. But Soviet communism was no normal world.

at some perceived enemy seeking to enter, but inward upon the unarmed, immiserated populace.

The ultimate symbols of that repression were the Berlin Wall, erected in August 1961 to keep the East Germans from fleeing to free West Berlin, and the fenced in people-zoo that was the Soviet Gulag, the prison system created by Lenin and Stalin.

Communism deprives individuals of their inalienable rights. It is a totalitarian, atheistic ideology pursued for the stated purpose of ushering in a classless utopia—a better, even perfect, world. This utopian promise has gone unfulfilled in every country that has attempted communism in any form. No ideology has so constantly, so abjectly, so horridly, so reliably failed to meet its central stated objective—instead achieving the precise opposite of an earthly utopia. From Stalin's Russia to Pol Pot's Cambodia to Hugo Chávez's Venezuela, communism has ushered in not the promised workers' paradise but the closest thing the world has known to hell on earth.

Swing a dead cat and you'll hit another pile of corpses left by a communist government. How many people did these gangsters and their deadly ideology kill? Seriously, what is the actual body count?

Counting the Bodies

The 1999 *Black Book of Communism*—a highly respected work published by Harvard University Press—attempted the thankless task of tabulating the total communist death toll in the twentieth century. It came up with a figure approaching a hundred million.[2] Here is the general breakdown:

- U.S.S.R.: 20 million
- China: 65 million
- Vietnam: 1 million
- North Korea: 2 million
- Cambodia: 2 million deaths
- Eastern Europe: 1 million
- Latin America: 150,000
- Africa: 1.7 million
- Afghanistan: 1.5 million
- The international communist movement and Communist parties not in power: about 10,000

The U.S.-based Victims of Communism Memorial Foundation, the preeminent institution for detailing communist crimes, agrees with the estimate of a hundred million deaths.[3]

But in fact, these frightening numbers are quite conservative.

Take the figure for the Soviet Union, where the *Black Book* records twenty million dead.[4] Most accounts of the total Soviet death toll exceed thirty-three million, and some estimates are twice that. Cold War historian Lee Edwards, citing the epic work on "democide" by political

A Book You're Not Supposed to Read

Marx & Satan (Crossway Books, 1986) is the title of a politically incorrect look at the life of the seminal communist philosopher Karl Marx by the late Richard Wurmbrand, a Christian minister who spent fourteen years imprisoned and tortured in communist Romania.

★ ★ ★

You Never Said a Truer Word

"We shall not enter into the kingdom of socialism in white gloves on a polished floor." —**Leon Trotsky**,[6] in what may be the understatement of the century

scientist R. J. Rummel, estimates that Soviet governments were responsible for the death of 61.9 million of their own people from 1917 to 1987.[5]

Alexander Yakovlev, a high-level Soviet official who became one of Mikhail Gorbachev's chief reformers and in the 1990s was given the official task of trying to tabulate the victims of Soviet communism, estimates that Stalin alone "annihilated... sixty to seventy million people." Yakovlev's estimate is consistent with the figures tabulated by dissident Alexander Solzhenitsyn.[7]

A similar level of bloodshed was wrought solely by China's Mao Zedong, who was responsible for the deaths of at least sixty million in China, and more likely over seventy million, according to the latest biographical-historical research.[8]

Also too conservative is the *Black Book*'s North Korea number, which does not include the two to three million who died in the famine of the late 1990s, a famine resulting directly from communist policies.[9] The *Black Book* went to press too early to include that figure in its twentieth-century total. (Give the communists a little more time, and they are sure to kill a few million more.) For a fuller sense of the devastation, two to three million dead was roughly 10 to 15 percent of the North Korean population.[10] That percentage of the American population would be forty million people. (America lost three hundred thousand dead in all of World War II.)

For an even worse death toll, consider the case of Cambodia, where the *Black Book* credits communism with two million deaths. That number, too, may well be higher, possibly rising to three million, though it is the percentage that is especially horrible: Pol Pot and his Khmer Rouge killed upwards of two to three million *out of a total Cambodian population of five to seven million in just four years.*[11]

The total deaths caused by communism in the twentieth century are closer to 140 million. That number equates to a rate of multiple thousands dead per day over the course of a century.

The 140 million figure was used by Professor Rummel, the late renowned expert of statistics on deaths caused by violent regimes.[13]

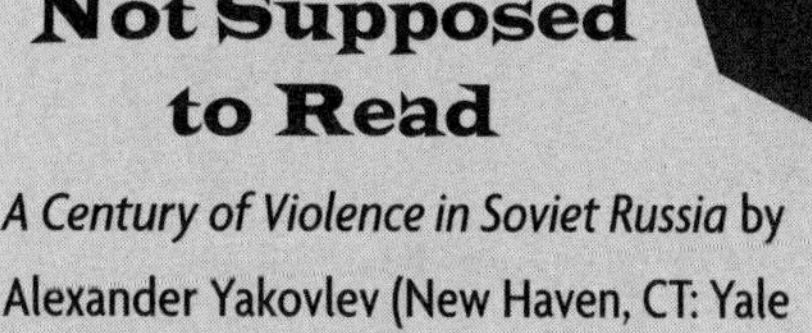

A Century of Violence in Soviet Russia by Alexander Yakovlev (New Haven, CT: Yale University Press, 2002).

Odious Comparisons

By comparison, Hitler's horrific genocide against Jews, Gypsies, the mentally disabled, and others he deemed "misfits" killed approximately ten million (six million of whom were Jews). Hitler was a master of death and evil, but his death toll doesn't approach that of Stalin or Mao alone, not to speak of what communist ideology en masse has done.

Another chilling figure for comparison: The combined dead from World Wars I and II—the most destructive conflicts in human history—was approximately fifty to seventy million. One must combine and then double the tolls of the two world wars to achieve numbers comparable to communism's mass slaughter.

★ ★ ★

The Dance of Death

"Ever more boldly I play the dance of death," are words Karl Marx put in the mouth of the title character in his youthful poem "The Player."[12] Here Marx proved himself a better prophet than poet. The ideas for which he would be famous, the philosophy that he scripted, the international communist symphony for which he composed the opus, represented a grand dance of death that left well over a hundred million people dead in the name of the ideology that bears his name.

★ ★ ★

Take Hitler and Start Multiplying

"And so many bodies! Not six million but 60 million, or 100 million—in any case scores and scores of millions. Too many ever to number." —**Jonathan Rauch**[16]

The highest estimates on the death produced during the entirety of the Spanish Inquisition, a period of some sixty years, come nowhere near the level of death in Stalin's purges—or merely Lenin's first year in power.[14]

As Jonathan Rauch has pointed out in *The Atlantic*, "The fact remains: communism, not Nazism or racism or whatever other ism you please, is the deadliest fantasy in human history, and even Americans, for all our struggles against it, have not yet looked it full in the face." Rauch quotes Alan Charles Kors, a historian of European intellectual history at the University of Pennsylvania: "The West accepts an epochal, monstrous, unforgivable double standard. We rehearse the crimes of Nazism almost daily; we teach them to our children as ultimate historical and moral lessons; and we bear witness to every victim. We are, with so few exceptions, almost silent on the crimes of communism. So the bodies lie among us, unnoticed, everywhere."[15]

Though feminists and others on the Left would object to including the abortion deaths in these numbers, and I have not done so, it would not be unjustified to do so, given that abortion was legalized first in the communist nations, beginning in Bolshevik Russia. To this day, China's coercive population control policy has devastating effects. The very worst abortion rates in the twentieth century, hands down, were in communist countries (the USSR, Cuba, Romania, Vietnam) and directly related to the communist policies prevailing there.

After seizing the ship of state in 1917, the Bolsheviks immediately made good on Lenin's June 1913 promise for an "unconditional annulment of all laws against abortions."[17] By 1920, abortion was legalized and provided free of charge to Russian women. In short order, the number of abortions skyrocketed. By 1934, Moscow women were having three abortions for every

★ ★ ★

Shocking Even Margaret Sanger

Planned Parenthood founder Margaret Sanger—a eugenicist who wished to rid America of "human weeds" and "morons" and "imbeciles"—was shocked by the prevalence of abortion during her 1934 Russian tour, but she was reassured by her hosts: "All the officials with whom I discussed the matter stated that as soon as the economic and social plans of Soviet Russia are realized, neither abortions nor contraception will be necessary or desired. A functioning Communistic society will assure the happiness of every child, and will assume the full responsibility for its welfare and education."[19]

live birth. In the 1970s, the USSR averaged a breathtaking seven to eight million abortions per year (according to official Soviet statistics), totaling seventy to eighty million deaths of unborn babies in just one decade in merely one communist country.[18] This far outpaced America's worst years of abortion after *Roe v. Wade*. To repeat: neither I nor others include these abortions in the total one hundred to 140 million killed by communism.

Under communism, totally different national cultures, from all over the globe, completely unrelated to one another, all experienced mass violence. The only common factor? Communism. The violence was always the standard, institutional policy of the new revolutionary order, carried out on a scale and with a degree of inhumanity far exceeding anything that had occurred in the past of these cultures.[20] The communists broke the mold.

It is hard to find even a disease that has killed that many people. Probably the most notorious epidemic in the twentieth century was the influenza of 1918–1919, which took at least ten to twenty million worldwide.[21] That's a mere sneeze, a head-cold compared to the Marxist menace.

Those who pursued such a deadly ideology worldwide—in the name of utopia, no less—were either moral monsters, monumental idiots, or people caught up in some form of insanity.

★ ★ ★

Good Question

"Mankind has survived all manner of evil diseases and plagues, but can it survive Communism?" —**Ronald Reagan**[22]

That's exactly what Ronald Reagan said: "Communism is neither an economic or a political system—it is a form of insanity."[23] He called the USSR the "evil empire"[24] and the "heart of darkness."[25] He said the Soviet leaders were "monsters."[26] And for his pains, Reagan was relentlessly mocked. His rhetoric was over the top, even dangerous. His anti-communism was unsophisticated and unrealistic.

But think about that death toll.

CHAPTER 3

When and Where It All Began

So communism has killed approximately 100–140 million people in the past hundred years—more than Hitler, more than both world wars, more than worldwide pandemics.

But just where did this horrifically lethal set of ideas come from in the first place?

Forerunners

It is hard to say when and where the idea of communism first gained currency. Certain elements of the communist collectivist mindset were present as early as Thomas More's sixteenth-century classic *Utopia* and even in Plato's ancient *Republic*. More's book is often pointed to as an example of pre-Marx communist thinking.

But More's book is not really a communist manifesto. Unlike most utopians who followed him, More was no God-hater; to the contrary, he was an extremely devout son of the Church, one who went to his martyrdom for his principled defense of the teachings of his faith. Priests, churches, and the worshippers who fill them are all held in great esteem in his utopia. It's

Did you know?

★ Lenin took the bloodthirsty Jacobins of the French Revolution as his models

★ Both Marx and Engels were virulent racists

★ *The Communist Manifesto* talks of the "abolition of the family" a far cry from Lenin's dystopia, where priests were lined up and shot by grinning executioners.[1]

Other popular utopian works followed in the centuries after More. But the first true precursors of the communist revolutionaries were the bloodthirsty Jacobins who turned the French Revolution into the Reign of Terror in the 1790s. Of the three ideals enshrined in the French Revolutionary motto—"Liberté, égalité, fraternité"—they, like their Marxist-Leninist admirers in the twentieth century, put all the emphasis on égalité—equality, the communist ideal. And it was a radical equality that soon ran amok, all the way to the foot of the guillotine. I had a professor in graduate school who always referred to the Jacobins as "the first communists," and not without good reason. They declared war on many of the same targets the Bolsheviks would place in their crosshairs: aristocrats, the wealthy, the religious, their political opponents. And they are best remembered for what communists are always known for: blood.

The Jacobins used the guillotine for their bloodletting, executing their enemies with an alacrity that would not be outdone until Lenin and the boys arrived on the world scene. They even devised an impressive canal-like drainage system to collect the blood rushing from the severed necks of the victims that served as case exhibits of the human cost of their utopian collectivist fantasy. The fanatics could not run a government, but they could manage the instruments of death with startling proficiency.

The "Committee of Public Safety"—a perfectly Orwellian name the French revolutionaries came up with a century and a half before Orwell—unleashed the Reign of Terror to enforce their utopian regime of "Virtue." Historians estimate that the Jacobins lopped off the heads of forty thousand French men and women in a single year, including the nuns whose hoisted blood-soaked skulls were a special prize. (Lenin would achieve a similar

★ ★ ★

The Jacobins Were *Hilarious*

What was their nickname for the guillotine? "The National Razor."

★ ★ ★

History Starts with Us

The Jacobins were the first to abolish the Christian calendar and start history over again with year one of their revolution. But they wouldn't be the last. Italian dictator Benito Mussolini—whose "everything within the state, nothing outside the state, nothing against the state" fascism has been branded "right wing" by the Left, but who was in reality such a perfect disciple of Karl Marx (whom he called "the father and teacher" and "the magnificent philosopher of working-class violence") that Lenin admired the Italian dictator's writings[3]—declared a new *era fascista* beginning with his 1922 March on Rome. And Pol Pot declared his own new year one after the murderous Khmer Rouge took power in 1975. For the record, the anti-religious Left's war on the Christian calendar has never ended. Notice how today BC (Before Christ) and AD (Anno Domini—in the Year of Our Lord) are being replaced by CE (Common Era) and BCE (Before the Common Era)?[4]

tally of murders in his first year in power. And both would be outdone by Stalin and Mao, the Kims and Pol Pot.)

The Jacobins were the first totalitarians—a concept that cannot be separated from communist ideology and governance. Totalitarianism is a form of politics and governance that asserts total control. A totalitarian government refuses to acknowledge any individual authority, margin of freedom, or source of value outside the regime itself. Neither religion, nor the law, nor tradition, nor family, nor even human nature is allowed to stand out against the dictates of the ideology. The revolution must overturn every source of authority or value outside itself. Thus the Jacobins threw out even the calendar. The year AD 1794 became year one in Jacobin France.[2]

The Russian communists would deliberately model themselves on "the most glorious of the Jacobins of the time of the Great French Revolution," as Soviet Comintern (Communist International) head Grigory Zinoviev put it.[5] Lenin praised the "great, ineradicable, unforgettable things provided by the Jacobins in the eighteenth century," and claimed that "the Jacobins gave France the best models of a democratic revolution."[6]

★ ★ ★

Not a Dime's Worth of Difference

In their classic study on totalitarianism, Carl Friedrich and Zbigniew Brzezinski list several characteristics exhibited by any totalitarian regime, which

- posits an official ideology, one that attempts to justify the actions of the government (no matter how harsh) in the name of some future state of happiness;
- governs by a single, hierarchical party that is intertwined with or superior to the government;
- employs an ever-present, lurking secret police to intimidate and control and that is willing to carry out campaigns of terror against perceived "enemies" of the state;
- secures a tight grip on the armed forces (i.e., the guys who have the guns);
- monopolizes the means of mass communication;
- establishes centralized control over the economy[7]

Totalitarianism or communism, what's the difference, exactly?

Fellow Bolshevik revolutionary Leon Trotsky—Lenin's closest ally—would compare Lenin to Maximilien Robespierre, the chief instigator of the Jacobin Terror, sensing in his own comrade a closet despot looking to turn the Communist Party into a Russian version of the murderous Committee of Public Safety. He called Lenin's methods "a dull caricature of the tragic intransigence of Jacobinism," whereby "the party is replaced by the organization of the party, the organization by the central committee, and finally the central committee by the dictator."[8]

Though the Jacobins were a model for the Soviet communists, scholars believe that the word "communism" wasn't coined until the 1840s—in Paris,[9] where it would have been one of innumerable asinine ideas emanating from the minds and mouths of the nattering nabobs in the salons and cafes of France. Leave it to a chattering class of effete intellectuals to give us something so dreadful.

The founding document for the communist movement is *The Communist Manifesto*, written in 1848 by Karl Marx and Friedrich Engels. The *Manifesto* refers to a pre-existing idea of "communism," but the term is not much older than that, and it is possible that Marx and Engels themselves had coined it a few years earlier. In any case, they certainly popularized it.

★ ★ ★

The Yankee Utopians

Between the French Revolution and Marx came a number of socialists and collectivists who are aptly dubbed the "Yankee Utopians" in Daniel Flynn's history of the American Left.[10] Not all were technically Americans, but all had their impact on American soil with the ideological colonies they established or inspired in the 1800s. Some were English; others (naturally) were French. They included Robert Owen, Charles Fourier, Albert Brisbane, and John Humphrey Noyes, who dubbed himself a "Bible communist."

The career of the English Robert Owen (1771–1858), who planted his shovel in the core of the American heartland two decades before Marx and Engels published their manifesto, illustrates the persistence—and some of the dangers—of certain communist ideas that were attractive even before the word "communism" was popularized, and that continue to seduce intellectuals and idealists who haven't learned anything from the abject failure of those ideas over the past two hundred years.

"I [have] come to this country to introduce an entire new state of society," Owen stated in his April 27, 1825, address at the public hall of his "New Harmony" utopian community. He came "to change it from the ignorant, selfish system, to an enlightened, social system, which shall gradually unite all interests into one, and remove all cause for contest between individuals."[11]

"Individual" was a dirty word to Owen. (He would have agreed wholeheartedly when President Obama deplored the American "bias toward individual action" and said that that Americans must unite in "collective action" and achieve "collective salvation.")[12] Owen said he had come "to change from the individual to the social system; from single families with separate interests, to communities of many families with one interest."

Owen marked the fiftieth anniversary of the Declaration of Independence with his own "Declaration of Mental Independence": "I now declare... to the world," proclaimed Owen, "that Man up to this hour, has been, in all parts of the earth, a slave to a Trinity of the most monstrous evils... to inflict mental and physical evil upon [our] whole race. I refer to Private, or Individual Property, Absurd and Irrational Systems of Religion, and Marriage, founded on Individual Property." He called for nothing less than a "revolution" to deliver mankind from private property, marriage, and religion.

Religion was worst of this "hydra of evils"—"All religions have proved themselves to be superstitions," scoffed Owen—but he didn't like private property or the family much better: "The forms and ceremonies of Marriage... were contrived and forced upon the people at the same time that property was first divided among a few leading individuals and Superstition was invented: This being the only device that could... permit them to retain their division of the public spoils, and create to themselves an aristocracy of wealth of power and of learning."

Owen's new society was a collectivist colony that pooled property, profits, and people, replacing the nuclear family with the collective family. Children were removed from parents into separate parts of the collective for proper "education."

The New Harmony colony floundered within just two years. Owen squandered most of his personal fortune on his failed colony, but his leftist vision remained alive. "The social system is now firmly established," he asserted.[13] Of course it was.

Even before it folded, Owen took frequent sabbaticals from his little commie commune. This is typical of communist utopians: they rarely abide by the standards they impose on the people in whose names they govern. Owen and Fidel Castro and Mao and the Kims and all the other champions of "the people" never live by the rules they apply to everyone else. And no wonder. Given the choice, no one wants to live by rules so completely at odds with human nature. So the stupid system is always for the stupid sheep, never for the shepherds. Collectivists can never tolerate collective life. The one saving grace of Robert Owen's "New Harmony" communist utopia was that he wasn't in control of the government, so he couldn't force people to stay in it.

Despite the failures, the true believers never give up the dream; they remain committed to the communist vision. Robert Owen's "New Harmony" utopia dried up, but dozens of others would spring up around the country in the mid-1800s. There were over forty of them by the mid-century, and rarely did any of them last more than four years.[14]

But the faith lived on. In fact, it still lives on in America today.

Marx and Engels met in August 1844 in the left-wing looney bin that was Paris, where Marx had moved a year earlier with his wife and begun studying the French Revolutionaries and other utopian socialists, attending workers' meetings, and engaging in other leftist activities.[15] In 1847 a secret society of German émigré workers organizing in Paris, Brussels, and London under the name the "Communist League" commissioned Marx and Engels to write, as historian Martin Malia has put it, a "programmatic statement" to serve as a sort of "revolutionary catechism." That was the origin of *The Communist Manifesto*,[16]—the original blueprint for the communism that has troubled the world ever since, in various guises in different nations, whether it has been called "Marxism-Leninism," as in Russia, "Maoism," in China, or "twenty-first-century socialism" in Hugo Chávez's Venezuela.

Marx the Moocher

As Aristotle observed, "Men start revolutionary changes for reasons connected with their private lives."[17] And in fact the world's ugliest ideology was delineated by one of history's most unattractive characters. As a family man—in fact, all around, simply as a human being—the founder of communism left much to be desired.[18] Marx's conduct as a son, a husband, a father, a writing partner is not without relevance to the noxious Marxist ideology.

First consider Marx's relationship with his parents. As a grown man, Marx was a leech on his poor father and mother, draining his hosts. Even after he was married and had children of his own—teenagers, in fact—the man refused to work, instead sucking as much income from his parents as possible. He was draining his parents' life savings dry. His long-suffering mother was ultimately driven to express the wish that "Karl would accumulate capital instead of just writing about it."[19]

But Karl preferred opining on his imagined communist utopia to working. He was too busy devising his vital (actually life-destroying) theories in his personal office or the public library to bother earning an income to provide for his family. He demanded that others provide his income.

Long before there was Minnie the Moocher, there was Marx the Moocher.

As anyone knows, the host in such a relationship eventually has no recourse but to cut off the parasite—to the parasite's writhing displeasure and lasting fury. And sure enough Marx was enraged when his parents

The Unknown Karl Marx, edited by Robert Payne (New York: New York University Press, 1971).

finally quit bankrolling his irresponsibility and laziness. When his parents could give no more and finally insisted on some tough love for their selfish son, Marx refused to see them thenceforth, ultimately refusing to attend his father's funeral out of spite.

But Marx's parents were only his first go-to source. Now that he needed a new host to draw financial nutrients from, he turned to Friedrich Engels, his partner in the communist ideology business. Engels, too, had sucked from the teat of his parents' wealth, which was larger than the Marxes'. But Engels too, eventually, tired of Marx using him for money. And as Engels slowed the spigot, Marx lashed out at him as well.

But naturally, the chief victims of Marx's refusal to work were his wife and children, who were made destitute by his laziness. His wife and kids lacked money, food, and life-saving medical attention. They couldn't even depend on having a roof over their heads. In November 1849, a year after he published his *The Communist Manifesto*, Marx's landlord evicted the Marxes. The landlord naturally wanted to be paid the rent, but he was also fed up with Marx's filthy personal habits. The communist ideologue exhibited a stubborn resistance to grooming and bathing. He stank. Karl drank too much, smoked too much, never exercised, and suffered from warts and boils from his refusal to bathe. "The boils varied in numbers, size and intensity," says Paul Johnson, "but at one time or another they appeared on all parts of his body, including his cheeks, the bridge of his nose, his bottom—preventing him from sitting to write—and his penis. In 1873 they brought on a nervous collapse marked by trembling and bursts of rage."[20]

Marx was lazy not only in his personal habits and when it came to supporting his family. He also took the easy way out in his research. He avoided the factories and farms on which he professed to be an expert and did his research exclusively in the library. No wonder there's a vast separation between his economic ideas and reality. He was typical of the Ivory Tower intellectuals who never bother intermingling with the rubes that they profess to speak for from their perch of expertise in the faculty lounge.

★ ★ ★

Tragically, We Do

Marx suffered from boils for nearly twenty-five years—including the period when he was writing *Das Kapital*, something that may possibly explain the sense of oozing pain that one feels when reading his *magnum opus*. "Whatever happens," he groaned to Engels, "I hope the bourgeoisie as long as they exist will have cause to remember my carbuncles."[21]

Even sympathetic sources on the ideological Left agree on Marx's failure to provide for his family. "He and Jenny, his wife, spent the majority of their life together in considerable and frequently miserable poverty, relying on contributions from supportive friends (most reliably Friedrich Engels)," says a writer at the left-wing *Salon*. "If this was hard on Marx, it was surely harder still on Jenny." Marx's wife had been raised as what we today would call a "limousine leftist," brought up in an aristocratic family in Prussia. She gave up her life of privilege for a life of poverty and squalor with Karl. The two of them lived in the expectation that Karl's masterwork, *Das Kapital*, might actually earn them some capital. But Marx, who was notorious for not completing assignments and for ignoring agreed-upon word limits, missed his deadline by sixteen years. The first royalty check for the book arrived sixteen years later still, at which point both Karl and Jenny had died; only their surviving children got some royalties.[22]

Their *surving* children. Four of Marx's six children died before he did. In the wretched winter of 1849–1850, the Marx family sought refuge in a dilapidated German boarding-house where their baby Guido succumbed to the elements. He perished a victim of his father's irresponsibility. As Paul Johnson writes of Marx's wife, "Jenny left a despairing account of these days, from which her spirits, and her affection for Marx, never really recovered."[23]

Then in 1855 Marx's eight-year-old son Edgar died of intestinal tuberculosis "exacerbated," as Mary Gabriel, author of a sympathetic biography of Karl and Jenny, explains, "by... unhealthy living conditions.... the revolutionary path [his parents] had chosen had killed him." Marx lamented to Friedrich Engels, "Every day my wife says she wishes she and the children were safely in their graves, and I really cannot blame her, for the humiliations, torments and alarums that one has to go through in such a situation are indeed indescribable."[24]

Then at least two of his daughters committed suicide,[25] one of them in a suicide pact with her husband, whom Marx had ridiculed. Marx detested his sons-in-law, seeing them both as idiots. But he particularly disliked Paul Lafargue, his daughter Laura's husband. Because Lafargue was Cuban, Marx denigrated him as "Negrillo" or "The Gorilla" on account of the "Negro blood" in his veins.

Marx's attitude towards women was not much more enlightened than his treatment of racial and ethnic minorities. To the devastation of his devoted wife, he had a sexual relationship with the family's longtime nursemaid, whom he apparently impregnated, though he refused to concede that the unfortunate child was his—or to provide a penny of child support.

And he vetoed careers for his daughters. Mary Gabriel writes that Marx's daughters "adored their father." They relished being born into Marx's "revolutionary household, with all the complications that entailed." They were educated according to "the values of Victorian society—music, art, literature, and languages" and were also were taught "a heavy dose of radical politics." And as soon as they were able, they became their father's assistants. Not until they were grown women, says Gabriel, did Marx's daughters fully grasp "the high price of being born a Marx." She notes that one daughter lost all three of her young children while devoting herself "to further her father's agenda." Another daughter gave up a cherished life as a journalist for a "miserable marriage" to one of her father's young French

★ ★ ★

All People Are Equal, but Some People Are More Equal Than Others

It's hard to argue with Walter Williams, the leading economist and well-known black conservative, when he states flatly that "Marx was an out and out racist and anti-Semite."[26] The founding father of communism freely dispensed choice epithets aimed at blacks and Jews (despite the fact that Marx himself was an ethnic Jew).[27] Marx referred to the labor organizer Ferdinand Lassalle as a "greasy Jew," "the little kike," "water-polack Jew," "Jew Braun," and "the Jewish Nigger" and wrote to Engels, "It is now perfectly clear to me that, as the shape of his head and the growth of his hair indicates, he is descended from the Negroes who joined in Moses' flight from Egypt." Lassalle's "cranial formation," said Marx, a proud Darwinist, was the giveaway—or perhaps "his mother or grandmother on the father's side was crossed with a nigger." Marx concluded, "This union of Jew and German on a Negro base was bound to produce an extraordinary hybrid."[28] And Engels wasn't much better; he deduced with scientific accuracy that Marx's son-in-law Paul Lafargue possessed "one-eighth or one-twelfth nigger blood." In 1887, Lafargue was a political candidate for a council seat in a Paris district that contained a zoo. In an April 1887 letter to Paul's wife, Laura, Engels opined, "Being in his quality as a nigger, a degree nearer to the rest of the animal kingdom than the rest of us, he is undoubtedly the most appropriate representative of that district."[29] No doubt Engels and Marx had a good chortle over that one.

followers. And the third became "ensnared by a man whom she believed to be worthy of her father," but who, in the end, drove her to suicide.[30]

Engels shared not only Marx's racism but his exploitative attitude toward women, callously juggling a number of mistresses, who pleaded with him to make honest women out of them, to take them to the altar rather than merely to bed. At one point in the 1850s, Engels seems to have begun referring to one of these women as his wife, though he would not legally marry her. When she died, he may have married another sexual partner—the sister of his late "wife"—but only on her deathbed.[31]

★ ★ ★

I Don't Remember That from the Bible

In a letter to Engels, Marx said, "Blessed is he who has no family."[32] It's a curious take on the Beatitudes; Jesus seemed to have left that one out.

Abolishing the Family

It's really no wonder that communism promotes pre-marital sex, non-committed relationships, and easy divorce. The ideological preferences of Marx and Engels were extensions of their personal preferences, as was apparent with the publication of Engels's *The Origin of the Family, Private Property and the State* in 1884. That was the year after Marx's death, but Engels explained in the preface that the book also represented Marx's views on family. Marx, said Engels, had eagerly wanted to undertake this crucial work and right up until his death had been writing materials that Engels had reproduced in the book "as far as possible." Indeed, Professor H. Kent Geiger, in his seminal Harvard University Press book on the subject, notes that "many of the ideas" in *The Origin of the Family, Private Property and the State* can be found in the first joint work by Marx and Engels, *The German Ideology*, which was not published during their lifetimes.

According to Geiger, *The Origin of the Family, Private Property and the State* was a "joint work" by the two founders of Marxism, based on an "impressive unity and continuity" across four decades of their mutual thoughts.[33] In that book Engels reiterated what both he and Marx had previously argued, namely that housework was yet another private thing that the communist state should seize control of, replacing it with collective labor managed by the state. Under communism, Engels explained, "The single family ceases to be the economic unit of society."[34] Mothers would be corralled into the fields and factories to do more meaningful work. Housework, from cooking to cleaning, would become a government industry, as would child care, which would become a communal affair. Mothers and wives would be liberated from the "economic bondage" of

The Devil Is in the Details

According to Robert Payne—a respected and thoughtful British professor of English literature and drama, biographer, linguist, and absolutely no right-winger, Karl Marx "could recite long passages of Goethe's *Faust* with gusto, with a special preference for the speeches of Mephistopheles"[35]—the devil who tempts Faust to sell his soul. Marx also wrote Satan-themed poetry as a young man, including a ballad in which a pure Christian maiden succumbs to the love of a dark figure who "takes[s] her heart by storm," and persuades her that her "soul, once true to God / Is chosen for Hell,"[36] and another poem in which "hellish vapors rise and fill the brain"[37] and a character says, "See this sword? The Prince of Darkness sold it to me."[38] Engels, who also wrote poetry, described Marx as

> A black man from Trier, a remarkable monster,
> He neither walks nor hops, but springs upon his heels
> And stretches high his arms into the air in anger
> As though his wrath would seize at once
> The mighty canopy of Heaven and tear it to the earth,
> With clenched and threatening fist he rages without rest,
> As though ten thousand devils had seized him by the hair.[39]

the traditional family.[40] "Private housekeeping is transformed into a social industry," Engels envisioned excitedly. "The care and education of the children becomes a public affair; society looks after all children alike, whether they are legitimate or not."[41]

"This removes all the anxiety about the consequences which today is the most essential social-moral as well as economic factor that prevents a girl from giving herself completely to the man she loves," wrote Engels. "Will not that suffice to bring about the gradual growth of unconstrained sexual intercourse and with it a more tolerant public opinion in regard to a maiden's honor and a woman's shame?"[42] You can see exactly why Friedrich Engels hoped it would.

Professor Geiger notes that Engels and Marx appeared to have "little to say" about the relationships between parents and children beyond the crucial recommendation that "they would not continue to live together, because society was to rear and educate" them. This collective rearing of children by the communist state would bring "real freedom" to all members of the family. Parenting would become the responsibility of the state.[43] This was all in aid of the "abolition of the family" that Marx and Engels had already written about in *The Communist Manifesto*.[44]

CHAPTER 4

The Communist Program—and Its Problems

"Communism wasn't responsible for any deaths. Crappy leaders were."

A frustrated James Kirchick of the liberal *Daily Beast* jotted down those words after hearing them from a friend. Kirchick knows better. He takes liberals to task for this attitude, which pervades the political Left. He asked his readers, "How many times have you heard some formulation of this viewpoint? 'Communism is an excellent idea in theory, it just hasn't worked in practice.' I wish that was the sort of sentiment I only remembered from college dorm room bull sessions."

Kirchick responded, *"OK. How many more millions of people have to die before we get it right?"*[1]

The notion that communist ideology is not responsible for the well over a hundred million deaths perpetrated by communist regimes has long been (as Kirchick says) "de rigeur among a broad segment of the intellectual elite." What's worse, it is gaining currency among Millennials and the American population as a whole—the population of the nation that won the Cold War and ought to know better.

Did you know?

★ Sixty-four percent of Americans agree with Marx's statement of the basic principle of communism

★ Twenty-five percent of Millennials have a favorable view of Lenin

★ *The Communist Manifesto* calls for the "abolition of the distinction between town and country"

In an October 2016 survey, only 37 percent of Millennials said they had a very unfavorable view of communism; 25 percent had a favorable view of Vladimir Lenin. One in five first-time voters (aged sixteen to twenty) said they would vote for a communist. And this delusional attitude isn't exclusive to dopy Millennials. Among Americans as a whole, 64 percent agreed with the basic principle of communism, as Marx put it in *The Communist Manifesto*: "From each according to his abilities, to each according to his needs."[2]

These findings are no surprise to those of us who have watched public opinion in recent decades. If I had a dollar for every nice thing some dummy told me about communism, I'd be one filthy-rich capitalist.

Again and again, you hear assertions along these lines:

Communism is a good idea.

The Communist Manifesto *is a pretty good book.*

Communists favor helping their fellow man. That's not a bad thing.

The communists' goals were positive. What's wrong with taking money from the rich and sharing it with the poor?

I could start a lucrative business of baloney bumper stickers touting the bogus virtues of Marxism-Leninism. I'd be one fat Wall Street one-percenter.

"What do you have against Karl Marx, dude?" an irritated liberal whined to me in college one day in November 1989—just as the Berlin Wall, that ultimate monument to Marx, built not far from the lousy university where he honed his craft, was being torn down. "Marx was just a little old man with a long beard sitting in a library writing books about philosophy."

Again and again, we're told that communist philosophy was never the problem. No, it was nasty leaders like Joe Stalin who have given communism a bad name. Stalin, you see, was an aberration. As were, presumably, Lenin, Trotsky, Latsis, Dzerzhinsky, Beria, Bulganin, Khrushchev, Voroshilov, Malenkov, Mikoyan, Brezhnev, Andropov, Chernenko, Chebrikov, Ulbricht, Ceausescu, Tito, Hoxha, Dimitrov, Zhivkov, Mao, Pol Pot, Ho Chi

Minh, Mengistu Mariam, Kim Il-Sung, Kim Jong Il, Kim Jong Un, Fidel, Raúl, and Che, not to mention the countess thousands of liquidators and inquisitors in the NKVD, the GRU, the KGB, the Red Guard, the Stasi, the SB, the AVH, the Securitate, the Khmer Rouge, the Sandinistas, the Sendero Luminoso, and on and on and on. That's a lot of aberrations.

The Devil Is in the Details

The Communist Manifesto begins, "A spectre is haunting Europe, the spectre of communism. All the powers of old Europe have entered into a holy alliance to exorcise this spectre...." And why shouldn't a holy alliance have wanted to drive out this very unholy spirit? What else do you do with a demon but exorcise it?

You would think at least one commie, somewhere along the line, would have gotten it right. Why such ugly results if the theory is so pretty? Can't these geniuses read?

Kirchick quotes Marion Smith, director of the vital Victims of Communism Memorial Foundation: "It is perhaps one of the biggest lies that exist in our culture today that the deadliest ideology in history is somehow not responsible for the regimes that it brought to life and the deaths that it caused. Ideas have consequences and there has never been a communist regime that did not end up killing its own people as a goal."

From the outset Karl Marx conceded, in *The Communist Manifesto* no less, that despotism would be necessary to implement his ideology. To wit: "Of course, in the beginning, this cannot be effected except by means of despotic inroads." Lenin, Trotsky, Stalin, and a long line of communism's leading lights, implementers, practitioners, advocates, flag-wavers, cheerleaders, plus gaggles of theorists, teachers, and tenured radicals in American universities—far beyond just a handful of "crappy leaders"—understood and candidly admitted that violence would be necessary to reach the communist utopia.

And how could it not be? *The Communist Manifesto* said that, "Communism abolishes eternal truths, it abolishes all religion, and all morality."[3]

★ ★ ★

A Material Guy

"[Marx] thought that once the economy had been put right, everything would automatically be put right. His real error is materialism: man, in fact, is not merely the product of economic conditions, and it is not possible to redeem him purely from the outside by creating a favorable economic environment."—**Pope Benedict XVI**[8]

Marx and Engels envisioned a new morality without God, one based on "the most radical rupture with traditional ideas."[4] The things that communism promises are entirely unnatural, completely contrary to what human beings had believed before, and even to their very humanity itself. It was intended to transform human nature so completely, and so committed to undermining everything from natural law to Biblical law to common sense and decency, that the ideology could never have been implemented without killing people. Lots and lots of people.

An Ideal, a Program, and a Regime

Richard Pipes, Harvard professor emeritus of Soviet history, writes insightfully and authoritatively in his indispensable *Communism: A History* that the word "communism" in essence refers to three related but distinct phenomena: an ideal, a program, and a regime set up to realize the ideal.[5]

The "ideal" of communism is equality in its most extreme form. The program is based on what Karl Marx and Friedrich Engels wrote in their 1848 *Communist Manifesto.* The regime is the global horror-show unleashed upon millions of innocents who simply wanted to live in peace, beginning with the regime of the ghastly Bolsheviks, led by Lenin, angry architect of "Marxism-Leninism," the totalitarian ideology that became the dominant strand of communism across the world in the twentieth century.

To get the gist of the communist program, as Marx himself laid it out, does not require years of scouring dusty old volumes in stacks at university libraries. *The Communist Manifesto,* Marx's most famous single expression of his philosophy, is very brief and very inexpensive—free, in fact, at http://www.marxists.org/archive/marx/works/1848/communist-manifesto/.

But for a more thorough grasp of the world's deadliest philosophy, you have to understand Marx's ideas on the so-called "dialectic" of history—explained at great length in *Das Kapital* (*Capital*), his magnum opus. As a student at the University of Berlin, Marx had learned from the philosophy of Georg Wilhelm Friedrich Hegel that history is a series of struggles between opposing forces, with each successive struggle unfolding on a progressively higher plane than the one that preceded it. Ultimately, according to Hegel, the truth is only revealed as the result of a dialectical unfolding in history. As one Hegel scholar wrote, this "dialectical unfolding ends in the revelation of God."[6]

Hegel's was an "ideational dialectic." But Marx, unlike Hegel, was not any kind of Christian.[7] He was an atheist and a materialist, and the "dialectic" he had in mind in was not on Hegel's "ideational plane." It was based on economics and classes—the material things that were the framework of what Marx believed in. For Marxist philosophy, the be-all and end-all was economic and material. It was a dialectical materialism.

Marx was highly critical of the industrialization of the nineteenth century, which indisputably had its abuses, excesses, and cruelties. And Marx was a skilled complainer. He could describe wretchedness as movingly as anyone. Describing misery, however, is much different from diagnosing a proper response to it. And Karl Marx was the last person for coming up with good solutions. Marx envisioned an apocalyptic revolution leading to the overthrow of capitalism by the impoverished working class, the common people, the masses—the so-called "proletariat." The stage in the revolutionary process immediately following this overthrow would be "the dictatorship of the proletariat." But that dictatorship would be only a way station on the road to the ultimate utopia: a "classless society." The state would simply die out; it would *wither* away.

★ ★ ★

Soviet-Era Humor

"A Brit, a Frenchman, and a Russian are viewing a painting of Adam and Eve frolicking in the Garden of Eden. 'Look at their reserve, their calm,' muses the Brit. 'They must be British.'

"'Nonsense,' the Frenchman disagrees. 'They're naked, and so beautiful. Clearly they are French.'

"'No clothes, no shelter,' the Russian points out, 'they have only an apple to eat, and they're being told this is paradise. They are Russian.'"[11]

In a classless society there would be no more economic inequality, no more class antagonisms, no more conflict. All would be peace and harmony. Of course, in order for this utopia to come into being, socialism would need to sweep the planet. It had to be worldwide. It would need to spread across the globe. The whole thing was the ultimate utopian pipedream.

What were the specifics for getting there? Were there any? Where were the detailed directions? The road map? The blueprint?

Marx grandiosely exclaimed that "Communism is the riddle of history solved, and it knows itself to be this solution."[9] Few ideologies, or ideologues, have been so self-boastful.

Marx fantasized, "In communist society, where nobody has one exclusive sphere of activity but each can become accomplished in any branch he wishes, society regulates the general production and thus makes it possible for me to do one thing today and another tomorrow, to hunt in the morning, fish in the afternoon, rear cattle in the evening, criticize after dinner, just as I have a mind, without ever becoming hunter, fisherman, herdsman or critic."[10]

It would be, according to Marx, a "leap from slavery into freedom; from darkness into light."[12]

This was no small project, and thus it would require no small changes. As a matter of fact, it would require the transformation of human nature itself. In *The German Ideology*, Marx called for not merely "the production on a mass scale of this communist consciousness" but "the alteration of men on a mass scale." This project is totalitarian in its scope. It envisions a complete overthrow of human nature as we know it. Marx explained that the communist "revolution is necessary, therefore, not only because the ruling class cannot be overthrown in any other way, but also because the class overthrowing it can only in a revolution succeed in ridding itself of all the muck of ages and become fitted to found society anew."

Engels also preached a gospel of fundamental transformation (to paraphrase Barack Obama). In his *Dialectics of Nature* Engels called for "the *alteration of nature* by men" (his emphasis) as "the most essential and immediate basis of human thought."[13]

The success of communism naturally depends on altering human nature because few things are more inherent in human nature than the ownership of property. This basic human right is as ancient as the Ten Commandments, where God ordained that "Thou shall not steal." The commandment implicitly acknowledges that persons have possessions and that they have an inherent right to that property—so it is thus not permissible for others to take it away from them.

But Marx and Engels weren't about to admit the right to private property that we find even in the Bible.

So what exactly was this "proletariat" that would be so refined by the communist revolution that it would be suited to "found society anew"? Engels defined communism as "the doctrine of the conditions of the liberation of the proletariat" and the proletariat as "that class in society which lives entirely from the sale of its labor and does not draw profit from any kind of capital; whose weal and woe, whose life and death, whose sole existence depends on the demand for labor."[14]

Marx viewed the proletariat as pitiable but also as the source of salvation—a redeemer class. As Martin Malia explains it, this victim-redeemer class was charged with a higher mission precisely because it was the most exploited and hence most dehumanized class in society. Marx thus defined the proletariat not as the body of factory workers but as the class destined to liberate

★ ★ ★

Property Is Theft

"Under private property.... Each tries to establish over the other an alien power, so as thereby to find satisfaction of his own selfish need. The increase in the quantity of objects is therefore accompanied by an extension of the realm of the alien powers to which man is subjected, and every new product represents a new *potentiality* of mutual swindling and mutual plundering." —**Karl Marx,** *Human Requirements and Division of Labour* (1844)[15]

the species from social inequality. Marx's revolution would commence once this victimized proletariat achieved sufficient "consciousness" of its dehumanized plight and emancipatory mission.[16] And of course, the intellectuals—Marx and his university pals—were the anointed ones tasked with raising the consciousness of the unenlightened. It was by the stripes of these chastised people that humanity would be healed.

This is a crucial insight not only about Marxists-Leninists and cultural Marxists but also into the far Left generally. To this day, the radical Left never stops looking for a new class of victims, whether it be disgruntled workers, purportedly excluded ethnicities, or supposedly oppressed "sexual minorities" whose plight needs to be identified and their consciousness raised by a more enlightened intelligentsia. Go to the website of any modern communist publication at any time and you will find the comrades pushing and prodding and hoisting the latest group of downtrodden victims in (allegedly) desperate need of the assistance of the far Left. It is through these pitiful sufferers that redemption must be delivered.

All Proletarians Are Equal, but Some Proletarians Are Less Equal Than Others

The proletariat will redeem the world and usher in the communist utopia. But not necessarily all the proletariat. What Marx called the lumpenproletariat is identified in one of his myriad of memorable diatribes. This was an unseemly layer of working-class rabble, incapable of ever achieving proper class consciousness and thus essentially useless to the noble goals of the revolutionary struggle.

The word "lumpen" derives from the German for "rag" or "miscreant." Marx described this smarmy caste in his *The Eighteenth Brumaire of Louis Napoleon*. "Alongside decayed roués with dubious means of subsistence and of dubious origin," sniffed Marx, "alongside ruined and adventurous offshoots of the bourgeoisie, were vagabonds, discharged soldiers, discharged jailbirds, escaped galley slaves, swindlers, mountebanks, lazzaroni, pickpockets, tricksters, gamblers, pimps, brothel keepers, porters, literati, organ grinders, ragpickers, knife grinders, tinkers, beggars—in short, the whole indefinite, disintegrated mass, thrown hither and thither, which the French call *la bohème*." Here we see Marx's tendency—shared by Vladimir Lenin as well—to debase and dehumanize entire types and groups of people. (Lenin called some groups of people "harmful insects.") Marx rounded them up with his typewriter; Lenin and Stalin and boys would round them up with bayonets.

Abolishing the Present State of Things

Another hallmark of communism and the far Left in general, in addition to its serial adoption of new victim groups, is its hostility to reality as it actually exists. No institution, no tradition, no facet of nature—no matter how worthy, decent, or even absolutely necessary to human flourishing—is safe from the revolution. From the avowed communists in the German universities of the early twentieth century to the cultural Marxists at American universities in the

★ ★ ★

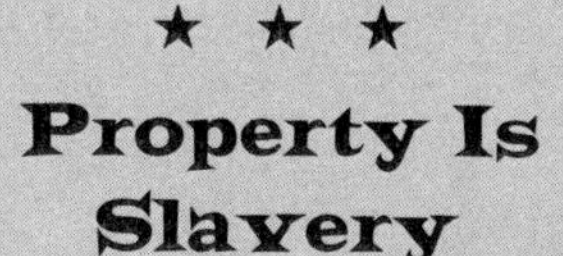

"The slave frees himself when, of all the relations of private property, he abolishes only the relation of slavery and thereby becomes a proletarian; the proletarian can free himself only by *abolishing private property in general* [emphasis original]." —**Friedrich Engels,** *Principles of Communism* (1847)[17]

twentieth century, the goal has been the abolition of the realities that underpin society as it actually exists.

"Abolition" is a word that appears frequently in the writings of Marx and Lenin. As Marx wrote in the *German Ideology*, "Communism is for us not a *state of affairs* which is to be established, an *ideal* to which reality [will] have to adjust itself. We call communism the *real* movement which abolishes the present state of things. The conditions of this movement result from the premises now in existence."[18]

Abolishes the present state of things. Those are significant words. This is why communism is a totalitarian ideology at its very root. Communists hate the very idea of permanent things. "To my mind," wrote Engels, "the so-called 'socialist society' is not anything immutable. Like all other social formations, it should be conceived in a state of constant flux and change."[19] You can see why communists like to refer to themselves as "progressives."

The essential elements of human life and society that the communists want to eradicate are countless, but they start with the ownership of property, marriage and the family, religion and traditional morality. According to Marx: "the theory of the Communists may be summed up in the single sentence: Abolition of private property."[20] Needless to say, the unequivocal rejection of such a fundamental aspect of human experience violates the most basic rights of all peoples, acknowledged from the cave to the courthouse, from primitive tribes to the most sophisticated philosophers of our Judeo-Christian civilization. As Marx himself acknowledged, his views on property stood undeniably contrary to the "social and political order of things."[21] The *Manifesto* offered a ten-point program of specific policy recommendations.[22] Here they are, in direct quotation:

1. Abolition of property in land and application of all rents of land to public purposes.
2. A heavy progressive or graduated income tax.

3. Abolition of all right of inheritance.
4. Confiscation of all property of emigrants and rebels.
5. Centralization of credit in the hands of the state, by means of a national bank with state capital and an exclusive monopoly.
6. Centralization of the means of communication and transport in the hands of the state.
7. Extension of factories and instruments of production owned by the state; the bringing into cultivation of waste lands, and the improvement of the soil generally in accordance with a common plan.
8. Equal obligation of all to work....
9. ...gradual abolition of all the distinction between town and country by a more equitable distribution of the population over the country.
10. Free education for all children in public schools....[23]

Marx and Engels conceded that this program would require despotism. They prefaced their ten points by insisting: "Of course, in the beginning, this cannot be effected except by means of despotic inroads."[24]

No kidding. Human beings were not going to give up their fundamental liberties—their natural rights—without some resistance. To take away everyone's property, rightly and fairly earned, would require a terrible fight. The communists—from Lenin to Pol Pot to Hugo Chávez—would need all their guns and their Gulags.

And the communists' work isn't done once they have seized everyone's property. Then they have to manage it. Communist economies are "command economies" or "centrally planned economies." The hallmark of communist economies—in contrast to free-market capitalist economies—is command and control via a central planning bureau, agency, or council. This group is tasked with the goal of managing and directing the whole of a nation's vast resources and means of production. The "Invisible Hand" of the free market is replaced by the omnipotent hand of the planning bureau. All major decisions regarding the resources used and the composition and distribution of the goods produced are dictated by the planning bureau.

This task, of course, would be hopelessly challenging for a small village. It is patently absurd to imagine that any bureaucracy could pull it off for a nation the size of the Soviet Union (which covered twelve time zones) or China (housing over one billion people) or for a "bloc" of countries comprising an entire region like Eastern Europe. Nonetheless, communist after communist—that is to say, one jaw-dropping economic ignoramus after another—has been undeterred, attacking this mission with glee.

Yuri Maltsev, who worked for the section of the Soviet planning bureau that set prices, recalls that his group had 328 staffers who were responsible for setting approximately twenty-three million prices in the USSR—for everything from potatoes and sausages to screws and cogs. They published a massive catalogue that contained this vast assemblage of information.[25]

Of course, as anyone with common sense knows, let alone a rationally thinking economist, no such catalogue could ever conceivably work. Just keeping it updated would be a pipedream. But the essential problem is that no group of individuals, unless they were literally omniscient, could begin to know the "right" price for each and every item. It was this problem that led Friedrich Hayek, the great Austrian School economist, to argue in his brilliant book *The Fatal Conceit: The Errors of Socialism*, published in 1988, that central planning is inherently unworkable. Hayek observed that centrally planned economies can neither be efficient nor even continue to exist in the long term because they lack the massive volume of intricate, minute, and dispersed knowledge that the free market makes available by means of prices negotiated by millions of producers and consumers acting on their own independent knowledge.

A similar argument had been made earlier by Hayek's Austrian School colleague, Ludwig von Mises, in his 1922 classic *Socialism*, which predicted the inevitable failure of communism. Free market capitalism, von Mises argued, constituted the only true economic democracy. The free market makes consumers sovereign. "Their buying and their abstention from buying decides who should own and run the plants and the farms," he wrote. "They make poor people rich and rich people poor. They determine precisely what should be produced, in what quality, and in what quantities." And these consumers are "merciless bosses, full of whims and fancies, changeable and unpredictable. For them nothing counts other than their own satisfaction. They do not care a whit for past merit and vested interests.... The consumers patronize those shops in which they can buy what they want at the cheapest price."

Indeed they do. Consumers, which comprise the *proletariat* and everyone else, are sovereign in the free marketplace. They are the bosses. They are the dictators. Under communism just the opposite is true. There, the consumers—the vaunted "masses"—are not sovereign but captive to the planning bureau and the unelected apparatchiks and dictators. They have little power.

What von Mises wrote is easily confirmed by everyday observation on the part of anyone with common sense and eyes to see and ears to hear. Communist central planning is a blanket violation of common sense and the natural order of things. Sadly, there are people who seem not to be able to see the problems inherent in communism—including a lot of people who enjoy life in the dynamic free world graced by Amazon and Walmart, Target and Starbucks, Home Depot and Trader Joe's. But to adapt Ronald Reagan quoting from Alexander Hamilton, those people are preparing themselves for a master—and they deserve one.[26]

The inevitable and utter failure of central planning is the cause of the abject poverty into which communists always drive their people. On top of

★ ★ ★

Everything to Lose

"The Communists disdain to conceal their views and aims. They openly declare that their ends can be attained only by the forcible overthrow of all existing social conditions. Let the ruling classes tremble at a communist revolution. *The proletarians have nothing to lose but their chains.* They have a world to win. Working Men of All Countries, Unite!"

—the stirring call to arms at the end of *The Communist Manifesto* is more than a little ironic considering the millions of people who have been reduced to desperate poverty by communism (not to mention stripped of their human rights, and frequently murdered)

the "fatal conceit" that bureaucrats will be able to manage the millions of pieces of information about every need and resource in an economy better than free individuals in a free market, there is also the problem of incentives. In the communist system, factories and farms are not owned by individual entrepreneurs but by government through collectives and state enterprises. And the whole point of the system is equality. So all workers—whether skilled or unskilled, industrious or lazy—are paid the same. Even the managers (there are no owners) of these collectives are paid the same, with no personal financial incentives or rewards for superior performance.

This no-incentive system, which you can see in a communist paradise such as Cuba to this very day, guarantees abysmal performance, whether at the level of the individual, the enterprise, or the national economy. Thus any communist economy is unable to respond to people's needs and desires. So in Havana you're one of the lucky ones if you're driving a 1950s-model car. In communist countries there are always shortages and long lines for the necessities of life, from transportation to plumbing fixtures to toilet paper.

Atrocities with No Shame

But communism is not just an abject economic failure everywhere it is tried. It is also a human rights disaster. Communists always end up violating human rights; their track record of persecution, imprisonment, torture, and murder is unrivaled in world history. It's not just that they inevitably find themselves using the brutal force of the state in their vain attempt to break human nature on the wheel of their utopian dreams. It's that they don't believe in objective right and wrong in the first place. Communists reject the very idea of moral absolutes; they frankly declare themselves unbound by them.

As Marx explained, "Law, morality, and religion are to him [the proletarian] so many bourgeois prejudices, behind which lurk in ambush so many bourgeois interests."[27] Under communism, all morality is subordinate to class interests. The collective stands superior to the individual. And the promised utopia justifies any violation of the rights of individuals and any breach of the moral law.

The Devil Is in the Details

"All the biblical descriptions of hell and the pains of Dante's *Inferno* are nothing in comparison with the tortures in Communist prisons," stated Richard Wurmbrand in his international bestseller, *Tortured for Christ*. He recalled, "I have seen communists whose faces while torturing believers shone with rapturous joy. They cried out while torturing the Christians, 'We are the devil!'" He remembered one torturer saying, "I thank God in whom I don't believe, that I have lived to this hour when I can express all the evil in my heart."

The inalienable rights claimed in the Declaration of Independence are alien to communism; they are antithetical to Marxist-Leninist thought. Bear in mind that in the Declaration Jefferson was borrowing from a Lockean tradition that also recognized property as a human right. The American founders believed that our rights to property, life, liberty, and the pursuit of happiness were "self-evident"—and self-evidently bestowed upon us by our Creator. Thus the Declaration of Independence gives governments merely the duty to help "secure" rights that are already there—not the authority to create them in the first place, much less the right to take them away.

But communists don't believe in a Creator. As Lenin said, "In what sense do we repudiate ethics and morality?...In the sense in which it was preached

★ ★ ★

Forgetting Freedom

"[Marx's] error lay deeper. He forgot that man always remains man. He forgot man and he forgot man's freedom."

—Pope Benedict XVI[29]

by the bourgeoisie, who derived ethics from God's commandments. We, of course, say that we do not believe in God."[28]

Tragically, the American Founders' understanding of liberty and human rights based on "the Laws of Nature and of Nature's God," which had spread around the world from the eighteenth century to the end of World War I, as many authoritarian governments gave way to freedom and democracy, was jettisoned by the Bolsheviks and their imitators. The real progress humanity had made beginning in 1776 came to a grinding halt in Russia in 1917. Beginning with the Russian Revolution, communist governments rejected every single one of these fundamental liberties: religion, conscience, speech, press, assembly, property, and, oftentimes, life itself.

To be sure, the level of suppression has varied from communist government to communist government, with some much worse than others. Not every Marxist—not even every Marxist dictator—was a Pol Pot. But the abrogation of civil liberties, the death of freedom, and the violation of human rights are hallmarks of every communist regime.

CHAPTER 5

Bolshevik Brutes

Communism moved from theory to practice in October 1917. It debuted with a bang, not a whimper, when the Bolsheviks—led by the fanatical troika of Lenin, Trotsky, and Stalin—took power and launched their global revolution of mayhem and murder. Neither Russia nor the world would ever be the same.

Vladimir Ilyich Ulyanov—"Lenin" was an alias—was the architect and pioneer of the first Marxist-Leninist state. He was born April 22, 1870 in Simbirsk, a town on the Volga River east of Moscow, which would be renamed Ulyanovsk after him in 1924. His parents were decent, civil people, both of them God-fearing—in fact, quite religious. His father, Ilya, was a pious and even conservative man. He died when his son was only fifteen years old.[1]

Lenin emerged from a somewhat complicated upbringing a devoted disciple of the teachings of Karl Marx. Lenin was arrested for sedition in 1895 and exiled by the Czarist government to Siberia until 1900. Immediately upon his release from Siberia, he moved to Germany, following the footsteps of so many socialists of the period. There he wrote quite a bit, formulating his ideas in writing.

Did you know?

★ Lenin called democracy "only one of the stages" on the road to communism

★ He preached the necessity of "mass terror"

★ Half a million Russians had already been killed by government repression before Stalin took over from Lenin

★ ★ ★

I Can Think of Something More Abominable

Lenin's contempt for religion began in his teenage years when, as he boasted, he had removed the cross he wore around his neck and "tossed it in the rubbish bin."[2] Later, as the leader of Bolshevik Russia, he would declare, "There's nothing more abominable than religion."[3]

In Germany, Lenin worked often with Julius Martov, sometimes in solidarity but usually (as was typically the case with Lenin) in opposition, division, and vituperation. In 1903, Lenin attended the Social Democratic Congress, also known as the Second Congress of the Russian Social Democratic Labor Party, starting in Brussels and ending in London, over a period of three weeks from July to August. This was a pivotal moment in history, though people at the time (especially those outside the assembly) had no idea just how profoundly dire the implications of the meeting would be.

With a plurality of supporters at the Congress, Lenin took for his faction the name "Bolsheviks," meaning "Majority." His opponents, led by Martov, became the "Mensheviks," or "Minority." Lenin, as was his habit in dealing with all his political opponents, hurled vicious names at the Mensheviks, denouncing them as "traitors" and, ironically, "liquidators"[4]—ironically because Lenin and his Bolsheviks would one day do with the Mensheviks what they accused the Mensheviks of wanting to do to them, and what the Bolsheviks would do to all their opponents whenever they had the opportunity: liquidate them.

Lenin's period as an expatriate would continue, ultimately running from 1900 to 1917, at which point the German government of the Kaiser put him in a boxcar to Russia and dropped him smack in the middle of St. Petersburg as a human bomb to annihilate the Germans' Russian enemy in World War I.[5] And the German plan worked—once the communists took over Russia, they signed an armistice with Germany and pulled out of the war. But the unintended consequences of Lenin's return to his native land at this critical point went far beyond World War I and beyond Russia, to every corner of the globe and into the longer century. That's because Lenin's arrival in Moscow made it possible, for the first time in history, for a communist ideologue, a disciple of Karl Marx, to seize power and gain control of a major nation.

The Devil Is in the Details

Look at photos of Lenin: the man is a dead ringer for the devil. The grim countenance, the goatee, the narrow face, the downward-pointing chin, the high forehead, the angular features, the beady eyes. The only things missing are the horns, the pitch fork, and engulfing flames. The man was right out of central casting. And no one can deny that Comrade Lenin subjected the Russians to hell on earth.

Keeper of the Flame

Vladimir Lenin was a true believer in communism as articulated by Marx and Engels. He believed that their writings had opened the door to utopia, and he judged himself the gatekeeper. The writings of Lenin, like those of Marx and Engels, are voluminous. But for probably the single best statement of Lenin's interpretation of Marx and Engels consider his classic, *The State and Revolution: The Marxist Theory of the State and the Tasks of the Proletariat in the Revolution*, written in August–September 1917 as he was in hiding from the Provisional Government, mere weeks before he spearheaded the October Revolution.[6] For a year at least, Lenin had been arguing the need for a theoretical work applied to practical realities, and this was his major stab at providing one. His original draft was titled simply, "Marxism on the State." He planned to write seven chapters but was able to complete only six before events overtook him and other priorities (such as running the actual state itself) demanded his full attention.[7] Lenin's *The State and Revolution* is essential for understanding communism.

Anyone reading anything by Lenin, from his letters to his pamphlets and books is immediately struck by his stridency. The man was a verbal bomb-thrower. Richard Pipes, who was editor of the Lenin letters that were declassified after the Soviet collapse, points out (citing, among others, Lenin

The Unknown Lenin: From the Secret Archive, edited by Richard Pipes (New Haven, CT: Yale University Press, 1999).

collaborator Peter Struve) that "the principal feature of Lenin's personality was hatred." Joyless hostility haunts not only his writings but the wider politics and history of the communist Left.[8] Lenin was an angry, vitriolic little man whose hatchet-edged prose reflected his nasty character and temperament.

Fittingly, in the opening sentences of the preface to *The State and Revolution*, Lenin twice used the word "monstrous," which he employed to describe the oppression of the workers by the state, but which actually better characterizes the communist revolution and the communist state that Lenin and his cabal would establish. Then this malicious man opened the first chapter of his book ("Class Society and the State") with vicious barbs that, inadvertently, better captured him and his movement than the intended targets of his smears. He used characterizations such as "savage malice," "furious hatred," "vulgarizing," and "lies and slander."

What was making Lenin so angry? Any attempt to water down Marx's full-blown revolutionary communism:

> What is now happening to Marx's theory has, in the course of history, happened repeatedly to the theories of revolutionary thinkers and leaders of oppressed classes fighting for emancipation. During the lifetime of great revolutionaries, the oppressing classes constantly hounded them, received their theories with the most savage malice, the most furious hatred and the most unscrupulous campaigns of lies and slander. After their death, attempts are made to convert them into harmless icons, to canonize them, so to say, and to hallow their names to a certain extent for the "consolation" of the oppressed classes and with the object

> of duping the latter, while at the same time robbing the revolutionary theory of its substance, blunting its revolutionary edge and vulgarizing it. Today, the bourgeoisie and the opportunists within the labor movement concur in this doctoring of Marxism. They omit, obscure, or distort the revolutionary side of this theory, its revolutionary soul. They push to the foreground and extol what is or seems acceptable to the bourgeoisie. All the social chauvinists are now "Marxists" (don't laugh!). And more and more frequently German bourgeois scholars, only yesterday specialists in the annihilation of Marxism, are speaking of the "national German" Marx, who, they claim, educated the labor unions which are so splendidly organized for the purpose of waging a predatory war!
>
> In these circumstances, in view of the unprecedentedly widespread distortion of Marxism, our prime task is to reestablish what Marx really taught on the subject of the state.[9]

Yes, "what Marx really taught." Lenin was anointing himself the enforcer of communist orthodoxy, the repository of revolutionary truth, the bearer of the Marxist torch. *The State and Revolution* is full of long quotations from the works of Marx and Engels, which Lenin acknowledged would render his text "cumbersome." But, he argued, the most essential passages from the works of Marx and Engels must be quoted as fully as possible so that the reader could secure "an independent opinion of the totality of the views of the founders of scientific socialism, and of the evolution of those views."

Lenin lit into what he termed the "petty bourgeois and philistine professors and publicists" who made "frequent and benevolent references to Marx" but who, in the infallible judgment of Pope Vladimir, had "distorted" the work of the great Marx and Engels. He was especially indignant at the "Socialist-Revolutionaries" who weren't on board with Engels's hallowed

★ ★ ★

Scientific Fraud

Note Lenin's use of the phrase "scientific socialism." Soviet officials would use those same words incessantly in the years ahead, applying the term "scientific" to a political theory that could never really truly be scientific. Marx himself had tried to make the case that his theories were "science." "Natural science will in time incorporate into itself the science of man," he claimed in *Private Property and Communism* (1844), "just as the science of man will incorporate into itself natural science: there will be *one* science."[10] For the record, the communists' claim to the mantle of science owes a great deal to the Darwinian theory of evolution popularized by monkey-man Charles Darwin in his 1859 *On the Origin of Species*, which Marx devoured immediately after its publication. (In his youthful poetry Marx spoke of his fellow men as "apes".)[11] Marx's "dialectic" has a lot in common with Darwin's "evolution": both are supposed to involve multi-step improvement by a process that their theoreticians claim is pushed along by purely material causes.[12] So great was the respect that the founding fathers of communism had for the theory of evolution that Engels invoked Darwin in his eulogy to Marx at Marx's graveside: "Just as Darwin discovered the law of development or organic nature, so Marx discovered the law of development of human history," claimed Engels.[13]

Trotsky was another huge fan of Darwin. "The idea of evolution and determinism," he wrote, "took possession of me completely. Darwin stood for me like a mighty doorkeeper at the entrance to the temple of the universe. I was intoxicated with his ... thought."[14]

Hardcore secular evolutionists like to imagine that if not for microscopic mutations in the gene pool, we'd all be monkeys jumping up and down slinging our feces at one another. Perhaps communism has simply never evolved beyond this stage?

words about the "withering of the state."[15] He quoted Engels: "The proletariat seizes from state power and turns the means of production into state property to begin with. But thereby it abolishes itself as the proletariat, abolishes all class distinctions and class antagonisms, and abolishes also the state as state." Thus, claimed Engels, "State interference in social relations becomes, in one domain after another, superfluous, and then dies down of itself. The government of persons is replaced by the administration of things, and by the conduct of processes of production. The state is not 'abolished.' It withers away."[16]

And as we all know that's what actually happened after Lenin took power in Russia. Once the revolution was complete and the proletariat took control, it merrily abolished itself and all the other classes, class hostility vanished, and the government faded away. Utopia was achieved.

Oh, wait. That's *not* what happened. Instead, Lenin waged a war of terror on the proletariat's supposed class enemies and used the full force of the most repressive police state the world had yet seen to stamp out any dissent from his communist program.

★ ★ ★

You Never Said a Truer Word

Lenin said that "there can be no question of specifying the moment of the future 'withering way.'" He assured his readers only that "it will obviously be a lengthy process."[18] No kidding. The Russian Revolution has now reached its hundred-year anniversary, inspiring numerous imitators across the globe in the century since 1917. So far, no communist state has yet withered away.

But the withering away of the state is what Lenin promised: "State interference... dies down of itself. The government of persons is replaced by the administration of things.... "[17]

The "administration of *things?*" The "government of persons" is replaced by some sort of "*administration of things?*" This, dear comrade, is pure gobbledygook. It is sophistry. It is ideological babble. It does not deserve to be taken seriously for a moment of fleeting discussion in a late-night dorm-room bull session, let alone as a serious proposal for implementation by a nation-state.

And of course even in the communist fantasy, the promised withering of the state is not the first thing on the program. The promised utopia is possible only *after* a bloody revolution destroys the present regime: "The supersession of the bourgeois state by the proletarian state is impossible without a violent revolution." Well, he got that one right. Lenin may have been wrong about the ultimate withering away of the state under communism, but he was absolutely correct in his belief that communism could never be imposed in the first place without violence. That's something that communists all seem to be on board with. They may have ferocious debates about the details of the zany blueprints for their crackpot utopian scheme, but the one thing they can agree on when they're plotting their takeover is the one thing they do best after they take power: violence.

Lenin's *The State and the Revolution* prattles on for page upon page—through headings such as "What Is to Replace the Smashed State Machine" and "Abolition of the Parasite State"[19]—of blistering attacks on his enemies. He excoriates not just the bourgeoisie and the other presumed enemies of the revolution he was trying to get started, but also any other *communists* who aren't 100 percent on board with his own reading of Marx. The *falsifiers* and *opportunists* must be kicked and kicked hard. "Let them howl!" Lenin exclaimed.[20]

The State and Revolution includes a chapter (chapter five, section two) on "The Transition from Capitalism to Communism." It begins with a quote from Marx: "Between capitalist and communist society lies the period of the revolutionary transformation of the one into the other. Corresponding to this is also a political transition period in which the state can be nothing but the revolutionary dictatorship of the proletariat."

Democracy, just like the (supposed, subsequent) withering away of the state, has to wait until some time after the revolution. Even after the proletariat takes over, "suppression" will still be necessary. As Lenin explains,

> Only in communist society, when the resistance of the capitalists have disappeared, when there are no classes (i.e., when there is no distinction between the members of society as regards their relation to the social means of production), only then "the state…ceases to exist," and "it becomes possible to speak of freedom." Only then will a truly complete democracy become possible and be realized,

> a democracy without any exceptions whatever. And only then will democracy begin to wither away, owing to the simple fact that, freed from capitalist slavery, from the untold horrors, savagery, absurdities, and infamies of capitalist exploitation, people will gradually become accustomed to observing the elementary rules of social intercourse that have been known for centuries and repeated for thousands of years in all copybook maxims. They will become accustomed to observing them without force, without coercion, without subordination, without the special apparatus for coercion called the state...Furthermore, during the transition from capitalism to communism suppression is still necessary, but it is now the suppression of the exploiting minority by the exploited majority. A special apparatus, a special machine for suppression, the "state," is still necessary, but this is now a transitional state. It is no longer a state in the proper sense of the word....[21]

Lenin was theoretically for democracy. But what did he mean by that term? Interestingly, Lenin used the word "democracy" in much the same way as leftists and progressives in the United States fling it around today—as a vague synonym for "equality." In their book, "democracy" can mean anything from "marriage equality" for gay people, to a guaranteed basic income from the government, to racial and "transgender" equality, to the minimum wage, to whatever other brands of snake oil the Left is lathering up to fundamentally transform the country. Like every part of their program, its meaning changes with the progress of the revolution. And at some point the revolution will have no more need of democracy. As Lenin wrote plainly,

> Democracy means equality.... But it is important to realize how infinitely mendacious is the ordinary bourgeois conception of socialism as something lifeless, rigid, fixed once and for all,

★ ★ ★

Not in the Instruction Manual

"[Marx] showed precisely how to overthrow the existing order, but he did not say how matters should proceed thereafter. He simply presumed that with the expropriation of the ruling class, with the fall of political power and the socialization of means of production, the new Jerusalem would be realized.... Thus, having accomplished the revolution, Lenin must have realized that the writings of the master gave no indication as to how to proceed. True, Marx had spoken of the interim phase of the dictatorship of the proletariat as a necessity which in time would automatically become redundant. This 'intermediate phase' we know all too well, and we also know how it then developed, not ushering in a perfect world, but leaving behind a trail of appalling destruction." —**Pope Benedict XVI**[23]

> whereas in reality only socialism will be the beginning of a rapid, genuine, truly mass forward movement, embracing first the majority and then the whole of the population, in all spheres of public and private life. Democracy is of enormous importance to the working class in its struggle against the capitalists for its emancipation. But democracy is by no means a boundary not to be overstepped it is only one of the stages on the road from feudalism to capitalism, and from capitalism to communism.[22]

Let me repeat that. In Marxism-Leninism, democracy is just "one of the stages on the road" on the way to communism. And somehow, in actual communist revolutions, that stage never seems to arrive. The bloody violence and brutal repression just go on and on, as far as the eye can see.

Communism in Practice

By the time of the October Revolution, leftist intellectuals and revolutionaries had been agitating for communism for roughly seventy years. But up to that point, it had been an imaginary utopia, an ideal state of affairs the communists could describe in whatever glowing terms they chose. Over the next seventy years, the world would learn exactly what communism was like in reality. To its sorrow.

The Cheka: Lenin's Political Police by George Leggett (Oxford: Clarendon Press, 1981).

Within ten weeks of launching their revolution in Russia in late October 1917, the Bolsheviks had already abolished all sorts of private property and individual rights, from factories to farms, from fur coats to bank accounts, from free speech and free assembly to newspapers, from religious education to religious worship services, and much, much more. Bank credit, dividends, and interest were also forbidden. Lenin accomplished this through a series of about a dozen extraordinary decrees from November through the end of December 1917. A fury of nationalization, centralization, collectivization was under way, with the abolition of property and a government monopoly on communication—with all the changes accompanied and facilitated by state terror.[24]

Because, believe it or not, the Russian masses in whose name this revolution was being carried out did not accept it without some serious resistance. From 1918 to 1921, Russia found itself in a horribly destructive civil war in which, according to historian W. Bruce Lincoln, seven million men, women, and children perished.[25] And after that huge loss of life, and after Russia's having lost more men than any other nation in World War I, the Bolsheviks celebrated their victory in the civil war by instituting a totalitarian dictatorship over the Russian empire and maintaining their power with terror.

"A Fight to the Death"

That terror would claim millions of victims. But Christians were among the first. "A fight to the death must be declared upon religion," asserted

Nikolai Bukharin, founding editor of *Pravda* and one of Lenin and Stalin's leading lieutenants. He was speaking for all Bolsheviks when he said, "Religion and communism are incompatible, both theoretically and practically.... Communism is incompatible with religious faith." And he was only echoing Marx: "'Religion is the opium of the people,' said Karl Marx. It is the task of the Communist Party to make this truth comprehensible to the widest possible circles of the laboring masses."[26] (Marx had also said, "Communism begins where atheism begins.")[27] Bukharin urged his fellow communists to "take on religion at the tip of the bayonet."[28] And that's precisely what they did.

By the end of 1918, the communist government had confiscated all the land and buildings of the Russian Orthodox Church, property that had belonged to the Church for centuries. Lenin's cronies ensured that church buildings were destroyed or turned into communist clubs, workshops, storage houses, offices, and obscene atheistic museums.[29] The Cathedral of the Archangel Michael on the southwest edge of Moscow, a beautiful eighteenth-century red-brick building crowned with five cupolas, was used to store grain.[30]

All church schools were also seized, and the Bolsheviks forbade religious instruction to anyone under eighteen years of age. Children were encouraged to turn in their parents if they taught them about God. Marriage was transformed into a strictly civil ceremony; weddings, baptisms, and funerals were converted into bizarre communist ceremonies: Infants were given social "godparents" who undertook to ensure that children were brought up to become worthy "builders of communism." The parents of newborn children would promise to raise their children "not as slaves for the bourgeoisie, but as fighters against it." Young mothers would declare, "The child belongs to me only physically. For his spiritual upbringing, I entrust him to society."[31] The "spiritual upbringing" for these children would be in the only approved faith: Marxism-Leninism. Moreover, the Russian Orthodox Church's long-standing prohibition against divorce was lifted—leading to an explosion in divorce, which wreaked havoc on the Russian family.[32]

Of the 657 churches that had existed in Moscow on the eve of the 1917 revolution, only 100 to 150 remained by 1976, according to official Soviet statistics. Of those, the Moscow Russian Orthodox Patriarchy said that only forty-six were still holding services by the mid-1970s.[33] And they were monitored by full-time, state-employed "church watchers," whose job was to spy and report on those who came to the church to pray.

★ ★ ★

Come On, Let Us Know What You Really Think

"All worship of a divinity is a necrophilia," Lenin snarled, averring that "any religious idea, any idea of any God at all, any flirtation even with a God is the most inexpressible foulness... the most dangerous foulness, the most shameful 'infection.'" (According to one Russian scholar and translator, Lenin was referring to venereal disease.)[34] "There can be nothing more abominable than religion," Lenin wrote to Maxim Gorky.[35]

In the war on religion they started in 1917, the Bolsheviks were taking on a gargantuan task. The USSR was a huge country that spanned twelve time zones. Within the Orthodox Church alone, there were over forty thousand churches and some hundred and fifty thousand priests, monks, deans, and bishops.[36] Churches could be turned into granaries or museums celebrating atheism, and recalcitrant priests and stubbornly faithful nuns could not be allowed to talk back; they would need to be carted off to Siberia, or executed. And tens of thousands of them were. Nuns were deliberately housed in special sections of the Gulag with prostitutes.[37] But the profits to the Bolsheviks were also gargantuan. "The booty is enormous," said Trotsky, salivating at the Church's "fabulous treasures."

Lenin was furious—a not unusual state of affairs—when the Church put up resistance to giving him and his cronies their icons and jewels and whatever else to sell or melt down. He instructed Trotsky and the Politburo to make sure that all churches were "cleansed," to "shoot ringleaders," and to implement "the death penalty for priests." Lenin predicted, "There is a ninety-nine per cent chance of smashing the enemy on the head with complete success and of guaranteeing positions essential for us for many decades to come."[38] The communists also staged show trials designed to make the priests and bishops, rather than the communists themselves, look like the greedy ones. The verdicts in the Moscow and Petrograd church trials of 1921–1922 were predetermined.[39] The Russian Orthodox Church's patriarch and sixteen other Church officials were all found "guilty" of not cooperating with the state. Of the seventeen defendants, eleven were ordered to be immediately shot. That was a damned good day for Bolshevism, as was the mass heist from the churches, which by November 1922 included 828,275 pounds of silver; 1,220 pounds of gold; 35,670 diamonds; and much, much more. Lenin rubbed his covetous little hands at the "hundreds of millions" of rubles before him.[40]

But the communists' chief aim in their war on religion wasn't booty; it was what Russia expert and onetime Librarian of Congress James Billington called "the extermination of all religious belief."[41] As Soviet historian Eduard Radzinsky said, the Bolsheviks created an "atheistic empire."[42] For those who feel that this language from critics of communism may be a bit over the top, it is important to understand that nary a former Soviet official would dispute these labels. "Just like religious orders who zealously convert 'heretics' to their own faith, our ideologues carried out a wholesale war on religion," wrote none other than Mikhail Gorbachev in his memoirs.[43] He affirmed that the Bolsheviks, even during the time of "peace" after the civil war ended, had "continued to tear down churches, arrest clergymen, and destroy them. This was no longer understandable or justifiable. Atheism took rather savage forms in our country at that time."[44] Close Gorbachev aide Alexander Yakovlev, given access to Communist Party archives as head of modern Russia's Presidential Commission for the Rehabilitation of Victims of Political Repression, has written of the "merciless mass terror" against the religious—so intense and insidious that Yakovlev used words like "evil," "infernal," and even "demonic" to describe it.[45]

The Devil Is in the Details

"Within the philosophical system of Marx and Lenin...hatred of God is the principal driving force." —**Alexander Solzhenitsyn**[46]

The Founding Father of Soviet Terror

Lenin was the preeminent founding father of the Bolshevik state that became the Soviet Union. It is a common misperception, long perpetuated in American universities, that if Lenin had not died a premature death in January 1924, paving the way for Joseph Stalin to succeed him, the bloodshed and tyranny that consumed Russia would never have happened. This is a fundamentally erroneous argument. In fact, Lenin created the Soviet totalitarian system. Lenin was the one who banished basic freedoms as soon as the communists seized control in Russia. And Lenin, not Stalin, created the network of prisons and concentration camps that would become known as the Gulag—what Yakovlev described as "the biggest cemetery on earth, as well as in history."[47] At the time that Soviet Russia became the most repressive totalitarian regime the world had ever seen, Stalin was still just Lenin's chummy sidekick.

W. H. Chamberlin, the journalist who became probably the first historian of the Russian revolution, estimated that by 1920 Lenin's secret police, the Cheka—the predecessor to the NKVD and ultimately the KGB—had already carried out fifty thousand executions.[48] By 1918–1919, the Cheka was averaging a thousand executions *per month* for political offenses alone, without trial.[49] This number was proudly self-reported by the Cheka, which apologized that its data was

A Book You're Not Supposed to Read

Doomsday 1917: The Destruction of Russia's Ruling Class by Douglas Brown (London: Sidgwick and Jackson, 1975).

★ ★ ★

Soviet-Era Humor

"An ex-inmate of the Gulag died and went to heaven. A few weeks after his arrival, he went on a bus tour around the different circles of hell. In the section reserved for the very worst people in history he found Hitler standing in a stinking lake of boiling mud up to his nose. Next to him was Stalin in the same lake up to his waist. The ex-prisoner was understandably angry and asked the devil taking them around, 'How come Hitler is in it up to his nose but Stalin is only in it up to his waist?' 'Ah.' replied the devil, 'but you see Stalin is standing on Lenin's shoulders.'"[50]

incomplete, and boasted that the number was likely much higher.

Historian Robert Conquest, drawing exclusively on Soviet sources, tallies a total of two hundred thousand executions at the hands of the Bolsheviks under Lenin from 1917 and 1923, and half a million when deaths from imprisonment and the suppression of insurrections are added.[51]

Lenin and all the leading Bolsheviks, across the board, preached the necessity of "mass terror." That call was echoed in *Pravda* and *Izvestia*, the Soviet Communist Party newspapers that controlled all print information in the USSR. Lenin approved of what he himself called "mass terror."[52]

All of this—including the founding of the Soviet secret police under Felix Dzerzhinsky—happened before Stalin took the reins of the communist revolution in his bloodstained hands. And the terror would continue even after Stalin was gone. One missionary sentenced to twenty-five years in prison and routinely tortured under Khrushchev—who denounced the "crimes of Stalin" in 1956—contended that while Khrushchev had "disowned" Stalin, he "continued to do the same thing. Half of the Russian churches that remained open in 1959 were reportedly closed.[53] The religious repression continued through the Brezhnev era, which lasted from the mid 1960s until the early 1980s. Not until Gorbachev and the end of the USSR did the Soviet repression of religion finally cease.

The cause of Soviet terror was not Stalin—or Khrushchev, or Lenin, or any one communist leader. It was communism. But Lenin was the one man most responsible for initially bringing communism—and terror—to Russia. Terror "was implicit in the regime from the start," wrote Orlando Figes in his history of the Russian revolution. "The ultimate aim of the Communist system was the transformation of human nature."[55] And it began with Vladimir Lenin.

"Terror was implicit in Bolshevism from the start." —**George Leggett**, *The Cheka*[54]

Lenin's role as the progenitor of Soviet terror is demonstrated in two recent books from Yale University Press's seminal Annals of Communism series (one by Soviet reformer Alexander Yakovlev and another by Harvard historian Richard Pipes). Lenin produced page after page of bloodcurdling directives ordering various groups and peoples—"kulaks," priests, and other "harmful insects"—to be hanged or shot.[56]

He especially reviled the kulaks, the better-off peasants who resisted the regime's forced confiscation and collectivization—also known as theft—of land and farms. "The kulak insanely detests Soviet authority," noted Lenin. He called them "the most beastly, the coarsest, the most savage exploiters," and said, "These bloodsuckers have waxed rich during the war on the people's want... These spiders have grown fat at the expense of peasants... These leeches have drunk the blood of toilers.... These vampires have gathered and continue to gather in their hands the lands of the landlords.... Merciless war against these kulaks! Death to them."[57] Notice how when the masses—inevitably—starve to death under communism, it's—also inevitably—somebody else's fault.

Lenin issued this decree to his henchmen administering a particular group of kulak districts: "Hang (hang without fail, so the people will see) no fewer than one hundred known kulaks, rich men, bloodsuckers." He demanded that Bolshevik authorities publish the names of the executed kulaks, that they "take from them [the kulaks] all the grain," and also take

★ ★ ★

A Useful Idiot

Author and respected British intellectual H. G. Wells was impressed by Vladimir Lenin, whom he called a "frank," "refreshing," and "amazing little man."[59]

hostages. "Do it in such a way that for hundreds of versts around the people will see, tremble, know, shout: they are strangling and will strangle to death the bloodsucker kulaks." He signed this letter cheerfully, "Yours, Lenin."[58]

The essence of Lenin's early "Red Terror" was described by Martin "M. Y." Latsis, a ferocious man Lenin appointed as chief of his killing machine. With deadly candor, Latsis affirmed that the Bolsheviks were in the process of "exterminating" whole classes of human beings: "We are exterminating the bourgeoisie as a class. In your investigations don't look for documents and pieces of evidence about what the defendant has done, whether in deed or in speaking or acting against Soviet authority. The first question you should ask him is what class he comes from, what are his roots, his education, his training, and his occupation. These questions define the fate of the accused."[60]

These were Latsis's orders to his comrades in the killing field. Like Nazism, Bolshevism was fueled by hatred; in the former case, race hatred; in the latter, *class* hatred.

Under Lenin, the Cheka introduced a quota method: each Russian region and district had to arrest, deport, or shoot a certain percentage of people who were deemed to belong to "enemy" social classes.[61] When this persecution inspired opposition, the Cheka only ramped up the level of the violence. As one Bolshevik official reported at the time, "I have checked up on the events surrounding the kulak uprising in the Nova-Matryonskaya *volost*. The interrogations were carried out in a totally chaotic manner. Seventy-five people were tortured, but it is impossible to make head or tail of any of the written reports.... The local Cheka leader [said]: "We didn't have time to write the reports at the time. What does it matter anyway when we are trying to wipe out the bourgeoisie and the kulaks as a class?"[62]

That question was not a sarcastic one. And the Cheka leader had a point: Why did it matter what crimes or disloyalties individuals were guilty of, given that the explicit goal, articulated repeatedly and without ambiguity by the Bolshevik leadership, was to wipe out entire classes?

The suffering of the Russian people in the early years of communism was unspeakable, and yet it would only get worse. The revolution Lenin had longed and planned for was underway. Only death would stop him—but not it.

CHAPTER 6

The Comintern: Taking the Revolution to the World

This vast array of violence, destruction, and dissolution that the communist revolution ushered in would have been bad enough in one place. Far worse, however, is that Lenin, Trotsky, Stalin, and their cohorts—and Marx long before them—had pledged themselves to world revolution. They wanted their communist vision advanced not just in one country but in every nation. Marx, after all, had exhorted the "workers of the *world*" to unite.

The Bolsheviks created an organization to carry out their "full-fledged political project: world socialist revolution": the Soviet Communist International (the Comintern). It was launched by Lenin in March 1919 at a congress in Moscow.[1] The objective of the Comintern was self-evident from its title, and made even clearer by Trotsky's description of it as "the General Staff of the World Revolution."[2]

In a March 6 *Pravda* article, the last day of the congress, Lenin wrote, "The founding of the Third Communist International heralds the international republic of Soviets, the international victory of communism." In his concluding address at the congress, Lenin proclaimed that with the founding of the Comintern, "the victory of the Proletarian revolution on a world scale is assured. The founding of an international Soviet republic is on the way."[3]

Did you know?

★ Lenin said it was impossible to achieve a socialist revolution in only one country

★ The American Communist Party was directly controlled—and financed to the tune of millions of dollars a year—by the Soviet Russian government

★ To join the Communist Party in 1935, Americans had to take an oath "to rally the masses to defend the Soviet Union"

★ ★ ★

Going Global

- "Workers of the world, unite!" —**Karl Marx** and **Friedrich Engels**, *The Communist Manifesto,* 1848
- "It is our interest and our task to make the revolution permanent, until the proletariat has conquered state power and until the association of the proletarians has progressed sufficiently far—not only in one country but in all the leading countries of the world." —**Karl Marx**, 1850 Address of the General Council to the Communist League[4]
- "We have always emphasized that one cannot achieve such a task as a socialist revolution in one country." —**Vladimir Lenin**, October 1920[5]
- "We knew that our victory will be a lasting victory only when our undertaking will conquer the whole world, because we had launched it exclusively counting on the world revolution." —**Vladimir Lenin**, November 1917[6]
- "We live not only in a state but in a system of states, and the existence of the Soviet Republic side by side with the imperialist states for an extended period is unthinkable. In the end either one or the other will conquer. And before this result, a series of horrible conflicts between the Soviet Republic and the bourgeois states is unavoidable." —**Vladimir Lenin**, March 1919 report to the Eighth Party Congress[7]
- "The ultimate aim of the Communist International is to replace the world capitalist economy by a world system of Communism."[8] —**The Communist International** (Comintern) Fifth Congress, January 1924

The Bolshevik hierarchy would run the Comintern with an iron fist. It exercised what it deemed "uncontested authority" over the Communist Parties established all over the globe—with centralized control in Moscow.[9] Every country with a Communist Party would have a representative in Moscow, and other liaisons connecting them. Moscow would be the physical headquarters, the high command. The leader of the Soviet Union was to be the conductor of the worldwide Marxist-Leninist symphony. The Comintern constituted an international association of national communist parties, all under the leadership of the Soviet government in Russia, and all directed toward sparking a global revolution for worldwide communism.

A Book You're Not Supposed to Read

Communism: A History by Richard Pipes (New York: Modern Library Chronicles, 2001).

The Bolsheviks wasted no time in agitating revolts and helping to foment full-scale civil wars in other countries. By January 1919, after only one tenuous year in power, the Bolsheviks had already instigated a revolt in post-WWI Germany, though it was quickly quelled. By the time of the second Comintern Congress in July 1920, the communists had sparked uprisings in Poland, Finland, and Hungary.

But the Comintern did not really get down to business until a little over year after its March 1919 founding, once Bolshevik victory in the Russian civil war seemed likely and Lenin and his comrades could focus on the larger prize: the world.[10] At that Second Congress, the Bolsheviks issued a manifesto proclaiming that "world Civil War" was the "watchword" and "the order of the day."[11]

Richard Pipes has noted that by 1920 Lenin had already left no doubt that he envisioned the Comintern as "a branch of the Russian Communist Party, organized on its model and subject to its orders." This was made unmistakably clear in the 1920 Comintern Congress, where foreign delegates submitted to "iron military discipline." Moscow imposed that discipline upon them, and they in turn would impose it upon Party members in their home countries. They were expected to both demonstrate and require complete loyalty and "the fullest comradely confidence." Their instructions were to take over mass organizations and especially trade unions in their home countries.[12]

The Comintern dictated that members of foreign communist parties—from Europe to America—who did not give total subservience to Moscow ("who

★ ★ ★

From *The Washington Post*: "America's Top Communists of All Time"

1. Earl Browder
2. Woody Guthrie
3. W. E. B. DuBois
4. William Foster and Jay Lovestone
5. J. Robert Oppenheimer
6. Alger Hiss
7. Whittaker Chambers
8. Paul Robeson
9. Elizabeth Bentley
10. John Reed
11. Julius and Ethel Rosenberg
12. Howard Fast
13. Eugene Dennis and Gus Hall[15]

reject in principle the conditions and theses put forward by the Communist International") were "to be expelled from the party." This was the infamous "party discipline" that was a hallmark of communist parties everywhere. It was dogmatically enforced within the domestic parties themselves, including in the American party, where the discipline took harsh forms. Wherever any communist party was—in America, Asia, or Africa—full submission to Moscow was obligatory. The 1920 congress was unambiguous. It laid down this line condition for admission and membership to the Comintern: "Every party which wishes to join the Communist International is obligated to give unconditional support to any Soviet republic in its struggle against counter-revolutionary forces." And befitting the vicious regime that was its source, the congress evoked war rhetoric as central to its mission, stating: "The Communist International has declared war on the entire bourgeois world."[13]

Communism, American-Style

Even before the Second Congress of the Comintern, the United States of America had a homegrown Communist Party. The show opened in America in September 1919, when two Communist Parties were formed in the United States, the "Communist Labor Party" (CLP) and the "Communist Party of America" (CPA), organized at a convention in Chicago during the first week of that month. After mergers and name changes, by 1929 the communists would be united in a single "Communist Party USA" (CPUSA), firmly under the control of the Comintern. The CPUSA was the political party for American communists throughout the Cold War, and it still exists today.[14]

A Book You're Not Supposed to Read

American Communism and Soviet Russia: The Formative Period by Theodore Draper (Viking, 1960).

It cannot be emphasized enough that American members of the Communist Party were subservient to the Comintern and to Moscow. The Communist Party in America was founded only months after the Comintern itself had been established in Moscow. The Comintern created an Anglo-American secretariat as its vehicle for micromanaging the Communist Party there, and a representative of the American Communist Party resided in Moscow as the liaison between the secretariat in Russia and the American Party, transferring information between the two and delivering orders from Moscow to American communists.[16]

As ex-communist Theodore Draper reported in his seminal work on the American Communist Party, when a new member joined the party in the 1920s, he or she signed a party registration card inscribed with these words: "The undersigned, after having read the constitution and program of the Communist Party, declares his adherence to the principles and tactics of the party and the Communist International: agrees to submit to the discipline of the party as stated in its constitution and pledges to engage actively in its work."[17] The mission of American communists who joined the Communist Party was obedience to the Soviets and work to forward the world revolution for communism.

By 1935 new CPUSA members also swore this loyalty oath: "I pledge myself to rally the masses to defend the Soviet Union, the land of victorious socialism. I pledge myself to remain at all times a vigilant and firm defender of the Leninist line of the party, the only line that insures the triumph of Soviet Power in the United States." That wording was—putting it mildly—difficult to square

★ ★ ★

New York City: Commie Central

J. Edgar Hoover's boys in the FBI were kept especially busy in New York City, which was commie central.

New York was home to the literal vast majority of American communists. It was the headquarters of Communist Party USA, the *Daily Worker*, and other publications such as *The New Masses*. It was the home of commie hot-spots such as Columbia University, not to mention the occasional communist cell at places like, yes, the *New York Times*.[18]

This was no secret to the FBI. A declassified March 2, 1948, document, addressed to assistant FBI director D. M. Ladd and titled "Redirection of Communist Investigations," notes that there were "approximately 30,000" Communist Party members in the New York City area alone. The document reported that "almost 50% of the Communist Party members in the United States are located in the New York area."

The New York Office of the FBI had accumulated 1,168 Security Index cards on these CPUSA members in New York. Americans placed on the federal government's Security Index were deemed "dangerous" or "potentially dangerous" because of the possibility of that they might collaborate with a foreign power against the United States—in this case, with Stalin's Soviet Union. If a war broke out between the United States and USSR, these people could have been placed under immediate arrest because of their loyalty oath to Stalin's Soviet Union, which they had sworn upon becoming Communist Party members.[19]

with the loyalties and duties incumbent upon American citizens. (Not to mention that at that point American Communists were swearing loyalty to Joseph Stalin, then in the midst of perpetrating "the Great Terror," a campaign of slaughter in which tens of millions would die.)

Comintern control of CPUSA was so total that when CPUSA picked leaders for its own Central Committee, a list was first sent to Moscow for approval. You can read these lists today in the declassified Comintern Archives. Other documents in those archives are equally revealing.

Take, for example, "Soviet Power and the Creation of a Communist Party of America," a so-called "Thesis of the Executive Committee of the Third

International," which was completed in the summer of 1919, just prior to the official formation of the original American communist parties in Chicago in September 1919. "The three-page document carries two important signatures: 'For the Bureau of the Communist International, N. Bucharin, J. Bersin (Winter).'"[20] The signatories are Nikolai Bukharin, one of the infamous Bolshevik founders, and Jan Berzin, later Soviet general and head of Soviet military intelligence, the GRU.

This document begins by establishing that the American party will not be independent from the Soviet Comintern: "1) For the purpose of attaining an immediate success of the revolutionary class struggle, of systematically organizing it, of uniting and co-ordinating all really revolutionary forces, and for the purpose of unifying principles and organizations, it is necessary to form a Communist Party which should be affiliated with the Communist International 2) The cardinal unifying and directing idea should be the recognition of the necessity for proletarian dictatorship, that is, Soviet power."[21]

A second key document in the Comintern Archives appears to have been issued at the Chicago convention of September 1–7, 1919. It is on the letterhead of the newly established Communist Party of America, at 1219 Blue Island Avenue, Chicago, Illinois. It is a brief celebratory salutation from the Communist Party of America's executive secretary, Charles Ruthenberg, along with attestation from two present "International Delegates," Isaac Ferguson and Alexander Steklitsky.[22] It contains four simple sentences:

> In the name of the Communist Workers of the United States organized in the Communist Party of America I extend greetings to the Communist Party of Russia.
>
> Hail to the Dictatorship of the Proletariat!
>
> Long live the Russian Socialist Soviet Republic!
>
> Long live the Communist International!

The level of loyalty in this letter, to what and to whom, speaks for itself.

A third revealing document in the archives is the November 24, 1919, application for Comintern membership by the Communist Party of America. The letter, signed by the party's international secretary, Louis C. Fraina, claimed a total party membership of "approximately 55,000 members."[23] This figure may (or may not) have been exaggerated. Nonetheless it is interesting that, even allowing for some padding of the membership rolls, it is considerably higher than the twenty-five-thousand-membership figure self-reported by CPUSA in 1934,[24] in the supposed heyday of the Party during the Great Depression.

The blind loyalty of American Communist Party members to the Soviet Union and its blood-stained leadership would last as long as the Soviet Union itself. As stated by Herb Romerstein, a former communist who for over fifty years was one of America's leading authorities on domestic communism, "from 1919, when it [CPUSA] was formed, to 1989, when the Soviet Union collapsed, it was under total Soviet control."[25] Romerstein called the American comrades "loyal Soviet patriots." Their legal citizenship might have been in the United States, but their hearts and minds belonged to the USSR.

Another bit of telling evidence of Soviet control emerged only after the Cold War ended. The CPUSA received funding from the Soviet communist government, beginning in 1919 and continuing until the collapse of the Soviet empire in 1989. These were not piddling sums; the financial support from Moscow was a lifeline that kept CPUSA afloat, to the tune of millions of dollars annually.[26]

In *The Secret World of American Communism*, Harvey Klehr and John Earl Haynes report that the American Communist Party had been "generously funded by the Soviet Union...from its inception in 1919." The subsidies from the Kremlin to CPUSA ultimately "reached $3,000,000 a year by the mid-1980s."[27]

Two Books You're Not Supposed to Read

The Secret World of American Communism by John E. Haynes, Harvey Klehr, and Fridrikh Igorevich Firsov (Washington, DC: Regnery, 2000).

Spies: The Rise and Fall of the KGB in America by John E. Haynes, Harvey Klehr, and Alexander Vassiliev (New Haven: Yale University Press, 2010).

Herb Romerstein concluded on the basis of documents from Soviet and CPUSA archives that the "Communist Party USA was receiving two to three million dollars a year until 1988"—essentially, until the end of the Cold War.

The support was there from the outset, even when the Bolsheviks had little cash to spare (as if they ever had). In the 1920s, the Comintern supplied the American communist movement several millions of dollars' worth of valuables—gold, silver, jewels—which had been stolen by the regime.[28]

The *Daily Worker*, the house organ of CPUSA, received heavy cash infusions from the Comintern from the earliest days of its existence.[29] The editor of the *Daily Worker* was approved by the Comintern. Soviet support of American communism was comprehensive, from day one.

A foreign nation, whose government was frankly attempting to overthrow the government and Constitution of the United States, was secretly and illegally funding an American political party. Today, none of this is a secret, but it is rarely taught in America's universities.

More disturbing facts have emerged from two excellent sources, one in the 1930s and '40s and the other after the end of the Cold War: Ben Gitlow and Morris Childs.

Gitlow shared tantalizing information in testimony before the U.S. Congress in the 1930s. He had been a top CPUSA figure, running twice as the Communist Party's candidate for vice president of the United States (1924 and 1928) and serving on the Executive Committee of the Comintern before

A Book You're Not Supposed to Read

The Venona Secrets by Herbert Romerstein and Eric Breindel (Washington, DC: Regnery, 2000).

leaving the party in 1929. After a long silence, Gitlow emerged to testify before Congress (1939) and write two major books, *I Confess* (1940) and *The Whole of Their Lives* (1948), in which he laid out a litany of disturbing facts about CPUSA's relationship with Moscow, from members' "fanatical zeal" for the Soviet Union and "its ultimate victory over the capitalist world," to espionage by American communists and Soviet funding of the American party. Gitlow testified that the Comintern had sent the CPUSA $100,000–150,000 annually from 1922 to 1929, given $35,000 to

★ ★ ★

The Rosenbergs

Julius and Ethel Rosenberg were the husband-and-wife team convicted of treason and executed for atomic espionage—that is, for helping Stalin's Soviet Union get the bomb. Sources as diverse as J. Edgar Hoover and the *Columbia Law Review* would call it "the crime of the century."[30] Predictably, liberals judged the Rosenberg case a travesty of justice and blamed it on the "hysterical" anti-communism of the 1950s. Nonsense.

Soviet espionage in the United States in the 1930s and 1940s was very extensive and successful, as both the Venona papers and the Harvard Cold War International History project have demonstrated. An estimated 350 Americans, including numerous high-level U.S. government officials and key scientists working on the Manhattan Project, were spying for Soviet intelligence. Beyond those was another group of helpers, a list of at least two hundred more.[31]

Soviet leader Nikita Khrushchev recalled hearing Foreign Minister Molotov tell Stalin that "the Rosenbergs had vastly aided production of our atomic bomb.[32]

The group of Americans most oblivious to the very real threat of such communist spies—including the Rosenbergs—was and remains liberals. Ironically, the Soviet code name for Julius Rosenberg, found throughout the Venona transcripts, was "Liberal."[33]

launch the *Daily Worker* in 1924, and paid tens of thousands of dollars to American union bosses, and that the funding continued at the time he was testifying.

A Book You're Not Supposed to Read

The Rosenberg File by Ronald Radosh and Joyce Milton (New Haven: Yale University Press, 1997).

Morris Childs was the ultimate first-person witness to the fact that that funding never stopped. He actually collected the money himself from the Kremlin in person in Moscow. Childs had risen to become the number two man at CPUSA, behind only Gus Hall, the head of CPUSA, who had succeeded previous communist leaders William Z. Foster and Earl Browder. The Soviets came to trust him completely and love him like a comradely brother. They awarded him the highest honors of the state. But Morris Childs had secretly become the highest-ranking informant for the FBI within CPUSA. His remarkable story is laid out in *Operation Solo*, the 1996 biography by John Barron.

Morris Childs and his brother Jack (who also worked undercover for the FBI) were conduits for Soviet funding of CPUSA through all of the 1960s and 1970s. During that period the Kremlin gave CPUSA millions of dollars in annual funding. The total approached $2 million annually by 1976—America's bicentennial—and rose to $2,775,000 by 1980. Barron's biography of Childs lists the exact amount each year, down to the penny. The FBI knew the precise amount because it counted every dime at a half-way house before Morris deposited it in a safe for Gus Hall. This was all illegal.

Stalin's Hollywood Stooges

Few parts of history have been rewritten by liberals quite like the story of the communists who penetrated the American film industry. The latest research, particularly by Larry Ceplair, Steven Englund, and Allan Ryskind,

★ ★ ★

Disinformation

The Soviets had spies in America and throughout the West—in fact, all over the world. And they also engaged in propaganda campaigns to foment conflict and smear the critics of communism. Pope Pius XII, who was such a formidable enemy to Soviet communism that Stalin and his goons labeled him "Hitler's Pope," was a chief target. In their 2013 book *Disinformation*, Ion Mihai Pacepa and Ron Rychlak chronicle the crass art of Kremlin deception, detailing communist campaigns to defame, malign, and slander religious individuals. Pacepa, a former Romanian general, was the highest-ranking intelligence official to defect from the Soviet bloc, and a witness to many of the events the book describes. As Pacepa and Rychlak show, so patently dishonest was the Soviet use of disinformation that even the Soviet definition of disinformation, published in the 1952 edition of the *Great Soviet Encyclopedia*, was itself a form of disinformation.

Pacepa and Rychlak gave special attention to the scandalously successful case against the vehemently anti-communist Pope Pius XII, who was public enemy number one to Stalin at the start of the Cold War. They show that the attack against Pius was launched with a 1945 Radio Moscow broadcast that first promoted the bald-faced "Hitler's Pope" smear. The Soviets understood that Pius XII was a mortal threat to their ideology and thus manufactured the big lie that Pius had been pro-Hitler. They embarked on an unholy crusade to destroy the pope's reputation, scandalize his flock, and foment division among Christians.

This was a standard tactic for the Soviets. They would sling the pro-Nazi charge at numerous Church figures including Cardinals Mindszenty of Hungary, Stepinac of Yugoslavia, and Wyszynski and Wojtyla of Poland.

And not just Catholic officials were targets. Pacepa and Rychlak revealed the loathsome anti-Semitism of the very conspirators behind the original "Hitler's Pope" campaign. The Kremlin deliberately spread the insidious *Protocols of the Elders of Zion* conspiracy theory. Pacepa and Rychlak detailed Yuri Andropov's anti-Zionism campaign, support of Islamic terrorism, and promotion of virulent anti-Semitism and anti-Americanism among Middle East Arabs. By 1978, the Soviet bloc had planted some four thousand agents of influence in the Islamic world, armed with hundreds of thousands of copies of the *Protocols of the Elders of Zion*—and military weapons.[34]

shows that there were two to three hundred communists operating in Hollywood in the late 1940s, always under concealment. Indisputably guilty were the screenwriters who made up the so-called Hollywood Ten. They were all card-carrying members of the Communist Party.

These comrades literally swore themselves to Stalin's Kremlin. Several of them followed Stalin even after the signing of the Hitler-Stalin Pact in 1939. Thus Allan Ryskind, son of Morrie Ryskind, an anti-communist screenwriter of the era, calls these dutiful comrades "Agents of Stalin, Allies of Hitler." Here are the Ten, along with the Communist Party card numbers of each:

John Howard Lawson: 47275.

Dalton Trumbo: 47187.

Albert Maltz: 47196.

Alvah Bessie: 47279.

Samuel Ornitz: 47181.

Herbert Biberman: 47267.

Edward Dmytryk: 46859. (He had two additional numbers on other cards.)

Adrian Scott: 47200. (He had an additional number.)

Ring Lardner Jr.: 47180.

Lester Cole: 47226.[35]

Communists knew that the film industry could be tremendously useful for propagating communist propaganda. Vladimir Lenin said that "of all the arts, for us the most important is cinema." Grigory Zinoviev, head of the Soviet Comintern, ordered that motion pictures "must become a mighty weapon of communist propaganda and for the enlightening of the widest working masses." In March 1928, the Soviets held their first Party Conference on Cinema.[36]

The Bolsheviks realized that nowhere was the movie industry as advanced and influential as the United States, especially in Hollywood's Golden Age. Their American comrades wholeheartedly agreed.

Two Books You're Not Supposed to Read

Red Star over Hollywood: The Film Colony's Long Romance with the Left by Ronald Radosh and Allis Radosh (New York City: Encounter Books, 2006).

Hollywood Traitors: Blacklisted Screenwriters—Agents of Stalin, Allies of Hitler by Allan Ryskind (Washington, DC: Regnery, 2015).

Working for a "Soviet America"

American communists were not dedicated to America. Their loyalty lay elsewhere. One of their first American general secretaries, William Z. Foster, openly advocated a "Soviet American Republic" as part of a "world Soviet Union." Foster spoke frankly of American communists' goal of creating a "Soviet America." In fact, the title of his 1932 book was *Toward Soviet America.*[37]

Members of communist parties around the world, including in the United States, saw themselves as loyal Soviet foot-soldiers. It was Moscow first. These communists served not America but the Soviet Union.

In the unforgettable words of Lincoln Steffens, the popular journalist for the *New Republic*, "I am a patriot for Russia; the Future is there; Russia will win out and it will save the world."[38] Langston Hughes, the celebrated African-American poet, agreed emphatically. "Put one more 'S' in the USA to make it Soviet," declared Hughes. "The USA when we take control will be the USSA."[39]

Herb Romerstein repeatedly stressed American communists' loyalty to Soviet Russia: "Communist Party members were loyal Soviet patriots.... Most were not qualified to be spies, but those who were qualified were recruited through Party channels and made available to Soviet intelligence for classic espionage, agent-of-influence operations, or as couriers." He said that "almost every spy" tapped by the Soviets was a communist and a member of the American Party.[40]

A telling display of this loyalty to the Soviet Union was a 1930 exchange between Republican Congressman Hamilton Fish of New York and William Z. Foster, longtime head of CPUSA and twice the presidential candidate of the Communist Party:

> Fish: Now, if I understand you, the workers in this country [America] look upon the Soviet Union as their country; is that right?
> Foster: The more advanced workers do.
> Fish: Look upon the Soviet Union as their country?
> Foster: Yes.
> Fish: They look upon the Soviet flag as their flag?
> Foster: The workers of this country and the workers of every country have only one flag and that is the red flag. That is the flag of the proletarian revolution....
> Fish: Well, the workers of this country consider, then, the Soviet Government to be their country. Do they also consider the red flag to be their flag?
> Foster: I have answered quite clearly.
> Fish: Do you owe allegiance to the American flag; does the Communist Party owe allegiance to the American flag?
> Foster: The workers, the revolutionary workers, in all the capitalist countries are an oppressed class who are held in subjection by their respective capitalist governments and their attitude toward these governments is the abolition of these governments and the establishment of soviet governments.
> Fish: Well, they do not claim any allegiance, then, to the American flag in this country?

Foster: That is, you mean, the support of capitalism in America—no.

Fish: I mean if they had to choose between the red flag and the American flag, I take it from you that you would choose the red flag; is that correct?

Foster: I have stated my answer.

Fish: I do not want to force you to answer if it embarrasses you, Mr. Foster.

Foster: It does not embarrass me at all. I stated very clearly the red flag is the flag of the revolutionary class, and we are part of the revolutionary class.

Fish: I understood that.

Foster: And all capitalist flags are flags of the capitalist class, and we owe no allegiance to them.

Fish: Well, that answers the question.[41]

It did indeed.

Representative Fish also elicited other interesting information from Foster:

Fish: Have you been to Russia?

Foster: Yes. Eight or nine times....

Fish: Do the Communists in this country advocate world revolution?

Foster: Yes; the Communists in this country realize that America is connected up with the whole world system, and the capitalist system displays the same characteristics everywhere—everywhere it makes for the misery and exploitation of the workers—and it must be abolished, not only on an American scale but on a world scale.

Fish: So that they do advocate world revolution; and do they advocate revolution in this country?

Foster: I have stated that the Communists advocate the abolition of the capitalist system in this country and every other country; that this must develop out of the sharpening of the class struggle and the struggle of the workers for bread and butter....

Fish: Now, are the Communists in this country opposed to our republican form of government?

Foster: The capitalist democracy—most assuredly. We stand for a workers' and farmers' government; a government of producers, not a government of exploiters. The American capitalist Government is built and controlled in the interests of those who own the industries and we say that the Government must be built and controlled by those who work in the industries and who produce.

Fish: They are opposed to our republican form of government?

Foster: Most assuredly.

Fish: And they desire to overthrow it through revolutionary methods?

Foster: I would like to read from the program of the Communist International at this point. The Communist International program says....[42]

At this point in his testimony, Foster paused to read from the Comintern document that he was holding: "The conquest of power by the proletariat does not mean peaceful capturing of ready-made bourgeois state machinery by means of a parliamentary majority. The bourgeoisie resorts to every means of violence and terror to safeguard and strengthen its predatory property and political domination. Like the feudal nobility of the past, the bourgeoisie cannot abandon its historical position to the new class without

★ ★ ★

Commie Kingpins

The Communist Party USA's chairmen:

William Z. Foster (1929–1934)

Earl Browder (1934–1945)

Eugene Dennis (1945–1959)

Gus Hall (1959–2000)

Sam Webb (2000–2014)

John Bachtell (2014–present)

a desperate and frantic struggle; hence the violence of the bourgeoisie can only be suppressed by the stern violence of the proletariat."

Foster's successor as head of the American Communist Party was Earl Browder, who was general secretary of CPUSA from 1934 to 1945. He, too, did not shirk from expressing where his true loyalties resided. "Above all," Browder stated in his 1934 CPUSA convention report, "we arm ourselves with the political weapons forged by the victorious Communist Party of the Soviet Union, with the mighty sword of Marxism-Leninism, and are strengthened and inspired by the victories of socialist construction won under its Bolshevik leadership headed by Stalin." The pro-Stalin, pro-Soviet patriot continued: "Our World Communist Party, the Communist International, provides us the guarantee not only of our victory in America, but of the victory of the proletariat throughout the world."[43]

His Communist Party colleague M. J. Olgin had written in 1933, "The Communist Party of the U.S.A. is thus part of a worldwide organization which gives it guidance and enhances its fighting power. Under the leadership of the Communist Party the workers of the U.S.A. will proceed from struggle to struggle, from victory to victory, until, rising in a revolution, they will crush the capitalist State, establish a Soviet State, abolish the cruel and bloody system of capitalism and proceed to the upbuilding of Socialism."[44]

The Comintern of the 1930s, during Browder's time, candidly told its members—which, of course, included CPUSA—that they "must render every possible assistance to the Soviet Republics in their struggles against counter-revolutionary forces. They should conduct an organized and definite propaganda to induce the workers to refuse to make or handle any kind of military equipment intended for use against the Soviet Republics, and should also carry on, by legal or illegal means, a propaganda among any troops sent against the Workers' Republics."[45]

The CPUSA itself said, "We want our Party to become like an army, a Bolshevik army, who while understanding the policy behind each decision is prepared to carry it out with military promptness, without any hesitation or question, and further, to carry out the decisions with Bolshevik judgment and maximum effectiveness."[46]

A Bolshevik army inside of America. *Forward!*

It's clear whose side the American communists were on, and it wasn't America's.

CHAPTER 7

Uncle Joe

When death knocked on Lenin's door in 1924, Joseph Stalin was ready to succeed him. And Stalin would kill far more than even Lenin managed to wipe out—perhaps merely because he lived longer than his predecessor and partner in crime. Give a communist more time, and more dead people will result. Stalin would rule the Soviet Union from the late 1920s until his death in March 1953.

Born in 1878 in the republic of Georgia, Stalin was originally named Joseph Dzhugashvili. "Stalin" was a pen name meaning "Man of Steel." He, like Lenin, had a religious upbringing. His mother Ekaterina was a pious woman who sent her son to parochial school and wanted him to become a priest. Stalin actually attended seminary, but was eventually kicked out. At that seminary, which was a liberal one, Stalin digested not only toxic socialist ideas but also Darwinism. Like both Marx and Lenin, Stalin would turn his back on God.

He would quickly become the greatest mass murderer in history, surpassed only by China's Mao Zedong. And Stalin took the lives of tens of millions of his own citizens through purges, the Gulag, a deliberately created famine, and more. Among these cruel campaigns, Robert Conquest

Did you know?

★ People were sent to the Gulag for being late to work

★ FDR's negotiating technique with Stalin was to "give him everything I possibly can and ask nothing from him in return"

★ Communists in the Eastern European nations subjugated by Stalin jailed bishops, crucified Christians, and forced Catholic priests to consecrate human excrement

The Devil Is in the Details

The papal encyclical *Divini Redemptoris*, issued by Pope Pius XI in 1937, during Stalin's Great Terror, called communism "pernicious," "Godless," "by its nature anti-religious," a form of "perversity," a "fury," "poison," an "extreme danger," a "deluge which threatens the world," a "collectivistic terrorism... replete with hate," and a "plague" that leads to "catastrophe." Communism was a "satanic scourge" that "conceals in itself a false Com-messianic idea." It was a form of "class-warfare which causes rivers of blood to flow," a "savage barbarity." Marxists were "the powers of darkness," orchestrating a battle against "the very idea of Divinity." Communism was a "truly diabolical" instrument of Satan and his "sons of darkness."[4]

would dub Stalin's 1934–1938 killing spree "the Great Terror" because it dwarfed even Lenin's "Red Terror" (circa 1918).[1]

The number of deaths in this period has been tallied by several sources, including Stalin's own successor, Nikita Khrushchev, who laid out the "Crimes of Stalin" in 1956, three years after Stalin's death. As just one indication of the scope of the carnage, consider these incredible numbers of victims from the Soviet military between 1936 and 1938. These were killed in the "Great Purge"—the part of the "Great Terror" that specifically targeted government officials, military officers, and Communist Party members:

- 3 of 5 Soviet marshals
- 13 of 15 army generals
- 8 of 9 admirals
- 50 of 57 corps commanders
- 154 of 186 division generals
- 16 of 16 army commissars
- 25 of 28 army corps commissars[2]

From May 1937 to September 1938, according to Soviet statistics, 35,020 military officers were arrested and expelled from the Red Army.[3] Tens of thousands were executed, often on Stalin's direct written order. This is not only a shocking crime but a shocking logistical feat. It boggles the mind that Stalin and a handful of select bullies could pull off such a wholesale purge of the men with the guns. But when it comes to killing, one could never underestimate communists. They always exceeded the worst possible scenarios.

Khrushchev and other Soviet officials understood that these actions by this tyrant not only directly killed thousands of their countrymen. Stalin's purge of the military also indirectly killed millions of Russian boys in World War II, as a hollowed-out officer corps put up ineffective resistance to the Nazi invasion of the Russian homeland, which came only a few years after Stalin's decimation of the military brass who knew how to fight a war.

★ ★ ★

The Wrong Number

Dr. Valentine Kefeli, who lived through the Stalin era in Russia, tells this story: It was three a.m., and there was a knock at the door of his family's apartment. His father got out of bed and said "I am ready." But as he answered the door, the men asked, "Is this apartment 52?" "No, it's apartment 50," he replied. They departed, and Valentine's father breathed a sigh of relief. "Everybody was ready to go to the gulag," recalls Valentine. "We knew that we were members of Animal Farm."[6]

Of course, it wasn't just the military. The purge numbers for Stalin's political rivals and for society as a whole were worse. Of the nearly two thousand delegates to the Seventeenth Party Congress of the USSR in 1934, more than eleven hundred would be shot between 1934 and 1938. Some 70 percent of the 139 members of the 1934 Party Central Committee were executed by 1938. Of the nation's eighty-one top-ranking political commissars, seventy-six were purged.[5]

As for Soviet society at large, the numbers were on an even ampler scale. Arnold Beichman, the late Hoover Institution expert on communism, estimates that one in every eight Soviet citizens—men, women, children, elderly—perished under Stalin's Great Terror. That would equate to about twenty million.

Millions of poor souls languished in the Gulag, the Soviet prison system that was a cold symbol of communist repression. Established throughout regions like Siberia, purposefully remote in order to deter inmates from trying to escape, the prison system contained millions of Soviet citizens who were sent to the Gulag beginning in the 1920s, starting under Lenin. They had been sent to the camps for the most minor *infractions*, ranging from expressing a desire for free elections to being late for work.[7]

★ ★ ★

You Don't Know Whether to Laugh or Cry

"A [Soviet citizen] went to the KGB to report that he lost his parrot. The KGB asked him why he was bothering them. Why didn't he just report it to the local police? Well, he answered, 'I just want you to know that I don't agree with a thing that parrot has to say.'" —joke told by **Ronald Reagan** in his remarks on the Strategic Defense Initiative to Martin Marietta Denver Astronautics Employees in Waterton, Colorado, November 24, 1987

Countless people perished in the Gulag, victims of the elements, malnutrition, disease, neglect, or execution. This vast prison system was described in *The Gulag Archipelago* by Alexander Solzhenitsyn, a survivor who lived to tell the world. Lenin and Trotsky started the Gulag system and referred to its "concentration camps" long before Hitler and the Nazis had set up any such thing,[8] but Stalin made even more effective use of the system than Lenin had. In the harsh conditions prisoners were subjected to, they died like flies.

And Stalin also killed millions outside the Gulag. One of his worst crimes was his forced collectivization of agriculture in the Ukraine, which led to the starvation of millions in the former bread basket of the Soviet Union. In this deliberately created famine—which Ukrainians call the Holodomor—huge number of "kulaks" were uprooted and had their land taken. Many of them were carted off to Siberia; many died in the Ukraine. Stalin made it a criminal offense, punishable by imprisonment, for anyone to mention the disaster. This man-made famine starved five to ten million people to death.[10]

★ ★ ★

Mass Murder without Shame

When Lady Astor asked him how long he was "going to go on killing people," Stalin answered, "When it is no longer necessary."[9]

How many deaths are attributable to Stalin, in total? For starters, there are his executions, purges, and imprisonments in often deadly conditions. Then there is the famine. Some observers also blame Stalin for the deaths of the tens of millions of Russian boys killed in World War II, primarily by the Nazi *blitzkrieg*—in which the Soviet Union lost upwards of twenty to thirty million soldiers, some thirty to forty times the combined death toll of British and American losses in the war. Stalin, after all, helped launched World War II in the first place. His August 1939 "non-aggression" pact—the so-called Hitler-Stalin Pact, or Molotov-Ribbentrop Pact—with Hitler enabled the September 1 invasion of Poland by Germany, which triggered World War II. (Later the same month, Russia also attacked Poland.) In June 1941, Hitler betrayed Stalin, sending his war machine into the USSR—and the rout was on. As we have seen, Stalin had so decimated his own military command that Russia lacked the veteran military leadership to slow Hitler—a major reason for the staggering Russian wartime losses.

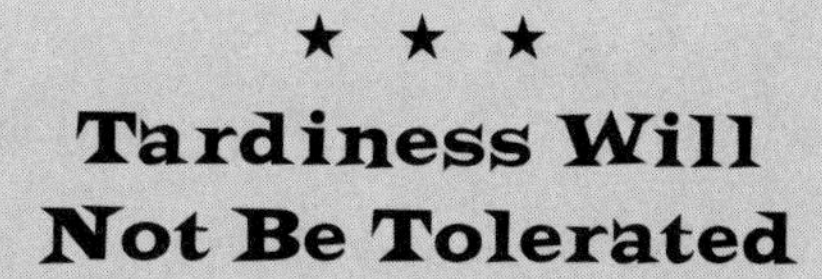

Tardiness Will Not Be Tolerated

"For five minutes late, you got an administrative write up—a memo in your records. For 20 minutes, you got the gulag."

—Valentine Kefeli[11]

The Russian people suffered horribly in the war that Stalin had helped start. But Stalin himself—despite having crippled his own military in the Great Purge—ultimately achieved many of his original goals in World War II. In a recently declassified Soviet document, a secret address by Stalin to the Plenum of the Politburo of the Central Committee of the All-Union Communist Party on August 19, 1939, mere days before the signing of the Hitler-Stalin Pact, the dictator averred, "The dictatorship of a Communist Party may be envisaged only as a result of a great war." As he explained, "It is in the interests of the USSR—the Fatherland of the Workers—that war should break out between the Reich and the Franco-British capitalist bloc." The "non-aggression" pact Stalin would shortly sign with Hitler was not about preventing a world war; on the contrary, it was meant to

The Devil Is in the Details

Besides taking the lives of millions, Stalin was guilty of destroying priceless artifacts. The Cathedral of Christ the Savior, Moscow's most ornate church, positioned on the banks of the Moscow River near the Kremlin, was dynamited at his behest.[12] Czar Alexander I had dedicated the church in gratitude to Divine Providence for saving Russia from Napoleon in 1812. It was the pride of Russia, with priceless artwork adorning the towering ceilings. In December 1931, Stalin had the ornate structure dynamited and reduced to rubble. The demolition was not simple: it took more than one blast, and it was not easy to find a construction worker willing to set it off. Rumors abounded in Moscow that Stalin set off the demolition explosion himself—and it would have been fitting for the most unholy man in Russia to do the dirty deed.

Stalin planned to replace the majestic structure with another monument to himself and his ideology. In the place of the cathedral, the communists would erect a sacred Palace of Soviets. But the incompetence of central planning—or perhaps an act of God—delayed construction, as the site was flooded with water from the nearby river. Ultimately, the mess was converted into a large municipal swimming pool.

bring it on and prolong it: "It is for these reasons that we must give priority to the approval of the conclusion of the pact proposed by Germany, and to work so that this war, which will be declared within a few days, shall last as long as possible."

Why did Stalin want a world war? Because he believed it would ultimately result in the spread of communism to the whole world: "We have before us a vast field of action to develop the world Revolution, Comrades!" The communist dictator imagined the possibility of a "Soviet Germany," of the "Sovietization of France," and much more.[13]

The signing of the Hitler-Stalin Pact in August 1939 achieved Stalin's initial goal: precipitating the Second World War. In short order, just as planned, on September 1, 1939, Poland was invaded from the West by Germany, prompting war declarations from Britain and France. Not long thereafter, Poland was also invaded from the East by the USSR. The world war that ensued would take the lives of upwards of forty to fifty million boys worldwide—ironically, as we have seen, more boys died from the USSR than any other nation. But, as we shall see below, it also enabled Stalin to achieve a good measure of his original purpose in precipitating the war. The "Sovietization of France" never happened, but he got half the "Soviet Germany" he wanted—plus all the nations of Eastern Europe.

Most estimates of Stalin's death toll leave out the wartime numbers, instead focusing on the tyrant's killing by famine, by execution, and within the walls of the forced labor-camp system. How many victims figure in this list?

As we have seen, Alexander Yakovlev, the lifelong Soviet apparatchik who in the 1980s became a chief reformer and close aide to Mikhail Gorbachev, and who, in the post-Soviet 1990s, was tasked with the grisly assignment of trying to total the victims of Soviet repression, estimates that Stalin alone was responsible for the deaths of sixty to seventy million people, a stunning number (and two to three times higher than the tally in *The Black Book of Communism*). Whatever the precise figure, Stalin's cruelty was indisputably staggering. The Soviet dictator was a superb practitioner of the death he preached. Only the Red Chinese, who had many more potential victims at their disposal, killed so many innocent citizens.

★ ★ ★

War Crime

Stalin was also guilty of a large number of non-Russian deaths in the war, of course. He is responsible, for example, for the Katyn Woods massacre, one of the twentieth century's worst war crimes. When the Nazis and Bolsheviks jointly invaded, annihilated, and partitioned Poland, the Soviets seized thousands of Polish military officers as prisoners. Their fate was sealed on March 5, 1940 when Stalin personally signed their death warrant, condemning 21,857 of them to "the supreme penalty: shooting." We have the actual NKVD document ordering the massacre. The officers were taken to three execution sites, the most infamous of which is the Katyn Forest, twelve miles west of Smolensk, Russia. The Bolsheviks covered their crime with a layer of dirt.[14]

★ ★ ★

Mass Murder without Shame

"Death solves all problems. No man, no problem." —**Stalin**[15]

Duped by a Dictator

It was this bloodthirsty fiend that American president Franklin Delano Roosevelt fondly called "Uncle Joe"—and said had taught him how "a Christian gentleman should behave." FDR was immensely impressed by the communist dictator when the Big Three—Roosevelt, Stalin, and Churchill—met at the Tehran Conference in 1943. FDR wondered where Stalin might have acquired the virtue that FDR somehow saw radiating from this man, and speculated that it might have been the dictator's youthful training for the priesthood.

Roosevelt's faith in Stalin was blind. He resisted ample evidence of the dictator's real character and was deaf to the warnings of some of his own aides. William Bullitt, for example, FDR's first ambassador to the USSR, had once been so gushingly pro-Bolshevik that he planted a literal kiss on Stalin's cheek. But he had awakened to the unmistakable death stench that was Stalinism. He warned FDR against the bloodthirsty thug in the Kremlin, but the president wouldn't listen: "Bill, I don't dispute your facts [or] the logic of your reasoning. I just have a hunch that Stalin is not that kind of man. Harry [Hopkins] says he's not and that he doesn't want anything but security for his country, and I think that if I give him everything I possibly can and ask nothing from him in return, *noblesse oblige*, he won't try to annex anything and will work with me for a world of democracy and peace."

"If I give him everything I possibly can"? "*Noblesse oblige*"? "Will work with me for a world of democracy and peace"? FDR was referring to *Joseph Stalin.*

A stunned Bullitt argued with FDR, informing the American president that he was dealing not with a British duke but with "a Caucasian bandit, whose only thought when he got something for nothing was that the other fellow was an ass." Uncle Joe's jackass, if you will.

Bullitt tried to tell FDR that there was no "factual evidence" that Stalin was a good man. FDR, however, felt differently. He saw Stalin as a "kind" man, a gentleman, one he could work with to advance democracy and peace. The president told Bullitt: "It's my responsibility, not yours, and I'm going to play my hunch."[16]

A Book You're Not Supposed to Read

Dupes: How America's Adversaries Have Manipulated Progressives for a Century by Paul Kengor (Wilmington: Intercollegiate Studies Institute, 2010).

Roosevelt wouldn't believe either his own aide or the evidence on Katyn Woods either. The Soviet massacre there was first exposed by the Nazis—who by then had betrayed the Hitler-Stalin Pact—in April 1943. The Germans discovered the mass graves and immediately converted the atrocity into a propaganda coup to try to split the Big Three Allies. But Stalin and *his* goons attempted to pin the massacre on Hitler and *his* goons. Stuck in between was the civilized world, which sought to determine which devil had done the deed.

FDR was inclined to give "Uncle Joe" the benefit of the doubt. Nonetheless, he realized the need to take a close look. Thus, he dispatched George Earle, former Democratic governor of Pennsylvania, a war hero, a diplomat, and a presidential special emissary, to investigate.

In short order, Earle discerned the obvious, which was not what FDR wanted to hear. FDR needed Russia and Stalin to help vanquish the Nazis, and this killing field created by America's wartime ally would not look good to the American public. In any case, Roosevelt always wanted to think the best of Stalin.

Earle made his case: "About this Katyn massacre, Mr. President. I just cannot believe that the American president and so many people still think it is a mystery or have any doubt about it. Here are these pictures. Here are these affidavits and here is the invitation of the German government to let

★ ★ ★

More Useful Idiots

H. G. Wells raved about Stalin, "I've never met a man more candid, fair, and honest... Everyone trusts him." Wells said this upon his return from a meeting with Stalin in 1934 amid the launch of the Great Terror.[17]

Wells's fellow socialist, George Bernard Shaw, was also impressed. He reprimanded people in the West who dared to arrogantly judge their democracies superior to Stalin's state: "We cannot afford to give ourselves moral airs when our most enterprising neighbor [the Soviet Union] humanely and judiciously liquidates a handful of exploiters and speculators to make the world safe for honest men."[18] Shaw dismissed reports of famine in the USSR as a "lie" and as "inflammatory irresponsibility"—a "slander" of Stalin's Five Year Plan.[19]

Fabian Socialist, Bertrand Russell, also drank the communist Kool-Aid on his 1920 tour of the Bolshevik utopia: "I believe that Communism is necessary to the world, and I believe that the heroism of Russia has fired men's hopes," proclaimed the English intellectual. "Bolshevism deserves the gratitude and admiration of all the progressive part of mankind." Bolshevism, said Russell, was a "splendid attempt" on behalf of the future of humanity.[20]

the neutral Red Cross go in there and make their examination. What greater proof could you have?"

FDR replied, "George, the Germans could have rigged things up." Earle was frustrated. As he later put it in his testimony for a Congressional investigation of Katyn, Roosevelt was adamant that the claims were "entirely German propaganda and a German plot." The president told his special emissary: "I'm absolutely convinced that the Russians didn't do this." An amazed Earle responded, "Mr. President, I think this evidence is overwhelming."

But FDR refused to believe the evidence. Earle saw Roosevelt's denial of Katyn as a microcosm of how the USSR had "deceived" too many Americans; he later said he felt "hopeless" about the president's unwarranted faith in Stalin.[21]

Roosevelt and many other New Deal liberals were deceived by Stalin, who preyed on their naivety. But not everyone in his administration was so innocent. Consider the case of Harry Hopkins. This was the "Harry" whose assurances that Stalin was "not that kind of man" FDR had quoted to William Bullitt to defend his blind trust in the dictator.

Hopkins was born in 1890 in Sioux City, Iowa; his father was a small businessman and his mother a devout Methodist. As a young man he left the Midwest for New York City, where he took a bite of the Big Apple's rotten left-wing politics. By the 1920s, he was active in a number of progressive causes, with a special interest in social work. He became executive director of the Temporary Emergency Relief Administration under New York governor Franklin Delano Roosevelt, where his management of welfare policy impressed not only the governor but the governor's wife. Eleanor was a big fan of Harry Hopkins. When her hubby won the presidency, they immediately enlisted Harry's help.

In March 1933, in the new president's landmark Hundred Days, Hopkins was summoned to Washington to spearhead relief at the federal level. He had so much influence with FDR that he would become one of the principal architects of the New Deal, of particularly the relief programs within the Works Progress Administration. Under Hopkins, the WPA became one of the largest employers in all of the United States. Only after his death in 1946 did we begin learning concrete information on the dealings Harry Hopkins had with communists.

Evidence from the Soviet side began emerging in the 1960s. The sources include Oleg Gordievsky, a former KGB officer and one of the most knowledgeable defectors ever to leave the Soviet Union, and Iskhak Akhmerov, a high-level Soviet official who worked inside the United States during World War II. Gordievsky began working undercover for British intelligence a decade before his defection and continued to do so until he was reportedly exposed by CIA traitor Aldrich Ames.

Both of these Soviet officials called Hopkins an "agent," with Gordievsky calling him an agent of "major significance." Akhmerov, who was also in contact with Alger Hiss, described Hopkins as "the most important of all Soviet wartime agents in the United States." Akhmerov claimed to have been in contact with Hopkins well before Hopkins's first visit to Moscow in July 1941. In fact, one of FDR's closest aides was quite possibly working with the Soviets.

More information on Hopkins emerged decades later. Herb Romerstein and Eric Breindel, the principal researchers of the Venona transcripts—secret wartime communiqués between the Soviet Union and American communists decrypted by U.S. codebreakers—concluded that Harry Hopkins was a member of Lee Pressman's "study group" inside the Department of Agriculture (DOA). Pressman was a cell leader of one of the infamous Hal Ware's communist cells within the Department of Agriculture.

Involvement with the Pressman group would not necessarily mean that Hopkins was a communist, let alone a KGB mole. But Romerstein and Breindel also concluded that Hopkins seems to be the only member of the Pressman group who can be definitively linked to Soviet espionage.

There are many Venona messages to or from Hopkins. Hopkins was in contact with Soviet officials as high up as Ambassador Maxim Litvinov and even Andrei Gromyko. Hopkins eventually had repeated discussions with Stalin himself, including some in FDR's absence. Many of those interactions were appropriate to Hopkins's role in the Roosevelt administration, but others are suspicious.

One Venona report, dated May 29, 1943, and signed by Akhmerov, reports secret discussions between FDR and Churchill that were inappropriately channeled to the Soviet government. Those discussions were relayed by Soviet agent "19," who is believed to have been Harry Hopkins.[22]

There is still debate over whether Harry Hopkins was a communist spy, loyal to the Soviet Union, or another duped New Deal liberal.[23] The leading authority on Venona, however, was convinced that Hopkins served the other side. "He was a dedicated Soviet agent," Romerstein told me categorically. "He was both a spy, that is, he supplied information, and an agent of influence." Hopkins was not a dupe, said Romerstein, but one who sought out dupes.[24]

And he found one in the Oval Office. Hopkins was the president's right-hand man, chief political adviser, confidant, troubleshooter, and sometimes diplomat. FDR saw him more than he saw any aide. "You'll learn what a lonely job this is," said a vulnerable FDR to presidential aspirant Wendell Wilkie, "and you'll discover the need for somebody like Harry Hopkins, who asks for nothing except to serve you."

Hopkins alone arguably wielded more power than the State Department, given the total faith placed in him by Mr. and Mrs. Roosevelt. He accompanied President Roosevelt to the major conferences of World War II: Casablanca, Tehran, and Yalta. Nowhere was he more instrumental than on American policy toward the Soviet Union, including the Lend-Lease program. FDR sent him to Moscow to negotiate with Stalin. He may even have helped Stalin acquire nuclear weapons by securing uranium for the Soviet a-bomb.[25] And it's beyond dispute that he encouraged FDR in his naïve trust and admiration of Stalin.

The Cold War

Roosevelt's bizarre affinity for the mass murderer would be very costly for the peoples of Eastern Europe. Joseph Stalin viewed the chaos at the end of World War II as an opportunity. Surveying post-WWII Eastern Europe, Stalin salivated, "Whoever occupies the territory also imposes on it his own social system as far as his military can reach."[26] That was the edict sent forth to Stalin's commissars. Vyacheslav Molotov, Stalin's foreign minister, described his job: "I saw my task as minister of foreign affairs as being how to expand the boundaries of our Fatherland. And it seems to me that we and Stalin did not [do] badly in this task."[27]

Not badly at all. But Stalin was significantly helped along by Roosevelt, who essentially abandoned the nations of Eastern Europe to the hands of the communist dictator at the Yalta Conference, held on Stalin's home turf in Crimea from February 4 to 11, 1945. At Yalta, FDR was totally rolled by Uncle Joe.

FDR's hagiographers today try to excuse his decisions at Yalta, but the hard truth is that the president himself knew that the Yalta agreement was a very bad one. "I didn't say the result was good," he told his close adviser Adolf Berle when he returned home. "I said it was the best I could do." Admiral Bill Leahy complained to FDR, "Mr. President, this [agreement] is so elastic that the Russians can stretch it all the way from Yalta to Washington without technically breaking it." In response, FDR sighed, "Bill, I know it. But it's the best I can do for Poland at this time."

Merely six weeks after the conference, on March 23, 1945, FDR told Anna Rosenberg, "Averell [Harriman] is right. We can't do business with Stalin. He has broken every one of the promises he made at Yalta." By that point he knew that Stalin had taken advantage of him.

When the Soviets saw weakness, they preyed upon it. FDR was physically and mentally weak at Yalta—he would die just two months later—and, one might argue, was ideologically weak as well. He was another liberal who was vulnerable prey to a master communist manipulator like Stalin. Unfortunately, FDR realized that too late.

In a letter to Stalin on April 1, 1945, FDR lamented. "I cannot conceal from you the concern with which I view the development of events of mutual interest since our fruitful meeting at Yalta." Stalin surely chortled at that one.

But however concerned FDR was, the Eastern Europeans had much more cause for worry. When World War II ended, the Red Army permanently occupied the Eastern European nations from Poland to Bulgaria, setting up communist governments up and down the continent. Stalin violated the promises he had made to President Roosevelt and Prime Minister Churchill at Yalta to allow free and unfettered democratic elections in those nations.

Instead, Stalin forcibly extended Soviet communism into Eastern and Central Europe following World War II. The Comintern had been technically abolished (in name only) in the early 1940s in order to appease the Allies during the war, but the Soviets had not abandoned their mission of spreading communism to the whole world. How could they? That was Marx's mandate. And Stalin would have far greater success in the task than Lenin ever had.

The two principal Western leaders who opposed Stalin were President Harry Truman and ex-Prime Minister Churchill. Truman had succeeded Roosevelt in April 1945, and gotten a rude awakening about America's wartime ally. When FDR died suddenly, his vice president, Harry Truman, had to step into some very big shoes. Truman at first was not entirely sure of Joe Stalin's precise intentions. He didn't know exactly what he would be facing from Moscow, though he soon learned it wouldn't be good.

Truman became more skeptical of communism than FDR. His own private acronym for the USSR was "R.G.P.S.," for "Russian Godless Pervert System." "I've no faith in any totalitarian state, be it Russian, German, Spanish, Argentinian, Dago [Italian], or Japanese," he said. "They all start with a wrong premise—that lies are justified and that the old, disproven Jesuit formula, the ends justify the means, is right and necessary to maintain the power of government. I don't agree, nor do I believe that either formula can help humanity to the long hoped for millennium."

★ ★ ★

A Pox on Both Their Houses

"If we see that Germany is winning we ought to help Russia, and if Russia is winning we ought to help Germany, and that way let them kill as many as possible." —**Senator Harry Truman's** policy advice in 1941, at the time Hitler invaded the USSR[28]

Truman averred that an "Honest Communism," akin to something closer to what is "set out in the 'Acts of the Apostles,' would work. But Russian Godless Pervert Systems won't work."[29]

The first salvo across Truman's bow, exactly one year after Yalta, was Stalin's February 9, 1946 Bolshoi Theater speech, blaming capitalism and the West—not Nazism, or Stalin's own pact with Hitler—for causing World War II.[30]

With the war over, Stalin was unmasked and unafraid. Truman advisers like the distinguished Paul Nitze interpreted the Bolshoi speech as tantamount to a Soviet declaration of World War III. It was such a wake-up call that within only days of the speech, a young staff officer named George Kennan submitted what became known as his "Long Telegram," sent from the U.S. embassy in Moscow to the United States. That historic analysis by Kennan is credited with the doctrine of containment, which became the long-term U.S. policy for dealing with the Soviet Union until President Ronald Reagan's policy of "rollback"—that is, actively reversing the USSR.

The Bolshoi Theater speech came in the context of blatant Soviet violations of the Yalta agreement. Not only was Stalin reneging on his commitment to free elections. The Red Army, which had never left the portions of Eastern Europe it had "liberated" during World War II, was committing all sorts of heinous war crimes throughout defeated Europe, especially in the eastern portion of Germany, where, as historian Antony Beevor records, Red Army soldiers were guilty of an estimated two million rapes of German women, thousands of whom committed suicide. There was a 90 percent abortion rate among impregnated German women.[31]

By the time of the Bolshoi Theater speech, Winston Churchill was no longer prime minister of Britain. He and his fellow conservatives had been replaced the previous summer by Clement Attlee and the Labour Party. Churchill and his work, however, were hardly finished. He had been called upon to save Western civilization at the start of the decade, when vandals from Hitler's Germany were at the gates. Now, Churchill perceived new vandals on the rampage.

Worse, the West, lulled into complacency and understandably tired of fighting after losing tens of millions of precious sons in history's most brutal war, were slow to recognize the threat. So the former British prime minister took it upon himself to travel to the United States to issue a wake-up call to the free world. He gave his famous "Iron Curtain" speech in the

★ ★ ★

Containing the Soviets

George Kennan is one of the great names in twentieth-century diplomatic history. Kennan warned that when the Soviets put their signature to a document, it was for calculated purposes only, and should not be trusted. Kennan underscored the cynical relativistic thinking about morality that marred the Marxist mind:

> This means that truth is not a constant but is actually created, for all intents and purposes, by the Soviet leaders themselves. It may vary from week to week, from month to month. It is nothing absolute and immutable—nothing which flows from objective reality. It is only the most recent manifestation of the wisdom of those in whom the ultimate wisdom is supposed to reside, because they represent the logic of history.

"The Soviet concept of power," wrote Kennan, "requires that the Party leadership remain in theory the sole repository of truth.... The leadership of the Communist Party is therefore always right." Since "they alone knew what was good for society"—and since their word was absolute, "immutable," infallible, "secure and unchallengeable"—the Soviet leadership was "prepared to recognize no restrictions, either of God or man, on the character of their methods."

Kennan warned that the "Soviet governmental machine" would act without reservation to implement the expansionary doctrine (or whatever else) dictated by the leadership. "Like the white dog before the phonograph," wrote Kennan, "they hear only the 'master's voice.' And if they are to be called off from the purposes last dictated them, it is the master who must call them off."

town of Fulton, Missouri, on March 5, 1946, at the invitation of President Truman, whose home was not far down the road in Independence. The audacity of Churchill's words stunned America:

> Nobody knows what Soviet Russia and its Communist international organization intends to do in the immediate future, or what are the limits, if any, to their expansive and proselytizing tendencies....
>
> From Stettin in the Baltic to Trieste in the Adriatic, an iron curtain has descended across the continent. Behind that line lie all the capitals of the ancient states of central and eastern Europe. Warsaw, Berlin, Prague, Vienna, Budapest, Belgrade, Bucharest, Sofia, all these famous cities and the populations around them lie in the Soviet sphere and all are subject, in one form or another, not only to Soviet influence but to a very high and increasing measure of control from Moscow.

Churchill conceded that these were tough words on the "morrow of a great victory." They were not the words of peace the world desperately wanted to hear on the heels of a bitter but well-earned triumph over Nazism, a victory in which Stalin's Russia had been an uneasy ally to the United States and the United Kingdom. Nonetheless, said Churchill, the West should not be blind to reality, and should not try to wish away the danger that he judged was clearly present.

The former prime minister spoke the truth. But America didn't want to hear it.

President Truman was taken aback by the outrage that many Americans expressed toward the Iron Curtain speech. He himself had not yet evolved into the strong anti-communist that he would later become, but he was still surprised by the animosity toward Churchill. When confronted by angry

Soft on Communism, Hard on Churchill

Eleanor Roosevelt was furious at Churchill's Iron Curtain Speech. She accused the courageous prime minister of "desecrating the ideals for which my husband gave his life." She publicly sneered, "Perhaps it's just as well that he is not alive today to see how you have turned against his principles."

reporters, Truman distanced himself from the former prime minister.[32] According to historian James Humes, Churchill was so floored by Truman's lack of public support that he did not recover until he found a friendly smile (and a drink) at the Gettysburg home of World War II pal Dwight Eisenhower.

Journalist David Brinkley, who covered the Iron Curtain speech, recalled that his fellow pressmen were appalled; they thought Churchill had lost his mind.[33] That was also the conclusion of former first lady Eleanor Roosevelt, who responded to the speech by denouncing Churchill.[34]

Yet, while the rest of the world covered its eyes, Churchill sounded his trumpet. Churchill was no Johnny-come-lately to the Bolshevik threat. With bracing foresight, Churchill had said in April 1919, long before anyone else, that "of all the tyrannies in history," the Bolshevik regime was "the most destructive, the most degrading." He described the Bolsheviks as "ferocious baboons," and told the cabinet of Prime Minister Lloyd George that it "might as well legalize sodomy as recognize the Bolsheviks."[35] At that point, Vladimir Lenin was just getting started, and Joseph Stalin had not yet seized the helm as captain of the dictatorship.

While everyone remembers the "Iron Curtain" speech, few today recall that Churchill specifically called Soviet communism a threat to "Christian civilization." Churchill had hit the bullseye.

And we know the rest of the sad story.

In short, painful order came more affronts to freedom by Stalin. In the grim year of 1948 a communist coup in Czechoslovakia was followed by the Berlin Blockade, the latter a direct violation of Yalta, with the Red Army blocking all road and rail routes into Berlin, where the American, British, and French occupation zones comprised an island of freedom in the sea of Russian-controlled East Germany. It was a brazen, bellicose act. The Cold War was on.

In no time, the two sides—West and East Europe—were starkly divided into adversarial military alliances: NATO in the West, and the Warsaw Pact in the East.

The fall of Czechoslovakia and also Hungary to communism was a sad fate for two nations that had shown such promise in the years between World War I and II. For the newly created Czechoslovakia, in particular, the inter-war years had been a golden age, as the young nation seemed poised to offer the world an example of freedom and democracy to be emulated elsewhere. Stalin's subjugation made Czechoslovakia another kind of example: one of the new "captive nations" of Eastern Europe.

Captive Nations

The Eastern Europeans' plight was gruesome. Under their new communist governments, they were subjected to the same kind of persecution and terror that the Russian people had first experienced under Lenin, and that Stalin had only made worse. We have already met Richard Wurmbrand, the Christian pastor who endured fourteen years of hell in a Romanian prison. He detailed some of the unspeakable cruelty he witnessed in testimony before the U.S. Congress and in his famous *Tortured for Christ*, first published in 1967:

> Thousands of believers from churches of all denominations were sent to prison at that time. Not only were clergymen put in jail,

but also simple peasants, young boys and girls who witnessed for their faith. The prisons were full, and in Romania, as in all communist countries, to be in prison means to be tortured....

A pastor by the name of Florescu was tortured with red-hot iron pokers and with knives. He was beaten very badly. Then starving rats were driven into his cell through a large pipe. He could not sleep because he had to defend himself all the time. If he rested a moment, the rats would attack him.

He was forced to stand for two weeks, day and night.... Eventually, they brought his fourteen-year-old son to the prison and began to whip the boy in front of his father, saying that they would continue to beat him until the pastor said what they wished him to say. The poor man was half mad. He bore it as long as he could, then he cried to his son, "Alexander, I must say what they want! I can't bear your beating anymore!" The son answered, "Father, don't do me the injustice of having a traitor as a parent.

★ ★ ★

Defenestration in Prague

Stalin used brutal methods to subjugate the Eastern European nations to Soviet rule. When the Czech parliament voted to accept America's generous offer of Marshall Plan aid, which had been offered to all of Europe, West and East, after World War II, a seething Stalin summoned the Czech leadership to Moscow, including foreign minister Jan Masaryk, the son of the founder of the modern Czech state, and ordered them to return home and overturn the action of the parliament and reject Marshall Plan aid. On the plane home, Masaryk lamented that he had left Prague a free man and was returning a slave to Stalin. He would soon die in a "suicide" leap from his window—really a murder, it has long been suspected—amid the tumult in the communist coup that followed. Czechoslovakia's fate was sealed. By early 1948, the Red flag was flying over Prague.

> Withstand! If they kill me, I will die with the words, 'Jesus and my fatherland'." The communists, enraged, fell upon the child and beat him to death, with blood spattered over the walls of the cell. He died praising God. Our dear brother Florescu was never the same after seeing this.[36]

Wurmbrand's captors carved him in a dozen separate parts of his body. They burned eighteen holes in him.

"What the communists have done to Christians surpasses... human understanding," he wrote. Wurmbrand said that communist torturers often told him, "There is no God, no hereafter, no punishment for evil. We can do what we wish." Wurmbrand described crucifixion at the hands of communists. Christians were tied to crosses for four days and nights:

> The crosses were placed on the floor and hundreds of prisoners had to fulfill their bodily necessities over the faces and bodies of the crucified ones. Then the crosses were erected again and the communists jeered and mocked: "Look at your Christ! How beautiful he is! What fragrance he brings from heaven!"... [A]fter being driven nearly insane with tortures, a priest was forced to consecrate human excrement and urine and give Holy Communion to Christians in this form. This happened in the Romanian prison of Pitesti. I asked the priest afterward why he did not prefer to die rather than participate in this mockery. He answered, "Don't judge me, please! I have suffered more than Christ!" All the biblical descriptions of hell and the pains of Dante's Inferno are nothing in comparison with the tortures in communist prisons.
>
> This is only a very small part of what happened on one Sunday and on many other Sundays in the prison of Pitesti.

> Other things simply cannot be told. My heart would fail if I should tell them again and again. They are too terrible and obscene to put in writing....

The Devil Is in the Details

Bishop Fulton J. Sheen, one of the most influential Americans of the twentieth century, said that the communists had failed to convince the world that there is no God. Rather, he quipped, they had succeeded only in convincing the world that there *is* a devil.[37]

On December 26, 1946, the Hungarian communists celebrated the Christmas season by arresting Joseph Cardinal Mindszenty. They would devote the next twenty-three years to torturing and repressing and silencing him.

During a sensational communist show trial, Mindszenty "confessed" before his accusers, a confession widely believed to have been obtained through drugging and five weeks of torture at the notorious secret police headquarters in Budapest. The kangaroo court sentenced him to life in prison.[38]

Mindszenty spent the next eight years in solitary confinement. He was released in 1955 because of ill-health but kept under surveillance. During the 1956 Hungarian uprising, he was freed by rebel forces. Rather than flee, he took residency in the U.S. embassy, refusing to leave his country unless the communist government rescinded his conviction, which, under pressure from the Kremlin, it would not do. He offered up his suffering in the form of what Fulton Sheen would describe as "The Dry Martyr of Hungary."[39]

Mindszenty concluded that communism is "a kind of religion" that "knows no God, no immortal soul."[40]

Stalin put the brutal communist regimes throughout Eastern Europe in place, but they survived his death—and continued to persecute their people—until the late 1980s, when communism even in Russia was near collapse.

★ ★ ★

You Don't Know Whether to Laugh or Cry

"The strength of the Solidarity movement in Poland demonstrates the truth told in an underground joke in the Soviet Union. It is that the Soviet Union would remain a one-party nation even if an opposition party were permitted, because everyone would join the opposition party." —**Ronald Reagan**, address to the British Parliament, Royal Gallery at the Palace of Westminster, London, June 8, 1982

In October 1984, three thugs from communist Poland's secret police seized and beat Jerzy Popieluszko, then bound and gagged and stuffed him into the trunk of their Fiat automobile. This gentle priest was the courageous chaplain to Solidarity, the Polish labor movement that—along with the Polish pontiff, Pope John Paul II—was the core of Poland's crucial fight for freedom that would ultimately bring down Soviet communism.[41]

Father Jerzy's first beating that evening was so severe that it should have killed him. But somehow the priest was managing to survive as he fought for his life in the cold, dark trunk of the Fiat. He managed to untie the ropes that bound him and extricate himself from the car. He began to run, shouting to anyone who could hear, "Help! Save my life!"

He was run down by one of the goons, who unleashed his club upon the priest's head with a fury and ferocity as if he were possessed. Then the priest's tormentors grabbed a roll of thick adhesive tape and ran it around his mouth, nose, and head, tossing him once again in the vehicle like a hunk of garbage on its way to the dump. After that came yet another thrashing still, with one of the communist secret police ultimately delivering a deadly blow to the priest's skull.

The killers drove to a spot at the Vistula River. They tied two heavy bags of stones, each weighing nearly twenty-five pounds, to the priest's ankles.

They lifted his body above the water and then quietly let him go. It sunk into the blackness below them.

The killers felt an immediate sense of guilt. They drove away, downing a bottle of vodka to try to numb their consciences. "Now we are murderers," one of them thought to himself.[42]

They were indeed guilty of murder. Of course, so was the communist system they represented. Father Jerzy Popieluszko was one of countless martyrs of communism. The communists let flow a veritable river of blood.

And Stalin was the bloodiest tyrant among them—up to the time of his death.

Death Comes for the Dictator

Ultimately, the man responsible for the murder of tens of millions could not escape the great equalizer. Death came for the death-dealing torturer on March 5, 1953, and it wasn't pretty. He lay in unbearable pain, a severe stroke having rendered his right side paralyzed. Fittingly, considering the horrible deaths suffered by so many of his victims, it would be a three-day death by torture.

The final hours for the "Man of Steel" constituted a slow asphyxiation, a steady strangulation. His daughter Svetlana would describe his "horrible death agony," a true story that one commenter would describe as a scene right out of Dostoevsky.[43] During his last hours, his face altered and turned dark, his lips black, and his features unrecognizable.[44]

After having been unresponsive for hours, with his eyes closed, Stalin summoned his strength for a final effort. Looking as if he were hallucinating, and apparently trying to wave away the walls that he thought were closing in on him, the dictator suddenly opened his eyes and shot a terrified glance at the assemblage of atheist communists gathered in the room. Then, amid his last gasps, "something incomprehensible and awesome happened

★ ★ ★

Keep Clapping, Comrade!

There is no better account of the terror-cowed culture of Stalinism than Alexander Solzhenitsyn's classic, *The Gulag Archipelago*. On page sixty-nine of the first volume is this chilling account:

> At the conclusion of the conference, a tribute to Comrade Stalin was called for. Of course, everyone stood up.... For three minutes, four minutes, five minutes, "the stormy applause, rising to an ovation," continued. But palms were getting sore and raised arms were already aching. And the older people were panting from exhaustion. It was becoming insufferably silly even to those who really adored Stalin.
>
> However, who would dare to be the first to stop?... After all, NKVD men were standing in the hall applauding and watching to see who would quit first! ...
>
> [The comrades] couldn't stop now till they collapsed with heart attacks! At the rear of the hall, which was crowded, they could of course cheat a bit, clap less frequently, less vigorously, not so eagerly—but up there with the presidium where everyone could see them?
>
> The director of the local paper factory, an independent and strong-minded man, stood with the presidium. Aware of all the falsity and all the impossibility of the situation, he still kept on applauding! Nine minutes! Ten! In anguish he watched the secretary of the District Party Committee, but the latter dared not stop. Insanity! To the last man! With make-believe enthusiasm on their faces, looking at each other with faint hope, the district leaders were just going to go on and on applauding till they fell where they stood, till they were carried out of the hall on stretchers! ...
>
> Then, after eleven minutes, the director of the paper factory assumed a businesslike expression and sat down in his seat. And, oh, a miracle took place!... To a man, everyone else stopped dead and sat down. They had been saved!
>
> That same night the factory director was arrested. They easily pasted ten years on him.... After he had signed Form 206, the final document of the interrogation, his interrogator reminded him:
>
> "Don't ever be the first to stop applauding."[45]

that to this day I can't forget and don't understand," said Svetlana. The tyrant managed to raise half his body from the bed and then held up a defiant left fist as if he were shaking it at something in the heavens he had long ago forsaken and despised. "He suddenly lifted his hand as though he were pointing to something above," recorded Svetlana, "and bringing down a curse on us all."[46]

Those present—the cursed—included the highest hierarchy of the Soviet state: Bulganin, Malenkov, Kaganovich, Voroshilov, Khrushchev, and the diabolical secret police chief Lavrenti Beria, who Svetlana even amid her tear-filled account of her father's death could not resist describing as an "utterly degenerate," "obscene," "repulsive," "cruel," and "cunning" "monster."[47]

They all watched Stalin in horror as he screeched something inaudible. "The gesture was incomprehensible and full of menace," said Svetlana, "and no one could say to whom or what it might be directed." The very next moment, she said, after a final effort, "the spirit wrenched itself free of the flesh."[48] Stalin sunk motionless into his pillow, the body finally finished. The soul fleeing elsewhere, somewhere.[49]

"My father died a difficult and terrible death," said Svetlana. "God grants an easy death only to the just."[50]

CHAPTER 8

Mao and Other Monsters: Communism Assaults Asia

In 1949, as Stalin continued his conquest of Eastern Europe and the Soviets detonated an atomic bomb thanks to the help of American commie spies like Julius and Ethel Rosenberg and their comrades, the world's most populous nation went communist. Mao Zedong and his Red forces defeated Chiang Kai-Shek and his Chinese Nationalists, ending a battle that had raged since the late 1920s and been immortalized by the communists' nasty "Long March" in 1934–1935. But with the communists in control of China, the death counter really began clicking.

Did you know?

★ Western liberals enabled the conquests of communist dictators from Mao to Ho Chi Minh

★ Once Vietnam fell to communism, Cambodia and Laos followed, just as the "domino theory" had predicted

★ The North Korean government has fed its people bark and grass

Cheerleader for the Chairman

Chairman Mao did not pull off his amazing victory alone. He had plenty of help from his progressive friends, including cheerleaders in the American press corps. Foremost among them was Edgar Snow (1905–1972), a nearly forgotten left-leaning journalist—one of many who helped the cause of international communism.

Snow might seem an unlikely candidate for dupe to Mao Zedong. He wrote not for the *New York Times* or the *New Republic* but for the popular and conservative *Saturday Evening Post*. The love letters to Stalin by *New York Times* reporter Walter Duranty were one thing, but it was something else for a reporter at the anti-communist *Saturday Evening Post* to be infatuated by a communist revolutionary. Nonetheless, Snow's *Red Star over China* (first published in 1938) became what Cold War historians M. Stanton Evans and Herb Romerstein have accurately described as "an unabashed commercial on behalf of the communist Mao Zedong and his Yenan comrades."[1]

Snow's account was packed with intimate details from multiple lengthy first-person interviews with Mao himself. He had access that few to no other journalists had. He recorded twenty thousand words of interviews with Mao—and he accepted virtually all of what the communist leader said uncritically, while he was anything but uncritical of Mao's opponents, Chiang Kai-Shek and his nationalists. No wonder Mao was happy to give Snow exclusives.[2]

Today Mao is recognized for the mass killer that he was. But at the time he was preparing to commit his mass murders, Edgar Snow described Mao's bloodthirsty movement as a "thoroughgoing social revolution" and even "democracy."[3] He described Mao himself as a "rather Lincolnesque figure... with large, searching eyes" and an "intellectual face of great shrewdness." Snow portrayed Mao as an everyman. "The story of Mao's life was a rich cross-section of a whole generation [of Chinese]," recorded Snow. "There would never be any one 'savior' of China, yet undeniably one felt a certain force of destiny in Mao."[4]

This romantic figure was sure to become "a very great man." According to Snow, "everyone knew and respected" Mao. Snow, personally, had "never met anyone who did not like" or "admire" Mao. The Chinese communist leader had a "deep sense of personal dignity," and appeared "quite free from symptoms of megalomania" (in contrast to Chiang). He was an "ardent student of philosophy" and insatiably curious about international events and foreign affairs.

According to Snow, Mao saw FDR as a man that Red China "could cooperate with." The chairman was especially intrigued by the New Deal.[5] He was practically a Chinese New Dealer.

The youthful Mao, said Snow, had harbored "strongly liberal and humanistic tendencies." He carried from his youth an intense work ethic and an "iron constitution." He was blessed with an "extraordinary mind." Overall, said Snow, "Mao impressed me as a man of considerable depth of feeling. I remember that his eyes moistened once or twice when he was speaking of dead comrades."[6]

Snow framed the Red Chinese as anti-imperialist, anti-fascist, and even (at times) Christian. Snow spent time with them, hunting, fishing, smoking, laughing. They were one with themselves and nature. Chiang and his forces, on the other hand, were downright repressive; they were bandits, brigands, kidnappers, killers, fascists, dictators, cretins. They made Snow feel much less safe. The Reds simply wanted to "stop civil war." The communists were so genuinely kind and good-hearted that only they could be so caring as to spare Chiang's life. If Chiang ever desired to see compassion, he might look to the poor yet benign communist souls that he and his ilk had tormented for so long.[7]

Snow's book, which was translated and reprinted in multiple editions, contributed to the Chinese communists' ultimate victory. With very different results from the ones Snow had predicted.

Red Chinese Butcher's Bill

Within the first two decades of communist China's existence, upwards of sixty to seventy million people were killed. They died from purges, malnutrition, starvation, the collectivization of agriculture—and generally from the wrenching transformation of society under totalitarian communism. Most of the deaths happened under Mao's Great Leap Forward (1957–1960)

Hungry Ghosts: Mao's Secret Famine by Jasper Becker (New York: Henry Holt, 1996).

and Cultural Revolution (1966–1969). The former, Mao's collectivization of agriculture, reaped bitter fruits indeed—mass starvation without precedent in history, surpassing even what Stalin had done in the Ukraine. It was a famine due not to weather or natural disaster, but strictly to a political ideology.

Under Mao, the Chinese nation was forcibly transformed into one gigantic social laboratory. Private possessions were eliminated, from clothes and hygiene products to pots and pans. The Chinese were denied the most basic liberties, from freedom of speech and the press to conscience rights. Even "private fires" for cooking food were banned, with the only permissible smoke being that which emanated from collective kitchens.[8]

In Jasper Becker's *Hungry Ghosts*, there's a vivid depiction of the inmates of Mao's nation-turned-insane-asylum scavenging the fields during the day for seeds, frogs, salamanders, insects, tree bark, anything to eat, and at night wandering the paths in search of human corpses to devour. Similar accounts of the daily horrors of Red China are found in poignant books such as Nien Cheng's *Life and Death in Shanghai*, Li Zhisui's *The Private Life of Chairman Mao*, and Jung Chang's *Wild Swans: Three Daughters of China*. The sixty-five or seventy million dead under Mao estimated by *The Black Book of Communism* and the more recent, authoritative *Mao: The Unknown Story*, possibly exceeds the total dead among all nations in World War I and II combined—in just one nation.

Mao's "Sinification" of Marxism—his Chinese adaptation of the Marxist philosophy—had wider consequences, beyond China's borders. The Chinese dictator applied the teachings of Marx to the landowner-peasant agricultural society that was predominant in Asia, in contrast to the industrial societies of the West. His implementation of Marxism in China opened the

★ ★ ★

Mao, Family Man

Under Mao, the families were steered in to omnipresent communes, with children pulled from their parents. As China-watcher and Mao admirer John King Fairbank reported, all parents were to work twenty-eight days of each month and to eat in large mess halls, "while their children went into day nurseries. This would bring... all [China's] labor, including its womanpower, into full employment." At long last, Mao had emancipated China's women.

Meanwhile, he was having his way with them. His personal physician, Li Zhisui, notes that during the horrific period of communist re-education known as Cultural Revolution the aging despot was serviced by a harem of handpicked young girls, always the most desirable virgins plucked from nearby villages for the Marxist master's full-time satisfaction. Dr. Li says that his patient, who refused to bathe or brush his teeth and had chronic venereal disease, was "sometimes in bed with three, four, even five women simultaneously." The girls' parents were expected to support this contribution to the revolution cheerfully. Mao showed himself to be a sexual progressive; he seems to have taken some young men for himself as well.[9]

door for a wider extension of communism into Asia, the most heavily populated region of the world. Within just one year of Chiang's China becoming Red China, the Korean peninsula would find itself divided in two in a hot war between the communist north and the non-communist south. Soon Vietnam would also be divided, and Cambodia would be annihilated by an unspeakably brutal communist regime.

Korea and the Kims

Way back in 1919—not coincidentally, the same year the Comintern was established in Moscow—two communist parties were founded in Korea. Both claimed to be Bolshevik in origin. The Comintern intervened to try to force the two into one party in complete subservience to Moscow, and the battle became brutal, with many in both factions killed.[10]

But these events were obscured by the continued Japanese occupation of the Korean peninsula, which had begun in 1910 after Japan's victory in the Russo-Japanese War. This was the ravenous Japan of the bellicose Bushido code, the mad killing machine that left in its wake vicious war crimes from Bataan to Nanking—and would only be stopped by two atomic bombs in August 1945. With Japan's formal surrender to General Douglas MacArthur on the USS *Missouri* on September 13, 1945, Korea was finally freed from a horrific thirty-five-year occupation.

But not unlike the liberation of Eastern Europe, the freedom was short-lived. The question of what to do with Korea after the defeat of the Japanese had been debated at the wartime conferences of the Big Three. At Cairo in November 1943, the Allies had pledged that "Korea shall become free and independent."[11]

At Yalta, Stalin agreed to FDR's concept of a multilateral "trusteeship" for Korea among the Big Three[12]—with no U.S. troops placed in Korea and full U.S. trust placed in the Kremlin. Stalin knew a deal when he saw one. But by the time of Potsdam, six months after Yalta, Truman had replaced the deceased FDR, and the new president already knew better than the old one. So the U.S. War Department devised a plan to divide the Korean peninsula into two zones, one in the north to be occupied by the Soviets and the other in the South, by the Americans.

Stalin's troops invaded northern Korea on August 9, the same day that America dropped the second bomb on Nagasaki. Japan surrendered a few days later, and U.S. forces entered southern Korea on September 8.

Communist mischief ensued. Hyon Chun Hyok, jockeying for power with a young commander named Kim Il-Sung, was assassinated. The Soviet "trusteeship" took the form of remaking northern Korea in the Soviet image—a one-party communist dictatorship of complete mass centralization and collectivization.[13] The Kremlin refused pleas by the United States and the newly created United Nations for a national unification of the

Korean peninsula with free and fair elections. Elections were held only in the southern portion, under American protection, where the government of Syngman Rhee took charge. The Republic of Korea was formally established in the southern half of Korea in August 1948.

In the northern half, the communists declared a Democratic People's Republic of Korea under the leadership of Kim Il-Sung. It had Soviet backing, of course, and it would soon have the more crucial support of a communist China, after Mao's victory in October 1949.

Then, in late June 1950, Kim Il-Sung sent a massive military force of seventy-five thousand troops storming into the south. The United States, which had been fully unprepared for the assault under the poor leadership of Secretary of State Dean Acheson, scrambled to the aid and assistance of the south.

A mass mobilization of Western troops from over a dozen nations under the auspices of the United Nations headed to southern Korea, led by General MacArthur. They would battle the communists for three years. The Korean War was on.

From 1950 to 1953, millions of Koreans died in the war. One to two million North Korean and South Korean soldiers perished in combat, as did many Soviet and Chinese soldiers who got in on the act. And fifty-five thousand American boys gave their lives, equal to the number that would die in Vietnam over a much longer period. It was a tragedy that, like Vietnam, did not end in a victory for America and the forces of freedom. It ended in a stalemate armistice signed July 27, 1953, with the once proud nation divided at the thirty-eighth parallel, the infamous DMZ, or De-Militarized Zone, the Berlin Wall of Asia, the hottest spot in what is left of the Cold War. It ended with a population of nearly twenty million northern Koreans living in a totalitarian communist hellhole.

Which still continues to this day. The North Korean prison state has lasted so long that its lifespan is poised to exceed that of the erstwhile Soviet

Union. The Kim boys are going to out-Stalin Stalin. In some ways, they already have.

North Korea is often referred to as Stalinist. It is, indeed, a fitting monument to the late Soviet tyrant. And yet the level of repression there far surpasses even Stalin's control. Observers have had to reach for novel language to characterize this singular system.

Christopher Hitchens, atheist and ex-Trotskyist, called the entire North Korean nation a "concentration camp." He explained, "Every minute of every day, as far as regimentation can assure the fact, is spent in absolute subjection and serfdom. The private life has been entirely abolished." Even "slave state" is too generous a term for North Korea, he said, because at least slave owners fed their slaves. The only thing that really works there is the secret police. North Korea is *literally* a land of darkness; satellite photos show the northern half of the Korean peninsula as an island of darkness in a sea of the surrounding countries' electric lights.[14]

Republican Senator Pat Roberts of Kansas, who visited North Korea in the late 1990s, described it as a "theocracy."[15] Its leaders have elevated themselves to god-like status, demanding worship from the North Korean masses. Paintings of the Kims, North Korea's rulers since it became a communist country, adorn every street corner, factory, school, and home. Giant statues of these midgets of Marxism stand everywhere, and North Koreans have been made to literally prostrate themselves before them.[16]

North Korea is always at the bottom of every scorecard on liberty—Freedom House's ranking of countries' political rights and civil liberties, the international index of press freedom from Reporters without Borders, the Heritage Foundation's annual Index of Economic Freedom. All radios and televisions are fixed to receive only government stations. The government's Ministry of People's Security has spies in every workplace and neighborhood to inform on anyone who says anything less than adulatory about the regime, even at home. Hundreds of thousands of North Koreans—a common estimate is two hundred fifty thousand—are held in prison camps. Executions, often performed in public, are routine.[17]

The personality cult and leader-worship that is everyday life in North Korea commenced with the first Kim. "Thank you, Father Kim Il-Sung" is the first phrase North Korean parents were instructed to teach their children. From cradle to grave, North Korean citizens are still stalked by the omnipresent face of the "Great Leader" (and of his son, the "Dear Leader," Kim Jong Il). As one assessment put it, "The [Kim] dynasty is much more than an authoritarian government; it also holds itself out as the ultimate source of power, virtue, spiritual wisdom, and truth for the North Korean people."[18]

That's the fiction of the quasi-religious myth that these communist tyrants have forced down the throats of their people. The reality is bloody repression and every kind of corruption. As soon as Kim Il-Sung took power, he began—like the Bolsheviks and Mao before him—to purge his own ranks. He may have executed as many as ninety thousand in nine purges over the course of his rule[19]—in a country of only twenty million. And that is a small slice of the death that has filled the country under the Kims.

Also like communists elsewhere, he launched a brutal religious persecution. Before the division of the Korean peninsula in the 1940s, the northern portion of Korea had half the population of the south but three times the number of Christians. Missionaries referred to Pyongyang, the capital of the north, as the "Jerusalem of the East." There were so many Korean Christians that even today South Korea is second only to the United States among nations with the largest number of Christian missionaries.[20]

"From its inception, the brutal suppression of religious activity and rival systems of thought and belief was a systematic policy of the DPRK," states a report by the U.S. Commission on International Religious Freedom. "Thus, it is not surprising that religious groups were viewed as one of the chief

The Devil Is in the Details

"We [could not] turn into a Communist society along with the religious people. Therefore, we purged the key leaders above the rank of deacons in Protestant or Catholic churches and the wicked among the rest were put on trial. The general religious people were... put into prison camps.... We learned later that those of religion can do away with their old habits only after they have been killed." **—Kim Il-Sung**[22]

political competitors of Kim Il-Sung's Korean Workers Party. When Kim Il-Sung came to power, religious adherents and their families were labeled as 'counter-revolutionary elements' and targeted for repression."[21]

He also engaged in a vast campaign to indoctrinate North Koreans in what we have seen is essentially a new religion. The U.S. Commission on International Religious Freedom says that the religious cult created around the Kims has touched every individual in the ironically named "Democratic People's Republic of Korea" (DPRK). Students were made to memorize the "Ten Principles for the Establishment of the One-Ideology System of the Party." And every North Korean citizen was expected to attend one or more of an estimated (incredible) four hundred fifty thousand "Kim Il-Sung Revolutionary Research Centers" at least weekly for instruction, inspiration, and "self-criticism."[23]

All adult citizens were required to wear a button with Kim Il-Sung's picture on it. Today, every household in North Korean must maintain portraits of both the "Great Leader" Kim Il-Sung and the "Dear Leader" Kim Jong Il. Inspectors visit homes to chastise and fine families who fail to properly take care of the portraits. Every government building and subway car displays the two portraits.[24] Disloyalty to King Jong Il and his late father, Kim Il-Sung, is a punishable crime. Offenses include allowing pictures of either leader to gather dust or be torn or folded.[25] Former North Korean prisoner Kang Chol-hwan has described how his prison camp had a shrine to the Kim family; the inmates, otherwise dressed in tattered rags, were required to put on a special pair of socks before entering the holy of holies.[26]

The "Dear Leader," the second crazy Kim to rule this tragic nation of captive communist serfs, was Kim Jong Il, son of the "Great Leader." Fittingly, he was actually born in the USSR, where his father was in charge of a Soviet military brigade made up of Korean and Chinese Communist Party exiles. He assumed the leadership of North Korea in the summer of 1994 on the death of his father. His birthday is a national holiday. The regime teaches that a double rainbow and new star appeared in the sky at the moment of his birth. State media claimed that in the first round of golf Kim ever played, he broke the all-time world record for the best round of golf in history. The little man bagged five holes in one! The government press also reported that Kim composed more and better operas—and at a younger age—than anyone in history. Songs such as "Dear Leader Dispels Raging Storms" were karaoke hits in North Korea.[27] A North Korean newspaper described the Dear Leader as "an outstanding great master of witty remarks as well as the greatest man ever known in history."[28]

A Book You're Not Supposed to Read

The Aquariums of Pyongyang: Ten Years in the North Korean Gulag by Kang Chol-hwan (New York City: Basic Books, 2005).

The communist government of North Korea is guilty of every kind of corruption. Women were forcibly enlisted into Kim Jong Il's "Satisfaction Corps," to provide their omnipotent leader with sex. According to Professor Phil Williams of the University of Pittsburgh's Graduate School of Public and International Affairs and Ridgway Center, "This is a criminal state not because it's been captured by criminals but because the state has taken over crime." James Przystup of the National Defense University described North Korea under Kim Jong Il this way: "It's the mafia masquerading as a government." Journalist Allan C. Brownfeld characterized North Korea as a "vast criminal enterprise" that counterfeits currency and peddles illicit drugs.[29] North Korea grows and ships opium, heroin, cocaine, hashish, and ephedrine, the base for methamphetamine. Particularly disgusting, in July 1998,

★ ★ ★

Another Useful Idiot

"People are busy. They work 48 hours a week.... We found Pyongyang to be a bustling city.... And after working hours, they pack the department stores, which Rosalynn visited. I went in one of them. It's like Wal-Mart in American stores on a Saturday afternoon. They all walk around in there, and they seem in fairly good spirits. Pyongyang at night looks like Times Square. They are really heavily into bright neon lights and pictures and things like that." —**Jimmy Carter's** observations on life in North Korea"[31]

two North Korean diplomats passing through Egypt were discovered with five hundred six thousand tablets of Rohypnol, the sedative "date-rape" drug.[30]

Of course the profits from all this criminal activity are spent not on food for the starving masses but on luxuries for the Kims—and on the North Korean nuclear weapons program. The North Koreans first successfully detonated a nuclear device in October 2006, about twelve years after the so-called "Agreed Framework"—supposed to stop this vicious and unpredictable nation from acquiring the atomic bomb—was negotiated between the Kims and the Bill Clinton administration by Jimmy Carter.

Beginning in 1995—a year after Jimmy Carter had raved about the marvelous shopping opportunities in Pyongyang—the communist dystopia in North Korea managed to produce a famine that starved two to three million people to death in four years, out of a population of twenty million.[32] The famine was caused not by weather or natural disasters but rather what a UN official called "systemic dysfunction"— in other words, the predictable failures of communist central planning. "I hope and pray," said Andrew Natsios of World Vision, "that this is the last of the great totalitarian famines."[33] Well, pray as we might, there will continue to be totalitarian famines so long as there is totalitarian communism.

North Korea has 80 percent of the Korean peninsula's mineral resources, with more arable land and fewer people than South Korea. Yet capitalist South Korea thrives, its standard of living having soared to Western levels since the early 1990s, while communist North Korean starved.

★ ★ ★

Let Them Eat Bark

During the famine the North Korean government set up distribution centers where the masses had their choice between "brown cakes"—made from tree bark extract—or "green cakes"—made from grass.[34]

There were reports of cannibalism from Chinese authorities along the northwestern border of the Democratic People's Republic of Korea. Hundreds of millions of dollars in relief and food aid was sent by South Korea, the United States, and the United Nations, but much of it was pilfered by North Korean officials.[35] As the people starved, the Dear Leader sent his personal chef to Tokyo to buy fresh sushi, to Copenhagen for gourmet bacon, to Tehran to buy caviar, and to Paris for the finest wines and cognacs.[36]

All of North Korea is a prison state—with prisons inside it. The infamous Camp 22, for example, is a concentration camp. There, countless thousands of men, women, and children accused of political crimes are held. Prison guards stamp on the necks of babies born to prisoners, and the camp even maintains gas chambers, where horrific chemical experiments are conducted on human beings. Entire families are gassed together, left to agonizing, cruel deaths as state scientists in white coats watch through the glass, taking notes.[37]

After Kim Jong Il's death in December 2011—reportedly "in a fit of rage" over the communist state's inability to competently construct a dam (informed of a leak, he "rushed to make an on-site inspection of the facility" where he was "unable to contain his anger and died suddenly")[39]—he was succeeded by his son Kim Jong Un.

★ ★ ★

A True Believer

Kwon Hyuk, former chief of management at Camp 22 in North Korea, exposed the gas chambers there. He admitted, with painful honesty, that he had felt no pity for the victims: "At the time I felt that they thoroughly deserved such a death. Because all of us were led to believe that all the bad things that were happening to North Korea were their fault; that we were poor, divided and not making progress as a country.... Under the society and the regime I was in at the time, I only felt that they were the enemies. So I felt no sympathy or pity for them at all."[38]

The third Kim started off his reign with a bang, executing his vice minister of the army, Kim Chol, with a mortar round after assuming leadership from his pappy. On the orders of Kim Jong Un to "leave no trace of him behind, down to his hair," Kim Chol was forced to stand on a spot that had been X-ed out and was "obliterated" with a mortar round.[40]

Like his father and grandfather before him (and Mao, the granddaddy of all the Asian communist dictators, before them), the current Kim has an insatiable appetite for women, whom his secret police round up for his pleasure. Kim Jong Il's "Satisfaction Corps" has been replaced by Kim Jong Un's specialized "Pleasure Squad." Some of the girls are as young as thirteen, often plucked from their school classrooms by soldiers. Their families, who are not allowed to see or speak to their daughters from that point, are told that the girls are being used for "important government projects." This chain gang of sex slaves contains some two thousand North Korean girls.[41]

How much blood is on the hands of the Kims? That is difficult to say.

There are the carcasses of the two to three million who starved to death in the famine in the 1990s—some 10 to 15 percent of the total population. There are the nearly hundred thousand who died in party purges. *The Black Book of Communism*, which was compiled in the mid- to late-1990s, points to another 1.5 million dead in concentration camps. And then, as *The Black Book* also notes, there were at least another 1.3 million deaths from the Korean War, instigated and organized by the communists. Plus at least another half-million victims of the effects of the widespread malnutrition—somehow in workers' paradises, it's always a struggle to get enough to eat—prior to the great famine of the 1990s.[43] In total, then, we are looking at 5.4 to 6.4 million deaths thanks to communism in North Korea.

★ ★ ★

Another Useful Idiot

Paul Boyer's *The American Nation*, a civics textbook used in American public schools, includes only these two brief sentences on North Korea: "Kim's government, a Communist dictatorship, redistributed land to poor peasants and nationalized most industries. Although Kim's government limited freedom of speech, it expanded education and established formal equality for women."[42]

Vietnam

After North Korea fell to communism, other Asian nations followed. Another brutal but even lengthier war—again involving America—ensued in Vietnam. When that painful conflict ended in 1975, over fifty thousand American boys were dead, millions of Vietnamese had perished, and Vietnam was communist. Hundreds of thousands of "boat people" headed for the waters of freedom—many making their way to the shores of America—as a result of the communist persecution that continues to this day.

The communist revolution in Vietnam was started not in the 1960s or even the 1950s, but in the 1920s. And here again, the Comintern and Soviet operative Mikhail Borodin—tasked by Stalin with spreading Bolshevism through Asia—were influential. Communism first came to Vietnam by way of China in December 1924, when an international agent known as Lee Suei was sent by the Comintern to work as "secretary, translator, and interpreter" in Borodin's mission to help the Chinese Kuomintang in Canton. This man, "Lee," was the future Ho Chi Minh, the godfather of Vietnamese communism.[44]

★ ★ ★

Not Exactly What the Founders Had in Mind

In September of 1945, Ho, who had mastered the art of propaganda at the Lenin School, held a ceremony where he invoked the words of the American Declaration of Independence. Ho needed allies, and he knew that the likes of the late FDR and other liberals had a reputation for being both anti-French and anti-colonial. "Thus began Ho's courtship of the U.S. by citing the Declaration of Independence and appealing to the American ideal of liberty," notes historian Ron Radosh. Ho's biographer, William Duiker, explained that Ho's aim was to "induce the United States to support the legitimacy of his government, rather than a return of the French."[46]

Appealing to America's founding ideals is an oft-used communist tactic. In fact, communists and their sympathizers have frequently framed modern communist revolutionaries as virtual reincarnations of the American Founders.[47] To give just one example, in 1943 Howard Fast, a Stalin Prize winner and pal of Obama mentor Frank Marshall Davis (Davis regularly ran Fast's columns directly above his own in his *Chicago Star*, which followed the communist party line), had written a book entitled *Citizen Tom Paine*, portraying Paine, Dr. Benjamin Rush, and other American revolutionaries as akin to Fast and his fellow current-day communist revolutionaries.

During the Vietnam War, the CPUSA and its mouthpieces regularly compared Ho Chi Minh to the Founding Fathers, as if Ho were fighting not for the ideas of the Bolshevik Revolution but the American Revolution. Dr. Benjamin Spock, America's most famous pediatrician—and an infamous dupe of the communists—repeatedly referred to the Vietcong as "communist patriots" and wrote, "The Vietnamese people declared their independence from France, much as we declared our independence from England in 1776. Their war of independence was fought by a united front of various political groups and was led by the communist patriot Ho Chi Minh.... The motivation for revolution is the same today as it was in 1776: the desire for justice and a better life." Spock claimed that "Ho is sometimes called the George Washington of Vietnam."[48]

Ho's shrewd communist propaganda lived on after his own death, through the Vietnam War and into the twenty-first century. President Barack Obama once claimed, "Ho Chi Minh was actually inspired by the U.S. Declaration of Independence and Constitution, and the words of Thomas Jefferson."[49]

Like other leading Asian communists, Ho Chi Minh embraced the faith as a young, wide-eyed student in Paris in the late 1910s and early 1920s. From Paris he went directly to the USSR, refining the craft of revolution under the nurturing of Lenin's Comintern. He returned to Asia in 1924, the year of Lenin's demise.

German Marxist revolutionary Ruth Fischer met Ho in Moscow in the 1920s. Writing in *Foreign Affairs* in 1954, Fischer referred to Ho as a "disciplined Communist," one who had "proved time and again his profound loyalty to Communism."[45]

Ho Chi Minh was arrested in Hong Kong in 1931. The French officials who ran colonial Vietnam demanded that British officials in Hong Kong return him for execution, but the British refused, and Ho Chi Minh returned to the welcoming arms of Stalin and his sycophants in Moscow. By the time of World War II, he had infiltrated his way back to Vietnam, and shortly after the Allied victory he was able to install an independent communist government in Vietnam.

By 1946, Ho's forces were engaged in armed conflict with French forces. The war ended in May 1954 with the French defeat at Dien Bien Phu. In July 1954, a treaty divided Vietnam at the seventeenth parallel, with the north remaining communist. Millions of Vietnamese escaped to the south. Five years later, in May 1959, Ho Chi Minh and his forces, with the backing of the Soviet Union and Mao's China, invaded South Vietnam.

American involvement in Vietnam can be traced back to the Truman administration, but significant high-level involvement began only with President John F. Kennedy, who sent military advisers to South Vietnam, troops to provide training and combat support, and a massive infusion of new weapons. When Kennedy came to office in January 1961, the United States had fewer than a thousand advisors in South Vietnam. The new president quickly upped America's commitment, dispatching the 4400th Combat Crew Training Squadron to Bien Hoa Air Base outside Saigon in early November 1961.

★ ★ ★

Insight into Evil

The Roman Catholic Church—including several popes—has been among the most prescient and insightful critics of communism. We have already seen how Pius IX condemned the pernicious ideology in 1846, even before the publication of *The Communist Manifesto*. In 1878 Leo XIII called it "the fatal plague which insinuates itself into the very marrow of human society only to bring about its ruin." And in 1937 Pius XI described communism as "pernicious," "Godless," "by its nature anti-religious," a form of "perversity," a "fury," "poison," an "extreme danger," a "deluge which threatens the world," a "collectivistic terrorism... replete with hate," a "plague" that leads to "catastrophe, a "satanic scourge" that "conceals in itself a false messianic idea, a form of "class-warfare which causes rivers of blood to flow," a "savage barbarity," a "truly diabolical" instrument of Satan and his "sons of darkness," a false promise, and yet one more "sad legacy" of the fall of man.[50]

What JFK—and many other Americans—feared was that a communist takeover of Vietnam would allow the virulent ideology to spread to neighboring countries—a scenario known as the "domino theory." Kennedy, an intense anti-communist and defense hawk, seems to have been ready to draw a line in the sand, though historians debate the degree to which he might have increased U.S. involvement in Vietnam had he not been assassinated in November 1963. What is certain is that a severe escalation transpired under Kennedy's successor, the dreadful Lyndon B. Johnson, who was president until January 1969. By then, America was embroiled in full-scale, total war in Vietnam.

We should not pass over one tragic mistake by the Kennedy administration in silence—the betrayal of Ngo Dinh Diem, the president of the Republic of Vietnam from 1955 through 1963. Diem was an intense anti-communist, his understanding of the dangers of Marxism-Leninism stemming in part from his devout Roman Catholicism. He was a pious Christian who would have preferred a monastery to the leadership of Vietnam—better suited for the priesthood than presidency, and up for Mass at 6:30 every morning. Diem was a man of character, a principled politician as well as patriot who fully respected and honored the faith of his country's large Buddhist population.

But Diem was vilified by detractors in the United States. The communists in Vietnam knew that the respect that he had rightly earned from the populace was the greatest obstacle to their takeover of their country—with the collusion or at least the sanction (scholars still debate which) of the United States. The Kennedy team approved the *coup d'état* against Diem. Ironically, Diem was assassinated the same month that Kennedy himself was assassinated by a communist.

The best piece of recent historical scholarship outlining this travesty is Canadian author Geoffrey Shaw's superb *The Lost Mandate of Heaven: The American Betrayal of Ngo Dinh Diem, President of Vietnam*, which tells the sickening story of the demonization, slow and steady abandonment, and final betrayal of Diem by certain elements in the United States. Diem had his supporters, to be sure, from CIA station chief William Colby and secretary of state Dean Rusk to two excellent ambassadors, American Frederick Nolting and Briton Robert Thompson. Kennedy's vice president, Lyndon Johnson, also supported Diem (in a rare moment of lucidity for LBJ). After visiting Vietnam in 1963, Lyndon Johnson told Kennedy that Diem was "the Winston Churchill of Southeast Asia" and, "Hell, he's the only boy we got out there."[51]

Kennedy, too, initially liked Diem, but he was eventually turned against him by the incessant demonization of Diem by the *New York Times* (particularly from reporter David Halberstam) and esteemed liberal "wise man" Averell Harriman. "The actions of these men led to Diem's murder," Shaw grimly concludes. "And with his death, nine and a half years of careful work and partnership between the United States and South Vietnam was undone. Within a few weeks, any hope of a successful outcome in Vietnam—that is, of a free and democratic country friendly toward the United States—was extinguished. Truly, in order to solve a problem that did not exist, the Kennedy administration created a problem that could not be solved."[52]

After Diem's assassination, the war in Vietnam would spin out of control. Once Kennedy himself was also assassinated, LBJ began micromanaging and mismanaging the rapidly escalating conflict. "They can't bomb an outhouse without my permission," Johnson bragged.[53] Not that LBJ's intentions were bad. "Our purpose in Vietnam is to prevent the success of aggression," he said. "It is not conquest; it is not empire; it is not foreign bases; it is not domination. It is, simply put, just to prevent the forceful conquest of South Vietnam by North Vietnam."[54] This was a noble purpose. But how it could best be pursued, and whether it was achievable, were difficult questions.

The Vietnam War had a tumultuous effect in America's domestic politics. As the numbers of U.S. troops coming home in body bags rose (hitting upwards of thirty thousand dead by 1968)—as the draft commenced, and as the Civil Rights movement, drugs and sex, and the rise of the New Left and cultural Marxism all roiled the youth culture, the nation's universities erupted. America's campuses and streets saw unprecedented unrest, including violent attacks on the police. Opposition to the Vietnam War reached a fever pitch.

But the effect on the Vietnamese people was far worse. While flower children lost their virginity and blew their minds on LSD on college campuses and at Woodstock, and fifty-eight thousand American boys lost their lives in Southeast Asia, the people of Vietnam lost far, far more, from the property and basic civil liberties to their lives. Over a million were killed in this horrific war, and then still more under the communists, whose takeover followed the American withdrawal.

American policy makers—including both the Democratic Kennedy and Johnson administrations and Republicans Eisenhower and Nixon—had long feared that a communist takeover of Vietnam could set off a wider domino effect throughout Southeast Asia, with nations from Cambodia to Laos potentially falling into the communist camp. Chiang Kai Shek's China, the most populous nation on the planet, had already fallen to communism, as had North Korea, and America was now facing the prospect of more Asian nations becoming allies and proxies for either the Soviets or the Red Chinese. By the late 1960s, the Sino-Soviet split was in full force, the Chinese communists having fallen out with their former sponsors in Russia, and the United States knew that China could be looking to expand and extend its own communist empire southward.

And that is precisely what happened. "Cold War thinking was that if South Vietnam fell to communists, the rest of Southeast Asia would fall as well," writes Earl Tilford, a Vietnam War historian and veteran. "That happened in Cambodia and Laos less than six months after Saigon fell on April 29, 1975." A Chinese general told Tilford that he had been one of the hundred and forty thousand "People's Liberation Army" volunteers in North Vietnam in 1972. The Chinese army was building a road through northern Laos toward Thailand—as Tilford knows well, having been stationed at Udorn Royal Thai Air Base, Thailand in 1970 and 1971. This so-called "China Road" was loaded with antiaircraft guns. Tilford remembers, "An Air Force RF-4C Phantom reconnaissance aircraft was so badly shot up on April 10, 1970, that it crashed while attempting to land at Udorn. Both crewmen successfully ejected, the plane careened through two officers' hooches and engulfed a trailer housing the radio station. The screams of nine airmen inside were heard across the base before the transmissions—and the men—died."[55]

Tilford's account of Chinese activity in this particular theater of operations is just one of endless examples of both Chinese and Soviet mischief that could be cited here. The point is that fears of communist expansion in Asia were entirely justified. The Soviets hoped for communist ascendancy, even after the Sino-Soviet split in the late 1950s. At the very least, the Kremlin was cheering for a crushing U.S. defeat. And so the Soviets supplied military aid to the Vietcong, engaged in diplomatic troublemaking, and shamelessly incited terrible wars—including the June 1967 Six Day War in the Middle East—as well as launching "active measures" that included propaganda, disinformation, and assassinations across the world.

One of the best eyewitnesses to Soviet intentions in Vietnam was a great Cold War spy, the number two man at CPUSA, Morris Childs, who, as we have already seen, was secretly working for the FBI. He was very close to Leonid Brezhnev, who fully trusted him. The Soviet leadership was very candid with Childs, including on the subject that dominated American headlines: Vietnam. The Soviet leadership used facts and figures to reassure Childs that they were doing all they could to assist communist North Vietnam militarily and politically. The Soviets briefed him in great detail on the extent and nature of their military aid, as well as their exciting plans to enlist leftist Western intellectuals in a propaganda campaign to undermine U.S. forces in Vietnam and to try to prompt an American withdrawal. A central part of the Soviet disinformation campaign was to argue that the Vietnam War was really just another inevitable "nationalist" uprising by an indigenous force that was in no way a serious communist threat to American interests.

And ultimately communist propaganda did succeed in duping American liberals into believing that Vietnam's communists were just anti-imperialists who desired democracy as much as communism. Run-of-the-mill protestors against the Vietnam War may have been simply in favor of peace, and unaware of the international scope and dimensions of the war, obscured by the propaganda push to mislead them. And many of the protestors were understandably, and rightly, frustrated by the horrible mismanagement of the war, especially by the Johnson administration, whose toxic mistakes in the conduct of the war were killing tens of thousands of Americans and far more Vietnamese, with no end in sight. Protestors marched outside the White House shouting, "Hey, hey, LBJ, how many kids did you kill today?"

But some of the more radical protestors actively sympathized with the Vietnamese communists, whom they much preferred to American Democrats and Republicans. American communists like Columbia University's Mark Rudd, who headed the campus chapter of Students for a Democratic Society (SDS), complained, "Liberals, including Robert Kennedy, his martyred brother John, and LBJ had given us Vietnam in the first place." Rudd would shut down Columbia's campus in the spring of 1968, and it was just one of many campuses where the chaos was so volatile that classes had to be cancelled.

When SDS was not radical enough to achieve their objectives, Rudd and comrades like Bill Ayers and Bernardine Dohrn created more violent splinter groups, such as the Weather Underground. "We have only begun," promised the 1974 Weather Underground manifesto, *Prairie Fire,* which was dedicated to (among others) Sirhan Sirhan, the assassin of Robert F. Kennedy. They vowed that "the only possibilities are victory or death." The Weather Underground's "revolutionary program" was "to disrupt the empire" of "U.S. imperialism" and "incapacitate it." The Weather Underground invoked the words of Che Guevara: "In our own hemisphere," declared the authors, "Che Guevara urged that we 'create two, three, many Vietnams,' to destroy U.S. imperialism...and opening another front within the US itself."[56]

President Johnson refused to pursue the Democratic Party's nomination for the presidency in 1968. It was a sign of the political toll that the Vietnam War was taking inside the United States. Republican nominee Richard Nixon won the presidency and quickly pursued a policy to win the war, or at least to avoid losing. The Paris Peace Accords was signed in January 1973, formally ending the war, but not ending the actual fighting on the ground. Then in January 1975, the North Vietnamese launched a massive attack on

★ ★ ★

Freedom Man

When communism finally conquered Vietnam, persecution, mass executions, torture, and deprivation of civil liberties quickly followed. An estimated five hundred thousand to a million South Vietnamese underwent forced "re-education" from 1975 until roughly 1986, when they were returned home from brainwashing centers. Millions more fled to the jungles or took to the ocean. The "Boat People Exodus" ensued, with hundreds of thousands—perhaps as many as two million—"boat people" heading for the high seas, leaving behind their possessions in search of freedom and normal lives. Hundreds of thousands never made it; they drowned in the process.

President Ronald Reagan remembered them in his poignant January 1989 "Farewell Address," paying tribute to what America's attempt to stop communism in Vietnam and to the suffering people left behind:

> I've been reflecting on what the past eight years have meant and mean. And the image that comes to mind like a refrain is a nautical one—a small story about a big ship, and a refugee, and a sailor. It was back in the early '80s, at the height of the boat people. And the sailor was hard at work on the carrier *Midway*, which was patrolling the South China Sea. The sailor, like most American servicemen, was young, smart, and fiercely observant. The crew spied on the horizon a leaky little boat. And crammed inside were refugees from Indochina hoping to get to America. The Midway sent a small launch to bring them to the ship and safety. As the refugees made their way through the choppy seas, one spied the sailor on deck, and stood up, and called out to him. He yelled, "Hello, American sailor. Hello, freedom man."[57]

South Vietnam, which fell on April 30. The infamous fall of Saigon was captured by vivid images of American helicopters, mobbed by desperate crowds, pulling up and out of the city.

Today, Vietnam remains under communist despotism. Sources ranging from the Victims of Communism Memorial Foundation to the Harvard

University Press work, *The Black Book of Communism*, record one million dead Vietnamese victims of communism.[58]

The Killing Fields of Cambodia

Cambodia fell the same year that the last American helicopter lifted out of Saigon. What communism brought to Cambodia was unspeakably horrific, with the violent death of a percentage of the population that far surpassed the proportion killed anywhere else, even under the worst moments of Mao's bloody tyranny.

Cambodia succumbed to a man named Pol Pot and his brutal Khmer Rouge movement. Pol Pot was born Saloth Sar in the 1920s into a large and fairly well-off family. His estranged brother would later remark that "the contemptible Pot was a lovely child." The young Pol Pot and his sister were lucky enough to have a private religious education, studying at a Buddhist pagoda in the capital city, Phnom Penh. Pot did so well academically that he earned a college scholarship to study radio electricity in Paris. As in the case of other future Asian Marxist leaders, including Vietnam's Ho Chi Minh, it was in Paris that the young Pol Pot acquired a rabid interest in far-left politics, becoming a passionate communist. Of the eight or nine core individuals who founded the Khmer Rouge (Red Cambodians) with Pol Pot, nearly all had studied in Paris, where leftist European intellectuals taught them their Marxism-Leninism.

Pol Pot left Paris and returned to Cambodia in the early 1950s. As Cambodia gained its independence from colonial France, Pol Pot and his Marxist friends helped establish the Communist Party in Cambodia. He and his Khmer Rouge replaced the American-supported Lon Nol government in 1975. With that, communism was on in Cambodia.

Pol Pot and the Khmer Rouge were textbook totalitarians, seeking to change human nature itself. Their attack on the most basic human rights began with savage haste. Cities and urban areas were immediately evacuated, with Cambodians forcibly relocated into rural areas. Once they were separated from all their possessions and thrust into the countryside, collectivized into common farms and re-education centers, Cambodians' entire lives were regimented. Private property was eliminated, including even personal hygiene products.

Communism, at its essence, is class hatred, and Pol Pot and his Khmer Rouge quickly focused their energies on the elimination of entire classes and professions. The educated classes were targeted, with doctors and lawyers being shot. Of course, religion was despised. The vast majority of the Cambodian population was Buddhist. At the start of the Khmer Rouge's purge, there had been upwards of eighty thousand monks in the country. They were now forced to renounce their vows and marry, or face execution. It is estimated that as many as forty to sixty thousand were killed. By some accounts, there were as few as one thousand monks left in Cambodia after four years. The year 1978 was rechristened the year zero.

From 1975 to 1979, Pol Pot's governing Khmer Rouge harvested the most heinous "Killing Fields" in history, with roughly two million or more Cambodians perishing in a mere four years (estimates range from as low as 1.6 million to as high as three million). While that total does not match Stalin's or Mao's total death toll (or Hitler's), it actually exceeds the victims of butchers as a percentage of the overall population, which at the start of the Cambodian genocide stood somewhere between five and seven million. Some 20 to 40 percent of the Cambodian population may have been annihilated in just four years under Pol Pot and his Khmer Rouge.[59]

Sam Rainsy, a Cambodian politician who experienced the genocide firsthand, points out that the bloodletting done by Pol Pot and his Khmer Rouge in the late 1970s is historically "comparable only to the attempt to exterminate the Armenians during World War I, the holocaust of Jews committed under Hitler, and more recently the massacre of hundreds of thousands of Tutsis and Hutus in Rwanda."

The human faces behind the statistics tell an even grimmer story.

"My wife held the youngest of our sons in her arms," recalls one survivor of the Cambodian holocaust. "I held the hands of the other two. Our elbows were then tied. We were blindfolded and I knew we were about to be executed. I was able to untie myself and lift my blindfold. The Khmer Rouge were stuffing the mouths of those they were leading with rags and grass to prevent them from screaming and were cutting their throats like animals—the throats of men, women, old folk and children alike."

When the Khmer Rouge was not lining up people and slicing their throats, it was starving them to death. Hunger remains "an issue I can talk on for hours," recalls Bo Meng, who lost six siblings and his father during those years of starvation and execution. Now a restaurant owner in Pittsburgh, Pennsylvania, Meng recalls how single spoonfuls of corn kernels served as family meals. Another survivor, Loung Ung, tells in her gripping memoir *First They Killed My Father* of how her older siblings shook the trees at night "hoping to find June bugs" to eat while she and her younger brothers and sisters scoured the ground to catch frogs and grasshoppers for nourishment.

The horrors in Cambodia and Vietnam can be directly attributed to the communist ideology that the United States had hoped to halt in Asia during the Vietnam War, a noble albeit tragic cause that was far from flawlessly pursued. And while America's involvement in Southeast Asia will long be debated and questioned, there remains no question that Pol Pot and his Khmer Rouge turned Cambodia into hell on earth.

What communism brought to Asia was nothing new. It was what communism always brings: horrific suffering, death, and sorrow.

CHAPTER 9

Meet Fidel and Che, Two Vicious Commie Nuts Who Wanted to Blow Up the World

The United States did its best to keep the scourge of communism out of its own backyard—the Western Hemisphere. But in 1959 the Marxist menace crawled under the fence just a hundred miles south of U.S. shores, taking down one of America's closest allies: Cuba.

A tyrant named Fidel Castro proceeded to grab everything from private garden plots to fishing poles. His regime violated the full sweep of human freedoms and inalienable rights. The people of Cuba have endured hell since the Castro brothers, Fidel and Raúl, along with their twisted friend Che, seized control of the nation nearly sixty years ago. And communism has been a menace to the people of Latin America ever since—from the "Sandinista National Liberation Front" in Nicaragua to the chaos the people of Venezuela are living through even as I write.

Did you know?

- ★ A 1957 *New York Times* profile of Castro called his program "anti-Communist"
- ★ Che Guevara had construction workers tear out a section of a wall so he could watch executions from his office
- ★ Che and a team of Cuban terrorists were plotting to blow up Grand Central station and several New York department stores

Launching the Revolution

It all started with Fidel.

Born in Biran, Cuba, in August 1926, Fidel Castro was raised by a wealthy farming family on the eastern part of the island. His father owned a huge amount of land, though it was nothing compared to the millions of acres of Cuban soil that Fidel one day would seize for "the state" as well as his own. Fidel and his brother Raúl, born in June 1931, were two more mansion Marxists—well-to-do young men who become viciously hostile to every aspect of private ownership and free enterprise that had enabled their comfortable upbringing. They came to power declaring their solidarity with the little guy, then took the property of all and built themselves palaces.

Fidel's turn to the extreme Left came in college, at the University of Havana, where he studied law and was inculcated with radical revolution. By his mid-twenties he was ready to take on the island's authoritarian dictator, Fulgencio Batista—no democrat, but a friend to the United States and a staunch foe of the Soviet Union and communism.

Fidel Castro launched his revolution on July 26, 1953, when he and his rebels attacked the Moncada army barracks at Santiago, Cuba. There were upwards of several hundred of them, and close to a hundred were wounded or killed, and many taken prisoner, including Fidel himself. But the revolution would ultimately survive because Fidel survived. He was sentenced to fifteen years in prison, but served only about a year—one of innumerable examples showing how the unelected authoritarian Batista, corrupt and repressive as he was, was never as brutal as Fidel would be. There is no way the instigator of an uprising against Fidel would have been allowed to live, let alone leave prison so generously soon.

Fidel's Pal at the *New York Times*

Many in the United States—including the Eisenhower administration—wondered where this young rebel, Fidel Castro, stood on the big questions: the Cold War, America vs. the Soviet Union, democracy vs. communism. A remarkably influential page-one article in the Sunday, February 24, 1957,

New York Times sought to allay their fears. The *Times* tossed Fidel and his 26th of July Movement a lifeline.

Herbert Matthews was a *New York Times* reporter and editorial writer. A graduate of Columbia University, Matthews first demonstrated his sympathy for communist causes in his dispatches from Spain during the Spanish Civil War. His extraordinarily influential reports from Cuba in 1957 breathed entirely new life into Fidel's movement when the defeated rebels were languishing in the hills and the world had given up on them. Che Guevara himself would contend, "When the world had given us up for dead, the interview with Matthews put the lie to our disappearance."[1]

Castro's revolution had floundered since the Moncada debacle. It was by all accounts on the run and essentially done. International support and enthusiasm had waned. But Castro's fortunes were about to change, courtesy of the *New York Times*. The page-one, three-part series on Castro was a blockbuster.[2]

Matthews began his game-changer of a story by reporting that "the rebel leader of Cuba's youth," was "alive and fighting hard and successfully in the rugged, almost impenetrable fastnesses of the Sierra Maestra." Castro was winning against all odds, despite everything that Batista was throwing at him: "President Fulgencio Batista has the cream of his Army around the area, but the Army men are fighting a thus-far losing battle to destroy the most dangerous enemy General Batista has yet faced in a long and adventurous career as a Cuban leader and dictator."[3]

Matthews then touted his scoop: "This is the first sure news that Fidel Castro is still alive and still in Cuba. No one connected with the outside world, let alone with the press, has seen Senor Castro except this writer. No one in Havana, not even at the United States Embassy with its resources for getting information, will know until this report is published that Fidel Castro is really in the Sierra Maestra."

The Man Who Invented Fidel: Castro, Cuba, and Herbert L. Matthews of The New York Times by Anthony DePalma (New York: Public Affairs, 2007).

Matthews seemed to be celebrating his own personal victory against Batista. "This account, among other things, will break the tightest censorship in the history of the Cuban Republic.... Havana does not and cannot know that thousands of men and women are heart and soul with Fidel Castro and the new deal for which they think he stands."

Note that loaded word for the *New York Times* faithful: "new deal." Matthews was suggesting that Castro was a leader like FDR, who was a veritable political saint to millions of Americans, especially readers of the *Times*. Castro was also a democrat (small "d"):

> Fidel Castro and his 26th of July Movement are the flaming symbol of this opposition to the [Batista] regime. The organization, which is apart from the university students' opposition, is formed of youths of all kinds. It is a revolutionary movement that calls itself socialistic. It is also nationalistic, which generally in Latin America means anti-Yankee.
>
> The program is vague and couched in generalities, but it amounts to a new deal for Cuba, radical, democratic and therefore anti-Communist. The real core of its strength is that it is fighting against the military dictatorship of President Batista.[4]

Castro was not only "democratic"—he was "anti-Communist."

Thus began Matthews's apologia for the man who would become the Western Hemisphere's longest-running communist dictator of all-time. Matthews went on to frame Fidel as a constitutionalist, a beacon of liberty, an advocate of freedom and free elections, an anti-colonialist, an anti-imperialist, a champion of social justice...and an extraordinarily eloquent one at that:

> Senor Castro speaks some English, but he preferred to talk in Spanish, which he did with extraordinary eloquence. His is a political mind rather than a military one. He has strong ideas of liberty, democracy, social justice, the need to restore the Constitution, to hold elections. He has strong ideas on economy, too, but an economist would consider them weak.
>
> The 26th of July Movement talks of nationalism, anti-colonialism, anti-imperialism. I asked Senor Castro about that. He answered, "You can be sure we have no animosity toward the United States and the American people."
>
> "Above all," he said, "we are fighting for a democratic Cuba and an end to the dictatorship. We are not anti-military; that is why we let the soldier prisoners go. There is no hatred of the Army as such, for we know the men are good and so are many of the officers."
>
> "Why should soldiers die for Batista for $72 a month?" he asked. "When we win, we will give them $100 a month, and they will serve a free, democratic Cuba."[5]

Note how remarkably similar this language is to that of Edgar Snow's reporting on Mao.

And what source did Matthews cite for these remarkable claims? Fidel Castro.

Castro's subsequent actions would prove the Matthews article abysmally incorrect, but at the time it was a godsend for the communist cause. The *Daily Worker* itself could not have produced such a perfect piece of political propaganda. And such a piece would not have been believable coming from the *Daily Worker*, but the *Times* was the *Times*—daily bread for American liberals. The only interesting question is whether Herb Matthews was Castro's dupe or his co-conspirator, or just a complete fool. This much we do know: the impact of his article was huge, and a major blow to the efforts of anti-communists who wanted to save their island from a man who would soon take all their property and most basic civil liberties. The importance of Matthews' article cannot be understated.[6] Conservatives would joke that Castro had gotten his job through the *New York Times*.

Victory Lap in Manhattan

Fidel Castro was on his way. He would come to power two years later in a January 1959 coup against Fulgencio Batista, who got out of Dodge, boarding a plane to escape the country and the firing squad.

As Castro secured his hold on Havana in those opening weeks of 1959, he also prepared for a major visit to America. In April of that year he toured the United States, with appearances in New York City and Washington, D.C. New York City, still replete with more communists by far than any city in America, was the perfect setting for his victory lap. Ecstatic crowds cheered. New Yorkers gave him the ticker-tape treatment. They rolled out the red carpet.

Norman Mailer was smitten. The leftist novelist got goose bumps at the sight of Fidel: "So Fidel Castro, I announce to the City of New York that you gave all of us who are alone in this country... some sense that there were heroes in the world. One felt life in one's overargued blood as one picked up in our newspaper the details of your voyage." According to Mailer, "It was as if the ghost of Cortez had appeared in our century riding Zapata's white horse. You were the first and greatest hero to appear in the world since the Second War."[7]

The American Left's sickening adoration of Fidel Castro was nothing new. Many a communist thug has been a hero to them. Mailer's love-letter was just one of countless such testimonies from American progressives, running through the decades ahead. The sight of Fidel in his military-festooned glory excited hippy leader Abbie Hoffman: "Fidel sits on the side of a tank rumbling into Havana on New Year's Day," observed Hoffman, filled with pleasure at the ideological eye-candy. "Girls throw flowers at the tank and rush to tug playfully at his black beard. He laughs joyously and pinches a few rumps." (The Left doesn't seem to mind sexual harassment when its icons are doing the groping.) "The tank stops in the city square," recorded Hoffman, his excitement rising. "Fidel lets the gun drop to the ground, slaps his thigh and stands erect. He is like a mighty penis coming to life, and when he is tall and straight, the crowd immediately is transformed."[8]

That was after Fidel had revealed himself as an America-hating Marxist despot. During Castro's April 1959 visit to America, he was still hoping to curry favor with his hosts. So in an April 19 appearance on NBC's *Meet the Press*, Castro again promised Cubans, Americans, and people everywhere that democracy was his "ideal" for Cuba, where elections would soon be held. "Democracy is my ideal, really," Castro told NBC's Lawrence Spivak. "I am not a communist. I am not agreed with communism.... There is no doubt for me between democracy and communism."

Today, over fifty years later, the world is still awaiting free elections in Cuba. Fidel took his unfulfilled promises to the grave. He never implemented democracy. He created a totalitarian communist dictatorship, the most militarized, repressive nation in the Western Hemisphere, and ruled it as a despot for half a century.

As Castro was delighting American communists and liberals, he was sending tremors of fear among genuine democrats and lovers of liberty in Cuba. Even before wowing New York and Washington, he had taken a page from Stalin's purges, holding a mass show-trial in Havana in February 1959, for which some eighteen thousand spectators gathered (as in a Roman Colosseum) at the Palace of Sports to judge Batista crony Jesús Sosa Blanco, who had been charged with executions under the old regime. Fidel and his brother Raúl, minister of defense, organized the kangaroo court. The verdict was predetermined; there was no need for witnesses.

In a carnival-like atmosphere of communist hysteria, the frenzied mob stood and issued Blanco a giant collective thumbs down. That was it: guilty. The "people" had decided. The sentence: death. Before he was shot Blanco decried the sensational scene as "worthy of ancient Rome."[9] The only thing missing were the lions.

Fidel Castro did not need lions; he had Che Guevara.

Cold-Blooded Killer

Any history of the communist takeover of Cuba cannot ignore Che, a wolf of a man, today inexplicably and obscenely placed on a pedestal by legions of embarrassingly misled American youth stupidly sporting his snarling face on T-shirts and posters.

Ernesto "Che" Guevara was born into a wealthy family in Buenos Aires, Argentina. He became consumed not only with Marxism-Leninism but with hatred, with militarization, with the violent creation of "the New Man," and with murder and death. Che was one more in a long line of radical-left fundamental transformers, from the Jacobins and Marx and Lenin to Pol Pot and the Khmer Rouge and on and on. That twisted dream never dies. He met Fidel in Mexico in 1955, and the rest was history.

Ironically for a man celebrated by today's apostles of non-conformity and "diversity," Che preached the collective. "Youth should learn to think and act as a mass," he insisted. He denounced "those who choose their own path" as "delinquents" and "lumpen" (borrowing from Karl Marx's condescending description of the masses as the "lumpenproletariat"). He publicly vowed "to make individualism disappear from Cuba! It is criminal to think of individuals!"[10]

Like Vladimir Lenin, after whom Che named his son, Che preached "hatred as an element of struggle"—something that has not deterred modern agents of "tolerance" and "social justice" from slavishly admiring him. He urged an "intransigent" and "unbending hatred for the enemy, which pushes a human being beyond his natural limitations." The word "hatred" is littered throughout Guevara's writings. His final words were about hate: in his will Che praised the "extremely useful hatred" that turns men into "effective, violent, merciless, and cold killing machines."[11]

That is an apt description of Che himself. He was a cold-blooded killing machine. A writer at the liberal *Daily Beast* described him as a "mass-murdering sociopath."[12] A writer at the liberal *The New Yorker* agreed, characterizing Che as "a fanatic consumed by restlessness and a frightening abstract hatred," who "recognized only one moral value as supreme: the willingness to be slaughtered for a cause."[13]

Che luxuriated in violence and savagery. Álvaro Vargas Llosa, a veteran chronicler of Che's life, notes that the writings of the Argentinian communist are "peppered" with "rhetorical and ideological violence. For example, this is the way Che described himself in a January 28, 1957, letter he wrote to his wife (later published in her book *Ernesto: A Memoir of Che Guevara in Sierra Maestra*) when he was traveling with Fidel Castro from Mexico to Cuba aboard their boat *Granma* (one of the symbols of Fidel's revolution): "Here in the Cuban jungle, alive and bloodthirsty."[14]

Few statements so succinctly describe Che and the revolution he and Fidel and friends were uncorking. That same month, Che personally shot local guide Eutimio Guerra because he suspected him of passing on information. "I ended the problem with a .32 caliber pistol, in the right side of his brain," Che gloated in his diary. "His belongings were now mine."[15]

A perfect summation of communism in practice. The communist leader takes aim at the target, kills him, and then seizes his property, which then belongs not to the masses for whom the communist claims

★ ★ ★

Atrocities without Shame

Che gloried in the executions. "*Executions?*" he publicly exclaimed. "Certainly we execute! And we will *continue executing* as long as it is necessary! This is a war to the death against the revolution's enemies!"[19]

the property, but to the communist revolutionary himself.

When not carrying out actual executions, the sadist Che would often line victims up against a wall and simulate executing them as a method of psychological torture.[16]

Fidel quickly recognized in Che an ideal man to put in charge of his most torturous prison, La Cabaña. As Llosa sees it, Che's cruel behavior during the darkest period of the prison was "chillingly reminiscent of Lavrenti Beria," the raping monster who ran Stalin's NKVD-KGB, and whom Stalin boastingly described to the Nazis as "our Himmler."

Javier Arzuaga, the prison chaplain and a left-wing Catholic priest sympathetic to the early aims of Castro's revolution and to liberation theology, recalls constantly pleading with Che for the prisoners that Che was so hell-bent on executing. "Che did not budge," the priest recalled, after witnessing at least fifty-five executions at which Che had ordered the priest's presence. "Nor did Fidel."[17]

The priest had had enough. The orgy of brutality was too overwhelming. He managed to escape.

The great Cuban jazz musician Paquito D'Rivera lost a cousin in one of those executions, a Christian thrown in jail for his religious beliefs. "One of those Cubans [at La Cabaña] was my cousin Bebo, who was imprisoned there precisely for being a Christian," wrote D'Rivera. "He could hear from his cell in the early hours of dawn the executions, without trial or process of law, of the many who died shouting, 'Long live Christ the King!'"[18]

Sounding eerily like M. Y. Latsis, the ferocious Latvian who was the first and preeminent executioner for Lenin's NKVD, Che stated, "I don't need proof to execute a man. I only need proof that it's necessary to execute him!...Judicial evidence is an archaic bourgeois detail. We execute from revolutionary conviction."[20]

At La Cabaña, Che and friends invented a specialty item: tiny cells called *ratoneras*, or "rat holes" for certain targeted political prisoners.[21] These were inhumane, unlivable spaces. But really the whole place was one giant rat hole, with the rat-in-chief relishing every moment in charge of his miserable kingdom. In fact, Che had fallen in love with La Cabaña at first sight, seeing it as ready-made for his intentions. When he first surveyed the premises, he was attracted immediately to the moat around the old Spanish fortress, deeming it an ideal execution pit. He could work his firing squads in triple shifts filling the moat with floating, bobbing bodies. Actually, the place was more than ideal, given Che's thinking. When the great revolutionary guerrilla could not be on the spot to revel in the executions enacted on his order, or fire a bullet into a skull himself, he had could watch his firing squads at work from his second-story office in La Cabaña. Che even ordered a construction crew to tear out a section of the wall that was obstructing his view.[22]

"When you saw the beaming look on Che's face as the victims were tied to the stake and blasted apart by the firing squad," former Cuban political prisoner Roberto Martin-Perez told Humberto Fontova, "you saw there was something seriously, seriously wrong with Che Guevara." Martin-Perez noted that whereas Fidel Castro "ordered mass murder," the butchery "didn't seem to affect him one way or the other" because he was "a classic psychopath" who carried out the slaughter for practical reasons, to consolidate his power. Che, on the other hand, "relished the slaughter."[23]

How many Cubans were imprisoned by this psychopath and his sadist "chief executioner"? In 1959, Cuba had a population of 6.4 million people. According to Freedom House, half a million Cubans have passed through Cuba's prison system. Humberto Fontova argues that this was a larger percentage of the population than went through Stalin's Gulag in the Soviet

★ ★ ★

Their Hero

Che's contempt for America would be a turn-on to the '60s radicals in America who, like him, were hoping to take down the United States. Mark Rudd, infamous SDS leader at Columbia University and one of the founders of the Weather Underground, called Che their "revolutionary martyr and saint."[26] Che was the radicals' Jesus Christ. "Like a Christian seeking to emulate the life of Christ," wrote Rudd. "I passionately wanted to be a revolutionary like Che, no matter what the cost."[27] *Prairie Fire: The Politics of Revolutionary Anti-Imperialism*, the infamous 1974 manifesto of the "guerilla organization" Weather Underground authored by Bill Ayers, Bernardine Dohrn, Jeff Jones, and Celia Sojourn—"communist men and women, underground in the United States for more than four years," as they described themselves—sported "THE BANNER OF CHE." *Prairie Fire* contained full pages featuring loving illustrations of their Messiah-like Marxist hero, and pledged, "The only path to the final defeat of imperialism and the building of socialism is revolutionary war." That "war," the authors promised, "will be complicated and protracted. It includes mass struggle and clandestine struggle, peaceful and violent.... Without armed struggle there can be no victory." It was a direct echo of Che's own philosophy.[28]

Union. Fontova notes that it is no coincidence that Che, who adored the Soviet leadership and thoroughly emulated its methods, often signed his personal correspondence "Stalin II."[24]

America: The Great Enemy of Mankind

Che loved the Soviet Union and its aims (though, quite tellingly, it was North Korea, a country he visited during a long trip in late 1960, that he said impressed him "the most"). He constantly looked to the Kremlin for advice—particularly on the enemy he loathed the most: the United States of America.

In 1961 Che declared, "The U.S. is the great enemy of mankind!" He insisted, "Against those hyenas there is no option but extermination. We will bring the war to the imperialist enemies' very home, to his places of work and recreation. The imperialist enemy must feel like a hunted animal wherever he moves. Thus, we'll destroy him! We must keep our hatred against them alive and fan it to paroxysms!"[25]

Che's most significant visit to the USSR came in August 1962 when he visited with Nikita Khrushchev at none other than Yalta, the spot where FDR had been suckered by Stalin a decade and a half earlier. There they finalized details on bringing dozens of Soviet nuclear missiles and thousands of Soviet troops to Cuba, poised and ready to go to nuclear war with the hated United States.[29]

The Cuban Missile Crisis

The October 1962 Cuban Missile Crisis arose in part from Che's most nearly successful attempt to genuinely annihilate mankind and initiate some form of New Man. The soil of the land he reviled the most would be razed. The mushroom cloud over the United States would make his firing squads look like a sunny picnic at the beach. And the holocaust that he fantasized for America nearly came true.

It was a nightmare scenario that terrified all of humanity—except for Che and Fidel: the prospect of dozens of Soviet nuclear missiles fired from Cuba onto American soil, leading to hundreds more nukes fired in retaliation by the United States against Cuba and the USSR, and then the USSR against the United States, with Western Europe and Eastern Europe brought into the fray. Literally hundreds of millions of people would have been killed.

"If the nuclear missiles had remained, we would have fired them against the heart of the U.S., including New York City," Che gleefully admitted in November 1962 to Sam Russell of Britain's *Daily Worker*. "The victory of socialism is well worth millions of atomic victims."[30]

Perhaps the single most revolting thing about Che (which is really saying something) was his willingness to actually fire those atomic weapons at the United States and launch a nuclear war that he understood would lead to the nuclear destruction of Cuba too. The Argentine annihilator bragged that "this country is willing to risk everything in an atomic war of unimaginable destructiveness to defend a principle."[31]

Keith Payne, president of the National Institute for Public Policy, has recounted how "Che Guevara specifically said that he was ready for martyrdom" and "ready for Cuba, as a country, to be a national martyrdom." Payne quotes the response of an alarmed Anastas Mikoyan, the leading Soviet official under Khrushchev, who responded to the martyr-like fanaticism by telling the Cuban communists, "We see your willingness to die beautifully. We don't think it's worth dying beautifully." As Payne saw, Mikoyan and the Soviet leadership were "very deterrable," but the "ideological and political zealots" on the Cuban side "were essentially beyond deterrence in that case."[32]

Was Che really that insane? That unhinged? Yes, and so was Fidel.

If Fidel Castro had had his way in October 1962, Cuba would have ceased to exist. That is not an exaggeration. Fidel actually recommended to Soviet General Secretary Nikita Khrushchev that Cuba and the USSR together launch an all-out nuclear attack upon the United States, and even *urged* Khrushchev to do so if U.S. troops invaded the island.

This is no secret. Castro openly admitted it. Robert McNamara, President John F. Kennedy's secretary of defense during the Cuban Missile Crisis, was taken aback by Castro's candor when the two men publicly discussed the incident years later in an open forum in Havana. Fidel told him flatly, "Bob, I did recommend they [the nuclear missiles] were to be used."[33]

In total, said McNamara, there were 162 Soviet missiles on the island. The firing of those missiles would (according to McNamara) have killed at least eighty million Americans, which would have been half the U.S. population.

But the 162 missiles in Cuba were far from the sum total of missiles that would have been launched. The United States in turn would have fired on Cuba, and also on the USSR. President Kennedy made that commitment clear in his nationally televised speech on October 22, 1962: "It shall be the policy of this nation to regard any nuclear missile launched from Cuba against any nation in the Western Hemisphere as an attack by the Soviet Union on the United States, requiring a full retaliatory response upon the Soviet Union." In response, of course, the Soviets would have automatically fired on America from Soviet soil. Even then, the fireworks would just have been starting: Under the terms of their NATO and Warsaw Pact charters, the territories of Western and Eastern Europe would also start firing.

Once the smoke cleared, hundreds of millions to possibly over a billion people could have perished, and Western civilization would have been in its death throes. If Fidel Castro had had his way, he would have precipitated the greatest slaughter in human history.

Would that have been good for Cuba? Fidel weighed in on that one, stating the obvious to McNamara: "What would have happened to Cuba? It would have been totally destroyed."[34]

Fidel didn't care, and neither did his comrade Che. They were ready for martyrdom, with Cuba serving as the eternal triumphant symbol of the glorious fight against capitalism and American imperialism. As McNamara said of Fidel, "He would have pulled the temple down on his head."[35]

Nikita Khrushchev's son Sergei, in his seminal three-volume biography of his father, reported Fidel's fanaticism this way: "He had to inform Moscow as quickly as possible of his decision to sacrifice Cuba. Let them be aware, as they drew up their plans, that Cuba was ready to perish for the sake of victory."[36]

Even the Soviets were shocked by such unbridled zealotry. Khrushchev quickly realized he was dealing with lunatics and had better bring the missiles home immediately. The Soviet ambassador to Cuba, Alexander

Alekseyev, was so stunned at Castro countenancing a first strike on the United States that he stood frozen, holding his breath as he listened to Castro tell him, "It's either we or they" (that is, Cuba and the communist world or the United States). "If we want to avoid receiving the first strike," said Castro, "if an attack is inevitable, then wipe them off the face of the earth."

Alekseyev, writes Sergei Khrushchev, was "crushed" as he took in Castro's insane thinking. But without waiting for an answer from the speechless Soviet ambassador, Castro started writing his feelings on paper, which, in Sergei's estimation, "seemed like a last testament, a farewell."[37] Fidel was ready to go—go up in a giant mushroom cloud for Marxism.

Khrushchev knew he had to act without hesitation to get the nukes away from these madmen. He met with the top Soviet officials in the "code room" of the Soviet Foreign Ministry very late on a Sunday night and ordered, repeatedly, "Remove them, and as quickly as possible."

Now, Khrushchev felt common cause with his American capitalist adversaries, not his commie cronies in Cuba. "We now have a common cause, to save the world from those pushing us toward war," he told Foreign Minister Andrei Gromyko. Even Gromyko, the frosty old Stalinist, was relieved. Khrushchev ordered him to instantly contact the Soviet ambassador in Washington, Anatoly Dobrynin.[38]

As for Fidel, he was "furious," says Sergei Khrushchev—just as Che was. "Castro was mortally offended," recorded Sergei. "Why? Because he had not managed to engage in a fight with the Americans. He had made up his mind to die a hero, and to have it end that way." He now considered Nikita Khrushchev "a traitor."[39] Che was also incensed when the missile crisis was resolved without causing an atomic war. He lost faith in his beloved Moscow, appalled at Nikita Khrushchev's unwillingness to launch nuclear Armageddon.[40]

Thankfully, the world averted nuclear war, through the steady leadership of President Kennedy and thanks to Nikita Khrushchev removing the Soviet missiles from Cuba. And no thanks whatsoever to Fidel Castro and Che Guevara, two unhinged, unbalanced, vicious, rapacious commie nuts who were ready and willing to blow up the world in the name of their Marxist-Leninist nightmare.

Or, if they couldn't manage to incinerate the whole world, at least New York City. Che Guevara spearheaded a plot to carry out a brutal terrorist attack on New York City on the day after the Macy's Thanksgiving Day Parade in 1962. This was to be Che's retribution for not getting the mass flow of blood he had lusted for during the Cuban Missile Crisis the previous month. He could not get his hands on a nuclear weapon for the attack, but his team of Cuban terrorists had assembled five hundred kilos of TNT and a dozen incendiary devices to target Macy's, Bloomingdale's, Gimbels, and even Grand Central station. This was a massive amount of explosives. Thousands would have died. The plot was uncovered and foiled only the week before by the FBI, which traced it to Che's "Foreign Liberation Department."[41]

Everlasting Icon to the Left

And yet Che remains an icon for the American Left.

"He was the first man I had ever met whom I thought not just handsome but beautiful," wrote I. F. Stone, the "progressive" journalist lionized as the "conscience of investigative journalism."[42] "With his curly, reddish beard, he looked like a cross between a faun and a Sunday school print of Jesus...In a sense he was, like some early saint, taking refuge in the desert." Christ-like, Stone looked at Che and yearned with love and a sense of redemption: "In Che, one felt a desire to heal and pity for suffering." Stone also invoked

St. Francis: "It was out of love, like the perfect knight of medieval romance, that he had set out to combat with the powers of the world."[43]

The love for Che on the American Left has, quite amazingly, only increased over the decades, regardless of ever more information surfacing on his obvious homicidal tendencies.

Only in the detached-from-reality world of goofy Hollywood and modern academia could a mass murderer like Che Guevara be turned into something of a cult celebrity. As Álvaro Vargas Llosa puts it, "Che Guevara, who did so much (or was it so little?) to destroy capitalism, is now a quintessential capitalist brand. His likeness adorns mugs, hoodies, lighters, key chains, wallets, baseball caps, toques, bandannas, tank tops, club shirts, couture bags, denim jeans, herbal tea, and of course those omnipresent T-shirts with the photograph." That photo, of course, is now omnipresent on the T-shirts of blissfully ignorant college students and perverse leftists.

"Dammit, this guy is cool-looking!" said Oscar-winning actor Benicio del Toro, who played Che in a movie by the same name, recalling the first time he saw a picture of Che. "Groovy name, groovy man, groovy politics."[44]

Yeah, and groovy mass murder, dude.

Che was the subject of the Rolling Stones' groovy tune, "Indian Girl."[45]

The most cynical leftists who take pride in never succumbing to pop culture fashions find Che alluring. The late angry atheist apologist Christopher Hitchens, who had been a Trotskyist, conceded that to him and many other revolutionaries, "Che was a role model."[46]

Decades after his death, Che has become a logo of "revolutionary chic." The thirtieth anniversary of his death in 1997 was celebrated by no less than five new biographies. He was immortalized in a movie produced by leftist Robert Redford and titled, *The Motorcycle Diaries*, which remade Che into a roguish-hipster. Useful idiots Carlos Santana and Antonio Banderas went to the Academy Awards ceremony and performed the theme song from *The Motorcycle Diaries*. Santana showed up wearing a Che T-shirt and a crucifix. How's that for a perfect combination: Che and Jesus?[47] The prince of death and the prince of peace.

Nothing new, Carlos, the Weather Underground terrorists beat you to that one by decades.

Good Question

Richard Cohen, longtime liberal columnist for *The Washington Post*, asked of Santana's Che T-shirt, "What was he celebrating? Firing squads?"

Castro's Corpses

Mercifully, Fidel and Che did not succeed in destroying the world—or even New York City. Cuba was not so lucky. The Cuban people have lived (and died) under communist oppression for half a century. Though Cuba was not hit with an atomic bomb, Fidel Castro nevertheless managed to lay waste to the nation. His communist revolution brought Cuba's economy to a grinding halt. From the time of Castro's takeover through the remainder of the '60s and into the '70s and '80s truly nothing progressed in Cuba. Castro's serfs grasped in vain for any semblance of property or prosperity, dignity, or human rights.

How many people have been imprisoned and killed by the communists in Cuba?

Armando Valladares, who spent decades in solitary confinement for refusing to pledge allegiance to the Castro regime, reports that an estimated eighty thousand individuals were imprisoned in Cuba under Fidel from 1960 to 2000, and that seventy thousand of those were ultimately successfully broken down and forced to pay submission to Fidel. The remaining ten thousand (including Valladares) who refused to give in spent the best years of their

★ ★ ★

Spreading the Poison

Under Castro, Cuba became a client state of the Soviet Union—one of the world's leading exporters of Marxism-Leninism, sponsoring and helping to supply insurgencies from Central America to remote outposts in Africa and Asia.

★ ★ ★

You Don't Know Whether to Laugh or Cry

"[Fidel] Castro was making a speech to a large assembly, and he was going on at great length. And then a voice out in the crowd said, 'Peanuts, popcorn, crackerjack!' And he went on speaking, and again the voice said, 'Peanuts, popcorn, crackerjack!' And about the fourth time this happened, [Castro] stopped in his regular speech and he said, 'The next time he says that, I'm going to find out who he is and kick him all the way to Miami.' And everybody in the crowd said, 'Peanuts, popcorn, crackerjack!'" —joke told by **Ronald Reagan** in his remarks at the Fundraising Dinner of the Republican National Hispanic Assembly, Arlington, Virginia, September 14, 1983

lives in jail.[48] *The Black Book of Communism* estimates that the number of Cubans imprisoned under the first forty years of the Castro regime was at least one hundred thousand.[49] But the real truth is that no one knows for sure how many people were in prison in Cuba—or still are. The Castro regime will not permit human rights groups like Amnesty International or Human Rights Watch or teams of UN observers to visit the nation to inspect.

How many were killed? According to *The Black Book of Communism*, in the 1960s alone, when Fidel and Raúl established complete control with the help of their murdering buddy Che, seven to ten thousand Cubans were killed for political reasons.[50] And that was just the start.

Enormous numbers of repressed Cuban citizens—perhaps a hundred thousand individuals—have attempted the treacherous hundred-mile swim to Florida in shark-infested waters. As many as forty thousand of them have died from drowning. As they bob for breath, the Cuban government has on occasion employed the resources of the state to drop large bags of sand on top of them from helicopters hovering high above.[51]

Compare those numbers to the total number of Americans who have attempted the swim to Cuba—including all of the liberals raving about the wonderful "free" education and healthcare in Castro's collectivist utopia: zero.

Setting aside the tens of thousands who have died at sea, how many people has Fidel Castro killed by more direct methods—a bullet to the head, or confinement to one of his deadly prisons? Most credible estimates (including in *The Black Book of Communism*) place the total somewhere between fifteen and eighteen thousand dead.[52] That is a lot of people for a tiny island.

Never underestimate communism's capacity to kill people.

CHAPTER 10

"21st Century Socialism" (Read: Communism)

Communism has a bad reputation, and it's well deserved. Wherever it has been tried around the world, from Lenin and Stalin through Mao and Pol Pot to the Castros and the Kims, the communists have murdered huge numbers of people and driven economies into the ground, reducing the survivors to lives of grinding poverty and horrific political repression.

So communism is perpetually in need of re-branding. The Left is always coining some nifty new term for what is really the same old, same old—the execrable communist ideology that always leaves a stench in its wake. And a good number of liberal-left suckers are always duped, even as the results are always predictably the same.

Did you know?

★ Both the Soviets and the Nazis called themselves "socialist"

★ The head of the Venezuelan government price control agency explained, "The law of supply and demand is a lie"

★ Russian embalmers were consulted in a failed attempt to preserve Hugo Chávez's body for veneration like Lenin's

By Any Other Name

Take Latin American "liberation theology," for example, which tugged on the heartstrings of leftist "social justice" Christians in the 1980s. Or consider how Daniel Ortega and the Sandinistas in Nicaragua were the darlings of the American Left in the 1980s—righteous revolutionaries resisting bad-boy Ronald Reagan and his unsavory anti-communist administration. American liberals who would never have said they were for "communism" or defended the Soviet Union were swept up in the romance of the revolution in Nicaragua.

And yet the aim was the same: to end "oppression." The promise was the same: utopia for the masses. The program was the same: "land reform" (in other words, stealing property from its owners) and central planning of the economy by the new government. And as P. J. O'Rourke's eye-witness testimony shows, the results were (inevitably) the same:

> It doesn't matter what kind of awfulness happens in Latin America—and practically every kind of awfulness does—there are always chickens. No Peruvian mountain village is so poor that you can drive through it without running over a chicken.... But there were no chickens in Managua.
>
> And there was plenty of nothing else besides. In the vast market sheds, the government-allotted stalls with government-determined prices were empty. In the spaces between the sheds vendors had set up illegally with scanty piles of bruised fruit and little heaps of rice and maize. Every now and then, the vendors said, officials from the Interior Ministry cleared them out.... Yet there was plenty of money visible, fists-full of bank notes, which the dispirited crowd handled like so much toilet paper. I take that back. There's a shortage of toilet paper.[1]

Then there's "progressive." Many communists hide behind that label. When researching my 2010 book, *Dupes: How America's Adversaries Have Manipulated Progressives for a Century*, the biggest challenge was sifting through the numerous self-described "progressive" individuals and organizations to figure out if they were genuine liberals or closet communists. Any researcher faces this obstacle. When Congress published its major investigation of communist front groups in 1961, titled, "Guide to Subversive Organizations and Publications," one of the most popular titles listed in the massive index was "Progressive."[2] Communists have been calling themselves progressives since the 1930s, and they are still doing it today. It is not unusual (in fact, it is the norm) for the comrades at the website of Communist Party USA and in *People's World* to describe themselves and their ideas as "progressive" more often than as "communist" or "Marxist." That language is more palatable to the uninformed and easily misled. And take a look at the founders of the 2008 group Progressives for Obama. From Tom Hayden and Mark Rudd to Jane Fonda and the other fellow travelers, these "progressives" for Obama were really a who's who of '60s communists, cultural Marxists, SDSers, and Weather Underground revolutionaries, who as late as the 1970s, as we have seen, were calling themselves communists. And then there are left-wing scholars and professors (do we have any other kind these days?) who help the deception along by conflating communists and "progressives."[3]

A Book You're Not Supposed to Read

The Politically Incorrect Guide® to Socialism by Kevin Williamson (Washington, DC: Regnery, 2011).

But the most popular and perennial euphemism for communism is "socialism."

So what's the difference? Not much.

A Dime's Worth of Difference

Communists—revolutionaries whose true Marxist bona fides no one can doubt—have typically called themselves socialists. Vladimir Lenin, the godfather of Bolshevism, considered himself a democratic socialist before he called himself a communist. It wasn't until he had seized power in Russia

★ ★ ★

Question

What does the second "S" in "USSR" stand for? It stands for "Socialist"—Union of Soviet *Socialist* Republics.

that Lenin changed his party's name from "Social Democratic" to "Communist."

Decades later, the Brezhnev-era Soviet Union championed "real socialism," a term that was ubiquitous in Soviet publications such as *Pravda*, *Izvestia*, and other propaganda organs in the 1970s and early 1980s.

In fact, pretty much all communists are socialists to some degree or in some form or at some point along their merry way—at least in their own opinion. But are all socialists communists? That brings us back to the question: what is the difference?

"Socialism" was the most looked-up word at Merriam-Webster.com in 2015.[5] That reflected a growing interest in socialism with the shocking surge of lifetime socialist Bernie Sanders through the 2016 Democratic Party primary. But it also reflected an enduring confusion over what the word means—and generally over political taxonomy. Ask most students who have taken poli sci 101 and they will recall the day the professor drew a line on the chalkboard delineating the spectrum of political beliefs from the far Left to the far Right. The far Left is reserved for communist totalitarians such as Stalin, Lenin, Mao, Pol Pot, and the Kims. The far right is always

★ ★ ★

Socialists Embrace a Synonym

The World Socialist Party of the United States (headquartered in Boston) declares its overriding "object": "The establishment of a system of society based on the common ownership and democratic control of the means and instruments for producing and distributing wealth by and in the interest of society as a whole.... We call this 'common ownership,' but other terms we regard as synonymous are communism and socialism."[4]

more problematic. In terms of economic freedom versus government coercion, the professor should put libertarians or anarchists at that end of the spectrum—given that they believe in the least government (or none at all). But few would categorize a libertarian or anarchist as "far right." That term is typically reserved for fascists, Nazis, and ultranationalists and racists.

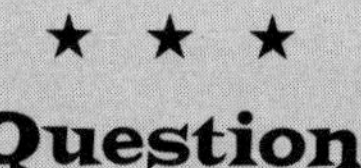

Question

What does Nazi stand for? National *Socialist* German *Workers'* Party.

But remember that both Hitler and Mussolini called themselves socialists, and Mussolini was a Marxist to boot. The Nazis absolutely favored centralized power.

Complicated? Yes, it is.

If you ask typical self-identified "socialists" in America or Western Europe today, they will vehemently object to any suggestion of similarity between their political beliefs and either Soviet or Nazi socialism. And in fact they cannot be compared with those tyrants. To do so would be unfair and a major mistake. That said, socialists generally, in America and the wider West, do share with the Soviets the general goal of government ownership of the means of production in some form. The famous Clause IV of the 1918 British Labour Party platform, which was repudiated by Labour Party reformer and future prime minister Tony Blair, called for "the most equitable distribution" based on "the common ownership of the means of production, distribution, and exchange."

"Socialism," states Merriam-Webster, is "government ownership of the means of production." At the time of this writing of this book, Wikipedia and other popular go-to sources say the same.

Let's go back to the drawing board and to that spectrum we were sketching. To simplify the discussion and get to the heart of the matter, we will stick to the Left side of the chalkboard. As the typical American would understand it, the communist at the far Left would favor complete

★ ★ ★

Let Them Speak for Themselves

I strongly recommend this exercise to readers: ask a self-identified "socialist" what the federal income-tax rate on the wealthiest Americans should be. I have never heard from a socialist (or from many liberals or "progressives") a tax rate below 40 percent. Most socialists have told me that their best-case scenario would be an upper-income rate in the 50–70 percent range, and some have told me far higher still.

government ownership of the entire means of production, with little to no private ownership. Individuals would not own factories or farms. In some especially hideous cases, including Kim's North Korea and Pol Pot's regime in Cambodia and Mao's Great Leap Forward and Castro's Cuba and still others, they might not be permitted to own their own homes, garden plots, pots, woks, pans, and candy.

Under "socialism," on the other hand—at least the modern version that most American and European socialists espouse—the government would have a large degree of ownership (or at least management so heavy-handed as to be virtually indistinguishable from ownership) of the means of production, and generally of certain forms of property throughout the society.

So not every avowed socialist is a communist. While socialists' schemes for redistribution and central management of the economy are doomed to failure, we should afford them the benefit of the doubt until they give us cause to believe that they're the kind of "socialists" (like Lenin and Stalin) who are willing to pursue that unworkable utopian vision by means of violent revolution, wide-scale starvation, and horrific human rights violations. Unfortunately, there are plenty of "socialists" who do look to the worst communist villains for inspiration.

In 2016, for example, the New York City district branch of the International Socialist Organization pointed to Lenin as its guiding star: "We stand in the tradition of one of the pre-eminent political strategists in world history. Lenin contributed enormously to our understanding of how we can best organize ourselves to both build working class movements, and at the same time a socialist cadre capable of helping to lead in struggle. Many of these ideas helped shape the Bolshevik party, the only group in the history of the world to lead a successful revolution from below."[6]

To lead from *below*? Sounds like an accurate characterization.

The Difficulties of Definition

As I write this book, *People's World*, the flagship publication of the American Communist Party, is conducting a regular "*People's World* series on socialism." I will share just a sampling of what they have published on that topic.

An April 6, 2016, piece on "21st Century Socialism" was written by former '60s radical Carl Davidson, onetime national secretary for Students for a Democratic Society (SDS) during its peak. Davidson became a member of the Weathermen with Bill Ayers, Bernardine Dohrn, Mark Rudd, Michael Klonsky, and crew, and by 2008 was an organizer for the newest radical collective: Progressives for Obama.[7]

In his *People's World* piece, Davidson recalls that when he was a philosophy major in the '60s, a professor offered his class a challenging exercise: students were to successfully define a concept before using it in a paper or a debate. The professor gave as an example "a good Christian" and pushed the class to come up with a common "objective" definition. The class failed, and the professor's point was made. This was a concept whose essence was "essentially contested," notes Davidson—and "so it is with socialism" as well.

Davidson observes that when his "revolutionary group in the 1970s" (presumably the Weathermen) was writing a "new program for a new

★ ★ ★

Accept No Substitutes

"Electricity will take the place of God," said Lenin in 1918.[8]

communist party," Davidson, whom the group considered well-read, was assigned the task of ferreting out a "true definition of socialism." After months, says Davidson, he finally gave up. He realized right away that even the "heroic figures" of "socialism" had said different things at different times. So, he personally simply picked the one he liked the best, which was a Lenin line describing socialism as "Soviet power plus electrification."

Davidson notes that by the late 1980s nearly every socialist recognized that there was a crisis in socialism, especially when the Soviet communist bloc collapsed (note that here Davidson used socialism and communism synonymously). Socialism, he says, was entering a new period of being "essentially contested...in a very big way for several decades to come," with every old model breaking up and every old dogma and "tried-and-tested truth" up in the air.

Davidson points to a new kind of modern socialist: Hugo Chávez of Venezuela, whom Davidson flagged as one of the first to break out of the old kind of socialism in crisis, and who first popularized the term "21st century socialism." Chávez, explains Davidson, stressed different things at different times, but his core idea was to bring "participatory democracy into socialism in dozens of new ways." Davidson and other old stalwarts from the '60s New Left immediately grasped the "importance" of what Chávez was touting and "held out high hopes" for it. (More on Chávez later.)

Another contributor to the *People's World* series, Geoffrey Jacques, in a piece titled, "What We Talk about When We Talk about Socialism," also concedes that a "satisfactory answer" to the question "What is socialism?" is much harder than people think. The socialist movement, he explains, has always "toggled between the burden of Utopia and the urgency of the fight for justice." And, too, definitions of Utopia and justice have varied among socialists—since the earliest days of the movement, when Marx and Engels wrenched the "socialist" label from the "ancient network of counterculture communities and coops they called 'Utopian' and then pinned the adjective 'scientific' to their own project."

As Jacques notes, other than phrases like "to raise the proletariat to the position of ruling class, to win the battle of democracy" in *The Communist Manifesto*, there is "very little" from Marx and his early followers about how the socialist dream would be realized. The "new society," avers Jacques, did not seem to look much different to Marx than it had to the traditional Utopians, with the only real distinction being the constant "squabbles" among socialists over the means to achieve the goal. He notes that for Marx and Engels, socialism would come when "all production has been concentrated in the hands of a vast association of the whole nation." This would constitute "an association in which the free development of each is the condition for the free development of all."[9]

Good luck with that one, guys.

Also taking a stab at defining socialism in the *People's World*'s series is Rick Nagin. In his April 20, 2016, piece, "What Does Socialism Mean? It Means Working Class Power," he observes,

> In everyday political discussions, "socialism" is used to describe policies in capitalist countries such as those in Scandinavia, where the means of production remain primarily owned by private individuals, but, through heavy taxation on excessive wealth and income, important social benefits like health care, education, and quality government services are provided to people....
>
> The essence of socialism is the replacement of the capitalist class and private corporate power by the working class and allied forces (family farmers, small businesspeople, self-employed

> professionals, etc.) as the dominant influence in society. When this coalition is the new ruling class, it can then begin to reorganize the economy. Such a reorganization would include social ownership of key industries such as finance, energy, and armaments....
>
> Socialism would still be a class society. But it would be one in which working class and trade union values become dominant—values like solidarity, equality, democracy, and peace.

But Nagin's "socialism" shades over into something uglier and more familiar. According to him, "the establishment and maintenance of socialism" and the building of "a new socialist society" would directly involve "Communist Parties" and "coalitions of Communists and other progressive forces and parties." And private property will be the target. Nagin provides a historical perspective (notice how he conflates socialism with communism, just as Lenin did):

> The first effort to do away with millennia of private property ownership and class power, in the Soviet Union, faced ferocious hostility in an international environment still dominated by private capital. Socialism's ability to flourish was, to say the least, greatly limited. The most serious challenge came with the rise of fascism and the Second World War unleashed by Nazi Germany and its anti-communist allies. Their goal was nothing less than the destruction of socialism in Russia and democracy everywhere else. Withstanding unprecedented devastation and loss of life, Soviet socialism overcame the Nazi onslaught, though, and an entire group of socialist-oriented states arose in Eastern Europe, North Korea, and China.

> With the support of the socialist countries and peace forces in the capitalist world, Vietnam established a unified country with a socialist government defeating the U.S. in a war that took over three million lives. Similar support allowed socialism to arise and survive in Cuba—despite invasion, repeated attempts to assassinate government officials, and economic sabotage conducted by the United States.
>
> Soviet socialism continued for decades under the conditions of the Cold War, but it was eventually destroyed because of both external pressure as well as internal corruption and mis-leadership.

Soviet socialism. Eastern European socialism. North Korean socialism. Chinese socialism. Vietnamese socialism. Cuban socialism. All failures of socialism, one might add. And all countries that we usually call communist (in fact, communist dictatorships) rather than socialist.

The Latest Model

Where do "socialists" go from here? "At present," insists Nagin, the "class struggle in the United States" must combat "right-wing extremism," but it must also seek the "full socialization of the economy, universal abundance, and the emergence of a classless, modern, democratic, and green communist society." American socialists "must establish a system where the socially-produced wealth is socially distributed. This requires progressive taxation of capitalist wealth and socialization of privately-owned means of production." And all of this can fully happen, he says, only if "the working people take over the apparatus of government."

The latest example of this name game is the "21st century socialism" that Hugo Chávez imposed on Venezuela. The Wikipedia entry for "21st century socialism" (it is instructive that there is an entry) is fairly accurate:

> **Socialism of the 21st century** (Spanish: *Socialismo del siglo XXI*) is a political term used to describe the interpretation of socialist principles advocated first by Heinz Dieterich in 1996 and later by Latin American leaders like Hugo Chávez of Venezuela, Rafael Correa of Ecuador, Evo Morales of Bolivia, and Luiz Inácio Lula da Silva of Brazil. Socialism of the 21st century argues that both free-market industrial capitalism and twentieth-century socialism have failed to solve urgent problems of humanity, like poverty, hunger, exploitation, economic oppression, sexism, racism, the destruction of natural resources, and the absence of a truly participative democracy. Therefore, because of the local unique historical conditions, socialism of the 21st century is often contrasted with previous applications of socialism in other countries and aims for a more decentralized and participatory planning process. Socialism of the 21st century has democratic socialist elements, but primarily resembles Marxist revisionism.[10]

Note the usual leftist litany of grievances—poverty, hunger, exploitation, economic oppression, sexism, racism, the destruction of natural resources—and the assumption that some enchanting left-wing genie can be summoned out of the collectivist bottle to zap them all with a magic wand. The "money line" (if communists will pardon that expression) in the Wikipedia definition is the final sentence: "Socialism of the 21st century has democratic socialist elements, but primarily resembles Marxist revisionism."

Bingo. It always does, and it always will, because there is never much difference between the hopes and dreams of the merry redistributionists who are kicking the ball around the leftist playing field today and those of the communists of the past. Whether they call it Marxism or democratic socialism, the goal is always the same—to miraculously solve every ill that human flesh is heir to with forced redistribution and collectivization.

Wikipedia continues, "Critics claim that democratic socialism in Latin America acts as a façade for authoritarianism. The charisma of figures like Hugo Chávez and mottoes like 'Country, Socialism, or Death!' have drawn comparisons to the Latin American dictators and *caudillos* of the past."

Put Marx in Your Head, Young Man

Hugo Rafael Chávez was born July 28, 1954. Not unlike Barack Obama, another leader of the Americas that he would come to admire, Chávez in his teen years came under the influence of a Marxist mentor: José Esteban Ruiz Guevara. Guevara was a leftist historian who introduced Hugo to everything from Jean Jacques Rousseau's dastardly *The Social Contract* to Karl Marx. "Put Marxism in your head, I told them," Ruiz recounted of Chávez and his other wide-eyed pupils.[11]

Hugo would do just that. He filled his mind with Marxist muck. The Dead White European Male (or "DWEM," as well-trained university leftists call European guys they *don't* like) would fuel Hugo's path all the way to the presidential palace in Caracas.

As with Fidel Castro in Cuba, Hugo's rise to power happened quickly. He was only forty-three years old when he was elected by Venezuelans eager to get their hands on the free stuff that Chávez and his cohorts were promising to ladle to the mouth-open masses from the giant collective soup kitchen that many hoped their state would become.

In 1998 Venezuela was no banana republic. But never underestimate the demand for free bananas if the people think the government will dole them out.

Chávez formed the United Socialist Party of Venezuela. He was elected three times (more or less)—often in disputed elections, and survived challenges and referenda. He secured for himself four terms in office (the last one very brief), with a "presidency" that ultimately ran from 1999 to 2013, when he left office the only way that communists ever leave office: death.

The prize before the Venezuelan redistributionist's hungry eyes was the vast reservoir of oil revenues bubbling up from the soil of his petroleum-rich nation. Chávez salivated over this black gold, tasting the possibilities to "spread the wealth" (as Barack Obama would put it) that it offered. But even all that oil would not be enough. There never is enough. Communism is capable of seizing and squandering infinite resources.

Chávez's government immediately began nationalizing key industries, creating what it gently called "Communal Councils," and inventing what it dubbed "Bolivarian Missions" to deliver "free" healthcare, expand education, and subsidize housing and food. Hallelujah! And of course Chávez promised the leftist panacea—"land reform." Those sacred buzzwords justify milking and bilking and stealing the private property of others to redistribute it on behalf of "social justice" for the poor. Who, under communism, always inevitably get ever poorer.

But of course, as always, liberals, progressives, and *New York Times* reporters never saw it coming. Just like Castro before him, and Mao before *him*, Chávez wasn't really a communist, we were told—at least not the nasty kind like Lenin and Stalin. This time, we were assured, the "reform" would work out great for the people. This time, socialism would save the poor, not starve them to death. This time, the revolution would be a boon to the whole world. The *Times* described Chávez's regime as a "populist" government and reported how he was using Venezuela's oil (which is always a bad thing) to help the poor (which is always a good thing) even in New York City—with the willing cooperation of Democrat Congressman José Serrano.[12]

It Happens Every Time

Chávez lifted his program straight from the communist recipe book. He nationalized Venezuela's oil industry—and ran it into the ground. Then he proceeded to destroy his country's domestic economy. Socialist regimes always annihilate markets and market prices, the fundamental institutions of an exchange economy, replacing them with artificially imposed prices controlled and dictated by government fiat. Chávez's Venezuela was a classic case: the benevolent "socialists" imposed prices below the natural market price in order to "help" the poor. (Lesson number one: when a socialist offers to "help," grab your wallet, hold onto your pants, and run for the hills.) The price controls started with "essentials" such as powdered milk, beans, sugar, coffee, and cooking oil. Then, in November 2011, Chávez announced that he was establishing price controls on no less than fifteen *thousand* additional goods.[13]

Was this really "21st century socialism?" It seemed remarkably like twentieth-century communism. The masses went running to the rapidly emptying shelves in stores to buy and hoard what they could before the central planners' "help" made them even more helpless. Hardest hit were the hygiene products, from deodorant to toothpaste to toilet paper, which always disappear first under communism. The scarcity of toilet paper was the sources of endless jokes in the Soviet Union, and it was hygiene products that vanished first in Cambodia and in Cuba. Venezuela would be no exception.

"I'm buying everything that's on the price control list that's going to be regulated," said retired schoolteacher Elena Ramirez, fifty-six, one of the millions of ordinary Venezuelans for whom Chávez and gang claimed to be the champions. Ramirez dashed to the Dulcinea supermarket in Caracas and nabbed twelve packages of toilet paper, each with four rolls. "Everyone is in the same game," she explained. "It's madness."[14]

Of course it's madness. It is always madness when "socialists" take charge. And when the inevitable failures, scarcities, and other disasters set in, the "socialists" blame everything and everyone but themselves and their ideology. So Chávez and his cronies naturally blamed the "hoarders," the evil companies, the nefarious private sector, and the rapacious market forces of supply and demand for the disaster they had imposed on the hapless and increasingly hungry Venezuelan population.

★ ★ ★

Soviet-Era Humor

"At the May Day parade in Moscow there was the usual long parade of missiles, tanks, armored cars, personnel carriers, and the like, and then right at the end an open truck with three middle-aged men in baggy suits.

"One day the senior Communists on the podium turned to the minister of defense and asked, 'Who on earth are they?'

"'Ah,' said the minister, 'they are economists from the central-planning bureau. You've no idea how much destructive capacity they possess.'"[15]

Speaking on state television, Chávez proclaimed that he detected "capitalists" hoarding vast supplies of powdered milk, coffee, and cooking oil. He threatened to nationalize the unidentified faceless, evil companies and factories caught "stockpiling goods." He threatened, "I'm at the front of this operation, and we're going to occupy factories and companies.... We're going to nationalize what needs to be nationalized. The bourgeoisie hoard milk, sugar and cooking oil and then blame me. But it's their fault, the hoarders."[16]

Damn those bourgeoisie! Hoarders of milk!

In the Ukraine, they hoarded wheat. In Cambodia, rice. In Cuba, sugar. In Ethiopia, coffee. Kill the kulaks!

The only solution, insisted Venezuela's intrepid state planners, was more state coercion—more nationalization and still more price controls. The last thing needed was more market freedom. That was verboten. "The law of supply and demand is a lie," explained Karlin Granadillo, the head of a price control agency set up to enforce the vast new ocean of regulations, speaking on state-controlled television. "These are not arbitrary measures. They are necessary."[17]

¡Viva la revolución!

All the Right Friends

Chávez had proclaimed himself an anti-imperialist, and thus anti-American.

He was an especially anti-*Bush* anti-American. In 2006, Chávez denounced President George W. Bush before the United Nations as "the devil," saying, "the devil came here yesterday, and it smells of sulfur still today. . . ." He was also no fan of Bush ally, Tony Blair, Britain's prime minister, who Chávez (sounding a lot like his buddy Fidel Castro) derided as "an imperialist pawn who attempts to curry favor" with America. And he was no cheerleader for Israel, either, accusing the Jewish nation of a "new Holocaust" against Palestinians.[18] Chávez also regularly eviscerated the Roman Catholic Church, once dubbing its hierarchy "devils in vestments." Like a long line of previous comrades, he blasted the Church.[19]

Chávez regularly called his enemies "degenerates," "squealing pigs," and "counter-revolutionaries." He was a superb demagogue, excellent at agitprop. He could sling it as well as anyone in Latin America.[20]

Did Chávez like anyone? Oh, yes. He had become instant pals with the Castro cabal in Cuba and other socialist-Marxist revolutionary leaders littering, loitering, and looting Latin America, such as Daniel Ortega in Nicaragua. He loved Marxists dictators.

And he also adored Barack Obama. He made that clear the first year of Obama's presidency. In an extraordinary statement at the United Nations that September, Chávez sniffed, "It doesn't smell of sulfur here anymore"—a swipe at former President George W. Bush. Waxing almost spiritual, Chávez mused at the new freshness in the air wafting northward from 1600 Pennsylvania Avenue: "It smells of something else. It smells of *hope*."

"Hope and Change," of course, was the Obama campaign slogan.

Chávez was so attracted to Barack Obama that he immediately sought him out to give him some reading material. At the Summit of the Americas in April 2009, just weeks after Obama was inaugurated, Chávez strolled up to Obama, gave him a gentle tap on the shoulder and a loving handshake, and handed him a paperback copy of Eduardo Galeano's scurrilous 1973 work, *Open Veins of Latin America: Five Centuries of the Pillage of a*

★ ★ ★

A Shared Vocabulary

Chávez would have appreciated *Dreams from My Father*, Barack Obama's bestselling memoir. Words such as "colonial," "colonialism," "neocolonialism" and "imperialism" recur incessantly, and phrases in the book (sometimes from people Obama quotes) include "colonial administration," "colonial West," "white colonials," "serving the interests of neo-colonialism." There is even a line about Christian missionaries bringing not religion but colonialism. At Occidental College, Obama recalls "At night, in the dorms, we discussed neocolonialism, Franz [sic] Fanon, Eurocentrism."[22]

Continent, a fatuous tome that blames the industrialized countries of the West for every conceivable ill in Latin America for the last half millennium, from sour tequila and bitter mangoes to lousy beer and voodoo dolls. An appreciative Obama smiled and accepted the tract, later telling reporters, "I thought it was one of Chávez's books. I was going to give him one of mine."[21] Was there much of a difference?

After the Venezuelan president gave the new American president a copy of *Open Veins of Latin America*, Galeano acquired an instant international readership. The aging Latin American leftist's thirty-six-year-old diatribe became a sudden overnight bestseller. As news footage of their encounter was shown worldwide, the book skyrocketed in sales, soaring from number 54,295 on Amazon to sixth place within twenty-four hours. The capitalist-hating Galeano made a bunch of bucks as the anticapitalist Left went wild buying his anti-capitalist rant with their computers, phones, and credit cards. Liberals, progressives, socialists, and communists across the planet grabbed their plastic and silicone to order up the screed Chávez had recommended to the new American president of hope and change.

"I Am a Trotskyist"

Chávez sometimes described himself as communist, and other times not—always toying with reporters over the question. But he openly identified with hardcore communists on many occasions. Visiting Cuba in 1999, on the fortieth anniversary of Fidel's tyranny, Chávez explained that "Venezuela is travelling toward the same sea as the Cuban people—a sea of happiness, real social justice and peace."[23]

And what about the other sea, not so happy—the literal ocean between Cuba and Florida, to which a hundred thousand Cubans had taken in a desperate attempt to escape the communist hellhole Chávez was celebrating?

In China in 2008, Chávez told reporters how much he admired Mao Zedong, a mass murderer on a scale that Fidel could never match, who killed more than six times as many people as the entire population of Cuba.

Chávez professed to aim for a more *Jesus-like* communism. In a 2009 speech to his country's national assembly, he stated, "I am a Marxist to the same degree as the followers of the ideas of Jesus Christ and the liberator of America, Simon Bolivar." The next year, in 2010, he described himself as a Marxist more in the mold of Leon Trotsky than Jesus Christ. He related a conversation with his labor minister: "When I called him, he said to me: 'President, I want to tell you something before someone else tells you...I am a Trotskyist,' and I said, 'well, what is the problem? I am also a Trotskyist! I follow Trotsky's line, that of permanent revolution."[24]

"Oligarchs tremble," Chávez warned in Lenin-like language in 2000, "because now is when the revolution is going forward." He had just redrawn the constitution, and his econ 101 flunkies had seized the legislature. "This is going to be delicious," he promised. "We're going to deliver a knockout punch to the counterrevolution."[25]

The Knockout Punch

Chávez delivered a knockout punch, all right—but not to "the counterrevolution." His fatal blow went right into the gut of the Venezuelan

★ ★ ★

The Same Old Story

"Why and how does this happen in Venezuela or in any other country that embraces the false, deceitful, utopian promises of socialist politicians? The policies that socialist leaders invariably embrace turn their socialist dreams into nightmares."[26] —**Professor John Sparks,** Grove City College

economy. As always with communism, the result was predictable: economic ruin.

The price control regime of the "21st century socialist" regime created queues, inflation, stagnation, and unemployment, and did everything but make prices more "affordable" for the working man. Shortages inevitably resulted, as they always do, from the artificially low state-mandated prices imposed by economic ignoramuses elected by a duped citizenry hoodwinked into thinking that "socialism" would shower them with an invigorating cascade of "free" stuff.

Fifteen years under socialist Hugo Chávez, followed by three years under his socialist successor, Nicolás Maduro, "left the economy in shambles and the living standards of Venezuelans falling to a level that can only be described as intolerable," assessed Professor John Sparks of Grove City College in July 2016, a flashpoint when Venezuelan dominated international news headlines. The needy masses that the nation's benevolent socialists had promised to help were suddenly suffering what the Venezuelan government euphemistically called a "nutritional emergency."

Sparks shared the story of what had happened to Venezuela's coffee-roasting companies, which was a typical scenario: First, some coffee producers held back on production in the hope that the government would agree to price increases that covered their costs. In response, the government resorted to what communist governments always resort to: force. Chávez ordered the country's National Guard to "find every last kilogram of coffee" that was being "hoarded."

And in 2009 the Venezuelan government seized the country's two largest coffee-processing plants, accusing the companies of the sin of "hoarding" and "smuggling" coffee.

It was the typical communist pattern. And not only was it a clear violation of market freedom, but, predictably, a guarantor of market failure. "They [the government] expropriates the sugar companies, and you cannot find sugar," stated one Venezuelan market analyst. "They expropriate the coffee companies... and you cannot find coffee. They expropriate Owen-Illinois, and we cannot find packages."

★ ★ ★

You Don't Know Whether to Laugh or Cry

"Communism works only in Heaven where they don't need it, and in Hell, where they've already got it." —joke told by **Ronald Reagan** in his remarks to the National Federation of Independent Business, June 22, 1983[27]

While producers were harassed and victimized, noted John Sparks, so were Venezuelan consumers, who faced shortage after shortage, lining up in Caracas in the middle of the night waiting for state-run "grocery stores" to open in hopes of getting something, anything, before supplies ran out. It was a scene repeated from every Communist Bloc country in Eastern Europe throughout the Cold War, replete with citizens presenting their handy new "registration cards" to ensure they were not exceeding their blessed "fair share." National guardsmen were on hand to enforce the strict rationing laws of the socialist state.

Sparks observed how the empty shelves in Venezuela were eerily reminiscent of the empty shelves in Robert Mugabe's claimed socialist paradise, Zimbabwe.[28] *The Economist* provided side-by-side photos of grocery stores in the two countries illustrating the point.[29]

And why not? After all, Chávez's wondrous "21st century socialism" is not much different from Mugabe's turn-of-the-century socialism. It is the same old, same old.

The Mugabe model is a good comparison, especially given the hyperinflationary trajectory of the Venezuelan economy under its snappy "21st century socialism." Here again, Professor Sparks:

> What is it like for Venezuelans seeking to purchase essentials such as food, medicine, and the like? In 2015 it was bad. If a half-kilo of rice cost 10 BsF (Bolivars) at the beginning of the year, by year end—due to inflation—the price had risen to 28.60 BsF or an increase of 186 percent. However, that understates the inflation because 186 percent inflation is the "official" governmental rate. In actuality, the price would probably have risen more like 400 percent in a single year. The International Monetary Fund is predicting price inflation for 2016 of an astounding 720 percent....
>
> In a single month (February 2016) the Bolivar declined in value at the rate of 16.9 percent. Consequently, Venezuelans who must use or hold Bolivars for day to day transactions suffer a cruel inflation "tax." Worse yet, citizens who have savings in the form of Bolivars have the value that was once there effectively confiscated by the inflationary policies. Furthermore, the unpredictability of the value of Bolivars leads to bartering, that is, avoiding the use of a medium of exchange by trading one good or service for another.[30]

Much of this, Sparks noted, was the result of the unstable monetary policy pursued by the "socialist" economic illiterates running the Venezuelan economy. The artificial depreciation of the currency falsified the necessary market signals needed to minimized costs and prices, leading to runaway inflation that is disastrous for consumers, producers, workers, and the nation as a whole. But the catastrophe did not stop there. For example, foreign suppliers of goods, such as foreign pharmaceutical firms, were understandably refusing to sell much-needed medical supplies and equipment into Venezuela unless they were paid with the dollar. "They want no part of the risk they would have to take if they accepted the declining Bolivars as payment for goods," wrote Sparks. "Since most medical goods are imported, this effectively makes it nearly impossible for hospitals to provide basic care." He asked, "Has Venezuela entered into the final phase of monetary destruction, namely: hyper-inflation?"[31]

Very possibly. Venezuela is chasing the other twenty-first-century collectivist trendsetter, Zimbabwe, which since 1987 has been suffering in the grip of dictator Robert Mugabe. Chronicling its list of failures would require a chapter unto itself. In 2007, Zimbabwe became the first country of the twenty-first century to experience hyperinflation, achieving an astonishing inflation rate of 66,212 percent that year. Incredibly, that was just the starting point of an unprecedented trajectory. Believe it or not, by May 2008, the inflation rate had soared to 2.2 million percent. And the insanity had just begun.

In Zimbabwe today, a billion-dollar bill is not worth squat. The best thing you can do with it is blow your nose—or perhaps use it for toilet paper. (Yes, better choice, as socialists and communists always run out of toilet paper.)

"As of 14 November 2008, Zimbabwe's annual inflation rate was 89.7 Sextillion (10^{21}) percent," says Professor Steve Hanke of Johns Hopkins University.[32] Yes, that's right, quantifying the ruin that socialism has brought to Zimbabwe requires using not millions, or billions, or even trillions, but sextillions.

Venezuela is barreling toward the same disaster. In 2016 even the left-wing Amnesty International had no choice but to condemn the government's policy of "forced labor"—a decree attempting to ameliorate the food crisis by declaring that any Venezuelan employee could be drafted into farm work.[33] As for the masses, they are responding the way they always do to communism (or is it socialism?). They are voting with their feet. They are fleeing the country, until and unless their benevolent caretakers harness them with walls or with rifles.

★ ★ ★

A Total Rip-Off

In the summer of 2016, a literal "100 trillion dollars" banknote from the Reserve Bank of Zimbabwe could be purchased (basically as a novelty or gag gift) at Banknoteworld.com for $79.99.[34] When I informed a colleague of mine, a professor of economics, of this price, he told me that $79.99 was a "rip-off": "I have two $100 trillion Zimbabwe notes, and know I didn't pay over ten bucks for them. Even that represented a 99.9999% profit to the person who probably brought a suitcase full of them here from Zimbabwe. At $79.99, they're a total rip-off."[35]

Remind me again, what's the difference between "21st century socialism" and communism?

And yet, if you ask the left-wing intelligentsia, the problem in Venezuela is anything but socialism. One professor of Latin American studies, writing in the longtime pro-communist *The Nation*, claims that "Venezuela is suffering not from too much socialism, but from too little." The "Socialist Red Herring," says the good professor, is a "mythological entity." The problem has not been government intervention, you see, but the need for *better* government intervention by the central planners. "Venezuela's current woes," says the professor, "are due less to excessive social spending and stifling regulations than to the haphazard implementation of government policies in general, and the inflexible implementation of specific policies."[36] As always, socialism just needs one more chance.

Communism Kills

The chief product of socialism is death.

It has killed millions of innocent people. But it has also killed a lot of communists—including Hugo Chávez. The Venezuelan dictator's golden road to a new "21st century socialism" ended in his own death. He died on March 5, 2013, sixty years to the day after Joe Stalin died—prematurely, of cancer.

You have to give Chávez credit to his fidelity to the socialism cause. Chávez, in his late fifties and desperately ill, opted to go to Fidel's Cuba for cancer treatment. It was a surefire death sentence. Only the most devoted communist would be so naïve as to risk going to Cuba for the fabulous free healthcare that liberals in America rave about but never, ever resort to when they are seriously sick. But Chávez was a true believer. He was weighed down with vast wealth that he had confiscated from his people, but he effectively chose acupuncture over the vastly superior healthcare widely available anywhere in the capitalist West.

The Venezuelan dictator clung to his secular god. Hugo Chávez was faithful to the end. He went to Havana. Did he really think he would be healed there? He should have learned from the fate of hundreds of millions over the last century: communism kills.

Chávez's demise was marked by gushing praise from admiring "progressives" in America and throughout the world.[37] The breathless encomiums by liberals, progressives, socialists, communists, democratic socialists, and assorted fellow travelers were appalling, but hardly surprising. And then Chávez's disciples sought to enshrine his remains for veneration—literally.

Sadly, even this should not have come as a surprise. The far Left has never been shy about upholding its heroes as worthy of veneration and in some cases even worship—ironically, given that the subjects of veneration have been not just atheists but militant atheists. Vladimir Lenin's remains are still on display in Red Square.

Upon his death in January 1924, Lenin's body was embalmed and preserved in a tomb, actually a shrine at which the faithful could forever honor the Great One. Etched in the marble holding the Bolshevik godfather's body is this inscription: "Lenin: The Savior of the World." Following Lenin's

★ ★ ★

Atheist Religion

"Everywhere you went, there were statues everywhere of Lenin. They wanted you to worship Lenin." —**Olena Doviskaya,** a Ukrainian citizen, in conversation with me

death, poems and songs were written in praise of the "eternal" Lenin who "is always with us." The Soviet press reported that Yuri Gagarin, the first Soviet cosmonaut, visited Lenin's mausoleum immediately before his flight so he could meditate over Lenin's yellowing flesh and draw strength for his mission. Later, Gagarin returned to the sacred site to *report* to Lenin on his mission. "Lenin Corners," modeled on the Icon Corners of the Russian Orthodox Church, were established throughout the USSR. These mini-shrines included icon-like paintings of Lenin along with his words and writings.

This seems odd for an atheist state angrily committed to a war on religion. But it is precisely what we have come to expect from communist regimes.

"Leninization" made the Soviet state's spiritual life as pagan as it was atheistic. A "secular religion" was established, one that, as Lenin biographer Dmitri Volkogonov has noted, demanded "unquestioning obedience" from its disciples. So certain was the Party of Lenin's infallibility that in 1925, one year after his death, the Politburo established a special laboratory to remove, dissect, and study Lenin's inactive, smelly brain. The purpose, said Volkogonov, was to show the world that the great man's ideas had been hatched from an almost supernatural mind.

Lenin came from a Russian Orthodox country. Hugo Chávez hailed from a Roman Catholic country. In both the Roman Catholic and Russian Orthodox traditions, prospective saints—people who lived genuinely and heroically holy lives—have been placed in special tombs for purposes of veneration and to see if their dead bodies are incorruptible. These churches have taught that the bodies of some saints are uncorrupted, divinely protected on earth even in death.

And so the rush to enshrine Hugo Chávez's body should not have been surprising. He could become a sacred symbol of collectivism, wealth redistribution, and nationalization—a new little holy trinity, embodied in the sacrificial flesh of Saint Hugo. The canonization process seemed to be quickly underway, with little Hugo on the fast track to secular sainthood.

But alas, within only a week of Chávez's death, it was determined that his corpse could not be preserved. The man's new-fangled socialism for a new century could not even produce toilet paper and deodorant. How would it pull off the proper preservation of a dead body?

Fittingly, Russian embalmers, with unique expertise after over ninety years propping up the constantly molting corpse of Vladimir Lenin, were consulted. They told Chávez's "21st century socialists" to toss in the flag. The body had putrefied.[38]

The rot was an enduring symbol of what Hugo Chávez left behind in Venezuela. Like the Venezuelan economy under his "21st century socialism," decomposition set in immediately. Today, his body, his nation, and his ideology share the same destiny of decay.

CHAPTER 11

Why Doesn't Everybody Know Communism's Appalling Track Record?

If much of what you have read in the early chapters of this book is new to you, then you're not alone. If you didn't learn any of this history—the horrors inflicted on hundreds of millions of people by communism—in your school or university, join the club. Communism (also known as "socialism") has failed spectacularly everywhere it has been tried. But the true believers of the Left have been very successful elsewhere. They have effectively commandeered the education system in capitalist countries for their cause. No wonder their own crimes are not on the syllabus.

And not only have the leftists in control of American schools and universities succeeded in keeping young Americans in ignorance of communism's perfect record of failure and its appalling death toll. They are actually turning young Americans toward socialism.

Did you know?

- ★ More Millennials approve of socialism than of capitalism
- ★ Marx wanted to abolish private education and homeschooling
- ★ The most respected founding figure in the history of American public education inspired the Bolsheviks' education "reform"—and praised it

Feeling the Bern

A turning point of sorts came in 2011, when a major study by the Pew Research Center found that 49 percent of Americans aged eighteen to twenty-nine have a positive view of socialism, exceeding those who have a positive

★ ★ ★

Voting Out of Ignorance

Part of the reason for Millennials' favorable view of socialism is that they have no clue what it means. The Reason-Rupe survey found that Millennials who viewed socialism favorably tended to describe the ideology as one of "people being kind" or "being together." They viewed socialism as a generous "social safety net" where a grand, benevolent government "pays for our own needs."[2] Of course, the exact opposite has always been the painful reality.

view of capitalism. Pew had done the same poll in years before. The previous polls showed socialism catching up to capitalism in popularity, but in 2011 socialism finally eclipsed capitalism in America[1]—the world's leading bastion of capitalism and history's greatest example of capitalism's success and promise.

In 2014, a Reason-Rupe survey found that 53 percent of eighteen- to twenty-nine-year-olds viewed socialism favorably, and Gallup found that 69 percent of Millennials said they would be willing to vote for a socialist candidate for president.[3] Millions of them did just that, in the person of Bernie Sanders.

Ex-communist Ron Radosh, in an important piece for the *Weekly Standard* titled, "Rehab for Reds," observes that for a new generation of college-aged students, for whom the Cold War is a distant phenomenon, democratic socialism has been legitimized in the form of lovable, huggable socialist Bernie Sanders. "It is just one short step for this same generation to argue that if socialism is a goal worth fighting for, then perhaps communism too was a worthy endeavor. The millions murdered by Stalin, Mao, Fidel Castro, and the other Communist leaders may simply be something they are not aware of. I would suspect that perhaps only 1 percent of Bernie's supporters have even heard of, let alone read, *The Black Book of Communism.*"[4]

He points to a recent piece in the *New Republic*, which in the 1990s was an anti-communist publication on the liberal Left. The article, titled "Who's Afraid of Communism?," was written by an editor of the journal *The New Inquiry*, Malcolm Harris. Radosh lamented the author's effort to rehabilitate not just Soviet communism but American communism. Harris's revisionist

★ ★ ★

The Socialist Candidate

Running for president on the Democratic Party ticket in 2016, lifetime avowed socialist Bernie Sanders nabbed the votes of over thirteen million Americans.

After growing up in Brooklyn, Bernie spread his socialist wings, first landing at what Ron Radosh has described as a "Stalinist Kibbutz" in Israel in 1963—the Hashomer Hatzair kibbutz, whose members considered themselves "Marxist-Zionists."[5] Daniel Greenfield has reported that Sanders spent "months" on this "Marxist-Stalinist" kibbutz.[6]

After that, Sanders went to the University of Chicago to earn a degree in political science. There he worked with the Young People's Socialist League ("Yipsel"), the youth section of the (Trotskyist) Socialist Workers' Party.

The *Daily Beast* has reported that Sanders also "served as a presidential elector for the Socialist Workers' Party in 1980," something that Sanders acknowledged in a 1988 television appearance. The *Daily Beast* quoted Sanders: "I was asked to put my name on the ballot and I did, that's true."[7]

Bernie married his current wife in 1988, and the two then headed immediately for Mother Russia. They honeymooned in the Soviet Union.

In October 2015, MSNBC reporter Thomas Roberts asked Bernie point-blank about that trip: "Did you go on your honeymoon to the Soviet Union?" Sanders replied: "The fact is that I went to establish a sister city program with Yaroslavl, then in the Soviet Union, now an important city in Russia which is still in existence today. The purpose of that trip was a sister city. Did it take place after my marriage? It did."

Sanders dismissed as "silly" and "absurd" the notion that the trip revealed him as "some type of communist sympathizer."

Communist Party USA would beg to differ. Throughout the 2016 presidential campaign, they were "feeling the Bern." The official CPUSA newspaper *People's World* repeatedly carried headlines hailing Bernie Sanders's "revolution." Consider the instructive words of CPUSA head John Bachtell: "The campaign of Sen. Bernie Sanders is making a unique contribution... and has the potential to galvanize long-term transformative change. Seeds of change are being sown and foundations are being laid for deeper-going changes in the future.... The campaign is expanding the collective political imagination and injecting radical ideas into the body politic. It has legitimized democratic socialism in the national conversation."[8]

★ ★ ★

Bolsheviks for Bernie

Radosh's piece quotes my own slightly tongue-in-cheek observation that "the Sanders campaign could mass-produce bumper stickers boldly touting 'Bolsheviks for Bernie' sandwiched between grinning faces of Marx and Lenin, and our contemporary products of the American university would shrug and cheer." Radosh concedes that, sadly, my quip is "not far off the mark."[9]

piece proposed a reexamination of communism, especially the 1930s variety, as practiced from the USSR to Spain to the United States, where, Harris argues, it deserves to be commended for its "struggle against fascism and white supremacy." These supposed wondrous achievements by this global band of Stalinists, Harris bemoans, have slipped all too quickly from "our collective memory."[10]

Harris' piece begins with kudos to Bernie Sanders and his grand ideological resurrection. "Bernie Sanders has proven the word 'socialism' doesn't scare the next generation," heralds Harris, "a lot of us even seem to like the idea." They clearly do.

Just a few days after Radosh's article came out in the *Weekly Standard*, the CPUSA *People's World* published a review of *The High Title of a Communist: Postwar Party Discipline and the Values of the Soviet Regime*, a new book by Edward Cohn. The book focused on the infamous iron discipline applied by the Soviet Communist Party to its members, and the review was by Tony Pecinovsky, a *People's World* bureau chief.[11]

Pecinovsky praises Cohn's book for painting "a vivid picture of a Party-state seriously attempting to live up to its professed values, beliefs and moral code on the one hand, and the actual practices and flaws of its leaders—namely, communist officials—on the other." Cohn discusses the so-called "Moral Code of the Builder of Communism" in the USSR, which was announced at the 22nd Party Congress in October 1961. That charter emphasized the "public duty" of communists, one that "extended far beyond the workplace while helping to forge the New Soviet Person and maintaining the movement's moral principles."[12]

New Man, New Morals

Marxist-Leninist morality was defined by Vladimir Lenin himself, who asserted that "the only morality that we recognize is that which furthers class interests."[13]

One should bristle at the thought of the Soviet system's "moral principles." It didn't have any—at least not as we have long understood them. Communist morality has always been relativistic and self-serving. Traditional moral absolutes are inevitably subordinated to Communist Party needs. The "New Soviet Person" was a new person fashioned upon a new view of the human person, one in absolute opposition to traditional-Biblical absolutes.

But for our purposes the most interesting part of Pecinovsky's review is his commentary on the rising reputation of socialism with American youth:

> It has been roughly 25 years since the collapse of the Soviet Union; in other words, since the first experiment in the construction of socialism on a national level came to a dramatic end. But Americans' curiosity about socialism hasn't waned with the passage of time. Socialism has once again become part of the mainstream political discourse—especially among youth—with the emergence of Bernie Sanders as a serious presidential contender. Additionally, more people are looking anew at the practices, policies, successes and failures of the former Soviet Union.

Notice how fluidly this modern Communist Party member links the "socialism" of the Soviet Union (he does not use the word "communism") with modern American curiosity about "socialism," which has "once again become part of the mainstream political discourse," especially among our youth, with the emergence of Bernie Sanders. More and more people are "looking anew" not at, say, "the practices, policies, successes and failures" of modern Sweden or other Western socialist democracies, but at those of the defunct Soviet Union. Yes, American youth are looking anew at history's leading communist-totalitarian state.

Isn't our education system doing a fantastic job?

Educating for Hate

"Give me four years to teach the children," asserted Lenin, "and the seed I shall have sown will never be uprooted."[14] The education front has always been core to the success of the revolution. Marx and Engels knew this from the outset.

Lenin saw hate as part of the teaching process. "We must hate—hatred is the basis for communism," he told his education commissars. "Children must be taught to hate their parents if they are not communists." If the parents were not on the side of communists and their goals, said Lenin, then the children must be taught to "not respect them."[15]

Does that make you think of our universities today, where far-left professors teach impressionable freshmen that their parents' beliefs on everything from capitalism to marriage and the family to sexual orientation and gender are hateful, and where mobs of students prevent "haters" who would express those ideas from speaking—in the name of "tolerance" and "diversity," no less? Ironically, college students are taught to hate those they frame as the *haters*. In merely four years of an undergraduate education, the leftists who run the universities can undo eighteen years of what a child learned at home.

In the next chapter we will meet Herbert Marcuse, the cultural Marxist and guru who became an ideological mentor to the '60s New Left, who in turn became the tenured radicals in control of our universities today. Marcuse argued for what he called "repressive tolerance," which he claimed was actually "liberating." What he wanted was "intolerance against movements from the Right, and toleration of movements from the Left."[16] And that's exactly what we have on American college campuses today. Those who accept Western civilization's multi-millennia understanding of, say, marriage, family, sexual orientation, and gender—based on countless generations of knowledge of nature, tradition, reason, logic, experience, and natural and Biblical law—are not to be tolerated. These normal people of normal opinions that have prevailed among 99.99-plus percent of people since the dawn of humanity are suddenly political extremists, cultural outliers, "intolerant" "right-wingers." How convenient. "We must hate," said Lenin.

The atheist philosopher and educator Richard Rorty candidly stated that the job of professors like him is "to arrange things so that students who enter as bigoted, homophobic religious fundamentalists will leave college with views more like our own" and "escape the grip of their frightening, vicious, dangerous parents."[17]

Dewey's Children

But the tenured radicals at our universities are not the only problem. The public education system in America has some disturbing ties with communist ideology.

★ ★ ★

He Knew What He Was Doing

Rorty was a red-diaper baby.[18] His parents were not naïve dupes like the parents who hand over their children and life savings to the higher education system controlled by the likes of Rorty. His parents were communists. They raised him to spread their atheist-communist-secular gospel. Rorty would have made an excellent education commissar in Lenin's Kremlin. But he preferred the freedom of an American university, where he could be paid handsomely (with the protection of tenure and his faculty union) to teach his students to despise the ideas of their parents.

Point ten in Marx and Engels's ten-point plan in *The Communist Manifesto* called for "free" education for all children in public schools, which they found vastly preferable to private education, whether religious or at home. Marx and Engels raged against the "exploitation" and "home education" of children by their parents. "Do you charge us with wanting to stop the exploitation of children by their parents?" Marx asked rhetorically. "To this crime we plead guilty. But, you will say, we destroy the most hallowed of relations, when we replace home education by social." He fulminated against "the bourgeois claptrap about the family and education" and sniffed at "the hallowed correlation of parent and child," which he found "disgusting."[19]

But American communists, collectivists, socialists, and "progressives" also wanted to herd the wide-eyed youth into the collective—the mass public education collective. From there, they could be handed up to the likes of Richard Rorty and Herbert Marcuse and their comrades for further and more sophisticated forms of indoctrination.

The godfather of the American public school system was none other than John Dewey, an icon to American progressives and public educators. If we want to understand the collectivization, centralization, and nationalization of American education, we need look no further than John Dewey and his devoted disciples. He is the golden boy, the hero at America's teachers colleges. America's future teachers genuflect before the statue of Dr. Dewey upon entering the gateway of the education departments that serve as the temples for progressive ideology. And not surprisingly, those future teachers are never taught that John Dewey was pro-Soviet, pro-Bolshevik, pro-communist. This beloved founding father of American public education was a "progressive" pioneer who achieved great success advancing Marx and Engels's goal of "free education" for all children in public schools.

The startling truth is that Lenin and the Soviets embraced Dewey's program for their schools long before all of our American progressives did for ours. The Bolsheviks were big fans of the Columbia professor's work, and the Columbia professor was an early fan of them and theirs.

From the beginning, the Bolsheviks had studied and experimented with Dewey's educational ideas, as well as those of other American leftists: Helen Parkhurst, Edward Thorndike, John B. Watson, and Dewey's close Columbia pupils and colleagues William H. Kilpatrick and Thomas Woody. As another colleague, William Brickman, recounted in his gushing introduction to Dewey's *Impressions of Soviet Russia*, published by Columbia's Teachers College in 1964, "The number of translations of Dewey's works was quite impressive during the initial decade [of the Russian Revolution]."[20]

Yes, the Bolsheviks wasted no time getting Professor Dewey's words into Russian. In 1918, only three years after it was published in the United States, Dewey's *Schools of To-morrow* was published in Moscow.[21] Given what else was happening in Russia at the time, this is staggering: The Bolshevik Revolution had begun only months earlier, and the devastating Russian Civil War was in full swing. Millions of people were on the verge of starvation, and death by both war and execution was rife. The Bolsheviks were broke, and struggling to survive.

They did not have the money to be translating American educational books into Russian. They couldn't afford it, but apparently they saw it as worth whatever the cost. The Bolsheviks saw education as foundational to building the communist state. The fact that they managed to allocate resources to Dewey's work at such a perilous moment is a remarkable testimony to how indispensable Lenin, Trotsky, and Stalin considered John Dewey's educational ideas to raising the communist state.

Only a year after *Schools of To-morrow* came a Russian translation of Dewey's *How We Think* (1919) and then, in 1920, Dewey's *The School and Society*.[22] Again, this was at the height of the misery unleashed by the Russian Civil War (1918–1921), which, according to historian W. Bruce Lincoln, snuffed out the lives of *seven million* men, women, and children.

Nonetheless, Dewey's ideas were too crucial to receive short shrift, apparently judged as formidable to the revolution as any weapon in the arsenal of the Red Army.

Several more translations immediately followed, including, in 1921, a sixty-two-page pamphlet excerpted from Dewey's *Democracy and Education* by Professor Stanislav T. Shatskii, a leading Soviet educational "reformer."[23] This classic of American public education was embraced by the Bolsheviks before the Russian Civil War even ended. That fact deserves special attention: *Democracy and Education* remains Dewey's most significant work. It became the bible of Columbia Teachers College, which was the murky guiding light and model for teachers colleges across the country. It still remains the typical choice in schools of education as an introduction to Dewey's thought. The book became the lodestar of numerous educational students, teachers, programs, departments, and colleges. It was the book in which Dewey himself said he attempted to summarize his "entire philosophical position."[24] And yet it was a Bolshevik favorite; it had Lenin's ideological imprimatur.

Dewey's impact on the international communist movement was immediate and pervasive. One witness to his influence on the Comintern world was Anna Louise Strong, one of eight contributing editors to the flagship publication of the communist front group, Friends of the Soviet Union (along with the likes of Lenin chum Maxim Gorky, CPUSA head William Z. Foster, and Upton Sinclair, a prominent progressive hopelessly duped by the American communist movement). Strong made an early 1920s visit to the USSR, where she closely observed Soviet education.[25] She reported that contemporary school reform in Lenin's Russia had been "modeled more on the Dewey ideas of education than on anything else we have in America. Every new book by Dewey is seized and early translated into Russian for consultation. Then they make their own additions."[26]

The Soviets themselves said the same thing, quite candidly. Albert P. Pinkevich, rector of the Second State University of Moscow, stated in a 1929 book that Dewey had a "tremendous influence" on Soviet education. Comparing Dewey's impact to that of leading educators in Germany, where Marxism had equally enthusiastic proponents—German was often the first Western language of translation for Soviet documents[27]—Pinkevich said, "Dewey comes infinitely closer [than even the Germans] to Marx and the Russian communists."[28]

The Soviets were generous in their praise and credit. Stanislav Shatskii happily cited Dewey, telling Thomas Woody that he "drew greatest assistance" from Dewey, and was "deeply impressed by his [Dewey's] 'philosophy of pragmatism.'"[29]

In 1928 Professor A. G. Kalashnikov of the pedagogical department of Moscow Technical University sent Dewey a two-volume set of the most recent *Soviet Pedagogical Encyclopedia*, which owed a great debt to Dewey's work.[30] Kalashnikov included a warm personal note to Dewey, which read, "Your works, especially 'School and Society' and 'The School and the Child,' have very much influenced the development of the Russian pedagogy and in the first years of [the] revolution you were one of the most renowned writers." The "concrete shapes of pedagogical practice" that Dewey had developed, wrote an appreciative Kalashnikov, "will be for a long time the aim of our tendencies."[31]

Was Dewey embarrassed by the Soviet adoption and celebration of his work? Not at all.

When the apparatchiks who had commandeered the Soviet educational bureaucracy, dizzied by Dewey, begged the American education reformer to come pay them a visit, he did precisely that. The Soviets liked Dewey so much and saw him as such a kindred spirit that the Soviets invited Dewey to Moscow for a "tour." And Dewey, for his part, could not resist a pilgrimage to the USSR. Thus, in the summer of 1928, Dewey became a "traveler" to Stalin's Soviet Union as part of an unofficial delegation of twenty-five American educators from various universities.[32]

Dewey's "Impressions"

According to State Department records, Dewey and other fellow "travelers," including Columbia Teachers College colleague J. McKeen Cattell, sailed for Europe on June 23 and left Russia to return home on or around July 20.[33] In the Soviet Union, Dewey and his fellow progressives were paraded from Potemkin village to Potemkin village. The Soviet leadership hoped to sucker them into glowing impressions of Soviet Russia, which they would gleefully report in (misleading) dispatches to Americans back home. And Dewey did not disappoint. He swallowed it hook, line, and sinker, proclaiming the Bolshevik Revolution "a great success."[34]

Dewey filed a six-part series of reports with the *New Republic* from November 14, 1928, through December 19, 1928, and eventually they were compiled into an entire book on his "impressions" of the "revolutionary world."[35] The professor provided lengthy reflections on Soviet education. He saw in Russia nothing short of an "educational transformation," of which he wholeheartedly, enthusiastically approved—in fact, envied. He concluded, "The Russian educational situation is enough to convert one to the idea that only in a society based upon the cooperative principle can the ideals of educational reformers be adequately carried into operation."[36]

John Dewey hailed the collective over the individual. He understood that Russian schools were the "ideological arm of the Revolution," as he rightly put it, and that they indulged in propaganda, but he did not seem to sense the danger. Quite the contrary, given his own views about how public schools must serve primarily to socialize children—in Dewey's writings, no other educational goal is more important—into the society, the group, and the collective, and given that he wanted schools to be devoid of a religious foundation and moral absolutes. No wonder he appeared highly impressed with what he witnessed in Russian education. A wide-eyed Dewey thrilled that "the activities of the schools dovetail in the most extraordinary way, both in administrative organization and in aim and spirit, into all other [Soviet] social agencies and interests."[37] A seamless harmony between Bolshevik public schools and Bolshevik government institutions. How delightful!

Dewey was especially pleased at how "the present government" of Russia—that is, the Soviet dictatorship—seemed so willing to pursue educational reform, experimentation, and "progress"—all glorious buzzwords in American education departments and doctoral programs to this day. Dewey appreciated that Lenin's regime had "cleared the way" of impediments to the pedagogical reform that had been frustrated by the Tsars. Dewey misled his readers into believing that the Tsars had blocked Stanislav Shatskii from instituting reforms as benign as introducing football to young people.

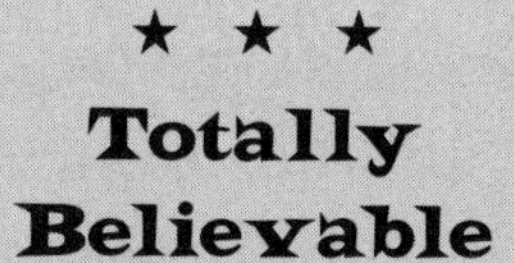

Dewey reported that the Tsarist authorities had concluded that instruction in football was really thinly veiled training for the art of bomb-throwing.[38] Dewey could have only learned this nonsense from his Bolshevik handlers.

The truth of the matter is that Shatskii, a committed communist and rabble-rouser, had been arrested by the Tsarist authorities for "trying to plant socialism in the minds of little children." Comrade Shatskii's crime was not teaching football but teaching totalitarianism—minor detail that Dewey did not share with readers of the *New Republic.*[39]

According to Dewey, all the educational closed-mindedness of the Tsarist era was in the past—dead with the *ancien regime.* Now, Dewey proclaimed, it was a new day for Russia. Shatskii, according to Dewey, now mercifully "found his advice and even his criticisms welcomed" by the open-minded, tolerant men who guided the new Russia.[40] (A painfully ironic note is in order here: Shatskii would be purged by these thoughtful, caring men in the Great Terror. He died in 1934.)

In Dewey's mind, this dawn of a new day for Russian education was extremely healthy for "the masses"—a phrase Dewey used often. Many "doors" were now opened to them "that were formerly shut and bolted." The Marxist-Leninist government, Dewey maintained, "is as interested in giving them access to sources of happiness," whereas the Tsarist government "was [interested] to keep them in misery.... This fact," explained the professor, "and not the espionage and police restrictions, however excessive the latter may be, explains the stability of the present government."[41] Apparently, Dewey wasn't in complete ignorance of the Soviet police state, but he thought the Bolsheviks' benevolent intentions toward the masses were more important.

For Dewey, education was a bulwark of that Bolshevik benevolence. He wrote glowingly of "the marvelous development of progressive educational ideas and practices under the fostering care of the Bolshevist government—and I am speaking of what I have seen and not just been told about."[42] The father of experimentalism in American public education was thrilled with the "experimentation" thriving in Russian public education, which he saw as "flexible, vital, creative." He longed for the same kind of experimentation in America. Dewey opined, "I think the schools are a 'dialectic' factor in the evolution of Russian communism."[43]

The Testimony of Bella Dodd

That was John Dewey, who would become honorary president for life for the National Educational Association, America's preeminent teachers' union. The truth is that the teachers' unions in America have been a magnet for left-wing planners, managers, fundamental transformers, "change agents"—and for communists. American communists flocked to the public schools and the teachers' unions in the hope of assembling an education front to advance the interests of the proletariat. One of them was Bella Dodd, a major CPUSA national player in the 1930s and 1940s.

Dodd was a nice little Catholic girl born and raised in New York by her Italian-immigrant parents. Baptized Maria Assunta Isabella, she attended

Hunter College. All was fine until the day that Bella and her friend Ruth Goldstein enrolled for courses at Columbia University. At Columbia, Bella explained in her book *School of Darkness*, she "discovered the John Dewey Society and the Progressive Education Association" and, of course, the Columbia Teachers College. She was especially influenced by Dr. George Counts, a John Dewey pal who likewise had made a political pilgrimage to Moscow to pay homage to the Motherland. She soon realized "what a powerful effect Teachers College would have on American education."[44]

Dodd also discovered what a powerful effect the Communist Party could have, as she moved into the education front and joined the Party (a natural next step after Columbia). She earned a master's at Columbia and then earned her law degree from NYU and became a self-described and highly engaged "card-carrying Communist." In March 1943, she consented to become "an open Party leader." In no time, her ideological commitment became a major hindrance to her married and family life. The comrades insisted that she could not be a good communist and have children. "The bourgeois family as a social unit was to be made obsolete," she was instructed. She obeyed. The Party pushed her into "industry."

Bella also turned her back on her faith, becoming "anti-clerical."[45] Religion was verboten; it must be destroyed. Bella would tell the chilling story of how communists infiltrated the churches—and how she personally helped recruit over a thousand communist men into the seminaries.[46] She would not crawl out of the pit of her communist atheism until years later, with the help of Fulton Sheen, who brought her back into full communion with the faith of her youth.[47]

Dodd became very disillusioned with the conniving and the evildoing, the harassing and intimidation by Party enforcers. But before she could leave the Party, her comrades expelled her. In one harrowing moment, Alexander Trachtenberg, one of the leading Party honchos, confronted her: "We want to ask you a few questions," said an accusatory Trachtenberg in his thick German accent. "We hear you attacked the Cominform" (the Cominform was the rebranded name for the Comintern after World War II). "I've been ill, Comrade Trachtenberg," Bella said in her defense. "I guess I'm all right now."[48]

That was the only reasonable explanation. Only a sick person, after all, would question the value of world revolution.

Trachtenberg was identified by Whittaker Chambers as the "head of GPU" in the United States. The GPU was the notorious Soviet military police, successor to the Cheka.[49] He was a charter member of the American Party and also its cultural commissar. He was also chief of International Publishers, which had a monopoly on the publication and distribution of Soviet books and pamphlets. "Trachtenberg once said to me," recalled Dodd in her memoir, "that when communism came to America it would come under the label of 'progressive democracy.' 'It will come,' he added, 'in labels acceptable to the American people.'"[50]

Education was where the dutiful comrade Bella Dodd did her Party work. She became a teachers' union leader and organizer. The teachers, said Dodd, "were used on many different fronts" by the Party. The goal was "to establish a Soviet America," the designation used by CPUSA leaders for the new

★ ★ ★

Wolves in Sheep's Clothing

"When we get ready to take the United States, we will not take it under the label of communism; we will not take it under the label of socialism. These labels are unpleasant to the American people, and have been speared too much. We will take the United States under labels we have made very lovable; we will take it under liberalism, under progressivism, under democracy. But take it we will." —**Alexander Trachtenberg** to Bella Dodd in 1944, according to her 1950 speech at Fordham University[51]

Comintern-directed country that would emerge upon their "victory in America."[52]

Dodd later greatly regretted what she had done. As a teacher, she was especially concerned about how communists manipulated children through the educational system. "There is no doubt in my mind that the Communists will use the schools and every other educational medium," she told the U.S. Senate. "They will use every educational medium . . . from the nursery school to the universities."[53]

Education Comrades

That educational push by communists has never subsided. It is not possible to give a full history here, but here are some recent examples.

When the American Federation of Teachers, the massive teachers' union, holds its conventions and conferences, it isn't front-page news anywhere but the union newsletter—and also at *People's World*, the flagship publication of CPUSA, where it is front and center. The comrades at *People's World* adore the AFT. It frames the teachers' union members as noble fighters and partners in the cause.

Any of the articles at *People's World* on these conventions and conferences would be illustrative, including the pieces from July 2015 and July 2016 that hailed the AFT endorsement of Hillary Clinton for president.[54] But to narrow the focus, consider the July 2014 AFT convention in Los Angeles, to which *People's World* devoted three long, excited news articles. No other event so dominated the Marxist organ's attention over a two- to three-week period surrounding the convention.

Most remarkable was how seldom education was mentioned in *People's World*'s coverage of the convention—a convention ostensibly focused on education. Instead, the teachers' convention was reported by an approving *People's World* as an endless rendition of calls for a living wage, for Obama-care, for gay rights, transgender rights, LGBTQ rights, women's rights, immigrants' rights, voting rights, and "social justice." The speakers demanded greater "democracy," denounced "right-wingers and privatizers," and excoriated the "Religious Right" for opposing taxpayer funding of abortion and the redefinition of marriage.

"I am so sick of a limited moral discussion [by] the so-called religious right who suggest that the only moral issues are abortion, prayer in the school and homosexuality," railed the keynote speaker, a pastor and civil rights activist from North Carolina. "I am so bothered by that because most of what they purport only has about five scriptures that would support it and four of them they misinterpreted." The faithful teachers thunderously applauded. He raged, "They say deny unemployment, deny labor rights, deny LGBT right[s], women's rights, immigrant rights and hold vicious rallies against immigrant children that that makes us a better America."[55]

The speaker did at least manage to mention education, as did some of the other activists. The AFT apparently did not like President Obama's education secretary, who was judged not "progressive" enough. "The American Federation of Teachers' convention has a blunt message for Obama administration Education Secretary Arne Duncan," said the lead in one *People's World* feature. "You flunk the test of helping the nation's schools and kids, so leave."

That lead ran aside a large photo of AFT women shouting and jumping with placards.

Clearly, *People's World* feels an intense solidarity with these brothers and sisters on the education front. The comrades are hailing the AFT as "an energized resistance to ongoing attacks on education."[56]

It is very revealing that America's communists remain so gung ho for the AFT, that they are so elated by the proceedings at the AFT convention—that they give it so much of their sustained attention and approval. They are portraying the union to fellow communists as kindred souls marching forward to the same fundamentally transformed America.

Here is another example, from March 2011. "More than 10,000 union members and supporters swarmed the State Capitol here," began an ecstatic *People's World*, describing the scene in Annapolis, Maryland. The masses assembled "to protest proposed changes to teacher's pensions and to respond to the recent attack on unions in Wisconsin." The CPUSA official media organ was there, reporting triumphantly, ready to storm the Bastille, arm in arm in solidarity with the workers against their evil oppressors.[57]

The article in *People's World*, self-styled "direct descendant of the Daily Worker,"[58] continued excitedly:

> The rally began at 6 p.m. as people began filing into Lawyer's Mall in front of the Statehouse, arriving from all corners of the state. When the mall was full and barriers broken down, people resorted to climbing trees to fit in.
>
> That's when the marchers arrived.
>
> Another 7,000 or so people came marching from the main boulevard. Standing at one end of the rally it was not possible to see the end of the procession that packed the whole four-lane street. The police ended up blocking traffic for blocks to accommodate the crowd....
>
> A local veteran of the labor movement at the rally said, "I've been coming to labor rallies in Maryland for over 25 years and I've never seen anything like it."...Another participant was a self-described "conservative" debating the merits of capitalism and the free market. Still, he was so energized by the recent movement by labor that he wanted to come support it....
>
> Speakers from the local labor movement pumped up everyone, leading up to the headliner, AFL-CIO president Richard Trumka.... Trumka had "a message for those who support the CEO agenda," warning, "Madison is just the beginning,

Cleveland is just the beginning. This right here tonight is only the beginning!"

The crowd roared. Trumka rallied the proletariat. "Tax the rich! Tax the rich!" chanted the workers.[59]

Here is one more recent example of CPUSA enthusiasm for the teachers' union, posted by *People's World* on December 6, 2013. The place was the auditorium of Cooperative Arts and Humanities High School in New Haven, Connecticut. *People's World* held its annual Amistad Awards ceremony there, where it honored three individuals: a former Democrat state representative, a current Democrat state senator, and a union president at Yale University. They were joined on stage by the previous award recipient, who today is president emeritus of the Connecticut AFL-CIO.

"From the opening video and drumming to the remarks of the awardees, songs, youth slide show and finale," began the report in *People's World*, "an atmosphere of unity and optimism inspired the entire multiracial audience at the 2013 People's World Amistad Awards, held in the auditorium of Cooperative Arts and Humanities High School." All the awardees, said the article, "praised the vision and work of the Communist Party in their communities."

The Amistad Awards are presented annually on the occasion of the anniversary of Communist Party USA. This was the ninety-fourth anniversary.

The proud winners for the year included former state senator Ed Gomes, a steelworker; state representative Edwin Vargas, a teacher; and Laurie Kennington, president of Local 34, the union of clerical and technical workers at Yale. They were "cheered on," said *People's World*, by family, friends, coworkers, elected officials, and union and community leaders.

State Representative Edwin Vargas had been a union president before his election to the state legislature. He had done all sorts of union work at local, state, and national levels. He chaired the Human and Civil Rights Committee for the American Federation of Teachers and became president of the Hartford Federation of Teachers. He spent thirty-five years teaching in Hartford public schools. He said that although he had received many honors and recognitions in those capacities, this commendation from the Communist Party was particularly fulfilling because "this is an award from people who are the hard core of the movement."

No question about that.

Vargas invoked the name of the great revolutionary saint and fighter for *social justice*: Che Guevara—the commie murderer and grimacing punk who wanted to blow up the world in October 1962. Quoting the "progressive" icon, Vargas asserted that "the true revolutionary is guided by a great feeling of love." Justice, he said, cannot be achieved without peace. To that end, one of Vargas' goals in the Connecticut state legislature is to figure out how the state can transition from an economy aided by military production to some better industry, one geared toward labor, peace, and the environment.

Naturally, Representative Vargas was a big supporter of Barack Obama. In 2008, the communist-award recipient organized Latinos for Obama. He was chair of the Hartford Democratic Party and is involved with the Democratic National Committee. He is a longtime member of the Democratic Socialists of America.

Amistad Award recipient Laurie Kennington, president of a union at liberal Yale University, praised the work of a local group called New Elm City Dream and the Young Communist League for their "commitment to fight unemployment."

Of course, the Young Communist League has long been committed to more than just unemployment. In the 1930s, it was committed to wavering not one inch from the Stalinist party line. The young American Bolsheviks in the YCL were completely subservient to the Soviet Union. They were loyal Soviet patriots. At the Seventh World Congress in Moscow in 1935, smack in the middle of Stalin's famines and mass purges, the Communist

International described "the Young Communist League of the United States" as "a great success."

Unfortunately, the Young Communist League did not die with the USSR and the Comintern. In fact Amistad Award winner Laurie Kennington still considers it a great success. And on this particular evening in New Haven, the comrades from the Young Communist League were there in attendance, gathered among the faithful. The young Marxists presented an inspiring slide show amid singing, drumming, chanting, shouting, and howling.[60]

Dewey's Ghost

No wonder the students in America's public schools are seldom taught the horrors of communism. Some of their teachers are still hoping to bring about a collectivist utopia here. And aside from any explicitly pro-communist teachers, far more teachers are mere clueless liberals, merrily oblivious to these slimy tentacles in the public education system. They are the ones that communists have always used as dupes.

But the American education system doesn't lean Left just because our schools and colleges employ a number of actual communists. A leftward bias has been built into our public education system since the days of the man who is still the most respected education "reformer" in U.S. history. The specter of John Dewey haunts American education. His impact on our schools over the past hundred years is difficult to overstate, especially through the instruction and training of college students to become unionized public school teachers. Dewey is celebrated as the "father" of both "pragmatism" and "experimentalism." We see the spirit of Dewey in the constant experimentation that prevails in the classroom, the never-ending, always-changing search for new methods, programs, terms, fads and fashion, and "research" into "improving" education.

We also see it in the aggressive secularism of our schools. Dewey favored that, too; when it came to rampant repudiation of moral absolutes in public schools, Dewey was ahead of his time.

And, most tellingly, we see the spirit of Dewey in public school students' "socialization" to the "collective" by means of the "environing forces" at work in our public school system—all of which Dewey argued and worked for.

Given the origins of the collectivist philosophy that governs our public education system in the thought of a radical reformer who was a close ally of the Bolsheviks, it should come as no surprise that our schools are turning out students highly susceptible to the siren call of "socialism"—the ugly twin of the communist ideology that has killed tens of millions.

Public education pioneer John Dewey judged that pursuing change through politics was frustratingly slow; doing so via education could be much quicker. This was a central theme in his best-known work, *Democracy and Education* (1916). The schoolhouse could be more efficacious than houses of legislatures in bringing about radical change.

That was the clarion call that compelled so many '60s radicals to earn graduate degrees in education, making them today's tenured professors. These revolutionaries ultimately eschewed politics for education. Given their extreme ideas, Americans would never elect former Weather Underground terrorists, denizens of the FBI's "Most Wanted" list, and self-avowed communists such as Bill Ayers, Bernardine Dohrn, and Mark Rudd. But young people have no choice but to take them seriously in the classroom. To learn more about what American college students are actually learning these days, turn to the next chapter and read about the particular strain of communism being pushed by the tenured radicals that have coopted our universities.

CHAPTER 12

Cultural Marxism and the New Left

Communists today sound surprisingly modern and hip. Just compare the old Soviet-backed and -funded *Daily Worker* to its successor publication, the official CPUSA media organ, *People's World*. Read *People's World* and you will be struck by just how on fire today's communist movement is for the "LGBTQ" agenda. It was not always that way.

A few short decades ago, the Communist Party USA did not exactly roll out the red carpet for the rainbow crowd. Quite the contrary. That's why gay rights pioneers like Harry Hay once had troubled relationships with the CPUSA, which at one point considered homosexuality deviant.[1] What changed?

Did you know?

★ "Frankfurt School" Marxists plotted to advance communism by destroying Western moral principles and traditional institutions

★ Unrepentant criminal New Left leaders who celebrated murder in the 1960s are educating American teachers today

★ Obama's CIA director voted for the CPUSA candidate for president in 1980

The Frankfurt School

Not blameless in this effort to redefine culture and sex is the Frankfurt School, an offshoot of Marxist-Leninist ideology that arose in Germany in the 1920s and 1930s and that has become enormously influential on American college campuses in the intervening decades. The pioneers of this movement were all about culture and sex and education. The founders of

★ ★ ★

Going Gay with Socialist Party USA and the DSA

The CPUSA is not the only far-left party on board with the LGBTQ agenda. The official platform of Socialist Party USA boasts a four-point plank calling for the legalization of same-sex marriage (already achieved) as well as (among other things) "adopting policies and procedures" to address the concerns of "GLBTQ people throughout the educational system."[2]

Even more aggressive in support of the LGBTQ agenda is the influential Democratic Socialists of America (DSA). The "About DSA" section at the group's website lists among its three planks the broad objective of seeking to "restructure gender and cultural relationships." The DSA passed a resolution calling for "the legalization of same-sex marriages in all the States and Territories of the United States of America" at its convention in November 2011, a year before Barack Obama and Hillary Clinton both came out in favor of same-sex marriage: This was merely point one in a comprehensive seven-point statement on "Lesbian, Gay, Bisexual, Transgender and Queer (LGBTQ) Rights" that also included "making public schools safe and bias-free for LGBTQ students, defending their free speech in school and allowing students to start gay-straight alliance clubs" and advancing "the rights of LGBTQ people to parent." Point four in the DSA statement insisted: "DSA advocates for local and federal non-discrimination laws and insists that religious beliefs cannot be used to justify bias."[3]

The Communist Party USA and its flagship publication, *People's World*, too have become giddy girly cheerleaders and exuberant pom-pom boys for the gay rights movement, and now consistently tout "gay marriage" and the entirety of the LGBTQ agenda, as can be seen on any given day in the headlines at *People's World* or in a search of the CPUSA website.

It is hard to pinpoint when exactly the CPUSA openly and publicly embraced homosexuals and gay marriage. At CPUSA's website at the time of this writing, there are numerous statements and archived articles that are retrievable on the topic. One crucial early example is an official June 21, 2006, statement released jointly by the Communist Party USA and the Young Communist League, titled, "Gay Pride Month: Communists stand in solidarity." It urges "celebration of the struggles and achievements of lesbian, gay, bisexual and transgender people in the United States," and charges that "we still have a long ways to go."[4] This has become a major united-front issue for communists.

the Frankfurt School were neo-Marxists, a new kind of twentieth-century communist less interested in Marx's ideas on class and economic redistribution than in remaking society through the eradication of traditional norms and institutions. They combined Marxist theory with psychology, sociology, and Freudian teachings on sex.

A Book You're Not Supposed to Read

Takedown: From Communists to Progressives, How the Left Has Sabotaged Family and Marriage by Paul Kengor (WND Books, 2015).

The Frankfurt School developed what has been described as a kind of "Freudo-Marxism," integrating the extraordinarily bad but influential twentieth-century ideas of Sigmund Freud with the extraordinarily bad but influential nineteenth-century teachings of Karl Marx. This was no match made in heaven, but quite the opposite. And the children of that demonic marriage—the flower children, the hippies, the Yippies, the Woodstock generation, the Haight-Ashbury LSD dancers, the sex-lib kids—would carry the entwined Freudian-Marxian ideology into the twenty-first century, as the nutty ex-sixties radical professors poured out the Kool-Aid for the Millennials, who would merrily redefine everything from marriage to sexuality to gender.

In the 1930s, the Frankfurt School was not issuing statements calling for, say, same-sex marriage—something that would have been considered pure madness in any time before our own. Nonetheless, their comprehensive push for an untethered, unhinged sexual openness with no cultural boundaries or religious restrictions opened the door for everything down the road. When God and tradition and ancient norms no longer exist, everything is permissible.

For the neo-Marxists, orthodox Marxism was too limiting; it was too narrow, too restrictive, too reactionary even, too controlled by the Comintern that strong-armed national communist parties from upon high in Moscow with its ironclad party discipline. This rigidity prevented these more freewheeling neo-Marxists from initiating the cultural transformation they craved, including revolutionary changes in marriage, sexuality, and family. These Frankfurt leaders were left-wing intellectuals who looked to the universities as the home base from which their ideas could be launched. They spurned the church and looked to Marx and Freud as the gods who they believed would not fail them. Rather than organize the workers and the factories, the peasants and the fields and the farms, they would organize the students and the academy, the artists and the media and the film industry.

One can look at the Frankfurt school's "cultural Marxism" not as a replacement for classical Marxism, but as the accelerator pedal that was missing from the wheezing, stalling vehicle of classical Marxism. It offered a gear shift into warp-speed. The cultural Marxist agrees with the classical Marxist that history passes through a series of stages on the way to the final Marxist utopia, through slavery and capitalism and socialism and ultimately to the classless society. But the cultural Marxist recognizes that the communists will not get there by economics alone. In fact, the classical Marxists would utterly fail to take down the West with an economic revolution; capitalism would always blow away communism, and the masses would choose capitalism. Cultural Marxists understand that the revolution requires a cultural war more than an economic war. Whereas the West—certainly America—is not vulnerable to a revolt of the downtrodden trade-union masses, it is eminently vulnerable when it comes to, say, sex or porn. While a revolution for wealth redistribution would be unappealing to the citizens of the West, a sexual revolution would be irresistible. Put the bourgeoisie in front of a hypnotic movie screen, and they would be putty in your hands. Thus, what was needed was a *cultural* Marxism.

Key figures of the Frankfurt School included Georg Lukács, Herbert Marcuse, Wilhelm Reich, Max Horkheimer, Theodor Adorno, Erich Fromm, Walter Benjamin, Franz Neumann, and the Soviet spy Richard Sorge. The formal school began in 1923 as the Institute for Social Research at the University of Frankfurt in Germany. But its foundations were laid the year before at the Marx-Engels Institute in Moscow. Lukács was present there, along with Karl Radek (a high-level Bolshevik leader and Lenin representative), Felix Dzerzhinsky (head of the Cheka, later known as the NKVD and KGB), and Willi Münzenberg (the so-called Red millionaire).[5]

"We must organize the intellectuals," exhorted Münzenberg. Marx and Engels had organized the workers in the factories; the neo-Marxists would organize the professors and students in the universities.[6]

Born in April 1885, Georg Lukács hailed from one of the wealthiest Jewish families in all of Hungary. His father was a self-made millionaire. Like many mansion Marxists who speak for the poor and oppressed masses, he was born with a silver spoon in his mouth, and he developed a red-hot hatred for the comfortable world in which he grew up—including its traditional gender roles, marriage, and family. "Woman," he sneered, "is the enemy. Healthy love dies in marriage, which is a business transaction.... The bourgeois family gives off swamp vapors."[7] The Marxist cynic exuded his own stench. At home, his foul ideas cost him his marriage; in public, they would pervade and corrode and erode the great values of the West.

For Lukács, Münzenberg, and the other founding fathers of the Frankfurt School, the key to undermining Western society was not the emancipation of the working classes but rather a revolution in the culture. And at the core of Western culture was a pesky morality that derived from the Old and New Testaments, a traditional understanding that freedom is not simply the license to do anything a person wants, a realization that one's passions occasionally need to be checked and restrained. To Lukács, the vital human traditions that had undergirded Western civilization and served it well for centuries were obstacles to the new society he and his comrades envisioned. "Of these obstacles," wrote Ralph de Toledano, one of the twentieth century's more insightful reporters on the communist movement and cultural Marxism, "the two greatest were God and the family.... The family was not only a receptacle of the continuity in values, but the cement which held society together—and Lukacs hotly hated both God and the family."[8] So Lukács took communism even further Left than Marx and Engels.

Antonio Gramsci

An important figure in the development of cultural Marxism who was not part of the Frankfurt School was Antonio Gramsci. At the age of thirty-five, in 1926, he was arrested in his native Italy by Mussolini (perhaps the only half-sensible thing *Il Duce* ever did), and he spent the last eleven years of his life in prison. Gramsci was arguably *the* founding father of cultural Marxism, and perhaps "the most dangerous socialist in history," in the words of insightful scholar Samuel Gregg.[9]

Whereas Marx and his original followers were all about class economics, seeing wealth redistribution and the seizure of the means of production as the key to their vision, Gramsci looked to culture. If the Left truly wanted to win, it needed to first seize the "cultural means of production." As Sam Gregg puts it, "Gramsci insisted that Marxists had underestimated the importance of culture-forming institutions such as the media, universities, and churches in deciding whether the Left or the Right would gain control (or to use his favorite word, 'hegemony')."

By Gramsci's estimation, these cultural institutions in his time served to advance capitalism, or at least a free-market society. Not until leftists came to dominate these institutions would they be able to convince enough people to support their Marxist revolution on class, wealth, and so forth. "This part of his thesis was like manna from heaven for many left-wing Western intellectuals," writes Sam Gregg. "Instead of joining a factory collective or making bombs in basements, a leftist professor could help free society from capitalist exploitation by penning essays in his office or teaching students."

And in a really radical stroke—one that was too radical for its own time, but that would ultimately succeed—Gramsci and his heirs insisted that these leftist intellectuals needed to question everything, including moral absolutes and the Judeo-Christian basis of Western civilization. They needed to frame seemingly benign conventions as "cynical bourgeois ploys" (Sam Gregg's description), as systematic injustices that must be exposed. This is where we got professors fulminating against everything from "the patriarchy" to "white imperialism" to "transphobia." By the twenty-first century, even biological sex was no longer considered a settled issue. As I write, the New York City council now offers public employees the option of choosing from thirty-one different gender identities.[10] Not two gender choices, or even three, four, five, six, or twelve, or twenty. But thirty-one. Of course, that's nothing compared to Facebook, which at various times in the last three years (as I write) has listed fifty-one gender options, fifty-three, fifty-six, fifty-eight, and seventy-one.[11]

Contradiction in Terms

Occidental College, Barack Obama's alma mater, has a Department of Critical Theory and Social Justice, which is blandly described on the college's website as an "interdisciplinary department drawing on ideas from across traditional disciplines."[12] Now there is some irony: "traditional" should never be used in the same sentence as "critical theory."

A slightly deeper dig into the description at the website, however, unmasks the real agenda, as the department promises to instruct its wide-eyed students in the principles of "Marxism, psychoanalysis, the Frankfurt School, deconstruction, critical race studies, queer theory, feminist theory, postcolonial theory . . ."[13] You get the picture.

There was no traditional institution off-limits to the cultural Left.

In fact, so "critical" was the cultural-Marxist Left of anything and everything that it would brand itself as "critical theory." It is a deceptively innocuous label. But it is also an apt label, because it is indeed a theory rooted in criticizing everything we once knew.

Michael Walsh, author of *The Devil's Pleasure Palace*, calls "the cult of critical theory," the instrument for "the subversion of the West."[14] Gramsci himself foresaw societal transformation coming about by a "march through the institutions"—that is, the capture of the cultural institutions of the West, one by one, for Marxism.

And alas, Gramsci was prophetic. In fact, he and the movement he launched have been so shrewd that truly the vast majority of those who are advancing the frontiers of cultural Marxism today—take, for example, the typical Starbucks-sipping supporters of same-sex marriage—have no conception whatsoever that they are complicit in the takedown of Western society. Accused of promoting "cultural Marxism," they would give a blank stare, or perhaps a hearty laugh at the paranoia of their accuser. Sam Gregg puts it very well: "The worst part of Gramsci's legacy is that it has effectively transcended its Marxist origins. His outlook is now blankly taken for granted by millions of teachers, writers, even churchmen, who have no idea that they are committed to cultural Marxism. So while the socialist paradises constructed by Lenin, Stalin and likeminded people imploded over 25 years ago, the Gramscian mindset is alive and flourishing at your local university and in more than a few liberal churches and synagogues." Gregg rightly concludes, "The vast structures of cynicism which Gramsci's ideas have built, which honeycomb Western society today, will prove much tougher to dismantle than the crude cement blocks of the old Berlin Wall."

They will indeed. The people of Berlin had no problem recognizing the wall that repressed them. But the people of the West today have no sense whatsoever of the contours of the cultural Marxism that has captured so many of our institutions and threatens our ruin.

Antonio Gramsci would die in prison in Rome on April 27, 1937. He was only forty-six. But the prison bars could not contain his ideas, which would proliferate throughout the West, thanks to the sexual-intellectual salons of Weimar Germany and the Frankfurt School.

A Book You're Not Supposed to Read

Dupes: How America's Adversaries Have Manipulated Progressives for a Century by Paul Kengor (Intercollegiate Studies Institute, 2010). In three chapters on John Dewey, I detail his role in bringing the Frankfurt School to Columbia.

Cultural Marxism Comes to America

The threat of Hitler's Germany drove the Frankfurt School out of Europe—into the welcoming arms of America's left-wing colleges. Many of the cultural Marxists in Germany were Jews who needed a safe haven in the 1930s. So they and their Institute came to New York City, specifically to the campus of Columbia, already a hotbed of communism.

Pleading the case for them at Columbia was the renowned educator-philosopher John Dewey, founding father of American public education, progressive fool, communist sympathizer, and useful idiot. Progressive education "reformer" Dewey and cultural commissar Lukács were a perfect match. Lukács and his Frankfurt School colleagues believed that neo-Marxism needed to be inculcated in the next generation of children—just as in the past the family had educated children in traditional values. Thus, their primary area of operation would be the educational system—the schools, the universities, and particularly the teachers' colleges. It was no coincidence that Columbia housed the nation's top teachers' college—a creation of John Dewey.

Lukács was only one of many of the Frankfurt-Freudian-sexual-Marxism school with his sights set on the family. Others included sexual fanatics such as Wilhelm Reich, A. S. Neill, Erich Fromm, William Steckel, and Otto Gross. Steckel and Gross were overboard for the tastes of even

Sigmund Freud, who described them as "morally insane" and a "complete lunatic." Really, that was a perfect description of cultural Marxism.[15]

The Wretched World of Wilhelm Reich

Wilhelm Reich, born in March 1897 in Austria-Hungary, was a key figure in the import of cultural Marxism to America. Reich was the perverse son of secular Jewish parents who did not raise him in the Jewish faith, or any faith—nor did they model virtuous behavior. Wilhelm's father, Leon, was cold, cruel, and uninterested in his son. The father was also neglectful of his wife, who responded to his lack of love with an intense sexual affair behind her husband's back. The affair was no secret to little Wilhelm. It made him feel ashamed but it also intrigued and titillated him, so much so that he strangely fantasized about jumping into bed with his mother and her lover and joining them.

Such odd, intense sexual inclinations began very early in the boy's life—he claimed that as early as four years old he had tried to have sex with the family's maid. Reich was extremely candid about these desires in his diary and later autobiographical writings, including his posthumously published *Passion of Youth*. He claimed that by the time he was just eleven years old, he was already having daily intercourse with another of the family servants. He admitted to borderline sadomasochism and near-bestiality. He ultimately became hooked on brothels, saying he could "no longer live" without them.

Things took a turn for the (further) worse for Wilhelm when he decided to inform his already perpetually angry father of his mother's affair with a younger man. Leon proceeded to beat his wife—nothing new, except that this beating was more severe, and the mother was so miserable that she killed herself. Her despondent husband ventured to do the same, but failed. He died a few years later from tuberculosis. Wilhelm, by then a tormented and neurotic teenager, took the blame for these deaths. Even Reich could not help but deem this disastrous state of affairs a "catastrophe."[16]

An apt description of cultural Marxism.

Wilhelm Reich's life was a mess. Tragically, the early twentieth century offered two poisonous medicines that he felt might provide a cure and some form of direction: Freudianism and Marxism.

In 1919, Wilhelm Reich found his first god when he met Sigmund Freud and asked him for a tutorial and list of writings on sexology. Freud obliged. Reich began working for Freud's psychoanalytic clinic in 1922. This new professional direction did not help his personal life. For Reich, there would be many women, many marriages, many extramarital affairs, many divorces, many wrecked lives, and much death, debauchery, and misery.

Wilhelm Reich would encounter his second god when he dug into the writings of Marx. He joined the Communist Party in Austria in 1928 and visited the USSR the next year, where he lectured and was received enthusiastically. To his communist brethren in the Soviet Motherland, Reich trumpeted psychoanalysis and Freud as things that good Leninists and Stalinists should embrace.

By this time, Wilhelm Reich was well on his way to a grand unifying theory of Freudianism and Marxism—a so-called "fusion" of the two. The budding Freudian-Marxist-fusionist began crafting a report on his visit to the Soviet Union, which ultimately would become his revolutionary sexual manifesto, *The Sexual Revolution*. The book made him famous. For Reich, full communist revolution required full sexual revolution.[17]

In 1930, Wilheim Reich moved to Berlin with his wife and two children. He established the Association for Proletarian Sexual Politics, and, with his marriage rapidly coming apart, found a more alluring romance with his ideological bedfellows at the Frankfurt School. They consummated an unholy marriage of the fallen angels of Marxism and psychoanalysis.

Every utopian has his key to utopia. For the New Left Marxists, especially Reich, it lay not in the boardroom but in the bedroom, not in the factory but the family. It was not about stimulating economic growth but stimulating the genitals. This also meant destroying the family. As Donald DeMarco and Ben Wiker note in their *Architects of the Culture of Death*, "Reich saw the family, with its inevitable patriarchal authority, as the chief source of repression. Therefore, the family had to be dismantled."[18]

Sadly, Reich would do that ideological-cultural dirty work in a great nation far away from the wretched Berlin that was slouching toward Gomorrah. He would do it to America. Reich fled Germany at the height of Hitlerism. He was persuaded to come to the United States by (naturally) a Columbia University comrade visiting and studying in Europe—Theodore P. Wolfe, a professor of psychiatry at Columbia. Wolfe not only offered to settle Reich and arrange a visa with the help of Franklin Roosevelt's heavily communist-penetrated State Department, but also assisted in cobbling together an offer for Reich to teach a course on "character formation" (yes, seriously) at The New School in New York, better known as The New School for Social Research, founded in 1919 by "progressive" educators, most notably John Dewey and (naturally) several other Columbia professors. Wilhelm Reich was on his way to America to spread his ideas in the home of the free and the brave.

Overall, how influential was Wilhelm Reich?

Time magazine in 1964 stated that Reich "may have been a prophet."[19] He has been called the "Father of the Sexual Revolution" by *The New Yorker*, among other sources.[20] As DeMarco and Wiker point out, his influence has been "particularly evident" among radical feminists, left-wing college students and professors, secular sex educators, and "enemies of the family."[21]

Herbert Marcuse and the New Left

Wilhelm Reich helped plant the seeds of the 1960s Sexual Revolution. Herbert Marcuse would help bring that Revolution to fruition. He would be dubbed the Father of the New Left because of his huge popularity and influence among the '60s generation.

Marcuse was born in Berlin in July 1898. By the early 1920s, the formative period for him, Germany's capital was a kind of modern European Babylon, a place of all sorts of moral-cultural-sexual excess, a chaotic mess, a haunt of demons.[22]

In 1922, Marcuse completed his doctoral work at the University of Freiburg. In 1924 he married Sophie Wertheim, his first of three marriages—typical of cultural Marxist family values. In 1933, Marcuse joined the Institute for Social Research, that is, the Frankfurt School, but like other Jews he was soon forced to flee Germany under the führer.

Marcuse searched for a professional home, and finally found one in America. There to roll out the red carpet was (naturally) Columbia University, where Marcuse began to really lay the foundation for his version of Marxist revolution. At Columbia Marcuse became the leading voice for the transplanted Frankfurt School, producing what some have called an "eroticized Marx," most notably in his 1955 work, *Eros and Civilization: A Philosophical Inquiry into Freud*. The book came just in time to be digested by faculty intellectuals and regurgitated for ready consumption by students arriving on campuses in the tumultuous '60s.

In 1964, just in time to provide the shock to the wave that became the radical '60s, Marcuse published his acerbic critique of capitalist society in his bestselling *One-Dimensional Man*.[23] It is a sorry sack of work, at once inane and impenetrable. Perhaps it was its abstruse nature that made the intellectual snobs and nattering nabobs in the universities assume that something "deep" was going on there—something higher and richer that they needed to try to understand. Balderdash. The book was a pile of Marxist tripe and relativistic twaddle. The last thing it deserved was to be taken seriously.

Marcuse advocated what he called "polymorphous sexuality." This psychoanalytic concept, also known as "polymorphous perversity," allows for sexual gratification outside the conventional channels of accepted sexual behavior—really by almost any possible means of sexual stimulation. As the entry on Marcuse at GLBTQ.com explains,

> According to Freud, adult sexual development is a progression from oral and anal eroticism in infancy to the final adult stage of genital sexuality. In response, Marcuse proposed sexual liberation through the cultivation of a "polymorphous perverse"[24] sexuality (which includes oral, anal, and genital eroticism) that eschews a narrow focus on genital heterosexual intercourse.
>
> Marcuse believed that sexual liberation was achieved by exploring new permutations of sexual desires, sexual activities, and gender roles—what Freud called "perverse" sexual desires, that is, all non-reproductive forms of sexual behavior, of which kissing, oral sex, and anal sex are familiar examples.
>
> Marcuse was himself heterosexual, but he identified the homosexual as the radical standard bearer of sex for the sake of pleasure, a form of radical hedonism that repudiates those forms of repressive sexuality organized around genital heterosexuality and biological reproduction....
>
> Marcuse, like other leading theorists of sexuality, such as Freud and Wilhelm Reich, argued that homosexuality was a form of sexuality of which everyone was capable—that in fact, everyone was fundamentally bisexual.[25]

Herbert Marcuse represents a significant step in the extension of Marxism into the wider cultural-sexual realm, including homosexuality, bisexuality, and new gender roles. His writings were a watershed. The GLBTQ.com entry on Marcuse concludes with some crucial information:

> Dennis Altman's *Homosexual: Oppression and Liberation* (1971), one of the earliest theoretical discussions of gay liberation and sexual politics, reflected the same assumption and relied extensively on Marcuse's work.... Like Marcuse, Altman also emphasized "polymorphous perversity," the undifferentiated ability to take pleasure from all parts of the body. "Anatomy," Altman noted, "has forced the homosexual to explore the realities of polymorphous eroticism." Thus, homosexual sex represented an expression of pleasure and love "free of any utilitarian ends."
>
> The Red Butterfly Collective, a Marxist faction of the Gay Liberation Front, also echoed Marcuse. The group stressed the importance of a democratic socialist perspective. "Human liberation," it noted in its comment on Carl Wittman's path-breaking *Gay Manifesto* (1969), "in all its forms, including Gay Liberation, requires effective self determination, i.e. democracy, in all spheres of social life affecting the lives of people as a whole." The group adopted as its motto the final line from the "Political Preface" of the 1966 edition of *Eros and Civilization*: "Today the fight for life, the fight for Eros is the *political* fight."[26]

One of Marcuse's former students, writing in the left-leaning literary publication *Boston Review*, sees in today's society a myriad of manifestations linked to Marcuse—more "diversity," more "tolerance," more multiculturalism, more feminism, and a culture in which "same-sex marriage rites become common." The former student explains, "Marcusean analysis is immensely useful in understanding the profusion of tattoos and pornography, the Internet and smart phones, coffee houses and art fairs, T-shirts and jeans, oral sex and divorce." The father of the New Left indeed had "enormous influence" in "deconstructing" traditional understandings of marriage, gender, and family.[27]

The long-term project of sexual-cultural revolution didn't take as long as you might think. Really, it only took a generation.

Walter Benjamin

Walter Benjamin is another Frankfurt School purveyor of wickedness worthy of mention. Benjamin was born in July 1892 in Berlin and raised in that same European Babylon. For his mis-education, he attended the University of Berlin and the University of Freiburg. His closest colleagues in the Marxist and cultural Marxist world were Bertolt Brecht, the playwright dubbed "Minstrel of the Soviet GPU" (Brecht was close to Hollywood's Reds), and Theodor Adorno, pioneer of "critical theory" and another man of destructive ideas. Via Adorno and Max Horkheimer, the mastermind behind the financing and operating and relocating of the Frankfurt School to America—Horkheimer secured crucial funding for the move from the Rockefeller Foundation[28]—Benjamin was able to secure Frankfurt School money for his projects. His most famous work was his final book, *On the Concept of History* (1940).[29]

Walter Benjamin, another Jewish neo-Marxist looking to escape Hitler and spread cultural Marxism in 1930s, fled to Paris, where for the first of several times he considered killing himself—a deed he finally accomplished in September 1940 in Catalonia, Spain, still fleeing the Nazis. Benjamin's ideas for the West were likewise suicidal. They would sow a sea of wanton rebellion by undoing the best traditions and timeless truths that the West had to offer.

The Devil Is in the Details

Walter Benjamin had a fascination with the "daemonic,"[30] which played a role in his conception of "critical practice," a form of critical theory. While some contend that he used the term "daemonic" in a political sense,[31] Benjamin was deeply influenced by the surrealists,[32] who dabbled in the Satanic. Surrealism had its origins in Dada, an artistic movement that critiqued "bourgeois culture" and launched attacks on Christianity. Dada was characterized by distain for established authority, especially the established religious order. Man Ray's *Monument à D.A.F de Sade* (1933), for example, featured an inverted cross which framed a female buttock.[33] Max Ernst's *The Blessed Virgin Chastises the Infant Jesus before Three Witnesses* depicted the Virgin Mary (complete with halo) holding down the infant Jesus while spanking his bare bottom.[34] (If these guys were around today, they would be prime candidates for a grant from the National Endowment for the Arts.)

By 1933 Benjamin was ascribing Satanic qualities to *Angelus Novus* (*New Angel*), the famous monoprint by Paul Klee—who was not a surrealist, but an artist who was influenced by the surrealists. This print is central to the work on the philosophy of history for which Benjamin is best known,[35] Benjamin went so far as to purchase the actual print, which is often referred to as Benjamin's "angel of history." His understanding of *Angelus Novus* evolved over time, but eventually he discerned "satanic features" in the Angel,[36] which became an "icon of the left."[37] Benjamin seemed to especially like *Angelus Novus* as a symbol of rebellion against the repressive status quo, especially the Western culture of "commodity."[38] He viewed Satan as a triumphant symbol of rebellion.

The Frankfurt School sought to dispel the traditional Christian understanding of society, to set society free from the constraints of traditional Western culture. As Max Horkheimer enthused, the goal of Critical Theory is "to liberate human beings from the circumstances that enslave them."[39] These "circumstances" are the traditional Western institutions and moral norms that have held the Judeo-Christian world together for millennia.

For the cultural Marxists, these institutions had to be taken down. To hell with them—literally.

Benjamin's "post-modern" worldview was heavily influenced by what he perceived as the failures of the "old way" of doing things. World War I demonstrated in Benjamin's mind that the traditional, capitalist economic-political order was doomed. The carnage of the war and Nietzsche's death of God moved him into aesthetic existentialism that left him hungering for a "great transformation."[40]

The Frankfurt School's Intellectual Godchildren

This noxious brand of communism is now a dominant ideology on U.S. college campuses—and pervades much of American culture at large. And it's being pushed by self-avowed communists who set off bombs and attacked and sometimes even killed their fellow citizens in a failed attempt to start a revolution in the 1960s and '70s.

The roster of '60s radicals, many of them now tenured radicals in our horrid universities, is too long to go through here. They include Barack Obama pals Bill Ayers and Bernardine Dohrn, Mark Rudd, Tom Hayden, and Robert Scheer. These unrepentant leftists belonged to groups like Students for a Democratic Society (SDS), '60s collectives like the Berkeley-based Red Family, and domestic terrorist organizations such as the Weather Underground, which, as Rudd put it, "had as its goal the violent overthrow of the United States government."

They are the '60s New Left. And they have transformed our society.

David Horowitz was intimately familiar with that movement. As editor of the radical publication *Ramparts*, he was—before a Black Panther murder caused him to begin rethinking and eventually abandon his leftist roots—one of the most influential young communists in the country. When I asked Horowitz to explain the cultural Marxists' long-term assault on marriage and family, he told me, "The phenomena that you're seeking to explain came when the Marxist working class model failed and the New Left started applying Marxist categories to gender. This started at the very end of the Sixties and was a phenomenon of the Seventies."[41]

Leading the charge were feminists such as Betty Friedan and Kate Millett, early faces of the National Organization for Women (NOW), who,

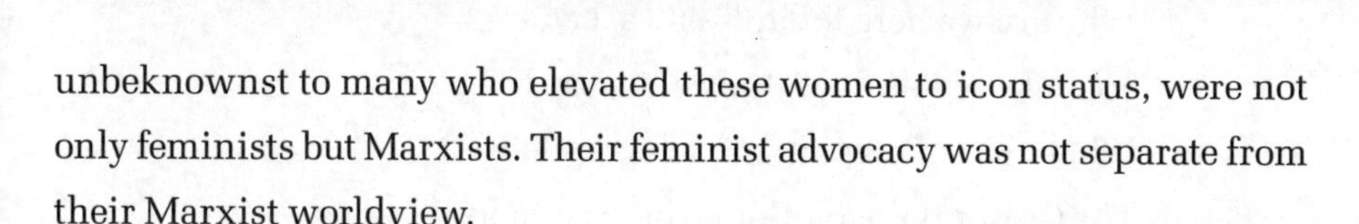

Two Books You're Not Supposed to Read

Radical Son: A Generational Odyssey by David Horowitz (Touchstone, 1998).

Commies: A Journey through the Old Left, the New Left and the Leftover Left by Ronald Radosh (Encounter, 2001).

unbeknownst to many who elevated these women to icon status, were not only feminists but Marxists. Their feminist advocacy was not separate from their Marxist worldview.

Kate Millett was the author of *Sexual Politics*, her dissertation at (naturally) Columbia, which became a cultural juggernaut when it was published in 1969, at the height of '60s mayhem and three years after Betty Friedan became the first president of NOW. The book landed Kate on the cover of *Time* magazine, which called her "the Karl Marx of the Women's Movement." As a committed Marxist-feminist, Millett picked up the torch ignited by the Frankfurt School ideological arsonists, decrying the "patriarchy" of the monogamous nuclear family.

Insight into Millett's mindset is provided by her younger sister, Mallory, who also became a Marxist but later rediscovered her Christian faith and pulled herself out of the clutches of the cultural-Marxist beast. During the late '60s revolution, Katie urged Mallory, who by then was a divorced single mom, to stay with her. "Come to New York," she urged. "We're making revolution!"[42]

And so Mallory became an eyewitness to history. She remembers,

> I stayed with Kate...in a dilapidated loft on The Bowery as she finished her first book, a PhD thesis for Columbia University, "Sexual Politics."
>
> It was 1969. Kate invited me to join her for a gathering at the home of her friend, Lila Karp. They called the assemblage a

"consciousness-raising-group," a typical communist exercise, something practiced in Maoist China. We gathered at a large table as the chairperson opened the meeting with a back-and-forth recitation, like a Litany, a type of prayer done in Catholic Church. But now it was Marxism, the Church of the Left, mimicking religious practice:

"Why are we here today?" she asked.

"To make revolution," they answered.

"What kind of revolution?" she replied.

"The Cultural Revolution," they chanted.

"And how do we make Cultural Revolution?" she demanded.

"By destroying the American family!" they answered.

"How do we destroy the family?" she came back.

"By destroying the American Patriarch," they cried exuberantly.

"And how do we destroy the American Patriarch?" she replied.

"By taking away his power!"

"How do we do that?"

"By destroying monogamy!" they shouted.

"How can we destroy monogamy?"...

"By promoting promiscuity, eroticism, prostitution and homosexuality!" they resounded.[43]

The comradely sisters then proceeded with a sustained discussion of how to advance these goals by establishing the National Organization for Women. "It was clear they desired nothing less than the utter deconstruction of Western society," Mallory said. How would they do this? They explained that their goal was to "invade every American institution. Every one must be permeated with 'The Revolution.'" (Gramsci and Lukács would have been so proud.) This included the judiciary, the legislatures, the executive branches, media, education—universities, high schools, K–12, school boards, even the library system.

Kate's sister Mallory notes tragically how she has met women in their fifties and sixties who fell for this creed in their youth and have cried themselves to sleep many countless nights grieving for the children that they will never have and that they "coldly murdered because they were protecting the empty loveless futures they now live with no way of going back." They ask her, "Where are my children? Where are my grandchildren?"[44]

Those children were sacrificed at the Marxist-feminist altar of abortion. Abortion is a holy sacrament in the church of radical feminism.

"Your sister's books destroyed my sister's life!" Mallory has heard numerous times. "She was happily married with four kids and after she read those books, walked out on a bewildered man and didn't look back." The man fell into despair and ruin. The children were stunted and deeply harmed. The family was profoundly dislocated and there was "no putting Humpty-Dumpty together again."[45]

Like many Marxists, Kate Millett incorporated her ideas on marriage and sexuality into her personal practices. Though she was married, she practiced lesbianism, becoming bisexual at (naturally) Columbia while writing *Sexual Politics*. This would, predictably, end her marriage.[46]

"We Sh-t on All Your Conventional Values"

Another Columbia radical of Millett's day created a fitting slogan for the New Left. "We're against everything that's good and decent," said John Jacobs, one of the leaders of the Weather Underground. Jacobs made this statement of the obvious at the infamous moment of iniquity that was the "War Council" held in Flint, Michigan, on December 27, 1969, attended by some four hundred "student troops."

Perhaps an even better, albeit cruder statement of the New Left's cultural Marxism came from Bernardine Dohrn at the same "War Council": "We're about being crazy motherf—ers!" So explained the charming and gracious Bernardine.

Mark Rudd, who had spearheaded the shutdown of (naturally) Columbia University in the spring of '68—the Left always devours its own—got caught up in the fervor at the War Council. "It's a wonderful feeling to hit a pig," he enthused. "It must be a really wonderful feeling to kill a pig or blow up something." Kathy Boudin, a red diaper baby who would later do prison time for murder after a Brinks robbery, and today is on the faculty of (where else?) Columbia University, declared all mothers of white children to be "pig mothers" and spoke of "doing some sh-t like political assassinations."

But the demure Bernardine Dohrn would go even further than that. The lovely Bernardine introduced what could be the brand label for cultural Marxism, the four-finger salute. Bernardine enriched the brethren with her ruminations on the brutal Tate-LaBianca murders, which had been committed by the satanic Charles Manson "family." The Manson clan's crime was horrific. The murderous lunatics ripped open Tate, a beautiful young actress who was eight and a half months pregnant. At the "War Council," Dohrn thrilled, "Dig it! First they killed those pigs. Then they ate dinner in the same room with them. Then they even shoved a fork into the victim's stomach! Wild!"[47]

They dug it. As Mark Rudd reported, the assembled "instantly adopted as Weather's salute four fingers held up in the air, invoking the fork left in Sharon Tate's belly."[48] One of the attendees, Larry Grathwohl, recalled the festive party-like atmosphere created by Bernardine's gesture. He remembered how, through the rest of the evening, as the peace-loving "flower children" danced, they gleefully held up their fingers in the four-finger salute, moving their arms up and down and back and forth, laughing joyfully.[49]

Mark Rudd captured what this moment meant to the '60s New Left: "The message was that we sh-t on all your conventional values.... There were no limits to our politics of transgression."[50] "We sh-t on all your conventional values." That statement perfectly captures the anything-goes nihilism, no-boundaries moral relativism, and death and destruction that is cultural Marxism.

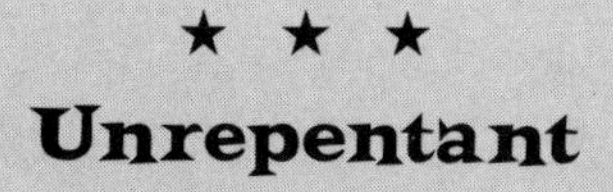

"I don't regret setting bombs.... I feel we didn't do enough." —**Bill Ayers**[52]

The victims of the Manson murders got no sympathy from Dohrn (a future childcare advocate). And as we have already seen in chapter nine, the Weather Underground revolutionaries—once they were on the run from the police—issued a manifesto calling themselves "communist men and women" and enthusing about Che Guevara.

Why were they on the run? Dohrn, Ayers, and Rudd and gang didn't just like to talk about violence. This "murderous core group," as one historian calls them, ended up on the FBI's "Most Wanted List" for violent crimes—including for their suspected roles in domestic bombings that killed Americans.[51]

And where are they today?

Bernadine Dohrn became a faculty member at Northwestern University School of Law, where the pioneer of the delightful four-finger salute specialized in children at the law school's Family Justice Center. It was an interesting appointment for a woman who once celebrated the bloody fork stuck into the pregnant body of actress Sharon Tate.[53]

Also joining Bernardine in the academy was her hubby, Bill Ayers, who taught in the education department at the University of Illinois–Chicago once he had received his doctorate from (of course) John Dewey's Teachers College at Columbia University after escaping jail time. Ayers became a distinguished professor of education and senior university scholar at the University of Illinois at Chicago.[54]

★ ★ ★

A Communist Appreciates America

"Guilty as sin, free as a bird. What a country!" —**Bill Ayers**, on escaping jail time for his violent crimes[55]

In the 1980s, John Dewey's celebrated intellectual home rolled out the red carpet for communist radical and domestic bomber Bill Ayers. Ayers had spent the previous decade fleeing the FBI as a fugitive. He lived in fifteen different states during that time, using the names of dead babies in cemeteries as aliases.[56] He wrote some of the most violent, insane screeds ever published in the United States. And after all that, in 1983 John Dewey's Columbia Teachers College offered him admission. Ayers deemed it a good fit; the college agreed. He earned his doctorate there.

Ayers then established himself in the education department at the University of Illinois–Chicago. Ayers, a self-styled "change agent," became a tenured professor of education, authoring (among other works) books on teaching "social justice," published by (you guessed it) Columbia Teachers College.[57]

Other former SDS and Weather Underground fanatics followed the same pattern.

Mark Rudd, Ayers and Dohrn's chief ally in the Weather Underground, also went into education. When the Columbia University alumnus is not behind his regular lectern at a university in New Mexico, he travels the country teaching "social activism" at other universities.[58]

Teaching Revolution

Still another SDSer running in these circles is Michael Klonsky, a close pal of Rudd's whom Rudd described as a "Stalinist" in their glory days.[59] Deeming the Communist Party USA too reactionary for his tastes, Klonsky became head of the New Communist Movement in the United States. He went to communist China, where he was disappointed in the free-market reforms pursued in the 1980s by Mao's milder successor, Deng Xiao Ping.

Where would Klonsky find a cultural-political-ideological milieu more to his liking? Where else, comrade? The American university system, of course.

Klonsky got himself a Ph.D. in (you guessed it) education and ended up in (you guessed it) Chicago, where he worked closely with his old Bolshevik buddy Bill Ayers. Klonsky and Ayers became what enthusiasts have described as "pioneers in small school development." Their "small schools" projects were funded to the tune of almost $2 million in grants underwritten by the Chicago Annenberg Challenge, where a young Illinois politician named Barack Obama served as chairman of the board, and by the Joyce Foundation and Woods Fund, whose boards Obama also served on.[60]

Klonsky and Ayers both joined the faculty at the University of Illinois–Chicago's College of Education. The two sold their wares under the rubric of "social justice," and published their work via (naturally) John Dewey's Columbia Teachers College. Among Ayers and Klonsky's works are *Teaching for Social Justice* (Teachers College Press, Columbia); *A Simple Justice: The Challenge of Small Schools* (Teachers College Press, Columbia); and *Handbook of Social Justice in Education* (Routledge, 2008).[61] The dynamic duo has co-authored many journal articles on education, which are being used in education departments nationwide to train future generations of "progressive" teachers.

Klonsky's wife, Susan, is one of the charter members of "Progressives for Obama," as is his brother, Fred. Not surprisingly, Susan and Fred are also involved in education. Fred, fittingly, serves as president of Park Ridge Education Association. If "Park Ridge" sounds vaguely familiar, that is because it is the native Chicago-area home of Hillary Rodham Clinton, where she and her fellow "social justice" warriors from the Methodist youth group were introduced to the political theology of Lucifer fan Saul Alinsky.

★ ★ ★

Better Call Saul

Hillary Clinton, the 2016 presidential nominee of the Democratic Party, had her own ties to the radical Left. Besides interning at the well-known Red law firm headed up by California communists Bob Treuhaft and Jessica Mitford, she was a great admirer of Saul Alinsky, an infamous socialist and the father of "community organizing" (which was once the job of her future boss, Barack Obama).

Alinsky claimed that he had never been a member of the Communist Party, but admitted that he did work with the Party. "I knew plenty of Communists in those days, and I worked with them on a number of projects," said Alinsky in his famous March 1972 interview with *Playboy* magazine. "Back in the Thirties, the Communists did a hell of a lot of good work." He added emphatically, "Anybody who tells you he was active in progressive causes in those days and never worked with the Reds is a goddamn liar. Their platform stood for all the right things." He contended that "the party in those days was on the right side and did considerable good."[62]

Notice that Alinsky was referring specifically to the Communist Party of the 1930s, the height of the Stalin era. This was precisely the period that American Communist Party members swore an oath of loyalty to Stalin's USSR and pledged to work toward the goal of a Moscow-directed "Soviet America." Those were the pals that Alinsky worked with, who *did a hell of a lot of good work.*

Hillary wrote her senior thesis at Wellesley on Alinsky and his tactics. On July 8, 1971, Clinton reached out to the aging Alinsky in a letter she marked "Personal."

"Dear Saul," she began warmly. "When is that new book coming out—or has it come and I somehow missed the fulfillment of Revelation?"

The new book that Hillary was excited about was *Rules for Radicals*, which begins with this curious epigraph:

> Lest we forget at least an over-the-shoulder acknowledgment to the very first radical: from all our legends, mythology, and history... the first radical known to man who rebelled against the establishment and did it so effectively that he at least won his own kingdom—Lucifer.

Hillary was looking forward to the new book because, as she told Alinsky, she had just had her "one-thousandth conversation about Reveille" (his best-known work at the time) and "need some new material to throw at people." She also informed Alinsky that she (Barack Obama-like) was pumped up to do some community organizing, telling him that she had "survived law school...with my belief in and zest for organizing intact."

"I miss our biennial conversations," Clinton said to Alinsky. "Do you ever make it out to California?" She wanted to see Alinsky. "I am living in Berkeley and working in Oakland for the summer and would love to see you," Clinton wrote. "Let me know if there is any chance of our getting together."[63]

And then there is the illustrative case of Angela Davis, one of the most notorious communists of the '60s era—a prominent early member of the Black Panthers, recipient of the Lenin Peace Prize, cheerleader for the Soviet invasion of Afghanistan, and candidate (twice) for vice president of the United States on the Communist Party ticket, where she ran alongside longtime CPUSA party secretary Gus Hall. (Among those who voted for the Hall-Davis Communist Party presidential ticket was John Brennan, Barack Obama's CIA director. Yes, Obama appointed as CIA director a man who had voted for the candidate of the Communist Party USA when it was still under the control of the Soviet Union!)[64]

Davis was one of the many academic disciples of Herbert Marcuse, Frankfurt School cultural Marxist, by whom she was "educated" at Brandeis University. In fact, Davis is arguably Marcuse's most complete and long-lasting success. He was nothing short of her mentor.[65] He took her under his wing at Brandeis in the early 1960s. In 1965, she honored her professor by retracing his steps to Frankfurt, Germany, spending two years at the University of Frankfurt. This was Marcuse's doing. Marcuse sent her to West Germany to study at his old haunt, the "Institute for Social Research" in Frankfurt. She returned to the United States in 1967 to continue her studies with Marcuse as her doctoral adviser.[66] At this point, Marcuse was teaching at the University of California–San Diego. He had also taught at (naturally) Columbia University.

Comrade Angela formally joined Communist Party USA the next year, 1968—the same year that Mark Rudd shut down Columbia University—and she would increasingly be involved in radicalism and violence. The year after that, 1969, she was recommended by Marcuse to UCLA's philosophy department, which hired her as an assistant professor, leading to a major clash with Governor Ronald Reagan and the California Board of Regents because of her CPUSA membership and advocacy.

Like any good communist, Davis's road to the revolution included breaking a few eggs along the way. She was soon pursued on charges of kidnapping, murder, and conspiracy for her suspected role in the August 1970 murder of a prison guard. Like Ayers and Dohrn, she landed on the FBI's Ten Most Wanted list. And like Ayers and Dohrn, she escaped jail-time "free as a bird" (as Ayers would boast), and then spread her wings in academia.

Today, like her late mentor, Herbert Marcuse, Angela Davis is a professor in the University of California system. She lists among her areas of expertise "critical theory," the formal academic front-name for cultural Marxism. And today, the official Herbert Marcuse website features a glowing biography of Angela Davis, one of the proudest legacies of the esteemed Frankfurt School figure.[67]

In June 2016, the Elizabeth A. Sackler Center for Feminist Art at the Brooklyn Museum feted Davis with its 2016 Sackler Center First Award, "honoring women who are first in their fields."[68] Among Angela Davis's firsts, of course, was to be the first female comrade to run on a communist presidential ticket.

There to witness the spectacle was veteran radical-watcher Roger Kimball. Kimball described the award ceremony in New York: The Iris and B. Gerald Cantor Auditorium at the Brooklyn Museum was "packed to overflowing." The celebration began with a songfest led by a large group of children from the Manhattan Country School, a "boutique 'progressive' institution," who sang verse after verse of "We Shall Overcome." Elizabeth A. Sackler, chairwoman of the Brooklyn Museum, introduced the evening, glowing with pride about her grandchildren who attend the school. She gushed that the name Angela Davis is "the embodiment of all we hold dear," and is "synonymous with truth." Also welcoming the students was Chirlane McCray, wife of New York's comrade mayor, Bill de Blasio. McCray is beloved by New York "progressives" not only for her radical politics but for her progressive bisexual lifestyle in her biracial marriage.

Bill Ayers and Bernardine Dohrn were not in attendance for the Davis celebration, but Kathy Boudin was. Boudin was one of their Weather Underground colleagues, one of the few who did not escape jail time. Kathy and her sister-in-arms Bernardine Dohrn planted a bomb in the ladies' restroom at the U.S. Capitol building in Washington in 1971.[69] They got away with that one. But Kathy did not escape punishment for her role in an infamous October 1981 murder, when she and her Marxist revolutionaries pulled off an armed robbery of a Brinks security truck in Nanuet, New York, and two so-called "pigs" (i.e., policemen) and a Brinks guard were murdered. A decade earlier, in March 1970, Boudin had almost lost her own life. She was the infamous radical who stumbled naked out the front door of a smoking Greenwich Village apartment after a homemade bomb accidentally detonated, killing her classmate Diana Oughton. Three Weather Underground members were fatally injured that day. The revolutionaries' original plan had been to detonate nail bombs at a military dance in Fort Dix, New Jersey, in order to murder young Vietnam vets reunited for an evening of happiness with their wives. The plan backfired.

Kathy was convicted of murder for the Brinks hit and went to jail before later going to earn her graduate degree in (you guessed it) education at (naturally) Columbia University's Teachers College. Boudin earned an Ed.D. from John Dewey's celebrated college and today is adjunct assistant professor at (naturally) Columbia University School of Social Work. As her bio at the university's website states, Boudin's work focuses on "Mother-child relationships," "criminal justice," "restorative justice," "health care," and

★ ★ ★

Under the Radar

Roger Kimball, after attending the event honoring Angela Davis in (of course) New York, asked several of his younger colleagues if they knew about Davis's background. Not one of them under the age of thirty-five had heard of her. That is no surprise. But too many young people are indoctrinated in college by the likes of Davis, thanks to their duped parents' handing over their lifetime savings for a six-figure university "education." These are the men and women educating the next generation of Americans at our universities today; this is how the communists are fundamentally transforming America. And lo and behold, old comrade Angela was recently trotted out of the radical closet to serve as no less than honorary co-chair of the historic January 2017 Women's March in Washington, where the militant Lenin Prize winner was applauded by a roaring crowd of dingbats wearing silly pink hats literally named after their genitals.[71] They, too, are the tragic byproducts of our modern higher education system. These girls screamed their approval as the former Communist Bloc cheerleader hailed Chelsea Manning, "trans women of color," "our flora and fauna," and "intersectional feminism," and denounced "white male hetero-patriarchy," misogyny, Islamophobia, and capitalist exploitation.[72]

"working within communities with limited resources to solve social problems."[70] Like Ayers and Dohrn, today she takes the revolution directly to the nation's children.

Today, Angela Davis, like Kathy Boudin, Bill Ayers, Bernardine Dohrn, Mark Rudd, Michael Klonsky, and virtually all their old comrades from the '60s New Left, champions the Occupy Wall Street movement, vigorously supported Barack Obama, is "feeling the Bern" for Bernie Sanders, and fights for same-sex marriage and the larger "LGBTQ" agenda to take down the natural-traditional-Biblical family.

These men and women, who have described themselves as communists and committed violent crimes to try to start a revolution in America, are still working for a communist revolution. They're just hoping to accomplish it in a different way. And whether you call it "cultural Marxism," "critical theory," "neo-Marxism,' or "the New Left," it's having much more success than the old-fashioned communism—and not just on colleges campuses, but across all of American society.

The American university has become a vital outpost for American communists, "democratic socialists," and pro-communist "progressives" and liberals. Universities in the United States now honor traitors and Soviet spies. New York's Bard College boasts an Alger Hiss Chair in Social Studies.[73]

What Santayana said is correct: those who do not remember the past are condemned to repeat it. For decades now, we have not taught the next generation what it needs to know. Instead, we have let communist revolutionaries and commie-sympathizing dupes cover up the crimes of communism and teach generations of Americans the lie that Marxism is a noble, idealistic ideology. And that is coming back to bite us.

CHAPTER 13

Communism Today

Marxists—particularly cultural Marxists—have been remarkably successful in miseducating Americans. But education is just one front in the ongoing struggle to bring communism to our country. An astonishing variety of organizations and movements in the United States today are still agitating for the promised communist utopia. An alarming amount of the violence and division we see in our country today can be traced back to the activism of communists and associated leftist dupes and fellow travelers. And there are disturbing connections between these hardcore communists and a number of "mainstream" American politicians.

Did you know?

★ President Obama's boyhood mentor was a card-carrying member of the Communist Party (card number 47544)

★ "Progressives for Obama" was founded by formerly admitted communists

★ The Communist Party USA urged support for the Democrats in the 2016 presidential election

Revolutionary Communists

To this day, the Communist Party USA—which was completely loyal to Stalin and continued to toe the line set by the communist government in Russia until the fall of the Soviet Union—remains the dominant party of communists in America. But it is not the only communist organization in America. There are plenty of variations and splinter groups, as there have long been. For instance, there remains a following of Trotskyites (or

★ ★ ★

Guilt by Association

The Militant achieved some infamy after a photograph surfaced of Oswald proudly hoisting the publication alongside his rifle before he consummated his love affair with communism by placing a bullet in the skull of JFK. Oswald posed for two pictures with his rifle and pistol, a copy of the March 11, 1963, issue of *The Militant* and a copy of the March 24, 1963, issue of the *Daily Worker*.[2]

Trotskyists), which once included the popular angry atheist Christopher Hitchens.[1] Trotskyists gravitate toward Lee Harvey Oswald's favorite newspaper, *The Militant*, the flagship publication of the Socialist Workers Party.

The Revolutionary Communist Party, USA, (RCP) is one radical group that is arguably to the Left of the Communist Party USA (no easy task). Its tactics are certainly more aggressive. Its beliefs include a dedication to a real revolutionary communism, with its members insisting that the dividing line between genuine communists and those who are not genuine is the commitment to real revolution.[3] RCP comrades call for the "overthrow" of the current "capitalist-imperialist" system, which is to be replaced with a "radically different system."[4]

The group's chairman and guru is Bob Avakian, a Maoist, for whom the RCP membership is asked to provide a loyalty reminiscent of the personality cults of Mao and Stalin. Avakian's group proclaims, "Just as, in 1975, being a communist meant being a follower of Mao and the path that he forged, so today being a communist means following Bob Avakian and the new path that he has forged."[5] And Mao isn't the only bloodthirsty communist tyrant popular with the RCP. As Paul Berman explains in his book *Power and the Idealists*, "The RCP was a California group mostly, but it was animated by an ambitious view of the proletarian revolution and a determination to cultivate fraternal ties with Maoist parties around the world.... The RCP's comrades devoted unusual energies to celebrating Stalin." This "Stalin-worship," this "cult of Stalin," writes Berman, reflected the influence of the Chinese communists, who believed that Stalin, unlike

Nikita Khrushchev, had not betrayed the world proletariat. Thus, "The RCP dutifully set about burnishing Stalin's reputation in the world of the American left."[6]

The RCP's living hero, known as "Chairman Bob," was raised in a middle class home. Bob Avakian was radicalized in the 1960s during his time in Berkeley when he hooked up with SDS, the Black Panthers, and buddies such as Bill Ayers. He co-founded the RCP with fellow radical Carl Dix in the mid-1970s, about the time that Ayers and Bernardine Dohrn (who, like Avakian, had left SDS) were fleeing law enforcement.

Avakian is now in exile in Paris (some reports claim this is a self-imposed exile). It is said that only his closest comrades know where he is living.[7] His RCP operates "Revolution Bookstores" in sixteen American cities, including New York (of course), Berkeley, Cambridge, and Seattle.[8]

Avakian's personal manifesto, a book titled *The New Communism*, promises a "radically new society" based on a fundamental transformation of the existing order. He and his comrades proclaim a "New Communist Manifesto," and their website lists six resolutions of the RCP as of January 1, 2016. These long, strange, and meandering resolutions repeatedly express the Party's militant dedication to revolution, and every one of them mentions Avakian's name.[9]

Spyridon Mitsotakis, an insightful and informed reporter of communist activities who in 2014 reported on the RCP's attempted takeover of a

★ ★ ★

Personality Cult

"Bob Avakian is Chairman of the Revolutionary Communist Party, USA. Like all Party members, he is subordinate to the collectivity of the Party overall, even as he has been elected by the Central Committee to lead the Party. At the same time, as the initiator and architect of a new synthesis of communism, he is also objectively 'greater than' the Party. It is crucial that our Party be grounded in and proceed on the basis of Bob Avakian's new synthesis of communism." —Revolutionary Communist Party Resolution 6,[10] explaining that the Party's leader is to be viewed as objectively greater than the party itself, something that is very reminiscent of the personality cult that surrounded Stalin.

Unitarian Universalist Church, describes the Revolutionary Communist Party as an "intolerant totalitarian movement."[11] John Rossomando, another keen observer, says of the party's acolytes, "They are worse than the CPUSA."[12]

And, as we shall see in the next chapter, the RCP—which continues to agitate for an actual communist revolution in the United States—has been involved in fomenting some of the racial violence we see in America today in connection with the protests of police shootings and the "Black Lives Matter" movement.

★ ★ ★

Bring Back the Show Trials!

Peter Wilson reports in the *American Thinker* that the RCP advocates the creation of "special Tribunals" (again, quoting the RCP constitution) to be "established to preside in cases of war crimes and other crimes against humanity" committed by "former members and functionaries of the ruling class of the imperialist USA and its state and government apparatus." As Wilson notes, these enemies of the state would "be imprisoned or otherwise deprived of rights and liberties." Further, "those who played a leading role in opposing the revolution" will not be "accorded citizenship" and will be "deprived of the right to vote."[13]

"Progressives" (Read: Communists) for Obama

The Revolutionary Communist Party, USA, makes no apologies and no excuses. It operates openly and boldly. It is a party of revolutionary communism, period. Other communist and pro-communist groups, however, are far less forthright about their intentions—and who they really are. Take "Progressives for Obama." A more honest name for the group would have been "Communists and Progressives for Obama."

This group of '60s Marxists, Maoists, and Che admirers came together in 2008 to support what they saw as a once-in-a-lifetime presidential candidate, a kindred ideological spirit: Barack Obama. They sought to ride with him on a magic red carpet to the fundamental transformation that would finally change the nation they had so long loathed. He would usher in the utopian paradise they had always been hoping for.

The radicals of the 1960s, as we have seen, went from campus activism to bombings and other violent acts to life "underground" on the run from the FBI to rehabilitation (without repentance) that put them in the position to shape the minds of America's college students and future teachers. But still they felt themselves to be in a kind of frustrated exile as adults. They had painfully endured the rise of Reaganism and the collapse of the Soviet Union. The likes of Tom Hayden and Mark Rudd had gone into an uneasy limbo, teaching at universities, trying to get into politics, but they were frustrated that neither major political party in America would nominate a presidential candidate of their liking. Of course they despised the Republicans, but they also disliked Democratic presidents such as Jimmy Carter and Bill Clinton, who were too *conservative* for them (just as in the '60s they had detested traditional and anti-communist Democrats like John F. Kennedy and even Bobby Kennedy).[14]

Well, in 2008 that finally changed. The Marxist children of the '60s were suddenly back on the public stage, this time calling themselves "progressives." They were filled with direction, elation, and a new sense of purpose by the presidential candidacy of Barack Obama. Their movement was alive again.

Whether Obama knew it or not, he was the man they hoped could be their Manchurian candidate. He was the one on whom they projected their ideals and vision for America and the world—a false utopianism that had long ago smoldered into ashes behind that fallen wall that once divided Berlin. He was their political Phoenix, through whom they believed they would ascend again. He was the first Democratic Party presidential nominee whose politics approached theirs.

And so they came together with renewed vigor in a formal group called "Progressives for Obama." It was, in effect, a twenty-first-century iteration of something that this collective of red-diaper babies knew so well—a classic communist front-group.

★ ★ ★

Card-Carrying Communist, Presidential Mentor

In Hawaii in the fall of 1970, nine-year-old Barack Obama was introduced to sixty-five-year-old Frank Marshall Davis. Obama's grandfather made the introduction because the boy was lacking a black male role model. Stanley Dunham chose a curious pick as a mentor for his grandson: Davis was a card-carrying member of Communist Party USA (card number 47544).

Frank Marshall Davis was a writer, poet, and political extremist who became the founding editor-in-chief of the *Chicago Star*. There he shared the op-ed page with the likes of Howard Fast, the "Stalin Prize" winner, and Senator Claude "Red" Pepper, who sponsored a bill to nationalize healthcare in the United States.

In his first *Star* column, on July 6, 1946, Davis urged the need for "fundamental change." Davis averred: "If history teaches us anything, it teaches that any fundamental change advancing society is spearheaded by strong radicals." Davis would impart this attitude to Obama.

Davis's politics were so radical that the FBI placed him under continued surveillance. He did Soviet propaganda work in his columns, at every juncture opposing U.S. attempts to slow Stalin in Europe and Mao in Asia. In December 1956, the Democrats who ran the Senate Judiciary Committee summoned Davis to Washington to testify on his activities. He pleaded the Fifth Amendment. The FBI placed him on the federal government's Security Index, which meant that he could be immediately detained or arrested in the event of a national emergency, such as a war breaking out between the United States and USSR. To repeat: in the event of a war between Russia and America, this future mentor to the future president of the United States—who would commit himself and his presidency to a campaign of "collective salvation"[15] and to "fundamentally transforming the United States of America"[16]—would have been placed under immediate arrest.[17]

The roster of Progressives for Obama was a veritable who's who of the 1960s Students for a Democratic Society (SDS). Bill Ayers and Bernardine Dohrn were thrust into the national spotlight during the 2008 presidential campaign when it became public knowledge that Obama's political career had been launched in the living room of the home of the former SDS-ers and fugitives from the FBI.[18] But Progressives for Obama flew under the radar, unnoticed even by the Right, and predictably ignored by the liberal mainstream media, which had no interest in hurting Obama by exposing the ignominious names that headlined this group of associated advocates.

It was fitting (and chilling) that the man spearheading Progressives for Obama was the same man who had spearheaded SDS: Tom Hayden. Hayden was one of the four "initiators" of Progressives for Obama, along with Barbara Ehrenreich, Bill Fletcher Jr., and Danny Glover. The group also featured a list of ninety-four formal "signers," including Mark Rudd, Vietcong go-go girl Jane Fonda, Carl Davidson, Thorne Dreyer, Daniel Ellsberg, Richard Flacks, John McAuliff, and Jay Schaffner. Columbia University was represented—by current faculty like Todd Gitlin, professor of journalism and sociology.

It is no exaggeration to say that the names on the list of Progressives for Obama resembled a roster of SDS-ers and Weathermen once called to testify before Congress for their subversive activities. These very same names appeared throughout the index of the transcripts from Congress's December 1969 SDS investigation.[19] In addition to the aforementioned names, there was also Bob Pardun, SDS education secretary from 1966 to 1967, and Paul Buhle, a professor who had recently sought to revive SDS.[20] Other SDSers-turned-Weathermen who were not formal signers for Progressives for Obama but signed online petitions supporting Obama's candidacy included Howard Machtinger, Steve Tappis, and Jeff Jones, one of the four co-authors of the 1974 Weather Underground manifesto *Prairie Fire*[21]—the statement in which, as we have seen, the signers frankly declared themselves "communist men and women, underground in the United States for more than four years" in "a guerilla organization" and called for "a revolutionary communist party in order to lead the struggle, give coherence and direction to the fight, seize power and build the new society."

Others who had been called before Congress in the 1960s, such as the pro-Stalin Maoist Michael Klonsky (co-author with Bill Ayers of books on teaching "social justice"), were represented in the 2008 list of Progressives for Obama by their relations: Anne Lowry Klonsky and Fred Klonsky. All of the Klonsky clan are involved in the field of education. In fact, the vast majority of these communists are now in education, including Ayers and Dohrn and Rudd. Along with Ayers and Dohrn, Rudd serves on the board of "Movement for a Democratic Society" (MDS), which he and others envision as a "new SDS," which he hopes to resurrect with his talks in college classrooms around the country. MDS was founded in Chicago in August 2006, and includes Jeff Jones and Barbara Ehrenreich on its board. Its chair is socialist Columbia University professor Manning Marable.[22]

Rudd, who specializes in teaching social activism, remains a stalwart proponent of communist Vietnam and Cuba, whose repressive systems he still admires. He also admires Barack Obama, whose election Rudd saw as a major "advance" and "opening" for his cause.[23]

Former SDS leader Tom Hayden—he wrote the infamous "Port Huron Statement," the SDS manifesto that marked the birth of "the New Left"—played a central role in Progressives for Obama.

After his early life establishing SDS, meeting with the Vietcong, and vigorously protesting America, Hayden went into politics, activism, and (what else?) education. Like Rudd, Ayers, Dohrn, Klonsky, and many others, Hayden came to view a quick "revolution" of the political system as too daunting, if not impossible. By 2008 he had become much more patient. He sought to advance the "progressive" cause within the established, respected Democratic Party.

Thus Hayden was thrilled about Barack Obama's presidential campaign. The man who had drafted the SDS's pivotal Port Huron statement now drafted mission statements for Progressives for Obama. Hayden wrote a piece titled "Obama and the Open and Unexpected Future," in which he raved, "I didn't

★ ★ ★

Would You Call This Progress?

Woodrow Wilson, Democratic president from 1913 to 1921, was the progressive's progressive. He has few fans among conservatives. But unlike today's progressives, he had no sympathy for communism—at least in the form he could see it taking in Russia during his presidency.

President Wilson described Bolshevism as an "ugly, poisonous thing." He alerted Americans that the Bolsheviks were engaged in a "brutal" campaign of "blood and terror," of "mass terrorism," of "indiscriminate slaughter" through "cunning" and "savage oppression." The Bolsheviks were "barbarians," "terrorists," and "tyrants." They were "violent and tyrannical." In fact, said Wilson, they were "the most consummate sneaks in the world."

Wilson warned a joint session of Congress that the Bolsheviks were pushing an "expansionist" ideology that they wanted to export "throughout the world," including to the United States.

"In the view of this Government," said Wilson's State Department in an August 1920 statement, "there cannot be any common ground upon which it can stand with a Power whose conceptions of international relations are so entirely alien to its own, so utterly repugnant to its moral sense.... We cannot recognize, hold official relations with, or give friendly reception to the agents of a government which is determined to conspire against our institutions; whose diplomats will be the agitators of dangerous revolt; whose spokesmen say that they sign agreements with no intention of keeping them."

Vladimir Lenin, in turn, despised Wilson, dismissing him as an "utter simpleton" and openly calling for the overthrow of the U.S. government.

see him coming. When I read of the young state senator with a background in community organizing who wanted to be president, I was at least sentient enough to be interested. When I read *Dreams of My Father* [sic], I was taken aback by its depth." Hayden celebrated the fact that Obama had given "his first public speech" at a rally organized by Students for Economic Democracy (the student branch of the Campaign for Economic Democracy that Hayden had chaired in 1979–1982) at Occidental College, where Hayden taught. Hayden was hooked.

Tom Hayden saw Obama's campaign as an opportunity for the fulfillment of the long-awaited hopes of "economic democracy"—what both he and Obama called "economic justice." Hayden hoped that "the Obama movement" would come to "shape progressive politics...for a generation to come." He hoped that the "progressive movement" also "might transform" Obama as well. Both could reinforce one another and fundamentally transform the nation—under the banner of "progressivism."[24]

When Obama won the election in November 2008—against John McCain, a former POW during the Vietnam War (when Hayden's pals were spitting on American soldiers and denouncing them as "fascists," "pigs," and "baby-killers")—Hayden was beside himself with joy, shocked that the American electorate had at long last voted for someone that Tom Hayden saw as his kind of president.[25]

It was a towering achievement for him and his fellow "progressive" commies in Progressives for Obama.

This group of commies and ex-commies had engaged in very shrewd strategizing to persuade moderates, independents, and traditional Democrats into voting for Obama in 2008. And that is exactly what happened. Barack Obama, red-diaper baby mentored by card-carrying Communist Party USA member Frank Marshall Davis, won the 2008 election by concealing his radicalism and winning over moderates, independents, and traditional Democrats.

Democratic Socialists, Socialist-Friendly Democrats

And President Obama is far from the only "mainstream" American politician who has been both enthusiastically supported and deeply influenced by the radical Left.

The Democratic Socialists of America (DSA) is another far-left group with disturbing connections to politicians we usually think of as mainstream. The DSA website states, "We believe that the workers and consumers who are affected by economic institutions should own and control them."[26] The Soviet leaders said just the same. (When the Soviets proclaimed that "the workers" were in charge, it merely meant that the government was in charge. The "workers," like the phrase "the masses," was merely a nebulous, wide-ranging label for a mass collective that the centralized authority was in charge of orchestrating.)

And yet, though most Americans don't know it, the DSA has some serious influence in the U.S. Congress. John Rossomando, a writer and researcher who has long investigated the DSA, estimates that some "50–60" members of the Congressional Progressive Caucus are members of the Democratic Socialists of America.[27] The Caucus is chaired by Democrat Representative Keith Ellison and, Rossomando says, "used to advertise its DSA connections a decade ago"—until more people in the general public learned about the DSA's far-left extremism. Rossomando has detailed connections between the DSA and the Democratic Party, the Congressional Progressive Caucus,[28] the Socialist International, and even Barack Obama's pre-presidential campaigns in Illinois.[29]

Asked what they really believe, most DSA members appeal to some form of so-called "democratic socialism," just as the name of their party implies. "Democratic socialists believe that both the economy and society should be run democratically," says the DSA website. Sounds good, right? Could that take place in America? Not as we know it. In the very next line, the DSA states that "To achieve a more just society, many structures of our government and economy must be radically transformed."

CPUSA Today

And then there remains that old standby of American Reds: the Communist Party USA. A review of material published by the CPUSA makes it possible to see where this top group of American commies—formerly Stalin's loyal foot soldiers in the United States—stands today.

★ ★ ★

New York City's Comradely Mayor

A striking case of a high-level comrade securing the support of millions of Democrat voters is Bill de Blasio, the current mayor of New York.

De Blasio spent his ideologically formative years stumping for the Marxist Sandinistas in Nicaragua, the nasty communist regime spearheaded by Daniel Ortega. The future New York mayor actually peddled subscriptions for the Sandinista regime's newspaper, *Barricada*, the Sandinistas' version of *Pravda*. That is not a matter of casual interest. De Blasio was, thereby, working for the communist Sandinistas, helping them spread their propaganda; their newspaper was their chief print propaganda organ. *Barricada*, as Paul Berman notes, "was the most hardline of the Sandinista publications," and was controlled by Sandinista Ministry of the Interior, Tomás Borge, the regime's enforcer, chief defense officer, and top liaison to the Soviet Bloc. It was subscriptions to this paper, the *New York Times* reported, that De Blasio spent time and energy "hawking" to other New Yorkers.[30]

De Blasio was among the leftist Catholics taken in by the ruse that was Latin American Liberation Theology. He had a queer attraction to communist tyrannies. The appeal ran so deep that he engaged in one romance in the Soviet Union and then, a decade later, he and his bride actually honeymooned in Cuba.[31] The couple somehow orchestrated their Havana honeymoon despite the U.S. embargo on travel long ago signed by President Kennedy. Bill de Blasio, regardless, went where his heart led him; he and his honey found Fidel.

And today de Blasio is no less than the Big Apple's chief political official. Now, De Blasio wages war on "inequality" and the evil rich, devoting himself to leveling incomes, just as the Sandinistas did in Nicaragua.

Immediately after the vote, one writer penned a piece titled "America's First Openly Marxist Big City Mayor."[32] Bill de Blasio shrewdly describes his ideology in the same way that American communists have cleverly done since 1917: he refers to himself as a good old-fashioned "progressive" pursuing "social justice." "Make no mistake," he declared in his mayoral victory speech, standing behind a large sign proclaiming "PROGRESS," "the people of this city have chosen a progressive path. And tonight we set forth on it—together."

That material is vast. It is available at www.cpusa.org and in the online pages of *People's World*. Especially enlightening is a glance at CPUSA's formal statements from its annual conventions, where the group's platform and priorities are regularly trotted out. Any number of these could be quoted, but a statement promoting a recent annual convention held (fittingly) in Chicago, the adopted town and ideological home of Barack Obama, and the city where the American Communist Party was founded in September 1919, is typical and telling.

The statements from that convention (and others) are strikingly like the talking points coming out of the mouth of your average left-wing Democrat these days. Portions of the promotional statement for the June 2014 Chicago convention, for instance, read like a press release from Elizabeth Warren's office, sound like a Bill de Blasio campaign rally, or smack of campaign slogans and remarks on the stump by Barack Obama, Bernie Sanders, or Hillary Clinton.

The CPUSA statement from Chicago in June 2014 began by demanding that the masses unite to "put people before profits" and then pledged to "transform" America:

> We live in a capitalist system where the 99% of people struggle every day to survive and the richest 1% control the vast majority of wealth and power. Capitalism cannot meet the needs of the vast majority.... Our schools are underfunded and essential public services are strapped and slashed. Home foreclosures are everywhere and millions of people are homeless and hungry in the richest country in the world. Racism, sexism, homophobia and all kinds of discrimination are commonplace.[33]

This is a classic anti-capitalist rant—with the addition of support for the LGBTQ agenda. As we have seen, today's communists are as likely to rally

★ ★ ★

Watermelons and Climate Communists

Why is April 22, 1970, significant? It was the first Earth Day—and the centenary of Vladimir Lenin's birth. Ever since, Earth Day has been celebrated on Lenin's birthday.

Lenin's hundredth birthday was a big deal to the communist movement (and anti-communists also find one hundred significant in relation to Marxism-Leninism—it reminds them of the hundred million dead victims of the communist ideology).

Given this interesting confluence of events, it seems more than ironic that so many former communists, when the Cold War ended, ran for the woods. Really, the environment was the perfect refuge. Rocks and frogs cannot tell the commie "environmentalist" to go jump in a lake. Trees cannot speak. Unfortunately, nature has no audible voice that can call communists tyrants and tell whiny activists to take a hike back to their air-conditioned offices in Manhattan or coffee shops in San Francisco. Thus, it makes an ideal constituency for communists. Plus, environmentalism is the perfect excuse for doing what communists already want to do: wield government power to control people and their property.

Both communists and environmentalists view people as a drain on limited resources. Both embrace mass collectivism and redistributionism—not to mention government control and seizure of property—as solutions. Moreover, communists and environmentalists alike remonstrate against capitalism, profits, corporations, industry, free markets, the West.

Old-line communists (especially the Soviet variety) didn't give a damn about forests and vast landscapes. The forest that the Soviets found most useful was the Katyn Woods, where they exterminated thousands of Polish military officers. The most useful landscape that the Kremlin protected was snow-covered Siberia, perfect for housing countless Soviet citizens begging for basic civil liberties. Sure, Moscow did some preservation—constantly re-embalming the jaundiced corpse of Lenin planted in Red Square. Actually, the post-death history of Lenin's body is a cautionary tale about the challenge of recycling: it is costly and does not work well.

For an example of just how polluting a system can be, look no further than the countries in the Soviet Bloc, where filthy water and air was everywhere.[34] Or at China today, where in some places people have to wear surgical masks whenever they go outside, just to breathe safely.[35] To genuinely clean up an environment, capitalism is the key. Wealthy countries have the disposable income to afford it. When a population is starving from communism, its concern is not "paper or plastic" but rice or an empty stomach.

If Marx and Engels were alive today, they would be writing manifestos on socialism and ecology at some silly university. Today, their disciples at *People's World* urge left-wingers everywhere to "Get on board the... Climate Train."[36] The head of the Communist Party USA hails modern ecological warriors as "climate justice activists" battling for "green socialism."[37] Today's climate commies have shrewdly found a way to cloak their red ideology in green camouflage. They are "watermelons": green on the outside, red on the inside.

against "homophobia" as against the free market. The cultural Marxists have as many if not more seats at today's Red dinner table as the traditional class-economic Marxists. (Joe Stalin and Nikita Khrushchev certainly were not gay rights guys. But today's communists fully grasp the advantage of issues like "gay marriage" as long-awaited wedges to separate or "abolish" or "transcend" the nuclear family—a goal that communists have touted since Marx's *Communist Manifesto*.)

"Climate change," too, has been eagerly embraced by communists. "We also face an urgent threat to the very survival of life on the planet," declared CPUSA's June 2014 statement. "Climate change is the byproduct of capitalism." Whatever it takes to bring down business and those evil profits.

Sounding like a run-of-the-mill university professor or a *New York Times* editorialist, the comrades at CPUSA lament that "It is working people, the poor and communities of color who face the most direct consequences of global warming and the poisoning of our environment."

And it never takes CPUSA long to zero in on the real enemy, which just happens to be the shared enemy of every liberal Democrat: the Republican Party and the "right-wingers":

The main obstacle to progress today is right-wing extremism. Right wing spokespeople and groups represent and are funded by the most conservative sections of the rich and powerful.

The extreme right, which now dominates the Republican Party, is seeking to roll back all the social and economic rights that working people fought for and won. They want to take the country back to a time before marriage equality, before voting rights, before women's reproductive rights, before the right to a union. It seems at times that they want to take us back to the days of slavery.

Democracy itself is under attack from this far-right group and their servants in the [sic] Washington and statehouses around the country.

It's increasingly clear to millions of people: another world is possible and necessary. Another U.S. is possible too. Capitalism cannot solve these problems, we need a socialist USA....

The Communist Party of the United States of America has a 95 year history of fighting for democracy, jobs, equality and socialism.

Our party reflects the diverse working class of our country. Our members are of all the races, ethnicities and nationalities that make up the rich fabric of U.S. society. We are native born and immigrant. We are men and women. We are young and old. We are straight and gay....

We join the fight against the right wing today and build for socialist tomorrow.

We are proud to announce our 30th National Convention, June 13–15, 2014 in Chicago, the city of our birth.

Leading up to our convention, we will discuss the challenges and opportunities that working people face today. We will share

> experiences and discuss how our party can more effectively help build a people's movement capable of transforming the country and making the future brighter for everyone....
>
> Onward to Chicago![38]

Note once more the communists' use of the words "socialism" and "democracy" as synonymous with their own communist goals. And note, yet again, the remarkable degree of overlap between the language and goals of the Communist Party USA and the language and goals of "mainstream" politicians in the Democratic Party. Presidential candidate Barack Obama talked about "fundamentally transforming the United States of America"; the CPUSA talks about "transforming the country." And on the economy, on gender issues, on the environment, the stated goals of the current leadership of the Democratic Party are frighteningly close to the statements coming from the Communist Party USA, which was the official representative of the Soviet Union until its late demise. No wonder the far Left can work in harmony with the current leadership of the Democratic Party and the chief Democrat who occupies or seeks the White House. There was a time when the American Communist Party despised and demonized even liberal Democrats like Woodrow Wilson and FDR,[39] not to mention more conservative Democratic Party standard-bearers such as Harry Truman and John F. Kennedy. That is no longer the case. Conservative Democrats seem to be an extinct species, and today's "liberal" or "progressive" Democrats are far to the Left of Democrats of the past—so far Left that they are kindred spirits to the communists in the CPUSA and allies in their "onward!" march to "transform" America.

Consider the gushing excitement expressed by CPUSA chairman Sam Webb (the predecessor to John Bachtell) after Obama's 2012 reelection. "We meet on the heels of an enormous people's victory," Webb reported to CPUSA's National Committee on November 17, 2012. "An African American president

★ ★ ★

My, How Times Have Changed

The Democrats were not always dependable allies to the communists. Unbeknownst to liberals who have elevated the Kennedy family to their progressive Mt. Rushmore, the early Kennedy clan was intensely anti-communist.

The family was close to infamous anti-communist Joe McCarthy, a fellow Irish Catholic who often visited the family compound in Hyannisport and even dated one of the Kennedy girls. Bobby Kennedy would choose Joe as the godfather to one of his daughters.

Bobby had been a staff attorney to McCarthy, whom he greatly admired.[40] When McCarthy died in 1957, Bobby was distraught. "Very upsetting for me," he wrote in his diary when he got the news. "I dismissed the office [staff] for the day. It was all very difficult for me as I feel that I have lost an important part of my life." Bobby quickly caught a plane to be at McCarthy's burial in Wisconsin, where he was weeping so hard that he could not leave his car.[41]

RFK was not only anti-communist; he had at best a love-hate relationship with liberals. "What my father said about businessmen applies to liberals," said RFK. "They're sons of bitches."[42] He said liberals were "in love with death."[43]

RFK was especially appalled at the naïveté of liberals when it came to communism. As was his brother.

"The communist," said Senator John F. Kennedy in June 1955, had a "fear" of Christianity and allowed "no room for God." For communists, "The claim of the State must be total, and no other loyalty, and no other philosophy of life, can be tolerated." They "have substituted dialectical materialism for faith in God" and endeavored "to make the worship of the State the ultimate objective of life."[44]

Once he became president, JFK warned Americans of their "atheistic foe" in Moscow, of the "fanaticism and fury" of communism, and the "communist conspiracy" that "represents a final enslavement." Kennedy declared, "The enemy is the communist system itself—implacable, insatiable, unceasing in its drive for world domination.... This [is] a struggle for supremacy between two conflicting ideologies: freedom under God versus ruthless, godless tyranny."[45]

was reelected to the Presidency, the Democrats unexpectedly strengthened their hand in the Senate and House, new progressive voices, like Elizabeth

Warren, are coming to Washington, and victories, including for marriage equality, occurred at the state level.... All this bodes well for the future." Webb was celebrating because "[f]inally," he and his fellow communists would be able to "build the Party"—the Communist Party, that is—with "confidence, spirit, and boldness."[46]

Obama offered a truly new day and new dawn for America's communists.

The Seventeenth International Meeting

Really, any statement from the many annual meetings and conventions of communists could be recapped here as a telltale sign of how silly and yet scary their proposals are—and how uncannily similar today's Marxists are to today's Democrats and liberals. Let me give another example, this one from the Seventeenth International Meeting of Communist and Workers' Parties, which was held in Turkey in November 2015. The words I will quote come from the CPUSA's official statement, which is still posted at the website of CPUSA. It was presented and submitted to the conference by Tony Pecinovsky of CPUSA's National Board.[47]

The statement opened with "heartfelt condolences" to "our Turkish comrades" for losses suffered "at the hands of reactionary forces in your country." "Reactionary forces"? What was he referring to?

An American reader might be prompted to wonder which group of Reaganite conservatives had done what to the people of Turkey. Who was Pecinovsky talking about? It turns out that "reactionary forces" was a reference to radical Muslim jihadists (though of course no such words were used in his statement—no one in the Communist Party, the Obama Administration, or the Hillary Clinton State Department would ever use that kind of language). "The cowardly suicide bombing of the Ankara peace rally illustrates the depths of barbarity to which right-wing forces will go to attempt to stifle the voice of the people," lamented Pecinovsky on behalf of the

American Communist Party. Islamist jihadists were not called out as Islamist jihadists but as "right-wing forces."

"For the left," said James Burnham, the great ex-communist, "the preferred enemy is always to the right." And thus, a Muslim suicide bomber is morphed into a handy "right-wing" enemy.

But jihadists were not the only "reactionary forces" that Pecinovsky talked about. The preferred enemy and focus of this Communist Party USA address in Istanbul, Turkey, was American conservatives: "My remarks will focus on four overlapping, interconnected items that are central components to the struggle against reaction in the United States," said CPUSA spokesman Tony Pecinovsky. "First and foremost, I will briefly touch on the upcoming 2016 U.S. presidential elections; second, the ongoing and emerging challenge to racism, exemplified by #BlackLivesMatter; third, the 'Fight For $15' and a union, led by fast food workers and their allies; and forth [sic], a few thoughts regarding the international situation."

★ ★ ★

Who's the Reactionary Now?

It's hilariously amusing to observe communists framing their *opposition* as reactionary when, in truth, it is communists who are fighting for the ideas of two dead nineteenth-century white German philosophers. It is equally ironic to see communists hoist the mantle of "progress," as they always do, given that their two-century-old ideology surely meets the definition of a regressive one. The word "reactionary" nonetheless has long been a pejorative that the American Left uses against anyone and everyone on the political Right, including American conservatives.

It was yet another official Communist Party statement that was hard to differentiate from the campaign agenda of the Democratic Party.

"The importance of the 2016 U.S. presidential elections cannot be exaggerated," insisted Pecinovsky. "Americans are increasingly upset about the growing economic inequality in our country." He hailed heroes of the modern Left, from communists to the Occupy Wall Street movement. (That movement epitomized the left-wing surge of the first two years of the Obama presidency, during the Nancy Pelosi–Harry Reid Democratic Congress, before so many Democrats in Congress were bounced out of office in the November 2010 election.)

"The Occupy Wall Street slogan of the 1 percent versus the 99 percent has taken root in public awareness of the mounting and glaring inequities of our current system," said Pecinovsky. "Continuing economic insecurity, declining standards of living, hemorrhaging of jobs, persistent structural racism evidenced in a variety of toxic forms, environmental degradation and insecurity, austerity cuts in essential public services, crises in education—these and more weigh heavily on the 99 percent of Americans who make up our working class."

It was a direct echo of the 2016 platform from the Democratic National Convention in Philadelphia. "A powerful extreme right has emerged in our country over three decades beginning with the Reagan and even Nixon years," said Pecinovsky. Sounding like DNC head Debbie Wasserman Schultz, the CPUSA spokesman added, "With the 2008 election of President Barack Obama, a liberal who is the nation's first African American president, this extreme right went into overdrive. Having achieved domination of the Republican Party, the far-right now controls both houses of Congress and many state governments, and has a big presence—often forming the majority—in our nation's highest court, the Supreme Court."

Pecinovsky was just warming up: "These elements, very well financed by the most right-wing sectors in our ruling circles, such as the oil industry, are viciously racist, militarist, anti-union, hostile to environmental protection, women, immigrants, sex and gender equality, and public services."

Sex and gender equality? This was a curious message to be vocalizing against Republicans in Muslim Turkey! Nonetheless, these days American communists wave the LGBTQ rainbow banner just as enthusiastically as American liberals, "progressives," and Democrats. So the CPUSA was going to wave the flag proudly even amid a sea of gay-denouncing Muslims in Istanbul.

Besides, noted Pecinovsky, the Republicans' "foreign policy is aggressive, shoot-first, racist," and they "are an obstacle to any social progress in our country. Having captured significant position of power, they have forced progressive movements into a defensive posture, fighting just to protect or even re-win past gains. Now they are intent on recapturing the White House, putting them in virtually total control."

And so, said the leader of the Democratic—nay, correction—*Communist* Party, "We consider the defeat of the far-right Republicans an essential first step in the struggle for a people's agenda and ultimately socialism." He insisted, "The race for the next presidency has already begun. In our two-party system, the race is between two parties, Republican and Democratic. One the one hand, we have the Republican Party, now dominated by rabid, hate-filled, racist, anti-worker, anti-immigrant, anti-women, anti-environment, anti-LGBT, anti-people, pro-corporate profit warmongers."

Surely the CPUSA spokesman must have been putting in his resume to apply for a job with the DNC.

"Domestically and internationally," he went on, "this group of reactionaries are unanimous. They want anti-immigrant border walls built, unions broken and women's rights smashed... They are racist, sexist, homophobic and anti-Muslim."

Hold on there, comrade! And Muslims are, what, homo*philes*?

One can imagine the raised eyebrows in the room as Comrade Tony continued to hammer the homophobes in the racist, sexist GOP, who also hate clean air and bathe in Big Oil: "With strong backing from Big Oil, they deny the reality of the emerging climate crisis. And their only loyalty is corporate profits."

The CPUSA guy even took time to inform the international comrades of Republicans' ongoing advancement of a dangerous "right-dominated U.S.

Supreme Court," who legally backed the (here was more Obama-ish rhetoric) "millionaires and billionaires."

"Make no mistake about it," he told the assembled communists, "the Republican presidential candidates work at the behest of unrestricted aggressive capitalism and imperialism."

And where are the angels in the political system? The Communist Party USA head pointed them out for the international Marxists: they were in the Democratic Party: "On the other side in our two-party system are a range of Democratic Party candidates who take a generally pro-worker, pro-women's rights, pro-immigrant, anti-racist, pro-environment, less militarist stance. They include Hillary Clinton, the frontrunner, a defender of capitalism who believes it must be curbed and regulated to be more people-friendly." Republicans, bad; Hillary, good. "She has stood up to vicious attacks from the ultra-right. If elected, she would break new ground as the first woman president of the U.S. They also include Bernie Sanders, an independent senator from Vermont who is a self-avowed socialist and calls for a 'political revolution.'"

Really, either Bernie or Hillary would do, as far as CPUSA was concerned. "Even if he does not win the Democratic nomination," the American Communist Party spokesman said of Bernie Sanders, "his grassroots campaign has attracted enormous excitement and very importantly has brought discussion of socialism out of the shadows and back into the political mainstream."

The Democrats are the good guys. "Opposing the Republicans, Clinton and similar Democrats represent a more reality-based, sober section of the U.S. ruling class, which sees a need for alliance with the working class on a range of issues. Sanders represents an emerging progressive/left/working and middle class section of American politics, which sees the Democratic Party as the best vehicle for electoral battles at this time in our two-party system. Together, they reflect a shift in public opinion and growing mass demand to seriously address mounting income inequality, persistent racism, the crisis of climate change, immigrant rights, stop attacks on women's rights, defend and expand voting rights and access, advance equality for LGBT Americans."

By the time he was finished, Pecinovsky was making very specific policy pitches that were exact echoes of the Democratic agenda—for "green jobs," Barack Obama's Cuba policy, Obama's Iran deal, and, naturally, the $15-per-hour minimum wage touted by Bernie and backed by Hillary and the vast swell of unions who supported the Democrats. He also made numerous pitches for Occupy Wall Street and Black Lives Matter. "Tellingly," he said, "the Obama administration and Sanders and Clinton have all called for a $15-an-hour minimum wage, while all of the Republican candidates oppose increasing the minimum wage—and some Republicans oppose having a minimum wage, period."

On and on the CPUSA statement went, with more and more of the same. Without any doubt, and no exaggeration whatsoever, the Communist Party USA statement was a statement on behalf of the Democratic Party in the 2016 election and against the Republican Party. CPUSA was on the same page as the Democratic Party at the seventeenth international communist congress.

Pecinovsky concluded his talk in Istanbul with this ringing call to support "fraternal parties": "The CPUSA and our sister publication the *People's World* are both eager to work with comrades and fraternal parties to accomplish the most rewarding of all tasks—the winning of socialism! In solidarity!"

And especially, in solidarity with the Democrats.

"How to Better Unite the Left"

Finally, one last look at how today's commies are vigorously pushing for a united front of the wider American Left. This is obviously an overriding priority.

The *People's World* edition of June 12, 2013, is just one of hundreds of examples that could be cited in which today's communists have heralded a hopeful new moment in uniting the American Left.[48] Emboldened by the election and reelection of Barack Obama, plus major victories on everything from Obamacare to the defeat of the Defense of Marriage Act to the Boy Scouts' rejection—under extreme outside pressure—of their historical moral-Biblical beliefs on sexuality, the Marxist Left is flying high. They are especially confident about the cultural issues, sure that everyday Americans will continue to give them the green light to fundamentally transform America.

And so, *People's World* ballyhooed a June 5 event in which the CPUSA, the Democratic Socialists of America, the Freedom Road Socialists, and the so-called Committees of Correspondence for Democracy and Socialism came together to discuss "how to better unite the left."[49] Playing host, fittingly, was the worst union in America, the one gleefully marching America toward Greece: the SEIU. All the fellow travelers packed the New York City union hall of SEIU 1199 United Healthcare Workers East.

People's World reported that the four organizations have been working together over the past several years in the "peace, labor, youth, racial equality and other movements" and had more recently initiated plans on how to "enhance left unity between the groups and more broadly."

One of the comrades, CPUSA rep Libero Della Piana, stated, "Left unity should always be the outcome of the struggle.... It should go without saying that left unity cannot distract us from the current democratic and class struggles... A bigger, broader movement more engaged in the struggles will create the conditions for a vibrant left of greater size and scope."

What does that mean? Who or what will be part of that "bigger, broader movement" of "greater size and scope?"

Or, to quote Maria Svart, national director of the Democratic Socialists: "How do we expand? We need to build a movement that is democratic; it needs to be rooted in American realities; it needs to learn from American movements e.g., civil rights, the feminist movement. We need to take power seriously and not be satisfied being a thoroughly marginalized movement." She likewise insisted on building a larger "movement for a longer term," seeking out "social forces within capitalism to change the system."

People's World concluded its report on the "unity" event with words of wisdom from one attendee, the founder of (no kidding) *Jacobin* magazine, who exhorted his fellow leftists, "We should take some of the spirit of Occupy Wall Street, where there was a fierce sense of urgency."[50]

Overall, the lesson and general thrust of the sentiments from these socialists and communists was that new allies must be carefully sought out, identified, upheld, tapped—in a word, used.

In that sense, today's commies are little different from yesterday's commies. They, too, are counting on a large enough pool of suckers—that is, liberal dupes who will wittingly or unwittingly help them advance their agenda of fundamental transformation.

That concept—echoed in Barack Obama's campaign promise that "We are five days away from fundamentally transforming the United States of America"[51]—is the heart of the radical-left project.

Fundamental Transformation

I will give the last word in this chapter on "Communism Today" to John Bachtell, chair of Communist Party USA, writing in the socialism series for *People's World* under the headline, "Envisioning a modern, democratic, peaceful, and green socialism."

Bachtell started with a quote from Marx's *The German Ideology*: "[Socialism] is for us not a state of affairs which is to be established, an ideal to which reality [will] have to adjust itself. We call [socialism] the real movement which abolishes the present state of things. The conditions of this movement result from the premises now in existence."[52] This is actually a better and more revealing definition of communism than one might sense at first glance.

Bachtell argues that the "idea of socialism" must be thought of in ways "different from the formulas we on the left may have relied upon in the past." He calls for "A revolutionary reorganization of society to one that is people-centered, democratic, peaceful, and in harmony with nature" (note the green-olatry). He believes that a "social revolution" will be precipitated not by a mass "general strike" or an implosion of the economy or the working class overthrowing the old ruling class and hoisting the red flag. In his view, a socialist revolution is not a single episodic event but, rather, "the product of a complex and contested process, a transition orchestrated by real people consciously and creatively shaping their conditions of existence to make their lives more livable, secure, enjoyable, and meaningful." It will involve no less than "multiple stages of radical systemic, economic, political, social, and cultural change that addresses urgent and concrete needs. And it will certainly be an ongoing process." Bachtell sees socialism coming in "waves": "I like to envision the historic realization of socialism as a series of epic waves, characterized by ebbs and flows, advances and defeats."

Bachtell lays out that history. He says that the first wave featured the "utopian socialist communities" in the United States during the nineteenth century, which he estimates (correctly) numbered in the hundreds. These presumably included the (failed) ideological colonies erected by the likes of Robert Owen, Charles Fourier, Albert Brisbane, and John Humphrey Noyes. The second wave, says Bachtell, "encompassed 20th century socialism, born during the stormy era of war and revolution beginning in 1917." This was Bolshevism, Marxism-Leninism, Stalinism. This wave, states Bachtell, was characterized by centrally planned economies and full state ownership of the means of production. "Among the great achievements," of these states, insists Bachtell, "were rapid industrialization, elimination of illiteracy, universal health care and education." He concedes that these totalitarian hellholes had a few "democratic shortcomings, including constitutionally-enshrined one-party rule, political repression, lack of an independent press, and dogmatic approaches to ideology." Yes, one supposes so.

And now, today, Bachtell foresees a modern dialectical evolution developing before our very eyes, a third wave unfolding amid a completely new historical context: "the post-collapse of 20th century socialism, the deepening crisis of late capitalism, extreme wealth inequality, the displacement of millions of workers through automation, and an ecological crisis that threatens mankind's very survival" (again, note the climate communism).

The current head of Communist Party USA believes that America is on the cusp of that third wave, which will include great strides for "women's equality; free speech; LGTBQIA equality; disability rights; immigrant rights; and climate justice movements." Leading these efforts will be "an even broader and more diverse future coalition of socialist forces."

Here, Bachtell gets detailed with very specific policy prescriptions, the list of which ought to scare the daylights out of anyone who loves limited government, private property, and America as it was founded:

> Ultimately it means transferring all natural resources and the energy production sector to public ownership managed under democratic authority. It means a radical reallocation of social expenditures needed to rebuild the nation's infrastructure from coast to coast, retrofitting for conservation, and converting to renewables.
>
> It means a guaranteed wage and retraining for new jobs for all those who are displaced during a just transition or whose jobs have been eliminated due to automation (although here more far reaching reforms are needed like a shorter work week with no

> cut in pay). It means allocating necessary resources to adapt to the inevitable changes wrought by global warming, including extreme weather events, coastal flooding, relocating entire communities, building massive infrastructure works, overcoming drought, and deforestation.
>
> The immense resources needed can only come through a redistribution of society's wealth, which will require a conscious and determined struggle against the capitalist class. The battle will be over who pays for it: the ruling circles or the working class and people?
>
> A similar redistribution struggle will be fought to ensure a $15/hour minimum wage or a living wage, universal health care, and free college tuition.
>
> This will be part of the process of developing mechanisms for directing social investment and imposing further restrictions on capital and the anarchy of the market economy. This implies the need to raise Earth consciousness and intertwine it with class, racial, and gender consciousness.

That is a good summary of the current communist agenda, from environmentalism to transgenderism to using sexism or racism or whatever other "ism" can be coopted for the grand takedown of the America founded by Jefferson and Madison and Hamilton and friends. But it is now also the agenda of countless "mainstream" American politicians—in fact, of one of our two major political parties. America has just survived eight years under a Democrat President who had communist influences and who did his best to implement certain of these goals—to fundamentally transform our country. Which brings us back to Marx.

John Bachtell wrapped up his analysis with probably the single most important quotation from Marx. If Marx ever said anything that was worth remembering about his idiotic and murderous ideology, it is this: "To again quote Marx," wrote Bachtell, "socialism is 'the real movement that abolishes the present state of things.'" That it does. That it does.

In communism, nothing is permanent, including the first things that should never be tampered with. All Marxists agree. Take her down, baby. Take her down. America—that is, America as you knew it—rest in peace. Fundamental transformation is the watchword of the Left's new revolution. Goodbye, America.

CHAPTER 14

Commies Just Love Blacks and Women

As we have seen in the last two chapters, communists have made great progress influencing the political and civil life of the United States. Marxist radicals from the '60s counterculture have dug in at our universities and particularly at the education departments that train the teachers who staff our public schools and educate every generation of Americans. Communists have more influence in the political process than they could have ever have dreamed in the days of the Cold War, or after the collapse of the Soviet Union. In Barack Obama, Americans elected a communist-inspired radical who worked to fundamentally transform the United States. Numerous other elected officials from the Democratic Party—and in fact that Party's current agenda—reflect communist aspirations.

But despite these successes, communists in the United States have not entirely given up their penchant for chaos. In fact, they have been present in the mob violence that has swept through American cities in response to shootings of young black men by white police officers. And this is only the latest chapter in a long, long story. Since the earliest days of the Bolshevik Revolution and the Comintern, both Russian and American communists

Did you know?

- ★ The Communist Party USA was planning to establish a Soviet "Negro Republic" in the American South
- ★ The black poet Langston Hughes visited the Soviet Union and decided to reject Jesus for Marx and Stalin
- ★ An African-American former member of CPUSA testified that the Party used white women as "political prostitutes" to control its "Negro lickspittles"

plotted to exploit tragic racial injustices and exacerbate dangerous racial tensions in America for the purpose of fomenting a revolution.

That's what communists do: pit one group of citizens against another group in the hopes of bringing on a class struggle (or, in this case, a race war) that will surely usher in the utopia they promise. And since the dawn of cultural Marxism, communists—who had already been at war with the traditional family since the days of Marx and Engels—have been attempting to convince women that they are an oppressed class that can win their freedom only by joining the revolution.

Actual physical violence is only one aspect of the communists' revolutionary plans. But it is still a part of their program.

Race-Baiting in Pursuit of Revolution

The Revolutionary Communist Party literally wants to divide America by race. Peter Wilson notes in the *American Thinker* that the Revolutionary Communist Party's 2010 constitution includes a call for black Americans to unite into a separate republic in "the southern part of the former imperialist United States of America." The formation of that republic would be by a "special vote, in which only African-Americans would be eligible to participate." This is part of a broader plan by the RCP to generate "autonomy" for "minority and formerly oppressed nationalities." Wilson lists two other core RCP objectives, which extend beyond African-Americans to other ethnic minorities. In Wilson's words:

- The same conditions hold for Mexican-Americans in "what was the southwest region of the former United States of America," and in other cities/regions with significant black or Hispanic populations.

- Native Americans will be granted autonomy with "the necessary territories but also the resources." In this, they would receive "special assistance and support."

As Wilson notes, while Bob Avakian and his RCP accuse "Amerikkka" of racism, they are fighting for the establishment of what would be explicitly segregated regions of blacks, Hispanics, and Native Americans.[1]

This is nothing new for communists, who have always claimed to speak for black Americans. They see themselves as the voice of the downtrodden. They are the self-appointed representatives of the teeming masses, the common man, the repressed minority. They have long insisted that they are at one with black Americans, their "Negro" brother and sister comrades.

Not a New Strategy

There has been a century-long push by communists—particularly the CPUSA—to get African-Americans into the Marxist-Leninist movement, if not as Party members then at least as supporters or as accomplices acquiescing to the objectives of the revolution. This aggressive campaign is largely unknown to the American public. Whether American communists have ever actually given a rip about black Americans is a good question, but there is no question they have pushed hard to try to enlist the support of this particular racial minority. Communists have worked to promote and exploit the image of African-Americans as hapless, helpless victims, the subjugated, suffering servants of a racist, rapacious, callous American capitalist system that would prefer them in chains or shot dead in the streets. This is the picture inevitably painted by communist groups—from the CPUSA in the 1930s to the Revolutionary Communist Party today.

The exploitation of African-Americans for world revolution goes way back to the early 1920s, and all the way to Moscow. It was one of the earliest initiatives of the Soviet Comintern.

From 1922 to 1930, the Comintern and its lackeys in the American Communist Party launched a long-term effort to target black Americans. The Comintern ordered the American Communist Party to identify black causes in the Jim Crow South in particular.[2] This push to recruit African-Americans is one of the most salient features of the declassified Comintern Archives on the Communist Party USA, easily viewable at the Library of Congress, which purchased a mass holding of Comintern archives from Boris Yeltsin's post-communist Russia in the early 1990s. Having read hundreds of reels of microfiche from these archives, I can report that the CPUSA's effort to recruit "Negroes" is one of the things that most consistently strikes and alarms the researcher.

In 1922, the Comintern approved a fat $300,000 subsidy to the American Communist Party for purposes of propaganda among black Americans. This was no small sum, especially for a communist state that was financing itself with stolen valuables from churches and whatever else could be pilfered. The Comintern was already actively fomenting uprisings in countries from Hungary to Bavaria. The Red Army had just gotten its collective butt kicked in Poland, a defeat that sent Lenin into yet more fits of whirling rage. The Bolsheviks were still licking their wounds after a bloody three years of civil war. So to be tossing this kind of cash at the American South was quite a statement of Marxist-Leninist priorities. And it was just the start.

In 1925, the Comintern selected twelve black American communists to come to Moscow for training. These "Negroes" were to be Marxist-Leninist apostles, disciples baptized at the Kremlin and readied for their great communist commissioning. The most trusted of the twelve disciples were returned home with more funds for further propaganda.[3]

Lovett Fort-Whiteman: "The Reddest of the Blacks"—and the Deadest

Among the small group of black Americans selected in 1925 by the Comintern to come to Moscow for training was Lovett Fort-Whiteman. No other African-American so impressed the Soviets. *Time* magazine had labeled him "the Reddest of the Blacks."[4] He was designated for special assignment at Moscow's prestigious Lenin School. Fort-Whiteman was a force.

In that same year he founded the American Negro Labor Congress in Chicago, a mobilization of black workers organized by the Party. The collection on Fort-Whiteman in Communist Party USA archives at Tamiment Library in New York reveals him convening the congress of "working class negroes" in Chicago on October 25, 1925. "The fundamental aim in calling the American Negro Labor Congress is to establish in the life of the American Negro working class an organization which may serve as a medium through which the American Communist Party may reach and influence the Negro working class," said Fort-Whiteman, "and at the same time constitute something of a recruiting ground for the party." He was among seventeen charter signers, at least six of whom (himself included) were Communist Party members.[5]

Their "call to action" was published in the *Daily Worker*, which was jazzed up by the prospect of recruiting African Americans to the cause. Its pages sang the hosannas of a "Negro Sanhedrin" that would organize the black working class.[6]

Fort-Whiteman traveled to Moscow for the Fifth World Congress of the Third International, initially under the name, "James Jackson." There he excitedly promised that "Negroes are destined to be the most revolutionary class in America." A delegate to the Sixth Congress of the Communist International, he was the second "American Negro delegate" to come to Moscow (after Otto Huiswoud)[7] and the first black American to undergo Comintern training at the Lenin School.[8]

In 1930, Fort-Whiteman moved to the USSR, proclaiming that he was "coming home to Moscow." But he ultimately found Stalin's Russia not quite as agreeable as he had thought. By the latter 1930s he had had enough and wanted to return to America, which apparently wasn't so bad after all. The Soviets, naturally, refused. The freedom to emigrate was one of those fundamental American rights that did not exist in the USSR.

Freedom of expression was another. And when Fort-Whiteman dared to express misgivings about Stalin's repression, the onetime loyal Soviet patriot was accused of counter-revolutionary activities. He found himself on a one-way, no-return trip to northeastern Siberia—specifically, the frozen hell that was the Kolyma region. He did not last long.[9] In 1939, Lovett Fort-Whiteman died of mistreatment and starvation in the Gulag, though the full story of his fate was unknown for a half-century.

Comrade Fort-Whiteman had been such a loyal apparatchik, the so-called "reddest of the blacks." He had founded the American Negro Labor Congress to organize and influence and recruit the black working class for the American Communist Party. He was a faithful son of the Kremlin. Was this how Stalin treated his dutiful lieutenants? Actually, yes, it was.

In the end, Lovett Fort-Whiteman was a black man treated the same way as white men in the Soviet Union: he was murdered by the communists, just like them.

A Soviet-American "Negro Republic"

From 1928 to 1930, the Comintern doubled down. It explicitly ordered the Communist Party USA to get active in what the Kremlin called the "Black Belt," that is, the American South.

In 1930, at a Comintern conference in Moscow, a resolution was passed calling for the creation of a Soviet-directed and controlled "Negro Republic" among America's Southern states. Yes, chew that one over: the Soviet Comintern, working through American communists, actually crafted plans for a "separate Negro state," a segregated "Negro Republic," in the South. The plan was to foment an African-American rebellion within the South, which would join forces with a workers' uprising in the North. Together, black Americans and communist Americans would then occupy and lay siege to the United States, reconstituting the entire nation as a Soviet sister state.

The U.S. government did not learn about this Soviet scheme for black Americans until years later, in Congressional testimony from sources that

★ ★ ★

Marx over Jesus

One enthusiastic African-American communist who fared better than Fort-Whiteman was the poet Langston Hughes, who famously said, "Put one more 'S' in the USA to make it Soviet. The USA when we take control will be the USSA."[10] Hughes urged the masses to rise up and battle for the "great red flag... of the [Communist] Internationale." The black poet made pilgrimage to Moscow, where he was smitten with the totalitarian state—and found his god. "There," he swooned, "it seemed to me that Marxism had put into practical being many of the precepts which our own Christian America had not yet been able to bring to life."[11] He penned this poem:

Goodbye Christ, Lord Jehovah,
Beat it on away from here, make way for
a new guy with no religion at all,
A real guy named Marx, Communism,
Lenin, Peasant, Stalin, worker, me.[12]

Just another ridiculously embarrassing fool for the Russkies. But the communist Langston Hughes had—and still has—influence among both his fellow intellectuals and apparently mainstream Democrats. He was quoted by Democratic Party vice presidential candidate Tim Kaine in commendation of Hillary Clinton for her historic presidential run in 2016.[13]

★ ★ ★

Thank the McCarthyites

For the revelations about how communists were exploiting black Americans and attempting to start a race war, we can thank the anti-communist investigators that liberals demonize and portray as slack-jawed red-baiters and McCarthyites: the House Committee on Un-American Activities, the Senate Judiciary Committee, President Harry Truman's office of attorney general, and the Left's longtime enemy, J. Edgar Hoover's FBI. Only as a result of their efforts did we learn about the Comintern's plans for the American South and the willing cooperation of the CPUSA.

had bolted the Party. As always, American communists concealed their revolutionary collaboration with the terroristic foreign regime in Russia.

Sworn testimony about the plan was provided by several formerly communist African-Americans to Congress beginning in November 1939 and continuing through the 1950s. Congress published the testimony in several reports, including a major December 1954 investigation titled "The American Negro in the Communist Party."

The best source was William Odell Nowell, a heroic black American who earned the eternal enmity of his erstwhile comrades when he told Congress about the secret Soviet-directed scheme. In 1929, Nowell had been sent to Moscow as a CPUSA representative, where he participated in several meetings held by the Comintern's "Negro department." Those discussions led the Comintern's executive committee to issue the resolution to the CPUSA formally establishing the program to bring about a "Negro Republic" in the American South, which, Nowell testified, would be under direct control of the Soviet leadership—that is, under the thumb of Joseph Stalin.

The plot included black American communists like Nowell and self-styled white "progressives" from the North, such as Sol Auerbach, a Communist Party hack who had trained in the USSR. Using his Party name, James S. Allen, Auerbach headed to the South in mid-July 1930 to launch a Party newspaper, the *Southern Worker*, to mobilize African Americans to separate from the rest of America.

Saluting the Scottsboro Boys

Once on the ground in the South, American communists searched for political, cultural, and social causes to exploit in order to sow racial division and portray America as the world's most racist country—and recruit black Americans to the banner of the Soviet hammer and sickle.

Their timing was exquisite. When a genuine civil rights tragedy, the case of the Scottsboro boys, hit in 1931, CPUSA was on site and ready for action. The comrades wasted no time converting the Scottsboro case into a major communist campaign.

Briefly, this is what happened at Scottsboro: On March 25, 1931, two white women, Victoria Price and Ruby Bates, were said to have been raped by nine black teens along the railroad from Chattanooga to Memphis. The black boys had hopped a train ride that day, as had the two girls, who were with two white boys. A fight broke out, with the white boys tossed off the train, leaving the white girls and black boys together. The white boys informed the nearest stationmaster that they had been in a gang fight with the black boys. At the next stop, a town called Paint Rock, Alabama, a group of local white thugs took the law into their hands and "arrested" the black boys, transporting them to jail cells in nearby Scottsboro. The charge was that they had raped the white girls.

As news spread, enraged whites gathered outside the jail, ready to form a lynch job. Local authorities guaranteed the seething vigilantes that justice would be hastily served, promising quick trials and verdicts. On cue, five days later, on March 30, 1931, an all-white jury indicted the nine boys.

The case of the Scottsboro Boys was a serious miscarriage of justice. And American communists saw it as a delicious opportunity to swoop in and promote their own agenda. They attempted to hijack the case and the cause of the Scottsboro Boys.

The goal was not only to attract black Americans to the Communist Party—and also liberals, "progressives," and various fellow travelers and

★ ★ ★

Some Communists Are More Equal Than Others

The House Committee on Un-American Activities reported that the white comrades were not exactly looking up to their black comrades; in fact, the white boys were looking down at the black boys, telling them what to do. Federal investigators found that of 5,395 leading members of CPUSA, only 411 were black, far below the percentage of black Americans in the population as a whole.[14] Negroes could become black commies, so long as they obeyed the white commies in charge.

naïve "social justice" types—but, most of all, to portray the United States as an inherently racist, unfair, and nefarious nation where miscarriages of justice are the norm. Only the world of wondrous Soviet communism and the ideals of the far Left could spare America from its malicious, repressive capitalist system.

And how fruitful were the communists' efforts?

The case of the Scottsboro boys succeeded in drawing some black Americans into the Party, but only some. Actually, very few. In its December 1954 report on "The American Negro in the Communist Party," the House Committee on Un-American Activities (also known as "HUAC") reported that after decades of attempts by the Comintern and CPUSA to try to recruit African Americans, to spawn revolution among them, and to give them their marching orders for a revolution to create a "Negro republic" under Soviet command in the American South, communists had failed miserably in their efforts to attract black Americans.

While the House Committee found no evidence that Communist Party USA and its Moscow masters had attracted a mass swell of black Americans, it is not necessarily the quantity of recruits that counts. It is the quality that matters. At least one African-American attracted to the Communist Party by the Scottsboro campaign was nothing short of a sensational success, with results that would pay off in unimaginable ways down the road. It was CPUSA's cynical Scottsboro campaign that first drew a young journalist and editor in Atlanta named Frank Marshall Davis to the Communist Party.[15] Decades later, as we have already seen, Davis would become a mentor to a Hawaiian adolescent named Barack Obama.

What a payoff! The significance cannot be overstated: one of the Scottsboro campaign recruits to the Party was a communist who would go on to mentor a future president of the United States of America. Communists in the 1930s could never have conceived of such a spectacular success.

A Book You're Not Supposed to Read

The Communist: Frank Marshall Davis: The Untold Story of Barack Obama's Mentor by Paul Kengor (New York: Simon & Schuster, Threshold Editions, Mercury Ink, 2012).

Black Lives Matter

Of all the far-left parties in the United States, the Revolutionary Communist Party in particular excels at racial agitation, reliably showing up at hot-spots such as Ferguson, Missouri, and other cities where there is racial violence. The RCP is always there to organize a march and throw gasoline on the fire. Communists invariably see the police as the bad guys, and they do not hesitate to say so—at least when it serves their purposes.

"This system sees police wantonly murdering people as part of the normal order of things," RCP co-founder Carl Dix told an AP reporter in Milwaukee in August 2016 amid a long night of violence and a blocks-long march through the streets, with the Party marching in solidarity with Black Lives Matter protestors. "The killer cops always get off. People are sick of that."[16]

The Milwaukee police quickly grew sick of the Revolutionary Communist Party. The commies "showed up, and actually they're the ones who started to cause problems," said Milwaukee police chief Ed Flynn.[17]

Well, sure. Of course, they did. That's their job.

Racial division is a specialty of the RCP, just as it was for Obama mentor Frank Marshall Davis and one of his pet front groups, the American Committee for the Protection of the Foreign Born, in the 1970s.[18]

But it is crucial to understand that communist race-rousing is not restricted to the RCP. When Ferguson burst into the news in August of 2014, communists nationwide were ready. Every single lead article (four of them) in the rotating window at *People's World* was dedicated to Ferguson, in addition to scattered articles (and photos) across the website. The official Communist Party USA website had Ferguson as its lead story, with a piece tellingly titled, "Let us turn grief and anger into action and change." This article pushed aside other leads that had been there for several weeks, including reports from CPUSA's annual convention. The conservative website *TheBlaze* published videos showing "Communists in Ferguson"—commie agitators on the scene, mostly from the RCP.[19]

For American communists in general, Ferguson was a golden opportunity. And they held on to it—hard. They did not want to let go. When the violence receded and Ferguson mercifully disappeared from the news, they did their best to keep it front and center. Two months after the shooting of Michael Brown, in October, the lead piece at the *People's World* website was (once again) further promotion to rile up the American Left for a Ferguson rally the coming weekend. It began with a heart-tugging quote from a woman in Ferguson: "We are praying and waiting, crying and waiting, talking and waiting.... Why do we have to go through all that? This is simply about what's right and what's wrong."

What was really wrong was communists once again cynically exploiting race (not to mention prayer). The siren was sounded at the pages of CPUSA's flagship publication: "A national call has been made to support the grassroots struggle for justice for Michael Brown and all young lives that have been unjustifiably cut short by law enforcement officers throughout the United States.... Reminiscent of the southern civil rights movement of the 1960s, there is a fierce determination that justice must prevail."

From there, the *People's World* piece went into the usual pattern of racial agitation. It pitted the "African American man," "African American people," "African American community" and "its allies" against "white police officer Darren Wilson," the "white political power structure," and the repressive establishment. The article laid out the agenda of the upcoming October 10–13 protests. "Everyone is needed!" the *People's World* correspondent exhorted. "If you absolutely cannot come to Ferguson, there are other ways to help. First and foremost, help spread the word about what is going on! Post it on your social media. Text: handsup to 90975 to get an accurate account of current developments. Financial contributions are desperately needed to help feed and house as many participants as possible."

The *People's World* piece concluded, "Remember, Ferguson is a small town with limited resources. If you live near Ferguson, housing and carpooling would be graciously received. For more information go to: fergusonoctober.com or handsupunited.org."[20]

For those who thought and hoped and prayed that the Ferguson fracas had cooled, well, it had—which is precisely why the Marxist faithful were doing their best to stir up more violence. The Marxist maxim is agitate, agitate, agitate—and that is precisely what today's Reds are doing with race.

Confederate Flag, No—Red Flag, Yes

In short, when it comes to race, communists have done their usual bang-up job fanning the flames of violence and fomenting division.

The race issue continues to be a reliable one for American communists to seize at any moment. It's a show they can take on the road outside their big city haunts on the coasts. To note just one more example, communists

★ ★ ★

Suddenly They're Patriots

A patriotic *People's World* suddenly revealed itself a teary-eyed, lump-in-the-throat lover of America, adding, "Chants of 'take it down' eventually morphed into chants of 'U.S.A.' as the flag was lowered." Old Glory, baby. Old Glory. What a crock. Communists would prefer a flaming American flag over a lowering Confederate flag any day. And most of all, they would prefer a rising Red flag. It was a typical display of Marxist mendacity.

rallied in South Carolina in the summer of 2015 to celebrate the removal of the Confederate flag from the state house, where they joined a wider swath of leftists chanting and singing "Na na na na, na na na na, hey hey hey, goodbye," as the Confederate flag was lowered.

There was giant hypocrisy here. What about the red flag the Marxist-Leninists have hoisted and saluted for a century? As we have already seen, William Z. Foster, Communist Party USA chairman, testified to Congress in the 1930s, "The workers of this country and the workers of every country have only one flag and that is the red flag."

For the record, as a lifetime Pennsylvanian, a "Northerner," and a great admirer of Lincoln, I have no sympathy with the Confederacy or its flag. But as long as we're rejecting banners that symbolize horrible injustices and human suffering, then the hammer and sickle needs to be renounced along with the stars and bars.

But never mind that. There was an issue to agitate, damn it—one with a deliciously divisive racial component—and the Reds were not about to miss their chance.

For several days the lead piece in the rotating window at the *People's World* website, accompanied by a photo of someone holding an Obamaesque placard declaring "CHANGE HAS COME," cheered the removing of the Confederate flag. "A huge and diverse crowd cheered," narrated the *People's World* reporter about the lowering of the flag. "A roar went up from the crowds as the flag lowered and they burst into song when it was finally down."[21]

Down with the Patriarchy!

Another "minority" target for communists is women.

Communists have long tried to recruit women as comrades in their cause, though not with the same careful schemes and due diligence they have made use of in their attempts to sucker and snooker black comrades. Still, the effort has been vigorous. And what is amazing is the extent to which it is generally accepted by even elements of the moderate Left—playing their handy role of dupes and useful idiots to communists—that communism is liberating for women. This whopping falsehood is now taught in our classrooms. They have put it in the lousy textbooks used to teach public school teenagers about history and government.

I saw this painful fact firsthand several years ago when I was doing a commissioned survey of high school civics texts for the state of Wisconsin. I reviewed dozens of texts used by school districts throughout the state, which, significantly, are the same texts used by school districts in states throughout the country. Wisconsin is no different from other states; it is a microcosm of what is happening nationwide. The authors of these texts are always academic historians, professors at American universities. And in those texts, there is not only no material on the horrific suffering of women under communism, but, quite the contrary, praise of communism as something good for women.

Most offensive is the downright bizarre claim—made in more than one textbook—that communism, whether in the USSR or Mao's People's Republic of China, was a historic triumph for women. Communism is portrayed as liberating for women, a boon for women's rights. As one of the textbooks, titled *Global Insights*, puts it, communism empowered women with "full equality with men."[22] Many texts claim that women "won equal rights" with men as a result of the changes by the Bolsheviks in the Soviet Union in 1917 and by Mao's communists following their 1949 takeover. Several texts hint at or flat-out make this claim. These include *Global Insights, Connections to Today, Perspectives on the Past,* and *Patterns of Interaction.*[23] Two texts,

★ ★ ★

Margaret Sanger's Mission to Moscow

Planned Parenthood founder Margaret Sanger is revered by modern liberals. If there was a progressive Mount Rushmore, her face would be chiseled there.

Sanger was a racial-eugenicist who preached a gospel of "race improvement," participated in a "Negro Project," and spoke at the women's branch of the Silver Lake, New Jersey chapter of the Ku Klux Klan in May 1926. She wished to rid America of its "human weeds" and "morons" and "imbeciles."[27]

In the summer of 1934, Margaret made a pilgrimage to the Soviet Union. In the June 1935 edition of her flagship publication, *Birth Control Review*, in an article titled, "Birth Control in Russia," Sanger shared her excitement at what she had found: "Theoretically, there are no obstacles to birth control in Russia. It is accepted... on the grounds of health and human right.... [W]e could well take example from Russia, where there are no legal restrictions, no religious condemnation, and where birth control instruction is part of the regular welfare service of the government."

Even Sanger, however, was aghast at the proliferation of abortions. But Bolshevik officials assured her that this was a mere temporary bump on the road to utopia: "All the officials with whom I discussed the matter stated that as soon as the economic and social plans of Soviet Russia are realized, neither abortions nor contraception will be necessary or desired," said a reassured Sanger. "A functioning Communistic society will assure the happiness of every child, and will assume the full responsibility for its welfare and education."[28]

Patterns of Civilization and *The World's History*, give special attention to the strides women allegedly made under both the Bolsheviks and the Chinese communists.[24]

The text that emphasizes this most strongly is *The World's History*—in at least three separate parts of the book. On page 618, the authors claim that "legally speaking, Russian women were better off than women anywhere in the world."[25]

What? The authors are talking about life under Lenin and Stalin in the 1920s. Which legal rights had Russian women gained that made them "better off" than women anywhere else? Certainly not property rights, nor freedom of speech, religion, press, or assembly. How could the authors' claim be remotely defensible? They give their explanation in the next sentence: Russian girls now had access to abortion. Among the great strides on behalf of Soviet women, explains the text, were "effective birth-control methods," including the right to abortion, which the text notes "became so common that it was once again outlawed for a time after 1936."[26]

What other right does a gal need?

What lady wouldn't trade free speech and the right to worship—not to mention having enough to eat—for the right to abort her child? All sins of the Soviet state are washed clean at the altar of "abortion rights."

The same textbook also makes the assumption that Soviet women were grateful to communism for ushering them into the labor force. It is presumed

★ ★ ★

Drink and Divorce

One key reason that so many Soviet women entered the workforce was the extraordinarily high rates of alcoholism among their husbands. Drinking by Russian men reached epidemic proportions under communism. By the mid-1980s, Mikhail Gorbachev's biggest propaganda effort was not merely *glasnost* but also his domestic anti-alcohol campaign. By the late 1990s, the British medical journal *The Lancet* reported that Russia appeared to be the first modern nation in danger of drinking itself to death. The life expectancy for Russian men had plummeted to fifty-six years.

Another reason so many Soviet women had to work was that the Bolsheviks lifted the prohibition against divorce when they seized power. At least two of the civics texts that I reviewed highlight the "benefit" of divorce rights for women. But while some women were enabled to break a bad marriage, the option of easy divorce was a curse rather than a blessing for many women. It enabled their husbands to abandon them, leaving them to fend for the family themselves, and forcing them reluctantly into the workforce. Divorce rates sky-rocketed under Soviet communism, blowing away the worst numbers seen in America today.

★ ★ ★

Child Hero

Soviet children were told to be like Pavlik Morozov and inform on their parents to the authorities for breaking any of the communists' laws. Pavlik was the heroic boy who was supposed to have turned in his own father, who was shot by the communists. The boy was said to have been killed by other family members in revenge for his noble deed—a martyr for Bolshevism.

that their entry into the workforce was desired and welcome, that it was neither coerced by the state nor by dire economic circumstances that left them no other choice.

For an idea of what Soviet communism really did for women, look to forced labor in the Gulag rather than exciting new careers in the office. From 1934 to 1938, one of every eight Soviet women, men, and children perished.[29] In the early 1930s in the Ukraine alone, millions of women starved to death as a result of Stalin's forced collectivization of agriculture. A typical form of labor for a Soviet woman was waiting in line for food.

A Russian bride saw the government turn her church wedding into a strictly civil ceremony. God was told to stay home.[30] This was Soviet communism.

The most ardent religious believers in the USSR throughout its existence were women, especially the old women, the so-called "babushkas," who were often also targeted for the most ardent persecution. It was illegal to teach religion to anyone under eighteen, including your own children and grandchildren.

"If Hell Really Exists... We Saw Its Image"

Alas, for insight into the real-world experiences of women under communism, I recommend bypassing the high school textbook fantasists and digging into accounts of actual women's lives.

Where to begin? Really, any accurate account of the life of a woman under Soviet communism—or communism generally—is a horror show. For insight into the Soviet experience, one can read about nuns and prostitutes in Soviet prisons in Solzhenitsyn's *Gulag Archipelago*. They were housed together in special sections of the Gulag because the atheist state deemed the nuns "whores to Christ."

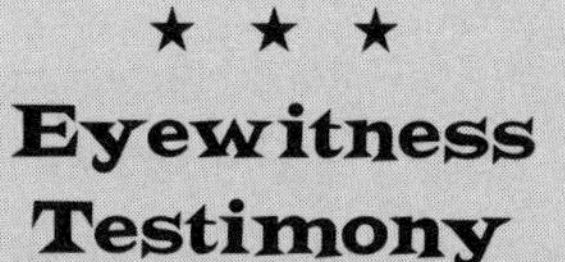

"The throats of our women are constricted with tears." —**Alexander Solzhenitsyn**,[31] an actual eyewitness to the lives of women in the USSR, not a pointy-headed academic opining from the faculty lounge

Or, one can peruse less-known works such as the recent (and chilling) *Children of the Gulag*, on Stalin's orphans, the tormented children taken from their mothers during the Great Purge after their fathers were jailed or murdered by the state.[32] Or take Lena Constante's *The Silent Escape*, about her eight years in solitary confinement in a Romanian prison. Or, for the Chinese experience, look at Jung Chang's *Wild Swans: Three Daughters of China* or Nien Cheng's *Life and Death in Shanghai: Communism in Mao Tse-tung's China*, Li Zhisui's *The Private Life of Chairman Mao* or Steven Mosher's *A Mother's Ordeal: One Woman's Fight Against China's One-Child Policy*. Or, for life under communism in Cambodia, see Loung Ung's heartbreaking *First They Killed My Father: A Daughter of Cambodia Remembers* or Chanrithy Him's *When Broken Glass Floats: Growing Up Under the Khmer Rouge*.

Among the many accounts, let me commend a worthwhile read that has received very little publicity, gaining nowhere near the readership of Solzhenitsyn's works on Soviet Russia. I will share just a few details. The book is Veronica Shapovalov's stirring *Remembering the Darkness: Women in Soviet Prisons*.

Shapovalov tells the stories of many women treated cruelly by the cold, clenched fist of the Bolshevik state—women who were, for the most part, highly educated with high ideals; that is, they were the very kind of new Soviet woman whose liberation from the old order our history textbooks want to celebrate. Many of them initially agreed with the Communist Party and its ideas, but they increasingly found it difficult to comply with communism in practice. They were self-proclaimed idealists, and the communist machine ultimately ground them up, deeming them as of just as little value as a kulak. In fact their high levels of education often contributed to their political troubles, as anything they had published before or during the communist takeover was subject to scrutiny. (As in Cambodia under the Khmer Rouge, and in communist countries, intellectuals were always very closely monitored by the Soviet state.)

Anna Petrovna Skripnikova, for example, was a well-known figure who was rounded up as part of a mass arrest. She had criticized the Soviet government under Stalin for its unpreparedness for the war with Germany. This marked her as a political "dissident." Highly educated, part of the national intelligentsia, she approached her prison stay as something unavoidable. She reasoned with the guards and did not fight, cry, or raise a fuss. She knew the facts she had to deal with: she had been arrested by the Cheka, and she was being transported through the country to Siberia. As an educated woman who understood the state of affairs in Soviet Russia, she knew that she had no control over her situation. When she was transferred to a communal cell in the first prison, her cellmates were confused by the fact that she did not cry upon her arrival. "Does one really have to cry?" she answered. "Could tears really help our situation?... When a warrant for your arrest has been issued and assigned to an agent, you will be arrested, and nothing in the world can save you."[33]

Veronica Shapovalov offers many such stories from the lives of women confined to the camps. In one section of her book, she shares accounts of women sent to the Gulag because of their family connections to political prisoners. The unfortunate designation of "wife of a traitor to the Motherland" was especially damning. Both physical and psychological punishment was doled out to women for their husbands' "misconduct." The fact that a crime (real or trumped up) by her *husband* could destine a woman to the cold hell of Siberia, Shapovalov points out, "testified to the real state of affairs in the country that had officially declared the equality and independence of women."[34] By viewing a wife as simply an extension of her husband's political mistakes, the communist regime was denying the autonomy of a woman as her own person with her own political ideals.

Feminism is dead, dear comrade, when it is a matter of state policy to punish women for the actions of their husbands.

Liudmila Ivanovna Granovskaia was one woman arrested for the "crimes" of her husband. Her husband, Liudmila said, was actually a loyal Party member, but he apparently must have angered the wrong person, leading to his arrest. And then her insistence that he was innocent led to her being arrested at her home. She was first sent to a crowded prison with other women, and there was an attempt to coerce her into signing a confession for her husband's crimes. When she asked what crimes *she* had committed, no charges were brought against her. She refused to sign the document but was still sentenced to five years in a labor camp. She described the living conditions as like those of a seventeenth-century prison: "rough, uncouth, clumsy, and heavy."[35]

Many of Liudmila's fellow prisoners were mothers who had been forcibly ripped from their children or had their babies stolen from them. Because of the psychological trauma, many of them had fallen into despair before they even arrived at the camp—wailing and screaming, agonizing dismally over the fate of their offspring.

But their experience was positively joyous compared to what other Soviet women faced. Shapovalov highlights the unique problems that women faced in the Soviet prison system, including sexual harassment, rape, and unwanted pregnancy.

Irina Pavlovna Vasileva was shoved onto an all-male train car—more specifically, a car full of all-male criminals. She was in fear for her life. She recalled her growing trepidation as the men realized there was a

★ ★ ★

"Political Prostitutes" and "Negro Lickspittles"

For testimony about how communists really viewed and treated both women and blacks, we can turn to the bird's-eye view of Manning Johnson, a well-known black communist who lived through the period when "Uncle Joe" Stalin tightly controlled the Communist Party USA. What Johnson saw led him to leave the Party in disgust.

As a leading African-American communist, Manning Johnson was placed on the National Negro Commission, an important subcommittee of the National Committee of the Communist Party. That commission, according to Manning, was created "on direct orders from Moscow to facilitate the subversion of the Negroes." He soon realized the full extent to which "the Negro is used as a political dupe by the Kremlin hierarchy." Top white communists such as James S. Allen (again, also known as Sol Auerbach), Robert Minor, and Elizabeth Lawson were placed on the commission and really ran the show. These white communists, said Manning, "wielded more power than the nominal Negro heads of the commission. In a word, they are like white overseers." Moreover, "Every Negro member was aware of the fact that these white overseers constituted the eyes, the ears and the voice of the Kremlin."

The black man was expected to follow the dictates of Sol and his other white masters. Good Negro communists, you see, were unquestioning Negro communists, who sat quietly and did as they were told.

And black men and white women were given unique roles by the Communist Party ringleaders. "I observed how white women communists are used as political prostitutes," wrote Manning, "cohabiting with high-level Negro communists in order to spy on them." The white male communist masters would delegate the white communist females to give themselves sexually to black communists for a romp and pillow talk to pump them for information. "This information is invaluable to the red hierarchy in their relations with their Negro lickspittles," said Manning. "In top red circles, this is known as 'bedroom politics.'"

The information procured by the white female communists was then transmitted to the white male communists as handy blackmail material against the black male communists, in case they got out of line, maybe did some back-talking, or got a little uppity with the white folks. The black Reds were basically being used as Uncle Joe's Uncle Toms.

What Manning Johnson concluded about the communists' use of African Americans also applies to their exploitation of women, whether in America or the Soviet Union or elsewhere. He warned that "when communists unite with and support [blacks] today," it must be kept in mind that "it may be necessary to denounce them tomorrow and the day after tomorrow hang them."[36]

Thus, blacks and women were, in the end, treated like everyone else under communism.

woman among them and began to encircle her. There was no one to hear her scream, no one to call for help, and she was frozen with fear until a large convict stepped in front of her and threatened to kill anyone who laid a hand on her. Her savior, along with a few other men, then guarded her for the entire night, telling her stories of his previous life to calm her. In the morning, the guards opened the door to make sure all the prisoners were alive. She was removed and transported by herself for the rest of the trip, unsure even of her rescuer's name as she continued through the Gulag system and landed in a camp. It was only much later that she learned her rescuer's fate: he was pushed from the train by his fellow prisoners the next morning and killed.

Elena Semenovna Glinka observed mass rape in the hold of a transport ship when male criminals broke down a barrier separating them from the female prisoners. Frenzied women tried to escape to the deck; some, like Elena, succeeded and watched transfixed at the horrors that were transpiring beneath them. She struggled for words to describe the unspeakable evil she saw: "No human fantasy, even the most distorted and pathological, could come close to the disgusting and ugly orgy of cruel, sadistic, and shameless rape that was under way there.... In my childhood, I had read about slave transports from Africa to the New World, but there had been nothing like this." Elena conveyed the scene of violence:

> I don't know the capacity of the men's holds on that ship or how many men were packed into them, but those apes were still leaping through the gap in the bulkhead. Like wild animals, the rapists rushed in, hopping around, taking their places in line, climbing the bunk beds, crawling around, and demonically raping women who had already been raped. Women who resisted were executed on the spot: Many men had Finnish knives, razor blades, or homemade stilettos. From time to time, with wild whistles, whoops, and obscenities, they would throw the tortured, cut, and raped women down from the upper bunks. Some were playing cards, with the stakes being this or that woman's life. If hell really exists somewhere in the depths, we saw its image and likeness in that hold.[37]

This was the reality of women living under the Soviet state. In the communist system, constant fear plagued them because of their gender.

Olga Viktorovna Iafa-Sinakevich was a woman determined to find some measure of beauty in life in the Gulag Archipelago. It was not easy. She recounted a time that the head of a punishment cell received rubles from home and wooed the young female prisoners by promising them a ruble for a kiss. Olga looked out her window and saw the man chasing the girls, who were wearing their assigned summer dresses that barely covered their bodies, and attempting to grab them for a kiss as they ran away. Olga tried to imagine Pan in the forest frolicking with nymphs—anything she could to salvage something out of the ugliness. She would summon thoughts of Greek mythology and the poetry she had studied and liken the scenario before her to those idyllic scenes. Such was her dogged determination to find beauty in the midst of horror in the Gulag.[38]

This is just a glimpse of the real-world accounts of Soviet women under communism—from just one book.

If your child is using *The World's History* for insights into Bolshevik Russia, hand her Veronica Shapovalov's *Remembering the Darkness: Women in Soviet Prisons* instead. Liberate your daughter with truth, don't leave her to the mercy of left-wingers peddling old Bolshevik propaganda.

Bolshevism was not good for women. And neither is any kind of communism—for women, or for any human being, male or female, white or black, or anything in between.

CHAPTER 15

Stupidity on Parade

We started this book with two examples. There was the high school near Gettysburg, home of Lincoln's iconic address, where the student marching band delivered a merry half-time show stepping to the rhythms of "St. Petersburg 1917." The land of Lincoln goes Lenin. There was also the 2015 prom theme for a high school in Albuquerque: "prom-munism" was the cutesy title of the big dance for the year. Guys and gals could hop and bop to the dulcet tones of Marx and Engels or the quaint quartet of Lenin, Trotsky, Stalin, and Bukharin.

How tragic, but how fitting. The field of education is precisely the turf where this cacophony is played out. The ongoing parade of ignorance about the horrors of communism begins at the K–12 level and proceeds to get only worse at the college level, where the ideological indoctrination reaches mind-blowing decibels. It is the universities that are the vast left-wing indoctrination centers in modern America. This miseducation has generated an arid landscape of ill-informed Americans of all ages.

Consider these recent shocking findings. According to an October 2016 report by the Victims of Communism Memorial Foundation, almost one-third of Millennials (32 percent) "believe more people were killed under

Did you know?

★ One out of four Americans believe that George W. Bush killed more people than Stalin

★ The Empire State Building was lit up in Chicom colors to celebrate the anniversary of Mao's revolution, but the request to light it up for Mother Teresa was refused

★ The Obama White House Christmas tree featured an ornament with Mao's picture on it

George W. Bush than under Joseph Stalin."[1] And it isn't only those silly Millennials. More than one in four Americans generally (26 percent) believe more people were killed under Bush than Stalin. That is a deeply disturbing finding.

The report found that the vast majority of Americans (75 percent) underestimate the number of people killed by communist regimes, and a large majority (68 percent) believe that Hitler killed more people than Stalin. Forty-two percent of Millennials are "unfamiliar" with Mao Zedong.

Given these findings, it is not surprising that well over half (69 percent) of Millennials would vote for a socialist. As we have seen, that was reflected in the 2016 Democratic primaries, when Bernie Sanders, a lifelong self-professed socialist, received thirteen million votes. To give you a sense of how significant that number is, Donald Trump got fourteen million votes in the Republican primary—and that was a record for a Republican primary. (Saul Alinsky disciple Hillary Clinton got seventeen million votes in the Democratic primary.)

This is not a failure to teach history; it is a failure to teach communism—that is, the evils of communism. We haven't failed to teach that Nazism was evil, that Hitler was a mass murderer, that fascism is bad. But we long ago failed when it came to communism, Bolshevism, the USSR, Stalin, Lenin, Mao, Castro, Che, Pol Pot, the Kims, and on and on. And that failure often has been deliberate, arising out of ideological bias. Too often it's leftists who are doing the teaching. They do not suffer the same historical blindness when it comes to teaching fascism and Nazism. R. Emmett Tyrrell Jr., founding editor of *The American Spectator*, refers to this phenomenon as the political Left's "outrage imbalance."[2]

For years I have traveled to colleges nationwide giving lectures with titles like "Why Communism is Bad," "Why Ronald Reagan Hated Communism—And Why You Should, Too," and "Professor Marx? Anti-Anti-Communism and the Academy," sponsored by groups such as the Young America's

Foundation and Intercollegiate Studies Institute. I did a videotaped lecture titled, "Why We Fought the Cold War," for the Free Think University online curriculum in partnership with the Leadership Institute. When I speak at these colleges, I read passages directly from *The Communist Manifesto* and other primary sources. When I cite authoritative sources on the maimed and dead, the students are aghast, eyes wide open. Rarely are their professors in attendance. The students are riveted as I expound upon evils wrought by communist hatred, such as the unprecedented number of dead bodies produced by the ideology.

As I review the casualties, these students are amazed at what they are hearing. They seem especially struck that I always ground every fact and figure in reliable research and authorities—books published by top university presses, quotations from the likes of Mikhail Gorbachev and Václav Havel and Alexander Yakovlev, anti-Soviet appraisals from Cold War Democrats such as Harry Truman and John F. Kennedy and early liberals like Woodrow Wilson, anti-communist assessments by leftist intellectuals and esteemed Cold War historians and scholars of communism including Allen Weinstein, John Earl Haynes, Harvey Klehr, Ron Radosh, Sam Tanenhaus, Arthur M. Schlesinger Jr., George F. Kennan, and John Lewis Gaddis. I invoke ex-communists and former communists who knew the Party and ideology extremely well from first-person experiences. I rarely use conservative sources because I do not want the professors of these students to be able to later poke holes in my presentation.

On a handful of occasions I have had a professor in attendance. In one case, a British professor, who could not stop sighing, squirming, and rolling her eyes as I quoted the most heinous assessments of religion by Marx and Lenin, got up and stormed out of the room. In another case, a professor contemptuously glared at me as if the ghost of Joe McCarthy had flown into the room and leapt inside my body. That is the essence of their criticism: the *anti*-communism they are witnessing appalls them. Pro-communism doesn't bother them a lick, but anti-communism sure does. The latter is deemed unsophisticated, boorish, loathsome, illiberal.

American Education, or Chicom Agitprop?

Those same professors write the textbooks used by high schools. We have already gotten a taste of the bias in favor of communism in the texts used in public schools from my extensive review for the Wisconsin Policy Research Institute.[3] The treatment of communism in these texts is outrageous. The greatest abuse is the sins of omission: what is not covered. I could not find a single text that listed figures on the total number of deaths by communist governments, even though similar data was provided in other categories, such as war-time deaths or those killed by the Nazis, and despite the fact that widely publicized data on deaths brought about by communist regimes had been made recently available in major post–Cold War works like Harvard University Press's *The Black Book of Communism.*

These texts' failure to highlight the historical scourge of communism stood in stark contrast to their treatment of historical events such as the Inquisition, the Crusades, slavery, the internment of Japanese Americans, and other episodes that featured infinitely lower casualties. So-called "right-wing" dictators like Cuba's Batista and Chile's Pinochet were treated more harshly than Fidel Castro, who had persecuted and killed far more victims—and was still in power.

The material on communist China in these texts was especially appalling. There was nothing on the staggering death toll in Red China, nor on the stifling array of human rights travesties. There was not even a word on Tiananmen Square (which, ironically, is also purged from Chinese civics texts by the Chinese government), despite its being so recent in memory.

Several of the texts addressed the population situation in China. The first thing that should come to mind on the subject of communist China and population is the state's refusal to allow women to have more than one or two children. It is difficult to find a more crass example of depriving people of their most basic human rights. How dare any government tell its people that they are not allowed to have children? But shockingly, many of these awful texts present the one-child policy (recently revised to a two-child policy) as a prudent, caring government step to curb the looming catastrophe of "overpopulation."

"To slow the population growth," the authors benevolently tell students, "Chinese leaders have been trying to convince couples to have only one child."[4] Of course, the (unnamed) methods by which the communist government has been "trying to convince" the unwashed masses to obey its (compulsory) limits on the number of permissible children include forced abortion and mandatory sterilization.

Of the textbooks I reviewed, the worst on China's population policy was probably *Patterns of Civilization.* "China's rapidly growing population put severe strains on the economy," says the text categorically. "To achieve modernization, Chinese leaders pressed forward with a one-child-per-family policy."[5] This suggests that the cap on children is necessary for modernization. If so, then how can it be that every other nation in history that has modernized has done so without a one-child limit? Moreover, China now, today, has decided it must move away from the one-child policy because more people are needed as the state modernizes.

As we saw in the last chapter, these textbooks praise communism for liberating women and ignore their suffering and oppression under the communist system. *World Cultures: A Global Mosaic*, for example, credits China's communist government with granting women equality and celebrates their independence under the communist regime: "Today, Chinese women have become more independent. Almost all women work outside the home, and many hold high-level jobs in the Communist party or as factory managers. The government has set up day-care centers and nurseries so that young mothers can be free to work outside the home."[6]

The text includes no mention of the poverty and starvation of women under Chinese communism; the government cap on the number of children they can bear; the forced abortion and sterilization; the horrific mass numbers of abandoned baby girls; the lives of prostitution resorted to by countless Chinese women who believe they have no other effective means of income; or the fact that female infanticide is more prevalent (both absolutely and in relation to the population as a whole) in China than in any other nation. There is no mention that China has 20 percent of the world's women but 56 percent of the world's female suicides.[7] According to the World Bank and World Health Organization, about five hundred Chinese women kill themselves every day.[8] This is a long-term trend that has persisted in China for at least twenty years now.

Besides failing to address human rights crimes like the one-child policy, the texts offer rosy descriptions of life in the contemporary Chinese classroom and of "youth groups" like the Young Pioneers. One text, titled *Global Insights*,[9] served up this glossy sidebar on Chinese "Young People":

> Although Chinese students work hard at their studies, they still find time to participate in activities outside of school. Many young people are involved in youth organizations. The Young Pioneers is a children's organization to which about 50 percent of China's youngsters belong. Its purpose is to train children to be good citizens. The Communist Youth League, on the other hand, is an honor organization for high school students. To become a member, a student must be at least 15 years of age and have an excellent academic and political record.[10]

This brief cheery section, which includes no critical examination of the political indoctrination of Chinese children into history's most murderous ideology in these groups, is followed up by a touching profile of a Chinese Olympic gymnast. This American high school history textbook reads like official agitprop from the PRC's Central Committee. We should expect to see Chinese children reading this propaganda in their communist schools, not American children in their public schools.

The same text makes the indefensible claim that Mao's Great Leap Forward (which, it neglects to note, created the largest mass starvation in the history of the world, with roughly fifty to sixty million deaths in about four years) enabled China to "make significant economic gains under communist rule. By the mid-1960s, it was ranked among the ten leading industrial nations in the world."

Putting a Sunny Face on Oppression

And it's not just in our education system that communist atrocities get treated with kid gloves. Liberal dupes in the American media have white-washed communist revolutionaries and the oppressive regimes they created from the Bolsheviks to Fidel Castro to Hugo Chávez. A recent Associated Press piece titled "One-Child Policy a Surprising Boon for China Girls" cutely, coyly credits China's perverse population policy with *helping* Chinese women to advance. The smaller pool of women, the article argued, has opened opportunities for women—at least, the women lucky enough to have not been aborted.[11]

Here is another picture of shameful ignorance, compliments of liberals in (where else?) New York City: In October 2009, New York City's Empire State Building was aglow in red and yellow. Why? To commemorate the sixtieth anniversary of the victorious communist revolution that established the People's Republic of China. This celebration took place not in Beijing, or Pyongyang, or Havana. It was done in New York City, in 2009, at the very symbol of the Empire State. New Yorkers were basking in the glow of the

Maoist ideology and government that killed more people more quickly than any nation in world history—the glorious colors of Chinese communism.

Had this happened in America sixty years before, Harry Truman would have thrown a fit. Joe McCarthy would have called hearings to find out who was responsible. And that was before Mao's killing-machine really got down to business.

New Yorkers were apparently oblivious to such implications as they strolled along Madison Avenue slurping smoothies and reading their *New York Times* under a blood red (and yellow) sky.[12]

Chairman Mao must have been chortling in his grave. And the old atheist was surely laughing even harder when the same gang of clueless New Yorkers rejected a request by the Catholic League to light up the Empire State Building for Mother Teresa on the centenary of her birth. They lit up for Mao, but not for Mother.[13]

This is the same New York City that honors Ethel Rosenberg, the American quisling who helped deliver atomic-bomb secrets to Stalin's Kremlin. In September 2015 the New York City Council enacted a resolution honoring convicted and executed spy Ethel Rosenberg on the centenary of her birth. The council declared September 28, 2015 "Ethel Rosenberg Day of Justice in the Borough of Manhattan." The enlightened New York City progressives commended comrade Ethel for her "great bravery." There could scarcely be a more apt gesture from a city that long housed Communist Party USA, the *Daily Worker*, and Columbia University, and whose current mayor is Sandinista propaganda peddler, Bill de Blasio.[15]

★ ★ ★

An Unlikely Combo

President Barack Obama's communications director, Anita Dunn, resigned not long after Glenn Beck had the temerity to broadcast her jaw-dropping affirmation, made in a church no less (at a high-school baccalaureate ceremony) that her two favorite philosophers were Mao Zedong and Mother Teresa.[14]

Wait, Stalin Liberated Normandy?

We expect such pro-communist political-ideological jackassery in New York City, but not in rural Virginia. But alas, the National D-Day Memorial in Bedford, Virginia, has one-upped the Empire State. The memorial has erected a statue of Stalin.

Flagging this outrage was the Victims of Communism Memorial Foundation, which created a website (www.stalinstatue.com) to call attention to this moral-historical slander. The site features a petition to remove the statue, with thousands of signatures from every state and dozens of countries, including some really upset folks from the former Soviet empire. Addressed to the National D-Day Memorial Foundation and President Obama's secretary of the interior, the petition demands that the "true history of World War II must be protected from distortion and misinformation which threaten to erase or alter well-established and documented facts." Among those facts: "neither Joseph Stalin nor Soviet forces played any part in the D-Day landing at Normandy."

And Stalin was morally complicit in the deaths of all those (non-Russian) boys who stormed the beaches of Normandy on June 6, 1944. As is detailed earlier in this book, it was the August 1939 Hitler-Stalin Pact that started World War II. Immediately after the pact's signing came the joint invasions of Poland, the Katyn Woods massacre, and Soviet support of and to the Nazis (until Hitler betrayed Stalin). Celebrating one of the world's most monstrous tyrants at the D-Day Museum simply makes no sense—outside the inverted values of the Left and the stunning ignorance of our education system.

But those inverted values prevail in large swaths of America today—wherever leftists have influence in America. The Obama White House considered banning a crèche at Christmas in 2009 while, simultaneously, sanctifying the White House Christmas tree with a most curious ornament. An article in the *New York Times* noted that inside the Obama

White House "there had been internal discussions about making Christmas more inclusive and whether to display the crèche." But while the display of a crèche was in question, happily hung on the historic White House Christmas tree was a rather novel ornament: a glistening, glimmering Mao Zedong.[16]

How's that for inclusion? Baby Jesus—maybe, maybe not? Chairman Mao, yes!

The bad boys at Fox News noticed the twinkling little chairman in the background of a warm and fuzzy photo of Barack and Michelle Obama in front of the White House Christmas tree. They blew the whistle. And of course the liberal faithful heaped righteous indignation on Fox, with the left-wing publication *Salon* blasting Fox for a "dopy right-wing attack" against poor President Obama.[17] It was another sin of anti-communism. (How would *Salon* feel if, say, the Christmas tree at the Trump White House had an ornament boasting a grinning Nazi?) Positive images of a mass murderer of tens of millions—adorning a Christmas tree no less—doesn't concern them; raising any objection to it, however, means you're a dopy red-baiting McCarthyite who sees communists hiding under every bed.

★ ★ ★

Not the Reason for the Season

Needless to say, Mao is not traditionally associated with Christmas. He persecuted Christians, hated Christianity, and did his best to wipe it out in China. One of the first things he did when taking over China in October 1949 was boot out the Western missionaries, which was a mere mild infraction and casual warm-up to his full-throttle persecution of religious believers, which continues in Red China to this day.

How We Lost the Cold War, After All

In the fight against communism, America has snatched defeat from the jaws of victory. We won the battle against communism on the world stage. But we lost the ideological battle here in the United States. We won the Cold War abroad but lost the war for truth at home—in our universities, riddled with '60s radicals; in our public school classrooms; and in the hearts and minds of the American people.

So those of us who understand the very real dangers of communism have a major fight on our hands. We can't afford to let the growing percentage of the American population that hankers for socialist distribution take American down the path of socialism or some form of pro-communism. But in these dire circumstances—with the universities and many of the public schools and much of the media doing the bidding for the other side—it may be encouraging to remember that America's victory in the Cold War was itself achieved despite the concerted opposition of much of the press and elite opinion.

Consider the reaction when President Ronald Reagan, speaking to a group of evangelicals in Orlando, Florida, on March 8, 1983, described the Soviet Union as the "focus of evil in the modern world" and called it an "evil empire."

If anyone was more upset by Reagan's words than the Kremlin, it was American liberals.

Anthony Lewis of the *New York Times* denounced the speech as "outrageous" and "simplistic," before ultimately concluding it was "primitive—the only word for it."[18] In *The Washington Post*, Richard Cohen called Reagan a "religious bigot."[19] Henry Steele Commager, historian at (where else?) Columbia University, judged Reagan's address "the worst presidential speech in American history," because of its "gross appeal to religious prejudice."[20] The *New Republic*, longtime flagship publication of the American Left, bellyached that the rhetoric of "Reverend Reagan" was "deeply divisive," and insisted that his history was "very poor."[21]

While the American press was denouncing Reagan's characterization of the Soviet Union as an "evil empire," those actually inside the Soviet Union—and particularly those inside the Gulag—had a very different reaction. Anatoly Sharansky, for example, a religious Jewish dissident and

★ ★ ★

The Exception That Proves the Rule

One Western journalist—an aging British gentleman named Malcolm Muggeridge—sent a letter of support to the president. Assuring Reagan that his history was not only *not* poor but right on target, Muggeridge recalled that when he was a young reporter in Moscow in 1932 he encountered "anti-God museums, the total suppression of the scriptures and related literature, the ridiculing of the person of Christ and his followers, the whole force of the most powerful and comprehensive propaganda machine ever to exist, including the schools and universities, geared to promote Marxist materialism and abolish Christianity forever." Muggeridge explained the fundamental difference between Christianity and Marxism: "Christianity happens to be true, and Marxism. . . .unresisting imbecility.'"[22]

an inmate of Permanent Labor Camp 35, upon learning what Reagan had said, jumped for joy inside his prison cell and tapped in Morse Code to his fellow prisoners the good news that "someone had finally spoken the truth."[23]

And once Soviet communism finally collapsed, we heard honest testimonials from Russian government officials who were finally free to speak their mind. In August 1991 Andrei Kozyrev, Boris Yeltsin's foreign minister, said of the USSR, "It was, rather, [an] evil empire, as it was put."[24] Sergei Tarasenko, the chief assistant to Soviet Foreign Minister Eduard Shevardnadze, summed up: "So the president said, 'It is an evil empire!' Okay. Well, we [were] an evil empire."[25]

But before that collapse, even some who saw the moral bankruptcy of communism as clearly as Reagan did despaired of ultimate victory. Ronald Reagan's favorite book was Whittaker Chambers's 1952 classic, *Witness*, a captivating memoir of one man's sojourn out of the clutches of atheistic communism and a life of duplicity as an agent for the Kremlin. (Chambers exposed a number of closet American communists, including State Department official Alger Hiss.)

A Book You're Not Supposed to Read

Witness by Whittaker Chambers (Regnery, 2014 reprint edition).

Reagan was taken not only by Chambers' gripping story, but also by the ex-communist's rich philosophical understanding of how communism violated the very nature of man. Reagan could quote passages from *Witness* verbatim off the top of his head. He shared these thoughts on Chambers in a March 1983 speech:

> Whittaker Chambers, the man whose own religious conversion made him a witness to one of the terrible traumas of our time, the Hiss-Chambers case, wrote that the crisis of the Western World exists to the degree in which the West is indifferent to God, the degree to which it collaborates in communism's attempt to make man stand alone without God. And then he said, for Marxism-Leninism is actually the second oldest faith, first proclaimed in the Garden of Eden with the words of temptation, "Ye shall be as gods."
>
> The Western World can answer this challenge, he wrote, "but only provided that its faith in God and the freedom He enjoins is as great as communism's faith in Man."
>
> I believe we shall rise to the challenge. I believe that communism is another sad, bizarre chapter in human history whose last pages even now are being written.[26]

Reagan insisted that he and his fellow Americans should rise to this challenge and defeat Soviet communism. It was up to them to save the world from this godless force. They could win the Cold War.

★ ★ ★

Come On, Let Us Know What You Really Think (Iron Lady Edition)

"A monstrous parasite which consumes the flesh of its host and leaves behind a shell which is designed to conceal the change by which the Party has itself become the State." —description of communism by **Margaret Thatcher** in an October 1991 speech at Jagiellonian University in Krakow, Poland, where a young priest and theologian named Karol Wojtyla, the future Pope John Paul II, had once taught

In this, Reagan differed from Chambers, who believed that he had left the Soviet side for the losing side. Reagan, the quintessential optimist, disagreed. Ronald Reagan believed that America could and would win.

Reagan's hope and determination—and that of his fellow Cold Warriors such as Pope John Paul II and British prime minister Margaret Thatcher—should inspire us. And in our current circumstances we could use inspiration!

The first generation of Americans born after the collapse of the Berlin Wall and USSR are now young adults. They did not live through the mass repression and carnage that was Soviet communism. They have no personal memories of Stalin's and Lenin's monstrosities or of Mao's and Pol Pot's mass murders, or any clue of what Fidel and Che really advocated. And, as we have seen, they have certainly not learned about any of these things in school. Nobody has drawn their attention to the communist horror stories still going on today in places like Cuba, North Korea, China, Venezuela, and Zimbabwe—even as these living museums to Marxist madness implode before our very eyes in our very times. Young Americans should have learned about these atrocities, just as they were taught about the evils of Nazism. But they didn't. And so we shouldn't be surprised if they're ready to march to the triumphal strains of the Bolsheviks' "Communist Internationale." God help us if stepping to that tune one day leads Americans anywhere near the same blood-drenched path that has been trodden by every people in history foolish enough to believe the communists' idiotic promises.

It's our nation's stupidity that is on parade.

A Book You're Not Supposed to Read

A Pope and a President: John Paul II, Ronald Reagan, and the Extraordinary Untold Story of the 20th Century by Paul Kengor (Intercollegiate Studies Institute, 2017).

Acknowledgments

In November 2015, the legendary Harry Crocker, whose name I've long held synonymous with Regnery Publishing, asked me if I would consider writing a *Politically Incorrect Guide® to Communism* to be released in 2017, the centenary of the Bolshevik Revolution that unleashed the global monster that is communism. The offer was too delicious to pass up.

I had read other books in the Regnery series of Politically Incorrect Guides®, including Robert Spencer's *Politically Incorrect Guide® to Islam* and Anthony Esolen's *Politically Incorrect Guide® to Western Civilization*. A number of people over the years have urged me to write a similar such book on communism, a subject that I teach, including in a full course on Marxism at Grove City College (and to some degree in all of my courses). As I noted in this book, for years I have traveled to colleges nationwide giving a lecture titled, "Why Communism is Bad." I've discussed communism and its consequences and horrors on countless talk shows. I have published hundreds if not thousands of articles on communism. I have written numerous books on the subject, many of them related to Ronald Reagan and the collapse of communism, several of which have been translated into foreign languages by international publishing houses. These included books with politically incorrect titles such as *Takedown: From Communists to Progressives, How the Left Has Sabotaged Family and Marriage*; *The Communist: Frank Marshall Davis, the Untold Story of Barack Obama's Mentor*; *Dupes: How America's Adversaries Have Manipulated Progressives for a Century*; and *The Crusader: Ronald Reagan and the Fall of Communism*.

I've also written many forewords, prefaces, and chapters in books on communism and the Cold War, including for the outstanding and very important work, *Disinformation*, by Ion Mihai Pacepa and Ron Rychlak. I've done reports on communism, surveys, white papers, journal articles. I had a fun "Commie Watch" column for the print edition of *The American Spectator*, which I continue for the online version.

None of this, I promise, is to toot my own anti-communist horn or puff up myself. Quite the contrary, it reveals a lot of time delving into the darkness. It is, frankly, pretty damned sad and depressing. It isn't fun. Believe me, I'd much rather write books about, oh, say, baseball. The point is that I've spent a lifetime suffering the lamentable occupational hazard of studying this stupid and genuinely evil ideology. Like Michael Corleone in *The Godfather II*, every time I try to get out from the communists' nightmare, they pull me back in. And alas, that's probably why I haven't stopped writing about this pernicious ideology: I feel a duty to warn the world not to repeat this horror show.

As I said, friends and colleagues have urged me for years to write some sort of politically incorrect critique of communism. Thus, when Harry Crocker suggested I consider writing precisely such a book as part of the world-renowned and witty Regnery Politically Incorrect Guide® series, how could I say no?

Not only did I feel I was the guy to write the *Politically Incorrect Guide® to Communism*... I basically *am* a Politically Incorrect Guide® to Communism.

I promised Regnery a "deliciously politically incorrect treatment of the subject." I hope I did not disappoint.

As for the good folks at Regnery, they have been terrific all along. I have not seen the faces or even caught the names of all of those involved in this manuscript, of which I'm sure there have been many, but I'd especially like to thank Elizabeth Kantor, my editor, who did a tremendous job with an initial manuscript that was too long. She took it under her wing and shaped it splendidly. She did a lot of moving, arranging, framing, labeling, and much more. She did excellent work, and she was always cheerful and so easy to work with. I am also grateful to Nancy Feuerborn for a fine copy editing job and Jason Sunde for the striking jacket design.

I would like to thank several Grove City College students who helped me with research on this book. Hannah Lutz and Ian Worrell were my go-to crack researchers anytime I needed something quick. They were my top assistants. I thank Lorenzo Carrazana, whose family of freedom fighters escaped the Castro dungeon that is modern Cuba. Hannah Wright provided an excellent compilation on women in Soviet prisons by distilling for me some of the heart-wrenching portions of Veronica Shapovalov's painful book. I thank Anthony Maniero for his assistance at the Tamiment Library in searching the files on Lovett Fort-Whiteman. I'm also grateful to Drew Brackbill and Annabelle Rutledge. And from outside of Grove City College, kudos two current homeschoolers, David Williams and Michael Williams, for digging up a bunch of funny (and yet not-so-funny) communist jokes.

Finally, I would like to finish with a nod to my wise nine-year-old son, John Dominic, who summed up the subject of this book best one Sunday evening in late November 2016. As I typed away at my keyboard, writing, adding, cutting, editing, John peered over my shoulder and read some of my lines and chapter titles and puzzled. The deluge of insanity before him overwhelmed him. "What kind of psychopath book are you writing?" he asked in disturbed bewilderment.

It was a perfectly reasonable question with a perfectly reasonable answer: "A book on communism, Johnny," I replied. "That's about as *psychopath* as you can get."

This book is for all the little Johns (and Janes) out there today, in the hopes of teaching them the truths about communism they will not learn in our wretched public schools and especially in our lousy, stinky universities. Here's to all the souls that can still be spared from the clutches of the false god that failed.

Notes

Chapter 1: Educating for Ignorance

1. Lysee Mitri, "Prom-munism: Seniors vote for Communism themed prom," KRQE (Albuquerque) News, March 5, 2015. http://krqe.com/2015/03/05/seniors-vote-for-communism-themed-prom/.
2. See Patrick Devenny, "The House of Kim," *The American Spectator*, November 15, 2005.
3. Sonni Efron, "Defectors Tell of N. Korean Drug Trade," *Los Angeles Times*, May 21, 2003.
4. See, among others, Li Zhisui, *The Private Life of Chairman Mao* (New York: Random House, 1994), pp. 98–106.
5. Mitri, "Prom-munism: Seniors vote for Communism themed prom."
6. Todd Starnes, "American High School Band Marches with Hammer & Sickle," Fox News website, September 2012. http://radio.foxnews.com/toddstarnes/top-stories/high-school-band-celebrates-russian-revolution.html.
7. Alonzo Hamby, *Man of the People: A Life of Harry S. Truman* (New York: Oxford University Press, 1995), pp. 313–14.
8. John F. Kennedy, "Commencement Address at Assumption College," Worcester, Massachusetts, June 3, 1955.
9. John F. Kennedy, *Public Presidential Papers*, (Washington, DC: U.S. Government Printing Office, 1962), Vol. 1, 1961, p. 341; and John F. Kennedy, "Speech of Senator John F. Kennedy to the Mormon

Tabernacle," Salt Lake City, Utah, September 23, 1960. See also Martin Walker, *The Cold War and the Making of the Modern World*, (London, 1993), p. 132 and Eric Hobsbawm, *The Age of Extremes: A History of the World, 1914–1991*, (New York: Pantheon Books, 1994), p. 231.

Chapter 2: How Many People Have These Bastards Killed?

1. Aleksandr I. Solzhenitsyn, *The Gulag Archipelago: 1918–56, Vols. I–II* (San Francisco: Harper & Row, 1973), pp. ix–x.
2. Stephane Courtois, et al., *The Black Book of Communism* (Harvard University Press, 1999), p. 4. Some contributors to the book, namely, Nicolas Werth and Jean-Louis Margolin, disassociated themselves with the hundred million estimate. See Ron Radosh, "The Black Book of Communism: Crimes, Terror, and Repression," *First Things*, February 2000 and Robert Stacy McCain, "Communism's Atrocities Detailed in 'Black Book,'" *Washington Times*, September 21, 2000.
3. Victims of Communism Memorial Foundation, http://victimsofcommunism.org/smith-joins-victims-of-communism/.
4. Courtois, *Black Book*, p. 4.
5. Lee Edwards, editor, *The Collapse of Communism* (Stanford, CA: Hoover Institution Press, 1999), p. xiii.
6. See: Tony Cliff, *Trotsky: The Sword of the Revolution: 1917-1923*, posted online at https://www.marxists.org/archive/cliff/works/1990/trotsky2/01-sovpower.html.
7. See Alexander Yakovlev, *A Century of Violence in Soviet Russia* (New Haven, CT: Yale University Press, 2002), 32; Alexander Solzhenitsyn, *Alexander Solzhenitsyn Speaks to the West* (London: The Bodley Head, 1978), 17; and Edwards, ed., *The Collapse of Communism*, xiii.
8. Jung Chang and Jon Halliday, *Mao: The Unknown Story* (New York: Knopf, 2005).
9. Barbara Crossette, "Korean Famine Toll: More Than 2 Million," *New York Times*, August 20, 1999.
10. Moreover, though the summary table on p. 4 of *The Black Book of Communism* lists two million deaths, the more specific tabulation on p. 564 suggests 3.4 million deaths, all before the famine of the late 1990s that killed yet another two to three million. The actual number of North Koreans killed by communism could be six million.

11. Many sources use numbers as high as two to three million deaths in Cambodia. Even more conservative figures use numbers approaching two million. The Cambodian Genocide Program at Yale University uses a figure of 1.7 million, which it equates to 21 percent of the population (see: http://gsp.yale.edu/case-studies/cambodian-genocide-program). At the time of this writing, the first sentence of the Wikipedia entry for the "Cambodian genocide" uses the figure "1.5 to 3 million" (retrieved June 2, 2017). R. J. Rummel uses a figure of 2,035,000 (posted online at https://www.hawaii.edu/powerkills/NOTE1.HTM).
12. Richard Wurmbrand, *Marx & Satan* (Wheaton, IL: Crossway Books, 1986), p. 15.
13. See Rummel's classic book, *Death by Government* (New Brunswick, NJ: Transaction Publishers, 1994), which is posted online at https://www.hawaii.edu/powerkills/NOTE1.HTM.
14. The highest early scholarly estimates of the death toll of the sixty-four-year Spanish Inquisition (1481–1545) were some 31,912 were killed. See J. A. Llorente, *A Critical History of the Inquisition of Spain* (1823), 575–83.
15. Jonathan Rauch, "The Forgotten Millions," *The Atlantic*, December 2003.
16. Ibid.
17. Vladimir Lenin, *Pravda*, June 16, 1913, republished in *Lenin, Collected Works*, (Moscow: Progress Publishers, 1977), vol. 19, pp. 235–37.
18. Paul Kengor, *Takedown: From Communists to Progressives: How the Left Has Sabotaged Family and Marriage*, ch. 3.
19. Margaret Sanger, "Birth Control in Soviet Russia," *Birth Control Review*, June 1935, p. 3.
20. See Martin Malia in *The Black Book of Communism*, pp. x and xvii-xviii.
21. Gina Kolata, *The Great Flu Epidemic of 1918–19 and the Search for the Virus That Caused It* (Touchstone, 2001).
22. "Ronald Reagan: Pre-Presidential Papers: Selected Radio Broadcasts, 1975–1979," January 1975 to March 1977, Box 1, RRL. For a full transcript see Kiron K. Skinner, Annelise Anderson, and Martin Anderson, *Reagan, in His Own Hand: The Writings of Ronald Reagan That Reveal His Revolutionary Vision for* America, pp. 10–12.
23. Ibid.

24. President Ronald Reagan, "Address to the Annual Convention of the National Association of Evangelicals," Orlando, Florida, March 8, 1983.
25. Reagan speaking before CPAC, February 6, 1977, Washington, D.C. The text of the speech appears in James C. Roberts, ed., *A City Upon a Hill: Speeches by Ronald Reagan before the Conservative Political Action Conference* (American Studies Center, 1989), p. 33.
26. Ernest Conine, "President Reagan: How Does *That* Sound?" *Los Angeles Times*, March 17, 1980, p. 5.

Chapter 3: When and Where It All Began

1. See Mark Levin, *Ameritopia* (New York: Threshold/Simon & Schuster, 2012), ch. 3.
2. There is some debate over the exact year, whether 1792 or 1794.
3. Paul Johnson, *Modern Times: The World from the Twenties to the Nineties*, rev. ed. (Harper Perennial Modern Classics, 2001), p. 57.
4. See William Safire, "B.C./A.D. or B.C.E./C.E.?" *New York Times*, August 17, 1997.
5. Grigory Zinoviev, "Lenin: Speech to the Petrograd Soviet Celebrating Lenin's Recovery from Wounds Made in the Attempt on His Life," August 30, 1918, posted at https://www.marxists.org/archive/zinoviev/works/1918/lenin/ch18.htm.
6. V. I. Lenin, "Can 'Jacobinism' Frighten the Working Class?" *Pravda* No. 90, July 7 (June 24), 1917, later published in *Lenin Collected Works*, vol. 25 (Moscow: Progress Publishers, 1977), 121–22, posted online at https://www.marxists.org/archive/lenin/works/1917/jul/07a.htm.
7. As cited in Thomas Magstadt, *Understanding Politics: Ideas, Institutions, and Issues*, 11th ed. (Cengage Learning, 2014), p. 66.
8. Quoted in Johnson, *Modern Times* (NY: HarperCollins, 2001), p. 52.
9. See Martin Malia introduction in Marx and Engels, *The Communist Manifesto* (New York: Penguin Signet Classics edition, 1998), p. viii.
10. Daniel J. Flynn, *A Conservative History of the American Left* (New York: Random House/Crown Forum, 2008), p. 19.
11. Robert Owen, "Address at the Public Hall," New Harmony, Indiana, April 27, 1825. Online transcripts for this and other remarks cited in this box can be found at http://www.indiana.edu/~kdhist/H105-documents-web/week11/Owen1826.html and http://historyproject.ucdavis.edu/lessons/view_lesson.php?id=29.

12. Paul Kengor, *11 Principles of a Reagan Conservative* (New York: Beaufort Books, 2014), pp. 61 and 152.
13. Flynn, *A Conservative History of the American Left*, pp. 30–32.
14. See Paul Kengor, *Takedown: From Communists to Progressives, How the Left Has Sabotaged Family and Marriage* (WND, 2015), chapters 2–5.
15. "Marx and Engels meet in Paris; this is the beginning of a lifelong friendship and joint work." August 28, 1844, entry at the authoritative Marxists Internet Archive, https://www.marxists.org/archive/marx/bio/marx/lifeandwork.htm.
16. See Martin Malia's outstanding introduction in his 1998 Penguin Signet classics edition of *The Communist Manifesto*, pp. 9–10.
17. See Aristotle's classic *Politics*. This translation is one used by my colleague Robert R. Reilly. The renowned Aristotle scholar Benjamin Jowett translated the same passage differently: "And since innovations [also translated as "revolutions" or "revolutionary changes"] creep in through the private life of individuals also, there ought to be a magistracy which will have an eye to those whose life is not in harmony with the government, whether oligarchy or democracy or any other." The Terence Irwin and Gail Fine translation is, "And since people's private ways of life also lead them to revolution.... " A strict Greek translation would be "on account of private lives." (I thank my colleagues in the Grove City College Department of Philosophy for their assistance on this issue.)
18. One of the most influential early accounts of Marx's family life was Otto Ruhle's *Karl Marx: His Life and Works* (New York: Viking Press, 1929). Among more recent works, see Francis Wheen, *Karl Marx: A Life* (New York: W. W. Norton, 2001) and Paul Johnson, *Intellectuals: From Marx and Tolstoy to Sartre and Chomsky* (Harper Perennial, 2007), ch. 3.
19. Ibid., p. 74.
20. Ibid., p. 73.
21. Ibid.
22. Troy Jollimore, "The private life of Karl Marx," *Salon*, September 18, 2011.
23. Johnson, *Intellectuals*, p. 77.
24. See Francis Wheen, *Karl Marx: A Life* (New York: Norton, 1999), p. 249, and also Mary Gabriel, *Love and Capital: Karl and Jenny Marx and the Birth of a Revolution* (New York: Little, Brown, 2011), pp. 5–7.

25. Some sources claim three daughters committed suicide; some claim only one. I believe that the correct number is two.
26. Walter Williams, "Marx's racism," nationally syndicated column, June 21, 2006.
27. Johnson, *Intellectuals*, pp. 62 and 789.
28. Dmitri N. Shalin, *Pragmatism & Democracy* (New Brunswick, NJ: Transaction Publishers, 2011), p. 197 and Johnson, *Intellectuals*, p. 62.
29. Shalin, *Pragmatism & Democracy*, p. 197, and Williams, "Marx's racism."
30. Mary Gabriel, "Marx's Not-So-Marxist Marriage," Daily Beast, September 21, 2011.
31. Richard Weikart, "Marx, Engels, and the Abolition of the Family," *History of European Ideas*, vol. 18, no. 5, 1994, p. 667.
32. Quoted in Weikart, "Marx, Engels, and the Abolition of the Family," p. 668. Marx's defenders will probably want to argue that he was speaking tongue-in-cheek, given the high cost of financially supporting a large family. Personally, I'm inclined to a less charitable interpretation, given the realities of Marx's behavior and attitudes.
33. See, among others: H. Kent Geiger, *The Family in Soviet Russia*, (Cambridge, MA: Harvard University Press, 1968), p. 11 and Weikart, "Marx, Engels, and the Abolition of the Family," p. 657.
34. Frederick Engels, *The Origin of the Family, Private Property and the State* (New York, NY: International Publishers, 1942), p. 67.
35. Robert Payne, ed., *The Unknown Karl Marx* (New York University Press, 1971), 57.
36. Karl Marx, "The Pale Maiden: A Ballad," *Early Works of Karl Marx*, https://www.marxists.org/archive/marx/works/1837-pre/verse/verse24.htm.
37. Payne, *The Unknown Karl Marx*, 59–60.
38. Richard Wurmbrand, *Marx & Satan* (Wheaton, IL: Crossway Books, 1986), p. 15.
39. Quoted in Mehring, pp. 92–93.
40. Weikart, "Marx, Engels, and the Abolition of the Family," pp. 665–56.
41. Frederick Engels, *The Origin of the Family, Private Property and the State* (New York, NY: International Publishers, 1942), p. 67.
42. Ibid.
43. Geiger, *The Family in Soviet Russia*, pp. 20–21 and 33.

44. Marx and Engels, *The Communist Manifesto* (Penguin Signet Classics edition, 1998), p. 71.

Chapter 4: The Communist Program—and Its Problems

1. James Kirchick, "Communism's Victims Deserve a Museum," The Daily Beast, August 25, 2014.
2. "New Report Reveals U.S. Attitudes on Socialism, Communism on Eve of 2016 Election," Victims of Communism Memorial Foundation, October 17, 2016, http://victimsofcommunism.org/new-report-reveals-u-s-attitudes-on-socialism-communism-on-eve-of-2016-election/.
3. Karl Marx and Friedrich Engels, *The Communist Manifesto*, p. 74.
4. Ibid.
5. Richard Pipes, *Communism: A History* (Modern Library Chronicles, 2003), p. ix.
6. Kenneth Alan, *Explorations in Classical Sociological Theory* (Thousand Oaks: Pine Forge Press, 2005), p. 72.
7. As one Hegel scholar explains, "Hegel is a Christian, but not an orthodox one by the Nicene Creed. He denies the precedence of the Father, from whom the Son and the Spirit proceed. He denies that lordship is the meaning of divinity, so that Christ manifests divinity only as the risen Lord. The true definition of divinity is Spirit. But Hegel is not an ancient Gnostic like Marcion or Valentinus. He does not denigrate the body as the kingdom of the devil. He affirms the incarnation and construes natures as the logos made flesh, as spirit, i.e., the infinite Christ. He is a modern, Joachimite Gnostic: world history is the story of the logos making itself flesh in the rational state and human rights.... [Hegelian philosophy] is still Christian even if not orthodox. To be a heretic one must after all first be a Christian." Clark Butler, *New Perspectives on Hegel's Philosophy of Religion*, pp. 139 and 141.
8. Benedict XVI, *Spe Salvi*.
9. Karl Marx, *The German Ideology* (1844), https://www.marxists.org/archive/marx/works/1844/manuscripts/comm.htm#44CC4.
10. Ibid.
11. Robert Machurek, *Humor from the Pulpit*, p. 14.
12. Thomas M. Magstadt, *Understanding Politics: Ideas, Institutions, and Issues*, 12th ed. (Boston: Cengage Publishing, 2017), p. 51, quoting Roy

Macrides, *Contemporary Political Ideologies* (Cambridge, MA: Winthrop, 1980), p. 180.
13. Friedrich Engels, *Dialectics of Nature* (1883), https://www.marxists.org/archive/marx/works/1883/don/ch07c.htm#alteration.
14. Engels, *The Principles of Communism.*
15. Karl Marx, *Human Requirements and Division of Labour under the Rule of Private Property* (1844), https://www.marxists.org/archive/marx/works/1844/manuscripts/needs.htm.
16. Malia, introduction to *The Communist Manifesto*, p. 15.
17. Friedrich Engels, *The Principles of Communism* (1847), https://www.marxists.org/archive/marx/works/1847/11/prin-com.htm.
18. Marx, *The German Ideology*, https://www.marxists.org/archive/marx/works/1845/german-ideology/ch01a.htm#p48.
19. Friedrich Engels, "Letter to Otto Von Boenigk" (1890), https://www.marxists.org/archive/marx/works/1890/letters/90_08_21.htm.
20. Marx and Engels, *The Communist Manifesto*, p. 67.
21. Ibid.
22. Ibid., p. 75.
23. Ibid., p. 91.
24. Ibid.
25. Yuri Maltsev as related to my colleague Mark Hendrickson and to me, August 28, 2013.
26. Ronald Reagan, "Time for Choosing Address," October 27, 1964.
27. Karl Marx and Frederick Engels, *Collected Works,* 40 vols. (New York: International Publishers, 1976), 6:494–5.
28. V.I. Lenin, *On Socialist Ideology and Culture* (Moscow, USSR: Foreign Languages Publishing House, 1981), 51–52.
29. Benedict XVI, *Spe Salvi.*

Chapter 5: Bolshevik Brutes

1. Dmitri Volkogonov, *Lenin: A New Biography* (New York: Free Press, 1994), pp. 5 and 12–13.
2. Quoted in Volkogonov, *Lenin: A New Biography*, p. 373.
3. Quoted in J. M. Bochenski, "Marxism-Leninism and Religion," in B. R. Bociurkiw et al, eds., *Religion and Atheism in the USSR and Eastern Europe* (London: MacMillan, 1975), p. 11.

4. Richard Pipes, *Communism: A History* (NY: The Modern Library, 2001), pp. 30–32.
5. Ibid., p. 33.
6. Lenin, *The State and Revolution*, published in *Lenin's Collected Works*, Vol. 25, pp. 381–492, posted online at https://www.marxists.org/archive/lenin/works/1917/staterev/.
7. See the introductory notes provided to *The State and Revolution* at www.marxists.org. The portions of the document that I quote from here are taken from the version published at that site.
8. Pipes, *Communism: A History*, pp. 29–30; and the entirety of Richard Pipes, ed., *The Unknown Lenin: From the Secret Archive* (New Haven, CT: Yale University Press, 1999).
9. Lenin, *The State and Revolution*, chapter I, section 1, accessible at https://www.marxists.org/archive/lenin/works/1917/staterev/ch01.htm#s1.
10. Marx, *Private Property and Communism* (1844), https://www.marxists.org/archive/marx/works/1844/manuscripts/comm.htm#44CC8.
11. Marx, in one of his grim poems, wrote of human beings as "Apes of a cold God." See, inter alia, Robert Payne, *The Unknown Karl Marx* (New York: New York University Press, 1971), pp. 60–61, and Paul Johnson, *Intellectuals: From Marx and Tolstoy to Sartre and Chomsky* (Harper Perennial, 2007), pp. 54–55.
12. Much has been written on this by many sources. For one source, see Ralph Colp, "The Contacts Between Karl Marx and Charles Darwin," *Journal of the History of Ideas*, April–June 1974, Vol. 35, No. 2, pp. 329–38. Also see: Pipes, *Communism: A History*, pp. 9–10.
13. Engels, "Speech at the Graveside of Marx," Highgate Cemetery, London, March 17, 1883, https://www.marxists.org/archive/marx/works/1883/death/burial.htm.
14. Quoted in Barry Lee Woolley, *Adherents of Permanent Revolution: A History of the Fourth (Trotskyist) International* (Lanham, MD: University Press of America, 1999), pp. 4–5.
15. See Lenin, *The State and Revolution*, chapter I, section 4, accessible at https://www.marxists.org/archive/lenin/works/1917/staterev/ch01.htm#s4.
16. Ibid.
17. Ibid.

18. See Lenin, *The State and Revolution* (1917), chapter I, section 5, accessible at https://www.marxists.org/archive/lenin/works/1917/staterev/.
19. These two sections are in chapter III of Lenin's *The State and Revolution.*
20. Lenin, *The State and Revolution*, chapter V, section 2, accessible at https://www.marxists.org/archive/lenin/works/1917/staterev/ch05.htm#s2.
21. See chapter IV of Lenin's *The State and Revolution* (1917), section on "Letter to Bebel," https://www.marxists.org/archive/lenin/works/1917/staterev/ch04.htm#s3.
22. See chapter V, section 4 of Lenin's *The State and Revolution*, accessible at https://www.marxists.org/archive/lenin/works/1917/staterev/ch05.htm#s4 .
23. Benedict XVI, *Spe Salvi.*
24. Paul Johnson, *Modern Times* (New York: HarperCollins, 1992), pp. 56–65.
25. W. Bruce Lincoln, *Red Victory: A History of the Russian Civil War* (New York: Simon & Schuster, 1989), pp. 11–12.
26. See chapter 11, "Communism and Religion," in Nicolai Bukharin's *The ABC of Communism*, written in 1920, first published in English in 1922, published by Penguin Books in 1969, and posted online at https://www.marxists.org/archive/bukharin/works/1920/abc/11.htm.
27. Fulton J. Sheen, *Communism and the Conscience of the West* (Indianapolis, IN and New York: Bobbs-Merrill, 1948).
28. Quoted in John Koehler, *Spies in the Vatican* (NY: Pegasus Books, 2009), p. 1.
29. "A Restored Look for the Long-Ignored Churches of Russia," Associated Press, July 23, 1976, p. 3.
30. Hedrick Smith, *The Russians* (London: Sphere Books, 1976), p. 396.
31. James Thrower, God's Commissar: Marxism-Leninism as the Civil Religion of Soviet Society (Lewiston, NY: Edwin Mellen Press, 1992), p. 64; Jennifer McDowell, "Soviet Civil Ceremonies," *Journal for the Scientific Study of Religion*, Vol. 13, No. 3, 1974, pp. 265-79; and Powell, "Rearing the New Soviet Man," in B. R. Bociurkiw, et al., eds., *Religion and Atheism in the USSR and Eastern Europe* (London: MacMillan, 1975), pp. 160–65.

32. W. Bruce Lincoln, *Red Victory: A History of the Russian Civil War* (New York: Simon and Schuster, 1989), pp. 476–77.
33. Ibid.
34. James Thrower, God's Commissar: Marxism-Leninism as the Civil Religion of Soviet Society (Lewiston, NY: Edwin Mellen Press, 1992), p. 39.
35. Bochenski, "Marxism-Leninism and Religion," p. 11.
36. Lincoln, *Red Victory*, p. 474.
37. Alexander Solzhenitsyn, *The Gulag Archipelago, 1918–1956* (New York: Harper and Row, 1974), pp. 37–38.
38. Volkogonov, *Lenin*, pp. 376–78.
39. Ibid, pp. 29, 325–27, and 345–51.
40. Ibid.
41. James Billington, "Christianity and History," 125th anniversary lecture series, Grove City College, Grove City, Pennsylvania, September 27, 2001.
42. Radzinsky speaking in interview for A&E Biography of Joseph Stalin, "The Red Terror."
43. Mikhail Gorbachev, *Memoirs* (New York: Doubleday, 1996), p. 328.
44. Mikhail Gorbachev, *On My Country and the World*, (New York: Columbia University Press, 2000), pp. 20–21.
45. Alexander N. Yakovlev, *A Century of Violence in Soviet Russia* (New Haven and London: Yale University Press, 2002), pp. 8, 87, and 158.
46. Alexander Solzhenitsyn, "Men Have Forgotten God," Templeton Prize Award speech, May 10, 1983.
47. Yakovlev, *A Century of Violence in Soviet Russia*, p. 26.
48. Douglas Brown, *Doomsday 1917: The Destruction of Russia's Ruling Class* (London: Sidgwick and Jackson, 1975), p. 174; George Leggett, *The Cheka: Lenin's Political Police* (Oxford: Clarendon Press, 1981), pp. 463–38.
49. Alexander Solzhenitsyn, *Alexander Solzhenitsyn Speaks to the West* (London: Bodley Head, 1978), p. 17.
50. "The Collapse of the World's Best Political Jokes," *National Review*, August 6, 1990, p. 32.
51. Robert Conquest, "The Human Cost of Soviet Communism" in Document No. 92-36, 92nd Congress, 1st session, U.S. Senate, Judiciary Committee, Subcommittee to Investigate the Administration of the

Internal Security Act and Other Internal Security Laws, July 16, 1971, pp. 5–33.

52. For only one example of Lenin specifically preaching the words "mass terror" (to Grigory Zinoviev) see Lenin, "To G. Zinoviev," June 20, 1918, *Sochineniya* (*Works*) (4th ed.) (Moscow: State Publishing House for Political Literature, 1951), p. 275. For transcripts of Lenin directives, see Pipes, ed, *The Unknown Lenin*, pp. 1, 3, 8–11, 13–16, 46, 50, 55–6, 61, 63, 69, 71, 116–21, 127–29, and 150–55.
53. Richard Wurmbrand, *Tortured for Christ* (Bartlesville, OK: Living Sacrifice Book Company, 1998), p. 65.
54. Leggett, *The Cheka*, p. 103.
55. Orlando Figes, *A People's Tragedy: A History of the Russian Revolution*, cited in Steven Merritt Miner, "A Revolution Doomed From the Start," *New York Times Review of Books*, March 9, 1997.
56. Alexander Yakovlev, *A Century of Violence in Soviet Russia* (New Haven, Conn.: Yale University Press, 2002; Pipes, *The Unknown Lenin: From the Secret Archive*. (Full citations listed earlier.)
57. Pipes, *Communism: A History*, pp. 46–47.
58. Pipes, ed., *The Unknown Lenin*, p. 50.
59. See, inter alia, H. G. Wells, *An Experiment in Autobiography: Discoveries and Conclusions of a Very Ordinary Brain (Since 1866)* (New York: Little, Brown & Co., 1984), pp. 215, 667, and 687–89. Wells made several trips to the USSR in the 1920s and 1930s. See: H. G. Wells, *Russia in the Shadows* (George H. Doran Company, 1921), pp. 160–62.
60. Stephane Courtois, et al, *The Black Book of Communism* (Harvard University Press, 1999), p. 8.
61. Ibid., p. 15.
62. Nicolas Werth, in Courtois, et al., *Black Book*, pp. 103–4.

Chapter 6: The Comintern: Taking the Revolution to the World

1. Stephane Courtois et al, *The Black Book of Communism* (Harvard University Press, 1999), pp. 271–75.
2. See Richard Pipes, *Communism: A History* (New York: A Modern Library Chronicles Book, 2001), p. 93.
3. V.I. Lenin, *Collected Works*, Vol. 28 (Moscow: Progress Publishers, 1965), pp. 477–80.

4. Barry Lee Woolley, *Adherents of Permanent Revolution: A History of the Fourth (Trotskyist) International* (Lanham, MD: University Press of America, 1999), pp. 12–13.
5. See Richard Pipes, *Communism: A History* (New York: A Modern Library Chronicles Book, 2001), p. 49. Pipes's source is A. G. Latyshev, *Rassekrechennyi Lenin* (Moscow, 1996), p. 40. Also see Leon Trotsky, *Socialism in a Separate Country*, "The History of the Russian Revolution, Appendix II" (London: Victor Gollancz Ltd., 1934), p. 1244, posted at https://www.marxists.org/archive/trotsky/1930/hrr/ch50.htm.
6. Pipes, *Communism: A History*, p. 49. Pipes's source is V.I. Lenin, *Polnoe Sobranie Sochinenii* (Complete Works), 5th ed. (Moscow, 1958–65), vol. 42, p. 1.
7. Quoted by Leon Trotsky, *The History of the Russian Revolution*, trans. Max Eastman (Ann Arbor: University of Michigan Press, 1932), p. 395.
8. The full quotations from this program are published by Brian Crozier, *The Rise and Fall of the Soviet Empire* (Rocklin, CA: Forum, 1999), pp. 38–40.
9. Among other sources, see Brian Crozier, *The Rise and Fall of the Soviet Empire* (Rocklin, CA: Forum, 1999), pp. 38–40; and Courtois, *Black Book*, pp. 275–56.
10. See Pipes, *Communism: A History*, p. 93.
11. *The Capitalist World and the Communist International Manifesto of the Second Congress of the Third Communist International* (Moscow: Publishing Office of the Third Communist International, 1920), p. 23. This is the English-language "American edition" published by the United Communist Party of America.
12. Ibid., pp. 94–95.
13. Jane Degras, ed., *The Communist International, 1919–1943: Documents*, vol. I (London, 1956), pp. 166–72.
14. The CLP and a faction of the CPA merged in 1920 to form the "United Communist Party." Later, the CPA and UCP merged under the name of the former—CPA. In 1921, this group changed its name to the "Workers Party of America," which changed again in 1925 to "Workers (Communist) Party of America." The name was changed once more in 1929 to "Communist Party USA" (CPUSA). Harvey Klehr, John Earl Haynes, and Fridrikh Igorevich Firsov, *The Secret World of American Communism* (New Haven and London: Yale University Press, 1995), pp. 334–35.

15. "America's Top Communists of All Time," *The Washington Post*, September 23, 2013. It is said that Harvey Klehr participated in the compilation of this list. Writer Dylan Matthews has objected that certain faithful commies were not included in the list, such as James P. Cannon, Max Shachtman, James Burnham, Max Eastman, Bayard Rustin, Hilary Putnam, Bernardine Dohrn, Bill Ayers, Pete Seeger, Harry Haywood, Harry Dexter White, and Angela Davis. All of these are excellent notable mentions. Fabulous commies.
16. A typical example was William Schneiderman, code-named "Nat" with an alias of "Sherman," who was an agent of the NKVD in the 1930s, and was later made head of the Communist Party of California, where he would come into contact with individuals as significant as J. Robert Oppenheimer, the chief scientist at the Manhattan Project. Herbert Romerstein and Eric Breindel, *The Venona Secrets* (Washington, DC: Regnery, 2000), pp. 258–68.
17. Theodore Draper, *American Communism and Soviet Russia: The Formative Period* (Viking, 1960), p. 162.
18. There was a communist cell operating at *The New York Times* in the 1930s. In 1938 it splintered from *The New York Times* and created a publication called *The New Times*, which was intentionally made to look exactly like *The New York Times*, from masthead to type style and size. Research into this cell has not been adequately pursued or published. Two researchers who both knew of the cell were the late Herb Romerstein and the Hoover Institution's Arnold Beichman. Congress was well-aware of the existence of the cell, so much so that Congress investigated it. There is today a full shelf of Congressional reports at the Library of Congress containing this information. The reports just sit there, with no academic researchers bothering to look at them. The Senate Subcommittee on Internal Security of the Senate Judiciary Committee tried to get into the Communist Party unit at *The New York Times*, but failed to get much information. Nonetheless, one can find material from the committee's hearings in a 1955 series by the Senate Judiciary Committee, titled, "Strategy and Tactics of World Communism, Recruiting for Espionage," parts 14, 15, and 16.
19. This March 2, 1948, document was an inter-office "Office Memorandum: United States Government," basically an official internal FBI document, written by J. P. Coyne and addressed to assistant FBI director D. M. Ladd.

20. This document does not contain a date, though it clearly was produced in the summer 1919. Communist Party USA in the Comintern Archives, Library of Congress, Fond 515, Opis 1, Delo 1.
21. Ibid.
22. Ibid., Delo 9.
23. Ibid.
24. Ibid., Delo 4065. The figures were reported in a confidential CPUSA document titled, "Additional Memorandum on Problems of CPUSA," under a section titled, "Building the Communist Party."
25. Email correspondence between the author and Herb Romerstein, April 16, 2007.
26. *Revelations from the Russian Archives: A Report from the Library of Congress* (Washington, DC: Library of Congress, 1993), p. 29; John E. Haynes and Harvey Klehr, "'Moscow Gold,' Confirmed at Last?" *Labor History*, Vol. 33, No. 2, Spring 1992, pp. 279–93 and Vol. 33, No. 4, Fall 1992, pp. 576–68. Haynes and Klehr actually published receipts signed by Gus Hall, head of CPUSA. See also Harvey Klehr, John E. Haynes, et al., *The Secret World of American Communism*, p. 24, and Harvey Klehr, John Earl Haynes, and Kyrill M. Anderson, *The Soviet World of American Communism* (Yale University Press, 1998), p. 150. The most intriguing source documenting the funding from 1958 to 1980 is John Barron, *Operation Solo: The FBI's Man in the Kremlin* (Washington, DC: Regnery, 1996), pp. xv and 339–40. This book tells the remarkable story of Morris Childs, discussed later in this chapter, and gives more details on the funding of CPUSA by the USSR. Herb Romerstein has also reported on the funding in a number of publications.
27. Klehr, Haynes, et al., *The Secret World of American Communism*. See also Harvey Klehr, "Setting the Record on Joe McCarthy Straight," FrontPageMagazine, December 4, 2013.
28. Herb Romerstein, "From Henry Wallace to William Ayers—the Communist and 'Progressive' Movements," posted at www.usasurvival.org.
29. Sam Tanenhaus, *Whittaker Chambers* (New York: Random House, 1997), p. 58.
30. See Robert D. McFadden, "Khrushchev on Rosenbergs: Stoking Old Embers," *The New York Times*, September 25, 1990.

31. Haynes discussion with Paul Kengor and Herb Romerstein, June 18, 2007, Library of Congress, Madison Building; Romerstein and Breindel, *Venona Secrets*, p. 233.
32. See Ronald Radosh and Joyce Milton, *The Rosenberg File* (New Haven: Yale University Press, 1997), p. xi; and Robert McFadden, "Khrushchev on Rosenbergs: Stoking Old Embers," *New York Times*, September 25, 1990.
33. See, inter alia, Romerstein and Breindel, *Venona Secrets*, p. 233.
34. See Ion Mihai Pacepa and Ron Rychlak, *Disinformation*.
35. Allan Ryskind, *Hollywood Traitors: Blacklisted Screenwriters—Agents of Stalin, Allies of Hitler* (Washington, DC: Regnery, 2015); Larry Ceplair and Steven Englund, *The Inquisition in Hollywood: Politics in the Film Community, 1930–60* (Urbana and Chicago: University of Illinois Press, 2003).
36. Anna M. Lawton, *The Red Screen* (London: Routledge, 2002), p. 58.
37. William Z. Foster, *Toward Soviet America* (New York: International Publishers, 1932), pp. 272–73.
38. Paul Hollander, *Political Pilgrims* (New York: Harper & Row, 1983), p. 64.
39. Jean Wagner, *Black Poets of the United States: From Paul Laurence Dunbar to Langston Hughes* (Chicago and Urbana: University of Illinois Press, 1973), p. 435; Faith Berry, *Langston Hughes: Before and Beyond Harlem* (New York: Citadel Press, 1992), pp. 296–97.
40. Email correspondence between the author and Herb Romerstein, April 16, 2007, and June 23, 2007.
41. "Investigation of Un-American Activities and Propaganda," Special Committee on Un-American Activities, 75th Congress, House of Representatives, January 3, 1939, pp. 18–21.
42. Ibid.
43. Earl Browder, *Report to the 8th Convention, Communist Party* (New York: Workers Library Publishers, 1934), p. 104.
44. M. J. Olgin, *Why Communism?* (New York: Workers Library Publishers, 1933), p. 95.
45. "Conditions of Admission to the Communist International," *Party Organizer*, February 1931, p. 31.

46. "Structure and Function of Party Units," *Party Organizer*, February 1931, p. 2.

Chapter 7: Uncle Joe

1. Robert Conquest, "The Great Terror at 40," www.globalmuseumoncommunism.org.
2. These numbers come from *The Black Book of Communism* (p. 198), though other sources report very similar figures. See, among others, the extremely lengthy text of Khrushchev's 1956 "Crimes of Stalin" speech and also Robert Conquest, *The Great Terror* (New York: MacMillan, 1973), p. 485.
3. Courtois, et al., *The Black Book of Communism*, p. 198.
4. *Divini Redemptoris*, Encyclical of Pope Pius XI, March 1937, accessible at https://w2.vatican.va/content/pius-xi/en/encyclicals/documents/hf_p-xi_enc_19370319_divini-redemptoris.html.
5. Magstadt and Peter M. Schotten, *Understanding Politics: Ideas, Institutions, and Issues* (New York: St. Martin's Press, 1993), p. 69.
6. See Paul Kengor, "Stalin's Evil Empire: A Former Soviet Citizen Remembers," published at the website of the Center for Vision & Values, March 5, 2003, http://www.visionandvalues.org/2003/03/stalins-evil-empire-a-former-soviet-citizen-remembers/.
7. Janusz Bardach and Kathleen Gleeson, *Man is Wolf to Man: Surviving the Gulag* (Berkeley, CA: University of California Press, 1999).
8. See, inter alia, Mikhail Heller and Aleksandr Nekrich, *Utopia in Power: The History of the Soviet Union from 1917 to the Present* (New York: Summit Books, a division of Simon & Schuster, 1986), pp. 66 and 116; David Remnick, "Seasons in Hell," *The New Yorker*, April 14, 2003.
9. "Death in the Kremlin: Killer of the Masses," *Time*, March 16, 1953, http://content.time.com/time/magazine/article/0,9171,935828,00.html.
10. See, inter alia, Pipes, *Communism: A History*, p. 61; Werth in Courtois, et al., *The Black Book of Communism*, pp. 159 and 167; and the official website at the Library of Congress, https://www.loc.gov/exhibits/archives/ukra.html.
11. Kengor, "Stalin's Evil Empire: A Former Soviet Citizen Remembers."
12. See, inter alia, Steven Erlanger, "Moscow Resurrecting Icon of Its Past Glory," *The New York Times*, September 26, 1995; and "A Restored Look

for the Long-Ignored Churches of Russia," Associated Press, July 23, 1976, p. B3.

13. Brian Crozier, *The Rise and Fall of the Soviet Empire* (Rocklin, CA: Forum, 1999), pp. 519–21. Also see Kengor, *Dupes*, pp. 233–34.
14. Paul Kengor, *Dupes: How America's Adversaries Have Manipulated Progressives for a Century* (Intercollegiate Studies Institute, 2010), pp. 170–74.
15. Richard Pipes, "'Death Solves All Problems,' He Said," *New York Times*, November 10, 1991.
16. See Kengor, *Dupes*, p. 165.
17. H. G. Wells, *An Experiment in Autobiography: Discoveries and Conclusions of a Very Ordinary Brain (Since 1866)* (New York: Little, Brown & Co., 1984), pp. 215, 667, and 687–89. Wells made several trips to the USSR in the 1920s and 1930s. See: H. G. Wells, *Russia in the Shadows* (George H. Doran Company, 1921), pp. 160–62.
18. In the early 1930s, Shaw, who by then was in his seventies, visited the USSR for ten days. See George Bernard Shaw, *The Rationalization of Russia* (Bloomington, Indiana: Indiana University Press, 1964), pp. 73 and 112.
19. Letter to the editor of the *Manchester Guardian* published March 2, 1933. Shaw was the author and lead signatory of the letter, followed by twenty other signers. As the letter itself stated, Shaw and all of the twenty others had been "recent visitors to the USSR."
20. Bertrand Russell, *The Practice and Theory of Bolshevism* (Auckland, New Zealand: The Floating Press, 2013—the original edition was published in 1920), p. 4.
21. U.S. Congress, House of Representatives, Select Committee on the Katyn Forest Massacre. *The Katyn Forest Massacre: Hearings Before the Select Committee on Conduct and Investigation of the Facts, Evidence and Circumstances of the Katyn Forest Massacre*, 82nd Congress, 1st and 2nd Session, 1951–1952 (Washington, DC: GPO, 1952), pp. 2204–7; Laurence Rees, *WWII Behind Closed Doors: Stalin, the Nazis and the West* (New York: Pantheon, 2008), pp. 248–89.
22. See, inter alia, Herb Romerstein and Eric Breindel, *The Venona Secrets* (Washington, DC: Regnery, 2000), pp. 214–16 and 473; Eduard Mark, "Venona's Source 19 and the 'Trident' Conference of May 1943:

Diplomacy or Espionage?" *Intelligence and National Security*, Summer 1998, pp. 1–31.

23. Colleagues whom I greatly respect, including Ron Radosh, believe that Hopkins was a duped progressive and not a spy and not "Agent 19." See my discussion in *Dupes*, pp. 175–80.
24. Email correspondence with Herb Romerstein, February 13, 2009.
25. Here, too, see my discussion in *Dupes*, pp. 162–63 and also Romerstein and Breindel, *The Venona Secrets*, pp. 210–1.
26. Milovan Djilas, trans. Michael B. Pterovich, *Conversations with Stalin* (New York: Harcourt, Brace & World, 1962), p. 114.
27. John T. Rourke, Ralph G. Carter, and Mark A. Boyer, *Making American Foreign Policy* (New York: McGraw-Hill/Dushkin, 1994), p. 140. Also see discussion in Kengor, *Dupes*, pp. 233–35.
28. Quoted in David McCullough, *Truman* (New York: Simon and Schuster, 1992), p. 262.
29. Quoted in Alonzo Hamby, *Man of the People: A Life of Harry S. Truman* (New York: Oxford University Press, 1995), pp. 313–14.
30. The large headline on the front page of *The Washington Post* the next day (February 10, 1946) was "Stalin Blames Capitalism For 2 Wars."
31. Antony Beevor, *The Fall of Berlin 1945* (New York: Viking-Penguin, 2002), pp. 32–34 and 410–13.
32. James C. Humes, *Eisenhower and Churchill: The Partnership That Saved the World* (New York: Random House/Prima Publishing, 2001).
33. Brinkley speaking on C-SPAN's "Booknotes," November 8, 1995.
34. For a sample of reactions, see: Spencer Warren, "Churchill's Realism: Reflections on the Fulton Speech," *The National Interest*, Winter 1995–1996, pp. 42–44.
35. Paul Johnson, *Modern Times* (New York: HarperCollins, 1992), pp. 73–74.
36. Wurmbrand, *Tortured for Christ*, pp. 33–38.
37. Riley, *Fulton J. Sheen*, p. 149.
38. H. W. Crocker III, *Triumph: The Power and Glory of the Catholic Church* (New York: Three Rivers Press, 2001), pp. 407–8.
39. Fulton Sheen described Mindszenty's martyrdom as "dry" because the cardinal suffered primarily mental torture rather than a physical bloodletting. Sheen would say this many times, first during a 1957 broadcast of his popular television show, "Life Is Worth Living."

40. Jozsef Cardinal Mindszenty, *Memoirs* (New York: Macmillan Publishing, 1974).
41. The best book on Father Jerzy is Roger Boyes and John Moody's *Messenger of the Truth*, which provides these details at great length. See Roger Boyes and John Moody, *Messenger of the Truth* (Warsaw: Drukarnia Loretanska, 2013). The book was originally published by Boyes and Moody as *The Priest and the Policeman* (New York: Summit Books, 1987). Also see chapter 26 of Paul Kengor, *A Pope and a President: John Paul II, Ronald Reagan, and the Extraordinary Untold Story of the 20th Century* (Wilmington, Delaware: ISI Books, 2017).
42. Ibid.
43. Svetlana Alliluyeva, *Twenty Letters to a Friend* (New York: Harper & Row, 1967), p. 9; Arthur Schlesinger Jr., "Twenty Letters to a Father," *The Atlantic*, November 1967.
44. Alliluyeva, *Twenty Letters to a Friend*, p. 10.
45. Aleksandr I. Solzhenitsyn, *The Gulag Archipelago: 1918–56, Vols. I–II* (San Francisco: Harper & Row, 1973), p. 69.
46. Ibid.
47. Ibid., pp. 7–11.
48. Ibid., p. 10.
49. Ibid., pp. 8–10. A dramatic account from which I have drawn is provided by Ravi Zacharias in his 1992 Harvard Veritas Forum (audio cassette tape provided by RZIM Ministries, Norcross, Georgia, 1992). Zacharias was told the true story of Stalin's death by Malcolm Muggeridge, who heard it from a tormented Svetlana.
50. Ibid., p. 10.

Chapter 8: Mao and Other Monsters: Communism Assaults Asia

1. M. Stanton Evans and Herb Romerstein, *Stalin's Secret Agents* (New York: Simon & Schuster, Threshold Editions, 2012), p. 142.
2. Edgar Snow, *Red Star over China* (NY: Random House, 1968).
3. Ibid., p. 17.
4. Ibid., p. 90.
5. Ibid., pp. 90–94.
6. Ibid., pp. 95–96.
7. Ibid., pp. 59, 82–83, 104, 345–46, 359–60, 368–89, 386, and 445.

8. Jasper Becker, *Hungry Ghosts: Mao's Secret Famine* (New York: Henry Holt, 1996).
9. Li Zhisui, *The Private Life of Chairman Mao* (New York: Random House, 1994).
10. See, inter alia, Pierre Rigoulot, "Crimes, Terror, and Secrecy in North Korea," in Stephane Courtois, et al, *The Black Book of Communism* (Harvard University Press, 1999), p. 548.
11. The official text of the Cairo conference, released December 1, 1943, declared: "The aforesaid three great powers, mindful of the enslavement of the people of Korea, are determined that in due course Korea shall become free and independent." See text posted at http://avalon.law.yale.edu/wwii/cairo.asp.
12. See, inter alia, *Arnold A. Offner, Another Such Victory: President Truman and the Cold War, 1945–53* (Stanford, CA: Stanford University Press, 2002), p. 349.
13. Rigoulot, "Crimes, Terror, and Secrecy," p. 549.
14. Christopher Hitchens, "Worse Than 1984: North Korea, Slave State," *Slate*, May 2, 2005.
15. See Pat Roberts interview with CNN's Wolf Blitzer, "Late Edition," May 8, 2005, posted at http://www.cnn.com/TRANSCRIPTS/0505/08/le.01.html.
16. David Hawk, *"Thank You, Father Kim Il Sung:" Eyewitness Accounts of Severe Violations of Freedom of Thought, Conscience, and Religion in North Korea*, United States Commission on International Religious Freedom, November 2005, pp. iv–vi.
17. David Wallechinsky, "The World's 10 Worst Dictators," *Parade*, February 22, 2004.
18. Hawk, *"Thank You, Father Kim Il Sung:" Eyewitness Accounts*, pp. iv-vi.
19. Rigoulot, "Crimes, Terror, and Secrecy," pp. 552–53.
20. Anthony Faiola, "An Act of Subversion, Carried by Balloons," *The Washington Post*, August 10, 2005.
21. Hawk, "*Thank You, Father Kim Il Sung*," pp. iv–vi.
22. Ibid., *Eyewitness Accounts*, pp. iv–vi.
23. Ibid.
24. Bradley K. Martin, *Under the Loving Care of the Fatherly Leader: North Korea and the Kim Dynasty*, (St. Martin's Press, 2004).

25. David Wallechinsky, "The World's 10 Worst Dictators," *Parade*, February 22, 2004.
26. Hawk, *"Thank You, Father Kim Il Sung:" Eyewitness Accounts*, pp. iv–vi.
27. "North Korea's Funny Man," *Economist*, January 26, 1996.
28. Ibid.
29. Allan C. Brownfeld, "Ramblings," *St. Croix Review*, April 1999, Vol. XXXII, No. 2, pp. 13–14.
30. Ibid.
31. "The Carter Interview: Jimmy Carter's North Korean Notebook," *Atlanta-Journal Constitution*, July 3, 1994, p. A12.
32. Barbara Crossette, "Korean Famine Toll: More Than 2 Million," *New York Times*, August 20, 1999.
33. Ibid.
34. *MacNeil-Lehrer Newshour*, PBS, October 20, 1997.
35. "Fed Up in North Korea," *The Washington Post*, April 9, 2000.
36. James Brooke, "Kim Jong Il's Ex-chef Lifts Lid on Ruler's Fancy Tastes," *New York Times*, October 20, 2004.
37. Antony Barnett, "Revealed: The Gas Chamber Horror of North Korea's Gulag," *The Guardian*, February 1, 2004.
38. Antony Barnett, "Revealed: The Gas Chamber Horror of North Korea's Gulag" *The Guardian*, February 1, 2004.
39. Alex Gore, "Revealed: North Korean Leader Kim Jong-il 'Died in Fit of Rage after Being Told a Major Dam Had Sprung a Leak,'" *London Daily Mail*, December 30, 2012.
40. Julian Ryall, "North Korean Army Minister 'Executed with Mortar Round,'" *London Daily Telegraph*, October 24, 2012.
41. Gavin Fernando, "Inside North Korea's Secret Sex Parties," *New York Post*, April 28, 2016.
42. Paul Boyer, *The American Nation* (Austin, Texas: Holt, Rinehart, and Winston, 1998), p. 799. My thanks to Jillaine Lambach for sharing this gem with me.
43. *The Black Book of Communism*, p. 564.
44. Nguyen Bich, "Vietnam Under Communism," http://vietnam.museumoncommunism.org/content/history-7, retrieved June 8, 2017.
45. Ron Radosh, "Ho Chi Minh Gets White House Praise," *Wall Street Journal*, July 26, 2013.
46. Ibid.

47. See "Our Communist Founding Fathers" in Paul Kengor, *The Communist: Frank Marshall Davis: The Untold Story of Barack Obama's Mentor* (Mercury Ink, 2012).
48. Dr. Benjamin Spock and Mitchell Zimmerman, *Dr. Spock on Vietnam* (New York: Dell, 1968), pp. 15–17.
49. Ian Schwartz, "Obama: 'Ho Chi Minh Was Actually Inspired by the Declaration of Independence and the Constitution,'" RealClearPolitics, July 26, 2013.
50. Pope Pius XI, *Divini Redemptoris*, March 1937.
51. Seth Jacobs, *Cold War Mandarin: Ngo Dinh Diem and the Origins of America's War in Vietnam, 1950–1963* (Lanham, MD: Rowman & Littlefield, 2006), p. 124.
52. Geoffrey Shaw, *The Lost Mandate of Heaven: The American Betrayal of Ngo Dinh Diem, President of Vietnam* (San Francisco: Ignatius Press, 2015), p. 18.
53. Edwin E. Moise, *A to Z of the Vietnam War* (Lanham, MD: Rowman & Littlefield, 2005), p. 9.
54. President Lyndon B. Johnson, "Remarks on Receiving the National Freedom Award," February 23, 1966.
55. Earl Tilford, "Vietnam in the Rear View Mirror," posted at the website of the Center for Vision & Values, June 1, 2016.
56. Pascal Fontaine, "Communism in Latin America," in Stephane Courtois, ed., et al., *The Black Book of Communism* (Cambridge, Mass.: Harvard University Press, 1999), p. 652.
57. Ronald Reagan, "Farewell Address to the Nation," Washington, DC, January 11, 1989, http://www.presidency.ucsb.edu/ws/?pid=29650.
58. See Courtois, et al., eds., *The Black Book of Communism*, pp. 4 and 572–74 and the Victims of Communism website, http://victimsofcommunism.org/tag/vietnam/.
59. We discussed the various estimates earlier in this book. For a careful analysis of the figures, see the assessment by Jean-Louis Margolin in the chapter on Cambodia in *The Black of Communism*, particularly pages 588–91. *The Black Book* considers estimates ranging from Ben Kiernan's number of 1.5 million to a figure of 3.1 million cited by Pen Sovan, the former secretary general of the People's Revolutionary Party of Kampuchea, which took power in 1979. *The Black Book* settles on an estimate of two million, which it contends would equate

to one in four or five Cambodians (that is 20–25 percent of Cambodians). If the number is as high as three-plus million, it would equate to closer to 40 percent (or higher) of the pre-Khmer Rouge population.

Chapter 9: Meet Fidel and Che, Two Vicious Commie Nuts Who Wanted to Blow Up the World

1. Che Guevara, "One year of combat," *El Cubano Libre*, January 1958.
2. The definitive work on Matthews and Cuba is Anthony DePalma, *The Man Who Invented Fidel: Castro, Cuba, and Herbert L. Matthews of* The New York Times (New York: Public Affairs, 2007).
3. Herbert L. Matthews, "Cuban Rebel Is Visited in Hideout," *The New York Times*, February 24, 1957, p. 1.
4. Ibid.
5. Ibid.
6. For a good summary, see Jonathan Alter, "Taking Sides," *The New York Times*, Sunday Book Review, April 23, 2006—a review of Anthony DePalma's *The Man Who Invented Fidel.* Alter writes that by 1959 Castro had openly "credited" Matthews's articles with helping to bring him to power. In 1959, during his celebrated visit to the United States, Castro, writes Alter, "bragged that when Matthews met him in the mountains two years earlier his movement was down to 18 soldiers—one bedraggled column that walked in circles to fool the reporter."
7. Paul Hollander, *Political Pilgrims* (New York: Harper & Row, 1983), p. 236.
8. Ibid., p. 238.
9. Pascal Fontaine, "Communism in Latin America," in Stephane Courteos, ed., et al., *The Black Book of Communism* (Cambridge, MA: Harvard University Press, 1999), pp. 648–49.
10. Humberto Fontova, "Che Guevara Exposed: The Killer on the Lefties' T-Shirts," Townhall.com, January 21, 2010.
11. Fontaine, "Communism in Latin America," pp. 648–52; Alvaro Vargas Llosa, "The Killing Machine," *New Republic*, posted at the website of The Independent Institute, July 11, 2005.
12. James Kirchick, "Communism's Victims Deserve a Museum," The Daily Beast, August 25, 2014.
13. Paul Berman, "The Cult of Che," Slate.com, October 30, 1997.
14. Llosa, "The Killing Machine."

15. Ibid.
16. Ibid.
17. Ibid.
18. Ibid.
19. Fontova, "Che Guevara Exposed."
20. Ibid.
21. Fontaine, "Communism in Latin America," p. 656.
22. Fontova, "Che Guevara Exposed."
23. Ibid.
24. Ibid.
25. Ibid.
26. *Prairie Fire: The Politics of Revolutionary Anti-Imperialism* was released in 1974 by the Weather Underground, with the publisher listed as the Communications Company, based in Brooklyn, New York, and San Francisco. To read *Praire Fire* online, go to https://archive.org/stream/PraireFireThePoliticsOfRevolutionaryAnti-imperialismThePolitical/Prairie-fire_djvu.txt.
27. Fontova, "Che Guevara Exposed," pp. 41–42.
28. Ibid.
29. Llosa, "The Killing Machine."
30. Fontova, "Che Guevara Exposed;" Llosa, "The Killing Machine."
31. Llosa, "The Killing Machine," quoting Philippe Gavi, *Che Guevara* (Éditions universitaires, 1970).
32. "On the Brink of Nuclear War" (discussion between Robert McNamara, Keith Payne, and Terence Smith), *The Newshour with Jim Lehrer*, February 22, 2001.
33. Ibid.
34. Ibid.
35. Ibid.
36. Sergei Khrushchev, *Nikita Khrushchev and the Creation of a Superpower* (Penn State University Press, 2001), pp. 627–29.
37. Ibid., p. 628.
38. Ibid., p. 630.
39. Ibid., pp. 637–42.
40. Ibid.
41. Fontova, "Che Guevara Exposed."
42. Henry Weinstein and Judy Pasternak, "I. F. Stone Dies," *Los Angeles Times*, June 19, 1989, p. A1; Mona Charen, *Useful Idiots* (Washington,

DC: Regnery, 2003), p. 89. See also the many tributes posted at http://www.ifstone.org/on_his_death.php.

43. Hollander, *The Survival of the Adversary Culture* (New Brunswick, NJ: Transaction Publishers, 1988), p. 218.
44. Fontova, "Che Guevara Exposed."
45. Ibid.
46. Ibid.
47. Llosa, "The Killing Machine."
48. Mary Anastasia O'Grady, "Today's Cuba a Nicer Place? Ask Maritza Lugo," *Wall Street Journal*, April 21, 2000; Armando Valladares, "A Firsthand Account of Child Abuse, Castro Style," *Wall Street Journal*, May 5, 2000.
49. See: Fontaine, "Communism in Latin America," p. 664.
50. Ibid., p. 656.
51. Ibid., p. 663.
52. Such is the estimate in *The Black Book of Communism*. See: Fontaine, "Communism in Latin America," p. 664.

Chapter 10: "21st Century Socialism" (Read: Communism)

1. P. J. O'Rourke, *Holidays in Hell* (Grove Press, 1988), p. 214.
2. "Guide to Subversive Organizations and Publications (and Appendices)," revised and published December 1, 1961, to supersede Guide published on January 2, 1957 (including Index), prepared and released by the Committee on Un-American Activities, U.S. House of Representatives, Washington, DC, 87th Congress, 2nd Session, House Document No, 398.
3. See: Paul Kengor, "*The Nation*'s Top 50 'Progressives'... and Socialists and Communists," *The American Spectator*, March 30, 2012.
4. See the website of the World Socialist Party of the United States: http://www.wspus.org/sample-page/declaration-of-principles/.
5. Alex Adrianson, "Socialism Can Never Work," *The Insider* (Heritage Foundation), Spring 2016, p. 2.
6. "Lenin's Political Thought," posted at the website of the International Socialist Organization's New York City chapter, http://nycsocialist.org/2014/01/lenins-political-thought-book-club/, retrieved June 13, 2016. Also see: Spyridon Mitsotakis, "Inside the Leftist Religion That Worships Murder and Mayhem," Conservative Review, May 29, 2016.

7. Carl Davidson, "21st century socialism: What makes it different?" *People's World*, April 6, 2016.
8. See: Volkogonov, *Lenin*, pp. 372–74.
9. Geoffrey Jacques, "What we talk about when we talk about socialism," People's World, June 8, 2016.
10. "Socialism of the 21st Century," Wikipedia, https://en.wikipedia.org/wiki/Socialism_of_the_21st_century, retrieved July 6, 2016.
11. Juan Forero, "Hugo Chávez, Passionate but Polarizing Venezuelan President, Dead at 58," *The Washington Post*, March 5, 2013.
12. Jonathan P. Hicks, "Venezuela's Leader to Send Heating Oil to the South Bronx," *New York Times*, November 26, 2005, http://www.nytimes.com/2005/11/26/nyregion/venezuelas-leader-to-send-heating-oil-to-south-bronx.html?_r=0.
13. Nathan Crooks and Jose Orozco, "Chávez Price Caps Spark Panic Buying of Coffee, Toilet Paper," Bloomberg News, November 25, 2011.
14. Nathan Crooks and Jose Orozco, "Chávez Price Caps Spark Panic Buying of Coffee, Toilet Paper," Bloomberg News, November 25, 2011.
15. "The Collapse of the World's Best Political Jokes," *National Review*, August 6, 1990, p. 32.
16. Nathan Crooks and Jose Orozco, "Chávez Price Caps Spark Panic Buying of Coffee, Toilet Paper," Bloomberg News, November 25, 2011.
17. Ibid.
18. Forero, "Hugo Chávez, Passionate but Polarizing Venezuelan President."
19. Ibid.
20. Ibid.
21. Andrew Clark, "Chávez Creates Overnight Bestseller with Book Gift to Obama," *Guardian*, April 19, 2009.
22. Barack Obama, *Dreams from My Father: A Story of Race and Inheritance* (New York: Times Books, 1995), pp. 100–101.
23. See a very instructive analysis at the www.worldsocialism.org website, "Hugo Chávez: '21st Century Socialist' or Populist Strongman?" http://www.worldsocialism.org/spgb/socialist-standard/2010s/2013/no-1304-april-2013/hugo-Chávez-%E2%80%9821st-century-socialist%E2%80%99-or-populist-st, retrieved July 6, 2016.
24. "Hugo Chávez: '21st Century Socialist' or Populist Strongman?" World Socialism, http://www.worldsocialism.org/spgb/socialist-standard/2010s/2013/no-1304-april-2013/hugo-Chávez-%E2%80%9821st-century-socialist%E2%80%99-or-populist-st, contains very instructive analysis.

25. Forero, "Hugo Chávez, Passionate but Polarizing Venezuelan President."
26. John Sparks, "The Truth about Socialism (Part 1): The Venezuelan Disaster," The Center for Vision & Values, June 21, 2016, www.visionandvalues.org.
27. Ronald Reagan, "Remarks to the National Federation of Independent Business," Washington DC, June 22, 1983.
28. John Sparks, "The Truth about Socialism (Part 1): The Venezuelan Disaster."
29. "Venezuela Today Looks like Zimbabwe 15 Years Ago," The Economist, April 2, 2016.
30. John Sparks, "The Truth About Socialism (Part 2): Venezuela Destroys Its Currency," posted at the website of the Center for Vision & Values, www.visionandvalues.org, July 7, 2016.
31. John Sparks, "The Truth About Socialism (Part 2): Venezuela Destroys Its Currency," posted at the website of the Center for Vision & Values, July 7, 2016, www.visionandvalues.org.
32. Steve H. Hanke, "R. I. P. Zimbabwe Dollar," Cato Institute report, http://www.cato.org/zimbabwe.
33. "Venezuela: New Regime Effectively Amounts to Forced Labor," July 28, 2016, https://www.amnesty.org/en/latest/news/2016/07/venezuela-new-regime-effectively-amounts-to-forced-labour/.
34. "Zimbabwe 100 Trillion Dollars Banknotes, AA /2008, P-91, UNC,100 Trillion Series," http://banknoteworld.com/shop/Zimbabwe-100-Trillion-Dollar-Banknote.html?gclid=CN-68K6m5s0CFQkfhgodhF0I5A.
35. July 9, 2016, mail from Mark Hendrickson, economics professor at Grove City College.
36. Gabriel Hetland, "Why Is Venezuela in Crisis?" *The Nation*, August 17, 2016.
37. For a summary, see J. P. Carroll, "Flashback: All Those People Who Praised Chávez's Socialism," The Daily Caller, May 22, 2016, posted at http://dailycaller.com/2016/05/22/flashback-to-all-the-people-who-praised-Chávezs-socialism/ and Ben Kew, "10 Famous People Who Praised Venezuela's Descent Into Socialist Hell," Breitbart, May 4, 2017, posted at http://www.breitbart.com/national-security/2017/05/04/ten-influential-public-figures-praised-venezuelas-descent-socialist-hell/.

38. Daniel Miller, "Hugo Chávez Can't Be embalmed Because His Body Was Already Decomposing, Officials Reveal," *Daily Mail*, March 15, 2013.

Chapter 11: Why Doesn't Everybody Know Communism's Appalling Track Record?

1. See "Little Change in Public's Response to 'Capitalism,' 'Socialism,'" Pew Research Center, December 28, 2011, http://www.people-press.org/2011/12/28/little-change-in-publics-response-to-capitalism-socialism/.
2. See Emily Ekins, "Millennials Don't Know What 'Socialism' Means," Reason, July 16, 2014, http://reason.com/poll/2014/07/16/millennials-dont-know-what-socialism-mea; Emily Ekins and Joy Pullmann, "Why So Many Millennials Are Socialist," The Federalist, February 15, 2016, http://thefederalist.com/2016/02/15/why-so-many-millennials-are-socialists/; and Emily Ekins, "Millennials Like Socialism—Until They Get Jobs," *The Washington Post*, March 24, 2016, https://www.washingtonpost.com/news/in-theory/wp/2016/03/24/millennials-like-socialism-until-they-get-jobs/?utm_term=.c2b608327058.
3. See Ekins, "Millennials Like Socialism"; Aubree Poole, "Gallup: 69% of Millennials Ready for a Socialist President," Red Alert Politics, July 5, 2016, http://redalertpolitics.com/2016/07/05/gallup-69-millennials-ready-socialist-president/.
4. Ronald Radosh, "Rehab for Reds," *Weekly Standard*, May 16, 2016.
5. Ronald Radosh, "Bernie's Adventures on a Stalinist Kibbutz," *PJ Media*, February 6, 2016 https://pjmedia.com/ronradosh/2016/02/06/bernies-adventures-on-a-stalinist-kibbutz/.
6. Daniel Greenfield, "Bernie Sanders Spent Months at Marxist-Stalinist Kibbutz," FrontPageMagazine, February 4, 2016, posted at http://www.frontpagemag.com/point/261724/bernie-sanders-spent-months-marxist-stalinist-daniel-greenfield .
7. Tim Mak, "Bernie's Past with the Far Far Far Left," *The Daily Beast*, January 30, 2016.
8. John Bachtell, "The Sanders campaign, political revolution, and the 2016 election," *People's World*, February 25, 2016.
9. Ronald Radosh, "Rehab for Reds," *Weekly Standard*, May 16, 2016.
10. Malcolm Harris, "Who's Afraid of Communism?" *New Republic*, April 27, 2016.

11. Pecinovsky's bio page at the *People's World* website describes him as "the bureau chief of the Missouri/Kansas Friends of the *People's World*."
12. Tony Pecinovsky, "New book offers inside look at Soviet Communist Party discipline," *People's World*, May 19, 2016.
13. See, inter alia, V. I. Lenin, *Collected Works, Vol. 31: April-December 1920* (Moscow: Progress Publishers, 1977), p. 291; "On Soviet Morality," *Time*, February 16, 1981, p. 17; and my lengthy discussion of this quotation and Lenin's thinking in Paul Kengor, *Dupes: How America's Adversaries Have Manipulated Progressives for a Century* (Intercollegiate Studies Institute, 2010), pp. 371–76.
14. This quotation is well established. For a current source documenting it nicely, see Barry Popkin, who, among other bona fides, is a contributor to the *Oxford English Dictionary*. At his website Popkin lists at least a half-dozen contemporaneous books (all by reputable, leading publishers of their day, such as MacMillan and Viking) with very similar variations of the quote, including Harry Greenwall's *Mirrors of Moscow* (1929), Bruce Hopper's *What Russia Intends* (1931), Margaret (Reibold) Craig-McKerrow's *The Iron Road to Samarcand* (1932), Thomas Woody's *New Minds: New Men?* (1932), and Walter Duranty's *Duranty Reports Russia* (1934). Duranty, of course, was the Pulitzer Prize-winning (and infamous) *New York Times* correspondent on Moscow. Duranty reported the Lenin quotation this way: "Give me four years to teach the children, and the seed I shall have sown will never be uprooted" (*Duranty Reports Russia,* p. 175).
15. Lenin was said to have made this statement to his Commissars of Education in 1923. The full quotation: "We must hate—hatred is the basis for communism. Children must be taught to hate their parents if they are not communists. If they are, then the child need not respect them; need no longer worry about them." This quotation was cited in the *Congressional Record* of April 1, 1933, pp. 1538–39, in an insertion by Senator Arthur R. Robinson.
16. Daniel J. Flynn, "The Sixties' Road to Rutgers and Beyond," *American Spectator*, May 9, 2014; Ralph Toledano, *Cry Havoc!, The Great American Bring-down and How it Happened* (Washington, DC: Anthem Books, 2006), pp. 151–53, 159, 188, and 191; Jonah Goldberg, *Liberal Fascism: The Secret History of the American Left, from Mussolini to the Politics of Meaning* (Doubleday, 2008).

17. Rorty was bracingly candid in his message to parents: "We are going to go right on trying to discredit you in the eyes of your children, trying to strip your fundamentalist religious community of dignity, trying to make your views seem silly rather than discussable." Robert B. Brandom, ed., *Rorty and his Critics* (Oxford: Blackwell, 2000), pp. 21–22.
18. David Horowitz, *The Black Book of the American Left: Volume II: Progressives* (Los Angeles: Second Thoughts Books, 2013), p. 138.
19. Karl Marx and Friedrich Engels, *The Communist Manifesto*, ed. Martin Malia (Penguin Signet Classics, 1998), p. 71.
20. William W. Brickman, ed., *John Dewey's Impressions of Soviet Russia and the Revolutionary World, Mexico-China-Turkey 1929* (New York: Bureau of Publications, Teachers College, Columbia University, 1964), p. 17.
21. Ibid., pp. 17–18.
22. Ibid., p. 18.
23. Ibid.
24. Henry T. Edmondson III, *John Dewey and the Decline of American Education* (Wilmington, Delaware: ISI Books, 2006), pp. 10–11.
25. Strong's trip took place in either 1922 or 1923.
26. Brickman, ed., *John Dewey's Impressions*, p. 19.
27. Nearly every Russian document in the Comintern Archives of Communist Party USA, which I have viewed at great length in the holdings at the Library of Congress, has a German translation.
28. Albert P. Pinkevich, *The New Education in the Soviet Republic* (New York: John Day, 1929), p. vi.
29. Thomas Woody, *New Minds, New Men?* (New York: Macmillan, 1932), pp. 47–48.
30. During his trip to the USSR in the summer of 1928, Dewey attended an educational conference organized by Professor Kalashnikov. They apparently hit it off quite well. It was ten days after the conference that Kalashnikov sent Dewey the two-volume encyclopedia.
31. Quoted in Jay Martin, *The Education of John Dewey: A Biography* (New York: Columbia University Press, 2002), p. 354.
32. See my three chapters on Dewey in Paul Kengor, *Dupes: How America's Adversaries Have Manipulated Progressives for a Century* (Intercollegiate Studies Institute, 2010).
33. Brickman, ed., *John Dewey's Impressions*, pp. 19–20 and 58n.
34. Ibid., p. 72.

35. The collection of essays was published in 1929 by *New Republic, Inc.* They were reprinted in Brickman, ed., *John Dewey's Impressions*, which was published by the Teachers College at Columbia University.
36. Ibid., pp. 74 and 89.
37. Ibid., pp. 74–75.
38. Ibid., pp. 75–76.
39. Ibid., p. 75. Brickman supplies this information in a note to Dewey's essay.
40. Ibid., pp. 78–80.
41. Ibid., pp. 78–80.
42. Ibid., p. 79.
43. For the record, Dewey would later repudiate Stalin and Stalinism—but not Trotskyism. He was enlisted by a cabal of American liberals, "progressives," Trotskyites, and assorted fellow travelers and useful idiots in the mid-1930s to defend Trotsky as he was put on trial in absentia by Stalin. That made Dewey an anti-Stalinist. In April 1934, the year that Stalin's Red Terror rampage began, Dewey wrote a short essay titled, "Why I Am Not a Communist," published in *Modern Monthly*. It is clear from the essay that Dewey's problems were not so much with communism as a philosophy as much as official "Communism" as it was being pursued by Stalin and the Soviet Union at the time. In fact he said that he objected to "Communism, official Communism, spelt with a capital letter."
44. Bella V. Dodd, *School of Darkness* (New York: Devin-Adair, 1954), pp. 3, 33–35, 39–41, and 42–43. On George Countss' Moscow pilgrimage with John Dewey, see Kengor, *Dupes*, pp. 66 and 102.
45. Ibid. pp. 47, 60, and 159.
46. Many people have written on this subject. Dodd herself addressed her vigorous recruitment of communist seminarians in a speech at Fordham University and in her fascinating testimony before the U.S. Congress. See "Communist Leader, Dr Bella Dodd, Confesses to Infiltrating the Church & USA," Youtube, April 24, 2013, https://www.youtube.com/watch?v=37HgRWTsGs0. One of the leading authorities on the subject is Mary A. Nicholas, an expert on Dodd who has interviewed the legendary Alice von Hildebrand on this precise question of Dodd recruiting communist men for Catholic seminaries. Von Hildebrand (widow of the renowned German Roman Catholic

philosopher and theologian Dietrich von Hildebrand, who was persecuted by Hitler), who taught at both Hunter and Fordham and knew Dodd personally, says that Dodd told her that the number of men she recruited was "approximately 1,200." I have exchanged many emails on this subject with Dr. Nicholas in recent years. For a recent and accessible online piece in the mainstream Catholic press (which uses the number 1,100), see Matthew Pittam, "Fulton Sheen Will Be Canonized—but When?" *Catholic Herald*, October 4, 2015. Also see "Testimony of Bella V. Dodd," United States Senate, Subcommittee to Investigate the Administration of the Internal Security Act and Other Internal Security Laws, Committee on the Judiciary, March 10, 1953, pp. 511-46.

47. Sheen also brought *Daily Worker* editor Louis Budenz back to the faith. At the time of Budenz's reversion, his name was still on the masthead. His wife and three daughters also came into the Church. Thomas C. Reeves, *America's Bishop: The Life and Times of Fulton J. Sheen* (Encounter Books, 2001), pp. 170–73.
48. Bella Dodd, *School of Darkness*, p. 214.
49. Whittaker Chambers, *Witness* (Washington: Regnery, 1952), pp. 242 and 264.
50. Bella Dodd, *School of Darkness*, p. 150.
51. "Communist Leader, Dr Bella Dodd." See the 1:09:35 marker for this particular passage.
52. William Z. Foster, *Toward Soviet America* (New York: Coward-McCann, 1932). This is a very revealing book by the head of the CPUSA.
53. Ibid.
54. "American Federation of Teachers Endorses Clinton," *People's World*, July 14, 2015; "Teachers' Convention Celebrates History, Vision for Future, Clinton Support," *People's World*, July 25, 2016.
55. "Moral Monday Leader a Hit at AFT convention," *People's World*, July 14, 2014.
56. "At AFT Meet, Energized Resistance to Attacks on Education," *People's World*, July 17, 2014.
57. "Richard Trumka, 10,000 Union Members Flood Maryland State Capitol," *People's World*, March 15, 2011.
58. See "About Us" section at the website of *People's World*, http://www.peoplesworld.org/about-the-peoples-world/.

59. "Richard Trumka, 10,000 Union Members Flood Maryland State Capitol," *People's World*, March 15, 2011.
60. "Amistad Awards Inspire Unity, Struggle," *People's World*, December 6, 2013.

Chapter 12: Cultural Marxism and the New Left

1. Paul Kengor, *Takedown: From Communists to Progressives, How the Left Has Sabotaged Family and Marriage* (Washington, DC: WND Books, 2015), ch. 17, "Communists and Homosexuality."
2. "2015–2017 Platform," Socialist Party USA, http://socialistparty-usa.net/platform.
3. See "Lesbian, Gay, Bisexual, Transgender and Queer (LGBTQ) Rights: Passed at the DSA Convention November 2011," http://www.dsausa.org/lesbian_gay_bisexual_transgender_and_queer_lgbtq_rights.
4. Press Release, "Gay Pride Month: Communists stand in solidarity," Communist Party USA, June 24, 2006.
5. For an early document on the founding of the Marx-Engels Institute see L.B. "The Marx-Engels Institute (Translated from *La Critique sociale*, no. 2, July 1931pp. 51–2," http://www.marxists.org/archive/riazanov/bio/bio02.htm.
6. Ralph de Toledano, *Cry Havoc! The Great American Bring-down and How it Happened* (Washington, DC: Anthem Books, 2006), p. 27.
7. Ibid., p. 25.
8. Ibid.
9. Samuel Gregg, "The Most Dangerous Socialist in History," *The Stream*, July 25, 2016.
10. See Peter Hasson, "New York City Lets You Choose From 31 Different Gender Identities," *The Daily Caller*, May 24, 2016, http://dailycaller.com/2016/05/24/new-york-city-lets-you-choose-from-31-different-gender-identities/. The list of gender identities for New York City is posted online at http://www.nyc.gov/html/cchr/downloads/pdf/publications/GenderID_Card2015.pdf.
11. See, inter alia, Rhiannon Williams, "Facebook's 71 Gender Options," *London Telegraph*, June 27, 2014, http://www.telegraph.co.uk/technology/facebook/10930654/Facebooks-71-gender-options-come-to-UK-users.html and Paul Kengor, "Girl Boy Scouts...and 71 Other 'Gender' Options," *Crisis*, February 9, 2017.

12. Critical Theory & Social Justice, Occidental College, www.oxy.edu/critical-theory-social-justice, September 30, 2016.
13. Ibid.
14. Michael Walsh, *The Devil's Pleasure Palace: The Cult of Critical Theory and the Subversion of the West* (Enounter, 2015).
15. Toledano, *Cry Havoc!*, pp. 96 and 105.
16. Wilhelm Reich, *Passion of Youth: Wilhelm Reich: An Autobiography* (New York: Farrar, Giroux, and Strauss, 1988), pp. 4–46 and Colin Wilson, *The Quest for Wilhelm Reich* (New York: Doubleday, 1981), p. 29.
17. See "Reich, Wilhelm (1897–1957)" Encyclopedia of Marxism, http://www.marxists.org/glossary/people/r/e.htm#reich-wilhelm.
18. Donald De Marco and Benjamin Wiker, *Architects of the Culture of Death* (San Francisco: Ignatius Press, 2006), p. 227.
19. "Morals: The Second Sexual Revolution," *Time*, January 24, 1964.
20. Ariel Levy, "Novelty Acts," *The New Yorker*, September 19, 2011. Another man who merits this title is arguably Alfred Kinsey, whose sexual anarchism was possibly to the left of even Reich.
21. De Marco and Wiker, *Architects of the Culture of Death*, pp. 222 and 231–12.
22. Toledano, *Cry Havoc!*, pp. 6–23; Martin Jay, *The Dialectical Imagination: A History of the Frankfurt School and the Institute of Social Research 1923-50* (Boston: Little, Brown, & Company, 1973), p. 28.
23. Ronald Aronson, "Marcuse Today," *Boston Review*, November 17, 2014.
24. Here the website provides a hyperlink to "polymorphous perversity," which defines it thusly: "Polymorphous perversity is a Freudian term referring to unfocused, infantile sexuality. In Freudian terms, as individuals mature, the focus of their sexuality passes from polymorphous perversity through oral and anal stages to culminate in adult, genitally focused sexuality. More generally, the term is used to indicate the ability to derive erotic pleasure from any part of the body."
25. Jeffrey Escoffier, "Marcuse, Herbert," GLBTQ Archive, 2004, http://www.glbtqarchive.com/ssh/marcuse_h_S.pdf.
26. Ibid.
27. Ronald Aronson, "Marcuse Today," *Boston Review*, November 17, 2014.
28. Toledano, *Cry Havoc!*, pp. 78–83.

29. Walter Benjamin, "On the Concept of History," 1940, https://www.marxists.org/reference/archive/benjamin/1940/history.htm.
30. Eric Jacobson, "Metaphysics of the Profane: The Political Theology of Walter Benjamin and Gershom Scholem" (New York: Columbia University Press, 2003), p. 245, n67.
31. Donna Roberts and Daniel Garza Usabiaga, "The Use of Lucifer: A Comparative Analysis of the Figures of Lucifer and Satan in the Writings of Roger Caillois and Walter Benjamin," http://www.academia.edu/6014358/The_Use_Value_of_Lucifer_A_Comparative_Analysis_of_the_Figures_of_Lucifer_and_Satan_in_the_Writings_of_Roger_Caillois_and_Walter_Benjamin_in_the_1930s.
32. Ibid.
33. Ray Man, "Monument a D.A.F. de Sade (1933)," Art Stack: The World's favorite art, https://theartstack.com/artist/man-ray/monument-a-d-f-de-sa.
34. Ernst, Max, "The Blessed Virgin Chastises the Infant Jesus Before Three Witnesses (1926)" artnet http://www.artnet.com/magazineus/features/kachur/kachur7-21-05_detail.asp?picnum=2.
35. Benjamin's interest in aesthetics and art criticism permeated throughout his works. This more esoteric, non-analytical approach to philosophy is characteristic of Benjamin's work.
36. David Biale, *Gershom Scholem: Kabbalah and Counter-History* (Cambridge: Harvard University Press, 1982), pp. 136-38 and n94; and Roberts and Usabiaga, *The Use of Lucifer*, p. 6.
37. See: Otto Karl Werckmeister, *Icons of the Left: Benjamin and Einstein, Picasso and Kafka after the Fall* (Chicago: University of Chicago Press, 1997), p. 9.
38. Roberts and Usabiaga, *The Use of Lucifer*, pp. 6–7.
39. Max Horkheimer, *Critical Theory* (New York: Seabury Press, 1982), p. 244.
40. Kam Shapiro, "Walter Benjamin, the Kabbalah, and Secularism," *AJS Perspectives: The Magazine for the Association for Jewish Studies*, Spring 2011.
41. Email correspondence between the author and David Horowitz, November 13, 2014.
42. See: Mallory Millett, "Marxist Feminism's Ruined Lives," *Front Page Magazine*, September 2, 2014.

43. Ibid.
44. Ibid.
45. Ibid.
46. Ibid.
47. Among many sources for the "dig it" quotation, see "The Seeds of Terror," *New York Times Magazine*, November 22, 1981.
48. See Paul Kengor, *Dupes: How America's Adversaries Have Manipulated Progressives for a Century* (Intercollegiate Studies Institute, 2010, pp. 338–39. In 1980, David Horowitz interviewed thirty members of the Weather Underground who had been present at the "War Council." He said not one of them doubted that Dohrn was serious. David Horowitz, "Allies in War," FrontPage Magazine, September 17, 2001, http://archive.frontpagemag.com/readArticle.aspx?ARTID=24446.
49. Grathwohl shared this with me on two occasions, including at a July 2012 event at the National Press Club the summer before he unexpectedly passed away. I have written about Grathwohl in my 2010 book *Dupes* and in a tribute published after his death: Paul Kengor, "RIP, Larry Grathwohl, Weather Underground Infiltrator," *American Spectator*, July 26, 2013.
50. Mark Rudd, *Underground: My Life with SDS and the Weather Underground* (NY: William Morrow, 2009), p. 189.
51. The best and most recent work on the Weather Underground is by Bryan Burrough. For a good summary article, based on his important 2015 book, *Days of Rage*, see: Bryan Burrough, "Meet the Weather Underground's Bomb Guru," *Vanity Fair*, March 29, 2015.
52. Dinitia Smith, "No Regrets for a Love of Explosives; in a Memoir of Sorts, a War Protester Talks of Life with the Weathermen," *New York Times*, September 11, 2001, http://www.nytimes.com/2001/09/11/books/no-regrets-for-love-explosives-memoir-sorts-war-protester-talks-life-with.html.
53. The directory page listing Dohrn, who appears to have recently retired, is located here: http://directory.northwestern.edu/?query=Bernardine+Dohrn.
54. See: https://billayers.org/biographyhistory/.
55. This is an infamous remark by Bill Ayers. As to its origins, see, among others: David Horowitz, *Radical Son* (New York: The Free Press, 1997), pp. 333–34.

56. Smith, "No Regret."
57. See, for instance: William Ayers, Jean Ann Hunt, and Therese Quinn, eds., *Teaching for Social Justice: A Democracy and Education Reader* (New York: Teachers College Press, Columbia University, 1998); and William Ayers, Michael Klonsky, and Gabrielle H. Lyon, eds., *A Simple Justice: The Challenge of Small Schools* (New York: Teachers College Press, Columbia University, 2000). More recently, and outside of Columbia University's press, see: William Ayers, Therese Quinn, and David Stovall, eds., *Handbook for Social Justice in Education* (New York: Routledge, 2008).
58. See Rudd's website: http://www.markrudd.com/.
59. Mark Rudd, *Underground: My Life with SDS and the Weathermen* (NY: William Morrow, 2009), p. 146.
60. "Duncan Praised as 'Bona Fide Reformer' of Chicago Education System," FoxNews.com, December 16, 2008.
61. See previous citations, especially: William Ayers, Michael Klonsky, and Gabrielle H. Lyon, eds., *A Simple Justice: The Challenge of Small Schools* (New York: Teachers College Press, Columbia University, 2000).
62. Alinsky said this in his 1972 interview with *Playboy* magazine. It is known as "The Interview with Saul Alinsky, Part Ten," and available on many admiring progressive websites.
63. These letters were disclosed in September 2014 by the Washington Free Beacon. For a detailed analysis of Hillary and Alinsky and Saul's peculiar interest in Lucifer, see my piece: Paul Kengor, "The Hillary-Alinsky-Lucifer Connection," The American Spectator, July 26, 2016.
64. See Tal Kopan, "Polygraph Panic: CIA director Fretted [over] His Vote for Communist," CNN, September 15, 2016, http://www.cnn.com/2016/09/15/politics/john-brennan-cia-communist-vote/ . I wrote about this in Paul Kengor, "Did Barack Obama Vote Communist in 1980?," *American Spectator*, September 27, 2016, https://spectator.org/did-barack-obama-vote-communist-in-1980/.
65. "Interview: Angela Davis," Frontline PBS), spring 1997, http://www.pbs.org/wgbh/pages/frontline/shows/race/interviews/davis.html.
66. "Angela Y. Davis," Marcuse.org, http://www.marcuse.org/herbert/scholaractivists/AngDavisBioBib88.htm.
67. Ibid.

68. Roger Kimball, "Angela Davis and Radical Chic," *Wall Street Journal*, June 6, 2016.
69. Horowitz, *Radical Son*, p. 334.
70. The bio is posted at www.columbia.edu/cu/ssw/faculty/adjunct/boudin.html.
71. See the Angela Davis bio posted at the website of the Women's March: https://www.womensmarch.com/honorary-cochairs/.
72. See the transcript of Davis's remarks posted at http://www.elle.com/culture/career-politics/a42337/angela-davis-womens-march-speech-full-transcript/.
73. The actual title, as posted at the Bard College website, is "Visiting Alger Hiss Professor of History and Literature." See, inter alia, "An Alger Hiss Chair in Social Studies?" History News Network, January 22, 2004, posted at http://historynewsnetwork.org/article/2915.

Chapter 13: Communism Today

1. See Christopher Hitchens, "The Old Man," *The Atlantic*, July/August 2004.
2. "Report of the President's Commission on the Assassination of President Kennedy," better known as the Warren Commission report," chapter 7, pp. 404–5, http://www.archives.gov/research/jfk/warren-commission-report/chapter-7.html.
3. See "Welcome to the Revolution: The Voice of the Revolutionary Communist Party USA," http://revcom.us/.
4. "Six Resolutions of the Central Committee of the Revolutionary Communist Party," January 1, 2016, http://revcom.us/a/423/six-resolutions-of-the-Central-Committee-of-the-RCP-USA-en.html.
5. Ibid.
6. Quoted by Spyridon Mitsotakis, "Community Church of New York: Pacifists Suspended, Maoists Welcome," FrontPageMagazine.com, July 1, 2014.
7. Eric Owens, "Meet the Fringe Communist Agitators Who Are Trying to Bring Revolution to Riot-Torn Milwaukee," *Daily Caller*, August 17, 2016.
8. Peter Wilson, "The Revolutionary Communist Party's Little Yellow Book," *American Thinker*, October 18, 2011.
9. "Six Resolutions."

10. Ibid.
11. Spyridon Mitsotakis, "Maoist Church Saga," FrontPageMagazine.com, July 21, 2014.
12. Email correspondence between the author and John Rossomando, July 24, 2016.
13. Peter Wilson, "The Revolutionary Communist Party's Little Yellow Book," *American Thinker*, October 18, 2011.
14. See Mark Rudd, *Underground: My Life with SDS and the Weathermen* (New York: William Morrow, 2009), p. 43.
15. Brent Hellendoorn, "Barack Obama on Collective Salvation," Youtube, December 22, 2010, https://www.youtube.com/watch?v=lLgHlYjJvXk.
16. Paul Kengor, "How Obama Made Good on His Promise to Fundamentally Transform U.S.A.," CNS News, January 16, 2017, http://www.cnsnews.com/commentary/dr-paul-kengor/how-obama-made-good-his-promise-fundamentally-transform-united-states.
17. See my book on Frank Marshall Davis and his relationship with the future President Obama: Paul Kengor, *The Communist: Frank Marshall Davis: The Untold Story of Barack Obama's Mentor* (New York: Simon & Schuster, 2012).
18. See, inter alia, Scott Shane, "Obama and '60s Bomber: A Look into Crossed Paths," *The New York Times*, October 4, 2008, p. A1.
19. See index of "Investigations of Students for a Democratic Society," Part 7-A, Hearings Before the Committee on Internal Security, House of Representatives, 91st Congress, First Session, December 9–11 and 16, 1969.
20. Daniel J. Flynn, "Obama's Boys of Summer," *City Journal*, June 2008.
21. These four reportedly signed online petitions calling for an "independent grassroots effort" to strengthen Senator Obama's presidential campaign. In addition to the signers who hailed from Progressives for Obama, like Mark Rudd, these petition signers also included Howard Machtinger, Jeff Jones, and Steve Tappis. Aaron Klein, "4 Weathermen Terrorists Declare Support for Obama," WorldNetDaily.com, October 2, 2008.
22. Thomas Good, "MDS Conference Elects Manning Marable Chair of MDS, Inc.," *Next Left Notes*, February 20, 2007.
23. Cliff Kincaid, "Terrorists on Tour," Accuracy in Media, April 23, 2009. The words I quote were from an April 22, 2009 press conference on the

release of Rudd's book, *Underground: My Life With SDS and the Weathermen*, cited above.

24. Tom Hayden, "Obama and the Open and Unexpected Future," CommonDreams.org, June 8, 2008.
25. Ibid.
26. Congressional Progressive Caucus, https://cpc-grijalva.house.gov/.
27. Email correspondence between the author and John Rossomando, June 24–25, 2016.
28. Congressional Progressive Caucus.
29. John Rossomando, "Obama Campaigned before Socialist Group in '96," Breitbar, October 23, 2010.
30. Paul Berman, "Why Bill de Blasio's Nicaraguan Work Worries Me," *New Republic*, September 30, 2013.
31. "De Blasio Visited Communist USSR in College," *New York Post*, November 3, 2013.
32. See Cliff Kincaid, "America's First Openly Marxist Big City Mayor," http://www.aim.org/aim-column/americas-first-openly-marxist-big-city-mayor/.
33. "Announcing the Communist Party Convention, June 2014!," *Communist Party USA*, November 27, 2013, www.cpusa.org/article/announcing-the-communist-party-convention-june-2014/.
34. John Tagliabue, "Industrialized Eastern Bloc Faces Pollution Crisis," *New York Times*, October 25, 1987, http://www.nytimes.com/1987/10/25/world/industrialized-eastern-bloc-faces-pollution-crisis.html?pagewanted=all.
35. Vaness Piao, "Among China's Smog Worries, One More: Counterfeit Masks," *New York Times*, December 10, 2015.
36. Joelle Fishman, "Get on Board the CT Climate Train," *People's World*, September 15, 2014.
37. See John Bachtell, "Envisioning a modern, democratic, peaceful, and green socialism," *People's World*, June 15, 2016 and C. J. Atkins, "Clinton Will Win Nomination, but Sanders' Revolution Can't Quit Now," *People's World*, April 22, 2016.
38. "Put People before Profits: Help Build a Movement to Transform This Country: Announcing the 30th Convention of the Communist Party USA June 13–15, posted at http://www.cpusa.org/article/announcing-the-communist-party-convention-june-2014/.

39. See chapters 2, 7, and 8 of my book *Dupes*.
40. The best source on this is Ronald Steel. See: Steel, *In Love With Night*, pp. 27 and 46-50.
41. Steel, *In Love with Night*, pp. 49–50.
42. This quotation has been reported a handful times (without elaboration), including by: Steel, *In Love with Night*, p. 120; Sean Wilentz, "Bobby Kennedy, You Were No Bobby Kennedy," *New York Times Review of Books*, January 9, 2000; and Evan Thomas, *Robert Kennedy: His Life* (New York: Simon & Schuster, 2000), p. 316. The original full quotation is published in Edwin O. Guthman and Jeffrey Shulman, eds., *Robert Kennedy: In His Own Words* (NY: Bantam, 1988), p. 204. When read in full context, it isn't entirely clear what Kennedy meant by the "in love with death" assessment. My sense is that he was probably referring to intransigent liberals who were willing to kill an entire piece of (worthwhile) civil-rights legislation if they didn't get exactly what they wanted.
43. Steel, *In Love with Night*, p. 165.
44. Senator John F. Kennedy, "Commencement Address at Assumption College," Worcester, Massachusetts, June 3, 1955.
45. These words are taken from the *Public Presidential Papers* of Kennedy, specifically the volumes for the years 1961 (p. 341) and 1962 (p. 723n). Also see: Walker, Martin, *The Cold War and the Making of the Modern World*, (London, 1993), p. 132; and Hobsbawm, Eric, *The Age of Extremes: A History of the World, 1914-1991*, (New York: Pantheon Books, 1994), p. 231.
46. See Sam Webb, "Defeat for the Right, Victory for the People & Democracy," Webb's report to CPUSA's National Committee, November 17, 2012, posted at http://www.cpusa.org/article/defeat-for-the-right-victory-for-the-people-democracy/.
47. See "CPUSA Statement to 17th International Meeting of Communist and Workers' Parties," November 11, 2015, posted at www.cpusa.org.
48. See Gabe Falsetta, "Left Unity Championed at New York Meet," *People's World*, June 12, 2013, http://www.peoplesworld.org/left-unity-championed-at-new-york-meet/.
49. See the website of Committees of Correspondence for Democracy and Socialism: http://www.cc-ds.org/.
50. Falsetta, "Left Unity Championed at New York Meet."

51. Barack Obama speaking in Columbia, Missouri, October 30, 2008.
52. John Bachtell, "Envisioning a modern, democratic, peaceful, and green socialism," *People's World*, June 15, 2016.

Chapter 14: Commies Just Love Blacks and Women

1. Peter Wilson, "The Revolutionary Communist Party's Little Yellow Book," *American Thinker*, October 18, 2011.
2. Harvey Klehr, John Earl Haynes, and Kirill Anderson, *The Soviet World of American Communism* (New Haven, CT: Yale University Press, 1998), p. 219. This source specifically points to the 1928–1930 period. Beyond this source, one can see this reality abundantly evident in the materials from the late 1920s and early 1930s in the Comintern Archives on CPUSA. See also "The American Negro in the Communist Party," Committee on Un-American Activities, U.S. House of Representatives, 79th Congress, Second Session, Washington, DC, December 22, 1954, pp. 5–7.
3. J. Edgar Hoover, *Masters of Deceit* (NY: Henry Holt, 1958), pp. 250–51. This book, which was assembled by Hoover's staff, became a huge bestseller.
4. "Black and Red," *Time* magazine, November 9, 1925.
5. See: Lovett Fort Whiteman collection at Tamiment Library, Box 9, Folder 57.
6. Lovett Fort-Whiteman collection at Tamiment Library, Box 9, Folder 57; "The Negro Sanhedrin," *Daily Worker*, February 16, 1924, filed in Fort-Whiteman box at Tamiment Library.
7. He was born in Suriname and his last name is spelled in several different ways—as "Huiswoud," "Houiswood," and "Husswood"—in the Tamiment archives. He was one of the first members (if not *the* first) black of the American Communist Party.
8. Some sources describe this as a "Comintern school." See "Black and Red," *Time* magazine, November 9, 1925; Raymond Arsenault, "Forgotten Revolutionaries," *The Washington Post*, January 13, 2008; Klehr, Haynes, and Anderson, *The Soviet World of American Communism*, pp. 218–23; CPUSA files on Fort-Whiteman, Box 9, Folder 57, Tamiment Library, New York University; "Investigation of Un-American Propaganda Activities in the United States," Special Committee on Un-American Activities, House of Representatives, 78th

Congress, Second Session, on H. Res. 282, App. Part IX, Vol. 1 (Washington, DC: GPO, 1944), pp. 1001, 1282, 1452; and Theodore Draper, *American Communism and Soviet Russia* (1960), pp. 329–30.

9. Klehr, Haynes, and Anderson, *The Soviet World of American Communism*, pp. xi and 218–23.
10. Jean Wagner, *Black Poets of the United Sates: From Paul Laurence Dunbar to Langston Hughes* (Chicago and Urbana: University of Illinois Press, 1973), p. 435; Faith Berry, *Langston Hughes: Before and Beyond Harlem* (New York: Citadel Press, 1992), pp. 296–97.
11. Langston Hughes, *Essays on Art, Race, Politics, and World Affairs* (Columbia, Missouri: University of Missouri Press, 2002), p. 207.
12. Ibid. This infamous Hughes poem is titled "Goodbye Christ."
13. Paul Kengor, "Tim Kaine Commends Hillary with a Communist Poet," Crisis Magazine, November 11, 2016.
14. "The American Negro in the Communist Party," Committee on Un-American Activities, U.S. House of Representatives, 79th Congress, Second Session, Washington, DC, December 22, 1954.
15. See my extended, detailed discussion in Paul Kengor, *The Communist: Frank Marshall Davis: The Untold Story of Barack Obama's Mentor* (New York: Simon & Schuster, Threshold Editions, Mercury Ink, 2012) pp. 36–52.
16. Eric Owens, "Meet the Fringe Communist Agitators Who Are Trying to Bring Revolution to Riot-Torn Milwaukee," *Daily Caller*, August 17, 2016.
17. "Milwaukee Police Chief Blames Chicago-Based Activists for Violence toward Police," *Chicago Tribune*, August 5, 2016.
18. See Kengor, *The Communist*, pp. 220–25, 228, and 308.
19. "Communist in Ferguson," *TheBlaze*, August 20, 2014, posted at http://www.glennbeck.com/2014/08/20/video-prominent-communists-ratchet-up-rhetoric-in-ferguson/.
20. "National Four-Day Protest Set for Oct. 10–13 in Ferguson," *People's World*, October 6, 2014, http://www.peoplesworld.org/article/national-four-day-protest-set-for-oct-10-13-in-ferguson/.
21. "Confederate Flag Taken Down at South Carolina Capitol," *People's World*, July 10, 2015, http://www.peoplesworld.org/article/confederate-flag-taken-down-at-south-carolina-capitol/.
22. *Global Insights*, p. 196.

23. Larry S. Kreiger et al., *World History: Perspectives on the Past* (Houghton-Mifflin, 1997); Elisabeth Gaynor Ellis and Anthony Esler, *World History: Connections to Today* (Prentice Hall, 1999).
24. Roger G. Beck et al., *Modern World History: Patterns of Interaction* (McDougall-Littell, 1999); and Howard Spodek, *The World's History* (Prentice Hall, 1998).
25. Ibid., pp. 13–15.
26. Ibid., p. 618.
27. For a detailed discussion, see Paul Kengor, "Race and Margaret Sanger," *American Spectator*, September 14, 2015, https://spectator.org/64049_race-and-margaret-sanger/.
28. Margaret Sanger, "Birth Control in Russia," *Birth Control Review*, June 1935.
29. Arnold Beichman, the late Hoover Institution expert on communism, estimated that one in every eight Soviet citizens—men, women, children, elderly—perished under Stalin's Great Terror. The number is not inconceivable, as that would equate to about 20 million people at the time, a figure consistent with typical estimates of the death Stalin unleashed on his population.
30. Jennifer McDowell, "Soviet Civil Ceremonies," *Journal for the Scientific Study of Religion*, Vol. 13, No. 3, 1974, pp. 265–79; David E. Powell, "Rearing the New Soviet Man," in Bociurkiw and Strong, *Religion and Atheism in the USSR and Eastern Europe*, pp. 160–65.
31. Alexander Solzhenitsyn, *Solzhenitsyn Speaks to the West* (London: The Bodley Head, 1978), p. 70.
32. Susanne Klingenstein, "Stalin's Orphans," *The Weekly Standard*, September 7, 2015.
33. Veronica Shapovalov, *Remembering the Darkness: Women in Soviet Prisons*, p. 76.
34. Ibid., p. 205.
35. Shapovalov, *Remembering the Darkness: Women in Soviet Prisons*, p. 247.
36. See Manning Johnson, *Color, Communism and Common Sense* (The Alliance, 1958), chapter 1.
37. Shapovalov, *Remembering the Darkness: Women in Soviet Prisons*, p. 307.

38. Ibid., pp. 297–301.

Chapter 15: Stupidity on Parade

1. "New Report Reveals U.S. Attitudes on Socialism, Communism on Eve of 2016 Election," Victims of Communism Memorial Foundation, October 17, 2016, http://victimsofcommunism.org/new-report-reveals-u-s-attitudes-on-socialism-communism-on-eve-of-2016-election/.
2. R. Emmett Tyrrell Jr., "Outrage Imbalance," *Washington Times*, January 14, 2000.
3. Paul Kengor, *Evaluating World History Texts in Wisconsin Public High Schools*, Wisconsin Policy Research Institute, June 2002, Volume 15, No. 4, www.wpri.org.
4. Mounir A. Farah, et al., *Global Insights: People and Cultures* (Glencoe-McGraw Hill, 1994), p. 214.
5. *Patterns of Civilization*, p. 783.
6. Iftikhar Ahmad, *World Cultures: A Global Mosaic* (Upper Saddle River, New Jersey: Prentice Hall, 2001), p. 362.
7. Elisabeth Rosenthal, "Women's Suicides Reveal Rural China's Bitter Roots," *New York Times*, January 24, 1999.
8. See Yuan Ren, "Young Chinese Women Are Committing Suicide at a Terrifying Rate," *London Telegraph*, October 20, 2016, http://www.telegraph.co.uk/women/life/young-chinese-women-are-committing-suicide-at-a-terrifying-rate/.
9. Farah, et al., *Global Insights.*
10. Farah et al., *Global Insights*; Kengor, *Evaluating World History Texts*, p. 21.
11. See: Steven Ertelt, "AP Criticized for Article Praising China's One-Child Policy," LifeNews.com, August 17, 2011.
12. Clyde Haberman, "Bright Lights That Mask the Darkness," *New York Times*, October 1, 2009.
13. "Effort to Have Empire State Building Honor Mother Teresa Mobilizes 40,000," Catholic News Agency, June 9, 2010.
14. "Obama Aide Fires Back at Beck over Mao remarks," CNN.com, October 16, 2009.
15. "City Council Honors Ethel Rosenberg for 'Great Bravery," *New York Post*, September 29, 2015.

16. See: Sheryl Gay Stolberg, "The Spotlight's Bright Glare," *The New York Times*, December 4, 2009; and "White House Christmas Tree Décor Featuring Mao Zedong Comes Under Fire," FoxNews.com, December 24, 2009.
17. See: "The 6 dopiest right-wing attacks on Obama," *Salon*, September 25, 2014, posted at http://www.salon.com/2014/09/25/the_6_dopiest_right_wing_attacks_on_obama_partner/.
18. Anthony Lewis, "Onward Christian Soldiers," *New York Times*, March 10, 1983.
19. Richard Cohen, "Convictions," *The Washington Post*, May 26, 1983.
20. The Commager quotation has been widely quoted. See, inter alia, Charles Krauthammer, "Reluctant Cold Warriors," *The Washington Post*, November 12, 1999.
21. Editorial, "Reverend Reagan," *New Republic*, April 4, 1983.
22. This March 1983 letter from Muggeridge to Reagan is on file at the Ronald Reagan Library in the Presidential Handwriting File, Presidential Records section, Box 6, Folder 78.
23. Sharansky interview with the *Weekly Standard*, published as: "The View from the Gulag," *Weekly Standard*, June 21, 2004.
24. Kozyrev on *This Week with David Brinkley*, ABC News, August 25, 1991.
25. Tarasenko said this during a February 25–27, 1993 conference at Princeton University. See William C. Wohlforth, ed., *Witnesses to the End of the Cold War* (Baltimore and London: Johns Hopkins University, 1996), p. 20.
26. Ronald Reagan, "Remarks at the Annual Convention of the National Association of Evangelicals," Orlando, Florida, March 8, 1983.

Index

C

N

R

S

W

Y

Z